Fergus Lyne

D0119531

# THE
# HANDBOOK
## OF
# U.S. CAPITAL
# MARKETS

# THE HANDBOOK OF U.S. CAPITAL MARKETS

## Stuart R. Veale

*Veale & Associates, Inc.*

HarperBusiness
*A Division of* HarperCollins*Publishers*

International Standard Book Number: 0-88730-450-8

Library of Congress Catalog Card Number: 91-31568

Printed in the United States of America

**Library of Congress Cataloging-in-Publication Data**

Veale, Stuart R.
    The handbook of U.S. capital markets/Stuart R. Veale.
        p.     cm.

    1.  Capital market--United States--Mathematics--Handbooks,
manuals, etc.  2. Investment analysis--United States--Mathematics--
Handbooks, manuals, etc.  3.  Portfolio management--United
States--Mathematics--Handbooks, manuals, etc.  I.  Title.
HG4921.V43   1991
332´.0415´0973--dc20                                   91-31568
                                                              CIP


91 92 93 94 SRV/RRD 7 6 5 4 3 2 1

*To Linda*

# CONTENTS

## PART IV DERIVATIVE INSTRUMENTS 275

## PART V FIXED-INCOME PORTFOLIO MANAGEMENT 415

# ACKNOWLEDGEMENTS

The author would gratefully like to acknowledge the contributions of the following individuals, without whom this text would not have been possible. First, I would like to thank my assistant, Cyndi Nabors, who is responsible for turning my sometimes unintelligible scribblings into finished prose. Second, I would like to thank Martha Jewett and the other professionals from HarperCollins, Inc. whose patience and advice proved to be invaluable. Third, I would like to thank the many professionals who have attended my training programs over the years. Their comments and suggestions have greatly improved the logic, accuracy, and utility of my presentations--especially this one.

I would specifically like to thank the 1990 Associates Class of Lehman Brothers, Inc. for their many helpful suggestions. This class included: James Adamson, Haejin Baek, James T. Brett, Andrew C. Brummer, Edwin M. Cook, Jr., Doreen Davidow, Harumi Aoto Donoyon, Joseph Foley, Gianmarco R. Formichella, Todd Giamportone, Kenji Hirakawa, Kashuku Hirao, Rebecca Horowitz, Toshiyuki Ishida, Rie Kanematsu, Karin S. Katz, Hitoshi Kikuchi, George C. Y. Koo, Scott A. Lauretti, Susan Laws, Donald C. Lee, Theodore T. Lo, Akinori Matsui, Theodore Nacheff II, Toshihiro Nakashima, Ryosuke Ota, Nicholas Jean Pourcelet, Reiko Shinozaki, Daisuke Sano, Jennifer Faye Solomon, Koichi Takashima, Shohei Ueda, and Carol Ann Werther.

# INTRODUCTION

Unlike many of the texts currently available, this text was written to meet a specific need in the marketplace. There is no shortage of introductory level texts that discuss fixed income products and markets. Likewise, there is no shortage of research journals and advanced anthologies that present "advanced level" information. However, at the time this project was undertaken, there were no texts which served as a "bridge" between these two extremes. That is the purpose of this text.

Throughout this text I strove to achieve the following objectives:

- To explain the more difficult concepts in a clear, simple, and straight forward manner.
- To use examples to explain and reinforce the key concepts.
- To incorporate those topics which are of most practical benefit to CFOs, Treasurers, Traders, Bankers, Brokers, and other market practitioners.
- To provide a logical framework in which to evaluate new investment vehicles and strategies as they are developed.

Only you, the reader, will be able to judge the degree to which my objectives were achieved.

This book is still very much a "work in progress." In order to improve future editions, I would like to request your comments, critiques, corrections, and suggestions. They may be sent to me at the below address. Allow me to thank you in advance for your time, and your thoughts.

Stuart R. Veale<br>
Veale & Associates, Inc.<br>
8202 Farwick Court<br>
Cincinnati, OH 45249<br>
513-489-1622

# ABOUT VEALE & ASSOCIATES, INC.

Veale & Associates Inc. designs, develops, and delivers specialized training programs on all aspects of the global capital markets. All of Veale & Associates, Inc.'s training programs are designed to meet the specific training objectives of its clientele.

Veale & Associates, Inc. has the capability of utilizing stand up lecture, comprehensive outlines, case studies, workbooks, textbooks, straight and interactive video, computer based "multimedia" training, periodic newsletters, and on-going telephone support in order to accomplish its client's objectives.

Partial client list: American Express Private Bank Ltd.™, Citicorp Inc.™, Kidder Peabody Inc.™, Lehman Brothers Inc.™, Manufacturer's Life Inc.™, ManuLife Insurance Co. Inc.™ Metropolitan Life Inc.™, PaineWebber Inc.™, SEI Inc.™, The Trust Co. of America Inc.™

# PART I
## The Money Market

# 1
# INVESTMENT POLICIES FOR SHORT-TERM PORTFOLIOS

## INTRODUCTION

Managing short term (i.e., money market portfolios) has become far more complicated over the last few years due to the proliferation of short term investment vehicles, the increased volatility of interest rates, and the increased level of credit risk within the money market. Managing a short-term portfolio is a five-step process:

- Investors need to establish their investment goals and objectives.
- They should write an investment policy statement that is designed to help them achieve their goals and objectives.
- They should build the highest-yielding portfolio that they can within the limits of their investment policies.
- They should carefully monitor the performance of their portfolios.
- They should make changes in their portfolios as necessary.

## TRADE OFF BETWEEN RISK AND RETURN

The first need of investors is to balance their desire for a high return against their willingness to tolerate risk. The greater the risk investors are willing to take, the greater the potential reward. Similarly, when investors limit the amount of risk they are willing to take, they are also limiting their potential return.

In addition to the direct relationship between *risk* and *return*, there is also a direct relationship between *risk* and the *variance of possible return*. Thus, as the level of risk that investors take increases and their potential returns increase, the *predictability* of their potential returns decreases. For example, the relationship between risk and probable returns can be expressed graphically:

**Figure 1.1** *Risk versus Reward*

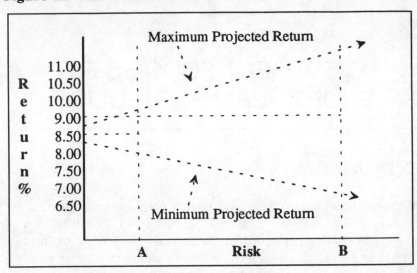

Thus, if an investor elects to build a portfolio with risk tolerance A, the investor's probable return will be 8.5%, with a variance of +/- 50 bp. Thus, the lowest return the investor might receive (statistically determined) would be 8%, and the highest would be 9%. However, if an investor elected instead to build a portfolio with risk tolerance B, the investor's probable return would rise to 9% to compensate for the higher risk. However, the variance of the possible returns would also increase to +200 bp/ -150 bp. Thus, the lowest return the investor might receive (statistically determined) would be 7.5%, and the highest would be 11%.

# RISKS IN THE MONEY MARKET

When investors are considering risk, in addition to considering the total level of risk they are willing to take, they also need to consider which *types* of risk they can tolerate. Short-term portfolios are generally exposed to three somewhat interrelated types of risk:

- Liquidity risk, which is the risk that the investor will be unable to quickly find a buyer willing to pay a fair price for the investment if the investor wants to sell.

- Credit risk, which is the risk that the investor will not receive the scheduled interest and principal payments in full and on time.

- Interest-rate risk, which is the risk that the market value of the portfolio will fall if market interest rates rise.

Depending on the investor's specific situation, the investor may be better able to take certain types of risk. For example, some investors are willing to buy instruments that are not liquid (and thereby accept liquidity risk) because they expect to hold all of their investments until they mature. However, these same investors may be unwilling to accept any credit risk because they have just enough funds to meet their future liabilities.

## INVESTMENT POLICY STATEMENTS

Once the investors have an idea of their investment objectives and their tolerance for the various types of risk, the next step is for them to clearly and concisely articulate their decisions in an investment policy statement. By writing and adhering to a sound investment policy statement, investors increase the probability that they will achieve their investment objectives. When the investor is a business or organization, there are some additional advantages associated with preparing a written investment policy statement.

First, having an investment policy statement eliminates confusion within the company. Surprisingly, in many companies, the individual(s) who have the responsibility for investing the surplus cash have no clear guidelines regarding how they are to invest the company's money. This places both the individual(s) and their company at risk.

Once the investment policy statement is prepared,

- the employees who are responsible for investing the company's money (and their supervisors) should sign it to acknowledge that they understand and will adhere to it.
- the company's senior managers should sign it to acknowledge their approval.
- the company's controller, as well as its outside auditors, should review it so that they can develop appropriate controls and audit procedures.

The second advantage of having this statement is that it should result in better service from the banks and/or dealers with which the company does business. By providing banks and dealers with copies of the company's current holdings and investment policy statement, the banks and dealers can limit their suggestions to those that would not violate the company's investment policy. This cuts down dramatically on the number of unwanted solicitations.

## Investment Policy Statement Issues

Some of the issues that have to be addressed in a company's investment policy statement include

- which investment vehicles are acceptable.
- the responsibilities and authority limitations of the company's money management personnel.
- the minimum and maximum maturities for each individual instrument, as well as for the whole portfolio.
- the credit quality required for each individual instrument, as well as for the whole portfolio.
- the degree to which the portfolio is to be diversified among vehicles and issuers.
- the required criteria for dealers and custodians.
- the procedure for obtaining exceptions to the preceding rules.

## Minimum and Maximum Maturity

The most common mistake that corporate money managers make regarding the maturity of their portfolios is keeping the weighted average maturity of their portfolios too short. In an effort to minimize their exposure to interest-rate risk, they sacrifice the higher returns that can generally be obtained from lengthening the weighted average maturity of their portfolios. To determine how long the weighted average maturity of a company's portfolio should be, companies first have to be divided into two categories: those that anticipate needing to draw down their cash reserves in order to meet projected expenses, and those that will not need to do this.

### *Institutions That Will Need to Draw Down Their Reserves*

Companies that anticipate that they will need to draw on their cash reserves in order to meet their projected expenses generally tend to keep the weighted average maturity of their portfolios very short, to avoid assuming any interest-rate risk and, in the process, sacrifice the higher returns generally offered by long-term instruments. Often, however, this sacrifice is unnecessary. Short-term portfolios are only exposed to interest-rate risk if an investment needs to be sold prior to its maturity. By properly managing the maturity of a portfolio, its weighted average maturity can often be extended without increasing the exposure to interest-rate risk. In order to lengthen the weighted average maturity of a portfolio without increasing its exposure to interest-rate risk, the maturity schedule of the portfolio should match the company's projected cash needs.

For example, suppose that a company has $5 million in cash and is entering an investment phase. The company's treasurer estimates that the company's future cash inflows and outflows will be as follows:

**Table 1.1** *Net Cash Shortfall (Thousands)*

| Time Frame | Cash Inflow | Cash Outflow | Net Cash Shortfall |
|:---:|:---:|:---:|:---:|
| in 7 days | $400 | $600 | $200 |
| in 30 days | $300 | $800 | $500 |
| in 60 days | $400 | $800 | $400 |
| in 90 days | $250 | $850 | $600 |
| in 120 days | $500 | $1,000 | $500 |
| in 180 days | $700 | $1,000 | $300 |
| in 270 days | $600 | $15,000 | $900 |

In order to avoid interest-rate risk, the treasurer must make sure that in each time frame, enough investments mature to meet the net cash shortfall. Thus, at least $200 thousand worth of vehicles must mature within seven days, an additional $500 thousand must mature within 30 days, and so on. Therefore, the longest weighted average maturity the portfolio can have without being exposed to interest-rate risk is the weighted average maturity of the company's projected cash shortfalls. Of course, the weighted average maturity of the portfolio can always be shorter.

(Note that there may also be times when a treasurer will elect to lengthen the weighted average maturity of the portfolio beyond the weighted average maturity of the cash shortfalls. In other words, there are times when the treasurer may believe that the yield advantage offered by long-term instruments more than outweighs the interest-rate risk; see "Riding Down the Yield Curve" in Chapter-2.)

Assuming in this instance that the treasurer does not want to assume any interest-rate risk, the next step is for the treasurer to determine whether the portfolio should have the maximum weighted average maturity or a shorter one. The answer to this question depends, to a large extent, on how large of a reserve account the treasurer wants to maintain, and the shape of the yield curve.

## Size of the Reserve Account

Most treasurers want to keep some of their company's funds in very short-term (usually seven days or less) investments to protect the organization against unexpected expenses or revenue shortfalls. How large this reserve account needs to be varies from company to company and depends on the reliability of the company's cash flow projections.

Any treasurer can make cash flow projections, but they are not guarantees. Some organizations have very predictable income and expense streams, whereas others have relatively unpredictable income streams and are susceptible to unanticipated expenses. The less predictable the company's cash flow, the larger the reserve account should be. Reserve accounts should generally be defined both in terms of dollars and as a percentage of the portfolio in the investment policy statement.

## Shape of the Yield Curve

Once the treasurer has determined how large the reserve account should be, the next step is to determine how long the weighted average maturity (WAM) of the balance of the portfolio should be. The weighted average maturity can be as short as one day or as long as the weighted average maturity of the cash shortfalls. The principal factor that should influence the treasurer's decision regarding the maturity of the remainder of the portfolio is the shape of the yield curve. The more positive the slope of the yield curve, the greater the incremental return for extending the portfolio's WAM.

In the following example, if the market is represented by "Yield Curve A," the incremental return for extending the maturity of the portfolio by 90 days is 25 bp. However, if the market is represented by "Yield Curve B," the incremental return for extending the maturity of the portfolio by 90 days is 100 bp.

**Figure 1.2** *Incremental Return versus Maturity*

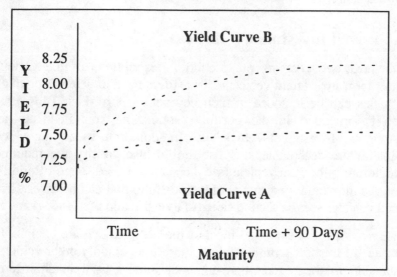

Because the treasurer receives a greater incremental return for assuming the same increase in interest-rate risk when the yield curve has a sharply positive slope, it makes sense to increase the maturity of a short-term portfolio when the yield curve becomes steeper, and to decrease the maturity when the yield curve becomes flat or inverted. In other words, *treasurers should increase the maturity of their short-term portfolios when, and only when, they get paid to take the higher interest-rate risk inherent in the longer maturity.* (As examined in "Riding Down the Yield Curve" in Chapter-2, as the slope of the yield curve becomes more positive, the exposure to interest-rate risk declines. Thus, as the slope of the yield curve becomes more positive, the return increases and the risk decreases.)

**Organizations That Will Not Need to Draw on Their Reserves**

For organizations that do not anticipate needing to draw on their cash reserves, the decision of what the minimum and maximum weighted average maturity of their portfolios should be is far more subjective. Treasurers can set their minimum and/or maximum maturity to be whatever they want based on their tolerance for interest-rate risk. Again, although it is important to control risk, it is also important to maximize return. Treasurers need the freedom and courage to lengthen the maturity of their portfolios when market conditions are favorable. If a company needs to raise cash, in addition to selling the vehicles prior to maturity, treasurers can also borrow against them.

## Approved Investment Vehicles

The next two chapters provide brief descriptions of the various short-term investment vehicles. Treasurers need to determine which vehicles can be included in their company's portfolios. Those that can be included in the portfolio should be compiled into an "Approved Investment Vehicle" list. In addition to specifying which vehicles are acceptable, this list should also specify the required credit rating for each vehicle (see the section called "Credit Rating") and the maximum percentage of the portfolio that can be invested in each vehicle (see the section called "Diversification").

Whereas this text examines most of the vehicles that are commonly employed in short-term portfolios, there are certainly other vehicles available in the market that are occasionally used in short-term portfolios. Also, as this is being read, new vehicles and variations of the old vehicles are undoubtedly being introduced. Thus, it is important for treasurers to periodically revise their approved list (see the section called "Revising an Investment Policy").

## Credit Quality of the Portfolio

After treasurers have determined the minimum and maximum weighted average maturities for their portfolios, the next step is to determine the credit quality they require their investments to have. Most organizations require that all their short-term investments be "investment grade," not because of an informed business decision, but because it is more expedient to specify that all investments be investment grade. Although it may be expedient, there are some disadvantages to treasurers taking this position:

- They preclude themselves from the possibility of investing in the growing number of non-rated instruments.

- They force themselves to sell any investment that is downgraded to a rating below investment grade while it is in their portfolios.

- They sacrifice potential return. Because most treasurers/money managers refuse to buy investments that have credit ratings below investment grade, *the yield differential between investment-grade and non-investment-grade instruments can be very substantial*.

When treasurers are establishing a credit policy, they need to specify

- the required weighted average credit rating of their portfolios.

- the minimum credit rating they require for each type of investment vehicle that they have on their approved lists.

- the maximum percentage of their portfolios that can be invested in non-rated paper.

Probably the easiest way to define the required credit ratings is to prepare a table that lists all of the approved investment vehicles and the credit ratings that they require with a footnote specifying the required weighted average credit rating of their portfolios, as well as the percentage of their portfolios that can be invested in non-rated paper. Some examples of these tables are presented in Chapter Six.

## Degree of Diversification

As mentioned previously, one of the factors that influences the total level of a credit risk for a portfolio is the degree to which the portfolio is diversified. When the diversification of a portfolio is increased, the portfolio's exposure to credit risk is decreased, and the predictability of the portfolio's return is increased. (Although it is impossible to quantify the default risk of a single instrument, it is possible to predict the default risk of a diversified portfolio by statistical techniques.) However, diversification also has some disadvantages:

At any time, only one investment vehicle will offer the highest risk-adjusted return. By diversifying a portfolio among different vehicles, the portfolio must, by definition, include vehicles that offer lower risk-adjusted returns than the maximum obtainable. Similarly, *within* each type of vehicle there is only *one issuer* that offers the highest risk-adjusted return. Thus, diversifying among different issuers also forces treasurers to accept lower risk-adjusted returns.

Also, because diversifying a portfolio will usually increase the number of individual securities transactions, the transaction charges will increase.

Because of the disadvantages of diversification, treasurers should avoid unnecessary over- diversification. As a point of interest, the higher the credit quality of a portfolio, the less diversification it requires.

Thus, when treasurers want to define the required degree of portfolio diversification, they need to specify the

- different investment vehicles, including the minimum and maximum percentage of the portfolio that can be invested in each type of vehicle.

- different issuers, including the minimum and maximum percentage of their portfolios that can be invested with any one issuer. (Without this limitation, a portfolio might end up being composed of Certificates of Deposit, Commercial Paper, Bankers' Acceptances and Repurchase Agreements that are all guaranteed by the same money center bank.)

## Personnel Responsibilities and Authority Limits

One of the most important components of any investment policy is to define clearly the responsibilities and authority limitations of the various personnel who are involved with investing the company's surplus money. For example, some of the policies that many companies consider implementing include

- limiting the amount of the investments that junior-level personnel can make without obtaining the approval of the senior manager.

- restricting junior-level personnel to only making investments in the vehicles in which they have proven expertise.

- granting each money manager "veto power" over investments that exceed a certain amount. In effect, requiring unanimous approval of large transactions by every member of the investment team.

- forming an investment policy committee to periodically review the investment policy.

- preparing appropriate controls and audit procedures.

## Required Criteria for Dealers and Custodians

An aspect of every investment program that is often overlooked and needs to be included in an investment policy statement is defining the banks, brokerage firms, and custodians with which a company will do business. Organizations generally choose one of the following alternatives when it comes to establishing dealer criteria:

- Dealing only with banks and securities dealers that the Federal Reserve Bank has designated "primary dealers," because they are generally too big to fail (see Chapter Five for a complete examination).

- Dealing only with banks and securities dealers that are on an approved list. The approved list is often prepared by the investment committee.

- Dealing with any bank or securities firm as long as all securities are paid for on a "delivery vs. payment" (DVP) basis. This means that a third-party institution holds the company's money until the securities are received, and thus largely eliminates the credit risk of dealing with smaller dealers.

(If possible, companies should try to keep politics out of the dealer selection process. Because a company is borrowing from a particular bank does not mean that the company should necessarily be buying securities from that bank.)

## Procedure for "Exceptions"

No matter how comprehensive and detailed a company's investment policy statement is, opportunities and situations will undoubtedly arise that will either not be covered by the investment policy or that would violate the investment policy. When these opportunities arise, the personnel responsible for investing the money will need a policy to deal with them. The most practical exception policy is to require that prior to entering into any transaction that violates the investment policy, approval must be obtained from the majority of the investment committee. In addition, a written record of every exception should be maintained so that they can be reviewed at the next investment committee meeting. Having too many exceptions is a clear indication that the investment policy needs to be revised.

## Revising an Investment Policy

Establishing an investment policy is not something that a treasurer can do once and be finished. Instead, treasurers will have to periodically revise their investment policies to reflect

- their organization's changing financial position.
- their organization's changing tolerance for risk.
- the introduction of new and/or redesigned investment vehicles.
- any changes in the structure of the market and any other changes that might occur.

The process by which the investment policy can be revised should be included in the investment policy itself. Usually, an investment committee consisting of a money manager, treasurer, and another senior manager is created and empowered to discuss and approve revisions. This investment committee should meet at least semiannually, and each member of the committee should be able to call a special meeting on short notice whenever necessary.

## Insuring Compliance

As mentioned previously, a copy of the investment policy should be forwarded to the company's financial controller and the outside auditors so that appropriate controls and audit procedures can be developed. In addition, the easiest way to insure compliance is to set up a spreadsheet for the short-term portfolio that automatically verifies compliance with your investment policy. For example, most companies have personal computer coordinators who can easily write macros that can automatically test a portfolio for compliance, and can point out any violations that need to be corrected.

# 2

# TAXABLE MONEY MARKET INSTRUMENTS

---

## INTRODUCTION

The traditional definition of a money market instrument is, *a high quality debt instrument that has an original maturity of a year or less*. Whereas this definition may have been useful in the past, it is now obsolete. Markets, including the money market, undergo constant change and innovation. Over the last decade the money market has undergone a tremendous amount of change and, now, any definition of money market instruments must include the following:

- Equities (especially those that were designed specifically to be money market instruments).

- Longer term debt instruments that are likely to have their lives shortened by call, put, or sinking fund provisions.

- Short-term debt instruments whose credit ratings are below investment grade.

- Long-term instruments with short remaining lives.

- The various floating rate instruments that are used as surrogates for the traditional instruments.

Unfortunately, none of these instruments is considered to be a money market instrument under the traditional definition. This chapter examines not only the traditional money market instruments, but also some of the more innovative vehicles and strategies that are commonly employed by short-term investors. Whereas the money market used to be somewhat sedate and mundane, today it is very dynamic and innovative.

# TRADITIONAL INSTRUMENTS

The traditional money market instruments include:

- Federal Funds
- Treasury Bills
- Certificates of Deposit
- Bankers' Acceptances
- Commercial Paper
- Repurchase Agreements

## Federal Funds

Federal Funds, commonly referred to as "Fed Funds," are funds that are immediately available that are held on deposit in a *reserve account* at a Federal Reserve Bank. (Commercial banks are required to maintain a non-interest bearing reserve account at their local Federal Reserve Bank. The balance in this account must equal a percentage of the deposits the bank accepts from its customers.)

Because Fed Funds do not earn the bank to whom they belong any interest, banks with more Fed Funds than they need to meet their own reserve requirements (i.e., excess reserves) usually choose to lend their excess reserves to other banks that have insufficient reserves. Lending excess reserves to another bank--at a competitive interest rate--is more sensible than allowing the funds to sit in a non-interest-bearing account (see the chapter on the Federal Reserve Bank for a more complete discussion of reserve accounts).

Banks usually lend their excess reserves for very short periods of time, often just overnight. Interbank loans of Fed Funds are referred to as "buys" and "sells," although they are really loans. For example, if a small bank lends Citicorp® $5,000,000 in Fed Funds on an overnight basis, the transaction would be described as a "sale of $5,000,000 in Fed Funds to Citicorp®."

The Fed Fund market is a very liquid market. Almost every bank is either a seller or buyer of Fed Funds on a daily basis. In addition, non-banking organizations can enter this market and lend their surplus cash funds to banks that need reserves. There is also a highly evolved broker market to facilitate the buying and selling of Fed

Funds. Because the Fed Funds market is so liquid, and because the term of most Fed Fund transactions is so short, the Fed Funds' rate tends to be one of the first market interest rates to change in response to changing market interest rates.

## Treasury Bills

A Treasury Bill, or T-Bill, is nothing more than a short-term U.S. Government Zero Coupon Bond. T-Bills are considered to be a safe investment because it is inconceivable that the government will default on its short-term debt obligations. The reason that a credit default is inconceivable is not because the government is particularly well-run, but because the government can simply print more dollars as needed. (Note that although T-Bills are not susceptible to credit risk, they *are* susceptible to political risk, which implies that the government can be shut down by a "budget impasse" and that, as a result, might fail to temporarily meet its obligations.)

Because T-Bills have no credit risk, and because of the huge volume of trade in the market, T-Bills are also very liquid instruments. The combination of credit quality and high liquidity makes T-Bills extremely attractive to investors with a low tolerance for risk.

The drawback of high liquidity and credit quality that T-Bills offer is their low yield. Normally, T-Bills offer the lowest yield of any money market instrument. Like other Treasury instruments, the interest on T-Bills is subject to Federal Income Tax, but are exempt from state and local income taxes.

### T-Bill Price and Yield Quotes

T-Bills are purchased for less than their face value. When T-Bills mature, the purchasers receive their face value. The difference between the T-Bill's purchase price and its face value is the investor's "interest." For example, if an investor bought a $100,000 T-Bill for $96,432, the interest the investor would receive when the T-Bill matures would be $3,568 ($100,000 minus $96,432). T-Bill discounts are normally expressed on an actual/360 basis (see the chapter on Money Market Mathematics for a more complete discussion).

## Purchasing T-Bills

The Treasury Department uses the Federal Reserve Bank to distribute its debt instruments, including its T-Bills. The FED distributes its T-Bills via public auctions. When they are first sold, T-Bills have original maturities of 13 weeks (91 days), 26 weeks (182 days) or 52 weeks (364 days). The 13-week T-Bills and the 26-week T-Bills are auctioned on a weekly basis, whereas the 52-week T-Bills are usually auctioned once a month.

Normally, the Treasury announces the number of T-Bills to be included in each auction approximately one week in advance of the actual auction date. The Treasury also announces how many of the T-Bills it plans to auction to simply refinance maturing T-Bills as opposed to how many are being sold to raise "new money." For example, the Treasury might announce that next week it will be auctioning $5.5 billion (face value) in T-Bills, $4 billion representing a refinancing of maturing T-Bills, and $1.5 billion representing new money that the Treasury needs to raise in order to finance the Federal Government's ever-present budget deficits.

## Bidding in an Auction

An investor can participate (i.e., bid) in a T-Bill auction in one of two ways: competitively or non-competitively. Usually, the FED sets aside enough T-Bills to fill all of the non-competitive bids and then holds a competitive auction for the balance. For example, if the Treasury were going to issue $5.5 billion in T-Bills in its weekly auction, and it received $1 billion worth of non-competitive bids, it would auction the remaining $4.5 billion *competitively*.

In the competitive portion of the auction, potential investors submit bids that include the face value of the T-Bills they wish to purchase and the discount rate they desire. The FED, after receiving all the bids, ranks the bids in order, from the lowest required discount to the highest. For example, assume that the FED received the competitive bids listed in Table 2.1. (Note that in a real auction, the FED receives thousands of bids.) Once the bids are ranked in order, the FED starts to fill the orders. It starts by filling the bid with the lowest required discount and then fills the bids with progressively higher desired discounts until it has allocated all of the T-Bills it has available for the competitive portion of the auction.

In Table 2.1, the FED would have run out of T-Bills after it filled bid #13. The discount rate on the last bid filled is referred to as the *stop*. Bids with discounts higher than 7.94% would go unfilled, and the investors who submitted those bids would have to buy their T-Bills in the secondary market.

The price that successful bidders pay for their T-Bills equates to the discount at which they bid. For example, the dealer who submitted bid #1 would pay $980,510.83/million face value for its T-Bills, whereas the investor who submitted bid #13 would pay $979,929.44 for the *identical* T-Bills. Thus, the investor or dealer who submitted bid #13 would pay $581.39/million *less* than the investor who submitted the first bid for the identical T-Bills. Thus, every competitive bidder wants to submit the last bid to be filled and to receive the highest discount rate.

For large investors, the difference in dollars between a good bid and a bad bid can be very substantial. Because there are so many dollars involved, large competitive bidders--primarily the major banks and securities firms--do a great deal of analysis before submitting their bids. They also wait until the last possible minute before submitting their bids so that their bids can reflect any last minute or sudden changes in market interest rates.

Once the competitive portion of the auction is completed, the FED calculates the weighted average discount of all the bids that were filled. This weighted average discount rate is then used to calculate the price that the non-competitive bidders pay for their T-Bills. Thus, the non-competitive bidders will receive a higher discount than half of the competitive bidders, and a lower discount than half of the competitive bidders. The difference between the weighted average winning discount rate and the highest winning discount rate (i.e., the *stop*) is commonly referred to as the *tail*. The smaller the tail, the more efficient the auction.

For those investors who lack the time, resources, expertise, and/or the inclination to deeply analyze the T-Bill market, the non-competitive bidding alternative provides a very practical and attractive way to acquire T-Bills. Recognizing that the competitive side of this market should be left to the "professionals," the FED requires that competitive bidders bid for a minimum of $200,000 (face value) of T-Bills per auction. Non-competitive bidders, on the other hand, can submit bids as small as $10,000 (face value), and are limited to maximum bids of $1,000,000 (face value) per auction.

**Table 2.1** *Bids in Hypothetical T-Bill Auction*

| Bid Number | Size of Bid (Millions) | Desired Discount Rate | Total Bids (Millions) |
|:---:|:---:|:---:|:---:|
| 1 | 200 | 7.71 | 200 |
| 2 | 300 | 7.72 | 500 |
| 3 | 400 | 7.72 | 900 |
| 4 | 500 | 7.74 | 1,400 |
| 5 | 450 | 7.75 | 1,850 |
| 6 | 150 | 7.75 | 2,000 |
| 7 | 250 | 7.76 | 2,250 |
| 8 | 550 | 7.77 | 2,800 |
| 9 | 600 | 7.81 | 3,400 |
| 10 | 700 | 7.91 | 4,100 |
| 11 | 100 | 7.92 | 4,200 |
| 12 | 150 | 7.93 | 4,350 |
| 13 | 150 | 7.94 | 4,500 |
| 14 | 250 | 7.95 | 4,750 |
| 15 | 400 | 7.95 | 5,150 |
| 16 | 600 | 7.98 | 5,750 |
| 17 | 700 | 7.99 | 6,450 |
| 18 | 300 | 8.01 | 6,750 |
| 19 | 250 | 8.02 | 7,000 |
| 20 | 400 | 8.03 | 7,400 |

Bids are submitted on the appropriate forms and must be accompanied by a certified check equal to the face value of the securities, in the case of a non-competitive bid, or by the purchase price, in the case of a competitive bid.

### The Usual T-Bill Auction Schedule

Currently, the FED auctions three-month and six-month T-Bills (usually in equal amounts) every Monday at 1:30 P.M. EST. The three-month and six-month T-Bills that are auctioned each Monday settle on Thursday of the same week. These same T-Bills mature in 13 or 26 weeks, respectively, (i.e., also on a Thursday). However, these T-Bills generally start to trade on the Tuesday of the week *before* they are auctioned. In other words, T-Bills can be traded before they exist.

These are referred to as *when issued* T-Bills. Thus, investors can sell T-Bills before they exist and use the auction to buy them to cover their short positions. Generally, *when issued* transactions settle when the auction settles (i.e., the Thursday immediately following the auction). The auction schedule for 1-year T-Bills is slightly different: they are auctioned on a Thursday and settle on the following Thursday.

## Certificates of Deposit and Time Deposits

The majority of Certificates of Deposit (CDs) that are sold in the United States are not technically CDs. The lobby of almost every bank or savings and loan institution in the U.S. has a sign that indicates the institution's CD interest rates. These are not really accurate, however. The difference is that actual CDs are negotiable instruments, i.e., they can be resold in the secondary market at whatever price the parties involved negotiate. However, the so-called CDs that most investors buy at their local bank or savings and loan institution are not negotiable; they cannot be resold prior to maturity.

Non-negotiable banking deposits are more correctly referred to as *Time Deposits* (TDs). Because TDs are non-negotiable, investors who must liquidate the investment prior to its scheduled maturity have to redeem it at the issuing institution and pay a penalty for early withdrawal.

Actual CDs are issued only by the money center banks. The minimum amount of a CD is $1,000,000, with $5,000,000 being the normal trading unit. CDs and TDs are usually sold on an interest-bearing, actual/360 basis.

## *Federal Deposit Insurance*

Deposits in banks and savings and loan institutions are currently insured for up to $100,000 of *principal and interest per depositor per institution,* by the Federal Government. (Banking deposits are actually insured by the taxpayers, because the government-sponsored insurance funds don't have enough reserves to cover even modest losses.)

Under the government's definition of *depositor*, every account with a different name is considered to be a separate depositor, and is therefore eligible for $100,000 insurance coverage. Thus, a family of four can have up to $900,000 in one institution and have it fully insured by opening nine accounts with different names:

1. Husband's account
2. Wife's account
3. Husband and wife--joint account
4. Husband, trustee for first child
5. Husband, trustee for second child
6. Wife, trustee for first child
7. Wife, trustee for second child
8. Husband and wife--joint trustees for first child
9. Husband and wife--joint trustees for second child

Organizations are not as fortunate. They generally open bank accounts in their own name only, and are therefore limited to $100,000 insured deposits per institution. Therefore, it is more difficult for organizations to manage the credit risk inherent in bank deposits (CDs or TDs).

Organizations have three ways of limiting the credit risk of their CDs and TDs:

- To buy CDs only from money center banks. The FED has stated publicly that the money center banks are too large to fail, and that it will do whatever is necessary to prevent a money center bank from failing. Thus, the general consensus is that there is no credit risk associated with placing money in a money center bank. Therefore, millions can be deposited in one institution in one name without assuming credit risk.

The disadvantage of buying CDs from money center banks is that they generally offer a lower yield than the TDs of smaller institutions. (Note that at press time, the FED was under pressure to retract its "too large to fail" policy.)

- To buy large TDs from smaller banks and savings and loan institutions. Whereas this alternative certainly exposes the organization to credit risk, careful research and analysis can partially mitigate this risk. Organizations that use this approach hope that the extra interest they receive for accepting the higher credit risk exceeds their actual credit losses.

(Note that some investors buy TDs from the same institutions that they borrow from, on the premise that they have no credit risk because they owe more to the institution than they have on deposit at the institution. However, this logic is flawed because if the institution fails, the court-appointed trustee will sue to collect the loan, whereas the organization may have little recourse regarding its lost deposits.)

- To buy $100,000 TDs from numerous smaller institutions. By limiting their deposits to $100,000 per institution, they need not be concerned about the credit quality of the institution. Thus, they can seek the highest yield while letting the taxpayers take the risk. The disadvantages of this approach are that wiring money to numerous institutions can be a very expensive and time-consuming process. Also, if the organization deposits $100,000 with each institution, only the principal is insured. If the institution fails, the organization may lose its interest. (This second problem can be avoided by buying only Zero Coupon Time Deposits that are worth $100,000 when they mature.)

At press time, there were several proposals before Congress to sharply limit deposit insurance protection.

## Variable Rate Certificates of Deposit

In addition to fixed rate CDs and TDs, banks also issue floating-rate CDs and TDs. These allow banks to lock in long-term financing without exposing the investors to the same degree of interest-rate risk as fixed-rate CDs and TDs. They become popular when investors expect interest rates to rise. Although there is a vast number of different types of floating-rate CDs and TDs, the two most common types are:

- six-month CDs with one-month resets.
- one-year CDs with three-month resets.

### *Eurodollar and Yankee Deposits*

When a bank outside the U.S. accepts a TD in U.S. dollars, the deposit is said to be a *Eurodollar Deposit*. The term is inappropriate because it implies that the deposit is in Europe. Actually, a dollar deposit in Hong Kong, Brazil, Mexico, or the Cayman Islands is also considered to be a Eurodollar Deposit. Dollar deposits outside the U.S. usually yield more than dollar deposits inside the U.S., because dollar deposits outside the U.S.:

- are not subject to the protection of the U.S. Judicial System.
- are exposed to sovereign risk (the risk that currency controls will prevent investors from repatriating their funds when their TD matures).
- are not backed by the "lender of last resort"--the FED.

"Yankee" CDs arc issued by the U.S. branches of foreign banks. Although these "Yankee banks" are owned by foreign banks, they must adhere to the same banking regulations and reserve requirements as domestic banks. "Yankee" CDs often offer a higher return than domestic CDs, usually because the name is unfamiliar to domestic investors.

## Bankers' Acceptances

In simple terms, a Bankers' Acceptance (BA) is created when a bank sells an investor an interest in a short-term bank loan that the bank has guaranteed. For example, suppose Chase Manhattan Bank® extends a 120-day $10,000,000 loan to one of its customers. When it executes this loan transaction, the bank receives an IOU from the customer which it carries on its books as an asset. (Normally, a short-term loan like the one described previously is created with a letter of credit and is used to finance an import-export transaction.)

The bank can elect to hold this asset until it matures or sell it to an investor. In order to facilitate the sale of its customer's IOU to an investor, the bank agrees to accept the credit risk associated with the IOU. Because the IOU is guaranteed by the bank, the investor can look to the bank for its credit guarantee, instead of having to research the credit quality of the actual borrower.

To verify that the bank has accepted the credit risk and will pay the IOU if the borrower defaults, the bank stamps *ACCEPTED* on the back of the IOU and has a bank officer sign it. The IOU will normally be sold on a discounted, actual/360 basis. Bankers' Acceptances are issued with maturities ranging from a minimum of approximately seven days to a maximum of 180 days. Multimillion-dollar transactions are normally broken into a combination of million-dollar "round lot" pieces and "odd lot" pieces. For example, if a bank had a $3,657,888 loan to a customer that it wanted to sell, it would break it into three $1 million pieces (the round lots) and one $657,888 piece (the odd lot).

When a bank sells a BA to the public, it is required by law to maintain a reserve account against the sale. This reserve account, coupled with the original borrower's credit guarantee, the bank's credit guarantee, and usually a lien against the merchandise being financed, makes BAs an investment with very little credit risk. However, they are not especially liquid and, thus, are not suitable for investors for whom liquidity is critical.

## Commercial Paper

Commercial paper (CP) is simply a short-term corporate IOU. Corporations borrow money from investors and give them an IOU which specifies when the loan will be repaid. Commercial paper is issued on both a discount basis and an interest-bearing basis and is priced on a 360-day basis.

By law, CP cannot have a maturity that is longer than 270 days. The reason for this limitation is that, under the Securities Act of 1933, any syndicated loan that is longer than 270 days is considered a security. As a security, the issuer would have to register the issue with the Securities and Exchange Commission (the SEC), produce a prospectus, etc., all of which would significantly raise the cost of funding. Most CP has an original maturity between seven and 90 days.

Like long-term investments, CP is rated by the major rating agencies as regards its creditworthiness. For example, Table 2.2 illustrates Standard & Poors'® CP ratings.

## Direct Paper versus Dealer Paper

Commercial Paper is issued in one of two ways: either directly by the issuing company, or indirectly by dealers (either commercial banks or investment banks) that are hired by the issuing companies.

Only those companies that frequently issue CP can justify the cost of maintaining an in-house marketing staff to sell its CP directly to investors. Thus, these direct issuers tend to be some of the largest issuers of CP. Because these direct issuers have more CP outstanding, their CP issues tend to be more liquid, and usually offer a lower yield than CP that is sold by dealers.

**Table 2.2** *Standard & Poors® Ratings System*

| Rating | Definition |
|--------|------------|
| A-1 | This indicates that the degree of safety regarding timely payment is either overwhelming or very strong. Those issues determined to possess overwhelming safety characteristics are denoted with a plus sign. |
| A-2 | Capacity for timely payment on issues with this designation is strong. However, the relative safety is not as high as for issues designated "A-1." |
| A-3 | Issues carrying this designation have satisfactory capacity for timely payment. They are, however, somewhat more vulnerable to the adverse effects of changes in circumstances than are obligations carrying higher designations. |
| B | Issues rated "B" are regarded as having only an adequate capacity for timely payment. However, such capacity may be damaged by changing conditions or short-term adversities. |
| C | This rating is assigned to short-term obligations with a doubtful capacity for payment. |
| D | This rating indicates that the issue is either in default or expected to be upon maturity. |
| +/- | Ratings may be modified by a plus or minus sign, reflecting the relative standing within the major ratings categories. |

CP dealers are generally hired by two types of issuers:

- Large companies that do not issue CP frequently and, thus, are not well known in the CP market.

- Smaller companies that have trouble securing an acceptable credit rating on their own.

## Letters of Credit (LOCs) and Commercial Paper

A specific issuer's CP often has two associated standby LOCs:

- The first protects the *issuer* against the risk that it will not be able to sell its CP. For whatever reason, if the company (or its dealer) is unable to sell or roll over the issuer's CP, the issuer will draw against its LOC in order to obtain funding. No corporate treasurer wants to risk missing payroll simply because they can't roll over their company's CP. Thus, the first letter of credit protects the issuer against liquidity risk.

- The second protects the investors against the risk that the issuer will default on its CP obligations. Commercial Paper with this type of backing is referred to as "bank-backed CP," although the credit guarantee is often extended by an insurance company instead of a bank (bank-backed CP is about 40% of the market).

  Issuers whose paper would be rated A-3 (or lower) by one of the major rating agencies generally have to obtain a letter of credit that guarantees their paper in order to make it marketable. By obtaining a LOC, CP that would have been rated A-3 is instead rated A-1, and A-1 CP is much more marketable. (Note that CP that obtains an A-1 rating via a LOC will generally offer a higher yield than CP that obtains an A-1 rating based solely on the credit strength of the issuer.)

The latest trend in the CP market is the growth of asset-backed CP including CP backed by real estate, other CP, receivables, inventory warehouse receipts. There are several reasons for this trend:

- Banks, and other extenders of financial guarantees, have become less willing to extend letters of credit to issuers of CP because they have become more credit-sensitive and because they now have to maintain a reserve requirement against their LOCs.

- Issuers have become less willing to make unsecured investments because of an increase in defaults.

## Repurchase Agreements

Repurchase Agreements (repos) are defined as the sale of a security coupled with an agreement by the seller to repurchase the security from the buyer at a slightly higher price, at a time agreed upon that is usually within one to 60 days, making the "sale" temporary.

The reason that the seller of the securities repurchases the same securities at a later date--and at a higher price--is to compensate the lender for the use of the lender's money. In effect, the differential between the price at which the security is sold and the price at which it is repurchased is the money lender's interest. The real purpose of a repo is to create a secured short-term loan.

For example, suppose that Merrill Lynch® wants to borrow money to finance its inventory of securities. Merrill Lynch® could, of course, borrow in the CP market, but because CP is an unsecured instrument and therefore has some credit risk, Merrill Lynch® would have to offer a yield on its CP that compensates investors for this risk. Instead of borrowing only on its own credit strength, suppose Merrill Lynch® also allowed its lenders to hold some high quality collateral, such as Treasury Bonds, in order to guarantee the loan. The loan would have much less credit risk and Merrill Lynch® would be able to borrow at a lower rate. Thus, in a repo the borrowers allow lenders to temporarily hold some securities as collateral so that they can borrow from the lenders at a lower rate. In order to effectively protect the lender against the risk that the borrower will default, and thus to insure that the lender will get its money back in full and on time, repo lenders have to follow certain procedures and guidelines.

### THE FIVE REPO COMMANDMENTS

- The securities used for collateral must have a very high credit rating in order to provide the lender with true credit risk protection.

- The securities used for collateral must be very liquid so that they can be sold quickly, if necessary.

- The market value of the securities must be greater than the amount of the loan (i.e., the loan must be over-collateralized). Typically, the loan will be over-collateralized between 1% and 10%, depending upon the credit strength of the borrower, the type of securities used as collateral, and the term of the transaction.

- If the borrower defaults, the lender needs to be free to sell the collateral in order to recoup its investment. The only way the borrower can be sure that the securities can be sold quickly is to either deliver the securities to the lender, or have the borrower deliver the securities to an *independent* third party. Repos in which the borrower holds the collateral as convenience for the lender defeat the whole purpose of establishing a repurchase agreement.

- The transaction must be properly documented. A prototype contract is available, without cost, from the Public Securities Association (PSA) in New York. The PSA can be contacted by telephone at (212) 809-7000.

**Figure 2.1** *Repo and Reverse Repo*

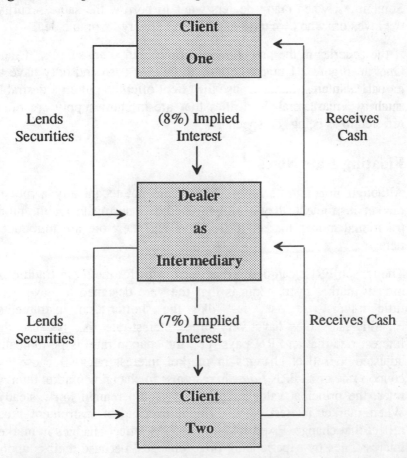

Recently, there have been some well-publicized problems with the repo market (ESM Securities®, Lombard Wall®, and others). However, in every case where lenders lost money in repo transactions, they ignored the preceding commandments.

Dealers are not the only ones who use repos to obtain low-cost financing. Investors can also borrow money at a very low rate from their banks and dealers by allowing their dealers to hold high-quality liquid securities as collateral. Transactions where the dealer receives securities and lends cash are referred to as *reverse repos*. Most dealers enter into regular and reverse repos and try to make a "spread" between the two transactions. In addition to investors initiating reverse repos in order to obtain short-term financing, dealers also initiate reverse repos in order to borrow the specific Treasury Securities they need to cover their short positions. Sometimes, when many dealers want to borrow the same security, the investors who own the security can cut very favorable deals.

If the security in the preceding example is in short supply, "Client One" in Figure 2.1 might be able to borrow cash and only have to pay a 1% interest rate, because the client offers to put up a desirable security as collateral. Securities that are in short supply are often referred to as being "on special."

## Floating-Rate Notes

Although floating-rate notes (FRNs) are not technically a money market instrument, they are often used as a surrogate for the more traditional money market instruments and therefore are introduced here.

The reason FRNs can be used as surrogates for the more traditional money market instruments is that they are designed to have very little interest-rate risk, just like the shorter-term instruments. Floating-rate notes have very little interest-rate risk because the interest rate that an FRN pays (i.e., the coupon rate) is periodically adjusted to reflect changes in market interest rates. Because the coupon rate of an FRN *floats* in response to changing market interest rates, the principal value of the note should remain fairly steady. When market interest rates change, every debt instrument must reflect that change. Fixed-rate instruments reflect changes in market interest rates by experiencing price changes, because their coupons are fixed. Floating-rate notes reflect changes in market interest rates by experiencing rate changes, allowing their market value to remain reasonably constant.

Because FRNs are designed to trade at (or near) value, some investors do not think it is important to really research the particular issues. They assume, erroneously, that one "A+"-rated FRN is the same as another "A+"-rated FRN. Unfortunately, there is quite a bit of diversity within the FRN market. Different FRNs that have different characteristics do not offer the same yield--nor do they offer the same value.

Floating-rate notes that have the same credit rating can still differ regarding:

- Index rate
- Caps, floors, and collars
- Reset period
- Spread over the index
- Spread quote
- Liquidity

## The FRN's Index Rate

The coupon rate of every FRN is tied to a specific index rate. When an FRN is originally issued, the index rate to which the note is tied and the spread that the note will pay relative to the index rate is fixed for the life of the note. Thus, the only principal variable that determines the coupon of an FRN is the index rate.

Although almost every short-term rate has been used as the index rate of an FRN, the most popular index rates are

- the yield offered by the six-month T-Bill.
- the six-month U.S. dollar Libor Rate.
- the prime rate.

At any given time, one index rate may prove to be the most attractive for investors and another index rate may prove to be the most attractive for issuers. As an illustration, consider the following example:

Suppose there are three FRNs (i.e., notes "A," "B," and "C"). The notes are identical in all respects (credit quality, reset period, and so on) except that they are tied to different index rates and have different spreads relative to their respective indices.

**Table 2.3** *Alternative Notes*

| Note | Index | Spread over Index | Current Index Rate | Note's Current Coupon |
|------|-------|-------------------|--------------------|-----------------------|
| A | T-Bills | +200 bp | 7.50% | 9.50% |
| B | Libor | +100 bp | 8.50% | 9.50% |
| C | Prime | -50 bp | 10.00% | 9.50% |

For all three notes, coupon rate is equal to the sum of the index rate plus the spread (i.e., 9.50%). Whereas all the FRNs currently offer the same coupon rate, this does not mean that they are all equally attractive.

The reason these three FRNs are not equally attractive, despite the fact that they offer the same coupon rate, is that the inter-index rate spreads will change over time. According to the preceding chart, the current spread between the T-Bill yield and the Libor Rate is 100 bp, which is why notes A and B currently have the same coupon. Recently, however, the spread between these two index rates has been as low as minus 15 bp and as high as plus 450 bp. As the spread between these two index rates changes, so does the attractiveness of Note A relative to Note B for both the issuer and the investor.

Thus, in order to determine whether Note A or Note B is a more attractive investment, an investor has to predict whether the spread between the T-Bill yield and the Libor Rate will widen or narrow. The principal factors that cause the spread between T-Bills and Libor to change are the degree of confidence that investors have, and the relative level of market interest rates.

Any time the world suffers a political or economic shock, investors usually respond by having a "flight to quality." Any time there is a shock to the system, investors pull money out of the Eurodollar market and instead buy T-Bills and other low-risk alternatives. By pulling dollars out of the Eurodollar market, investors cause the Libor Rate to rise (supply and demand), and by flocking to buy T-Bills, they cause the T-Bill yield to fall (also supply and demand). Thus, a shock to the system will cause the inter-index (Libor-T-Bill) spread to widen.

If the inter-index spread does widen, Note B will soon offer a higher coupon than Note A. If the inter-index spread rises by 50 bp, then Note B will yield 50 bp more than Note A. Because Note B yields more than Note A, the value of Note B will rise and the value of Note A will fall, making Note B a more attractive investment than Note A.

In addition, as interest rates rise, the inter-index spread between the Libor Rate and the T-Bill Rate also tends to increase. The spread widens so that the percentage difference between the two yields can remain constant. Consider the following example:

Assume that the T-Bill yield is 4% and the Libor Rate is 5%. Given these yields, it can be concluded that investors are demanding a 25% *incremental return* in exchange for taking the additional risk of having their dollars outside the legal jurisdiction of the U.S. (4% + 1% = 5%, 1%/4% = 0.25%). In order to maintain this 0.25% yield differential, if the T-Bill yield rises to 8%, the Libor Rate will have to rise to 10%. Thus, if the T-Bill yield rises to 8%, we would expect the inter-index spread to increase by about 100 bp--again making Note B relatively more attractive than Note A.

**Figure 2.2** *Impact of Rate Change on Spread*

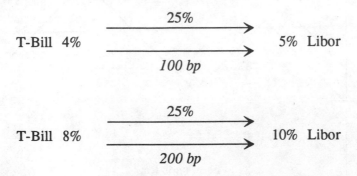

In addition to considering the factors that impact the spread between the T-Bill yield and the Libor Rate, investors also need to consider the factors that will impact the inter-index spread between the prime rate and the other index rates. There are two main factors that impact the spread between the prime rate and the other index rates: (1) the credit quality of the underlying bank(s), and (2) the speed at which the bank reduces its prime rate.

Consider the following example: Suppose a specific floating-rate note is tied to Chase Manhattan Bank's® prime rate. If the bank's credit quality declines, its cost of funding will increase. If the bank's cost of funding increases, it will have to increase its prime rate in order to maintain its spread. Thus, as the bank's credit quality declines, FRNs tied to the bank's prime rate become more attractive, relative to notes tied to other index rates (unless the notes are issued by the bank).

In addition, whereas all three index rates rise quickly in a rising interest rate environment, banks have been accused of being slow to lower their prime rate when interest rates fall. Although this lethargic behavior hurts borrowers whose loans are tied to the bank's prime rate, it helps investors whose FRNs are tied to the bank's prime rate.

**Figure 2.3** *Spread Between Prime and Fed Funds*

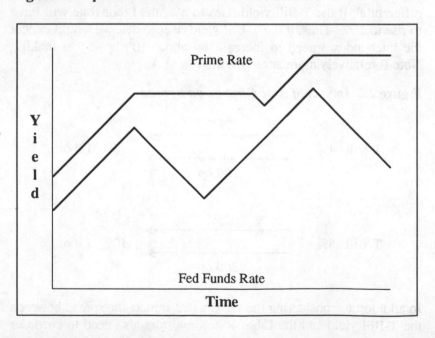

Suppose an investor's best projections were that:

- the Libor Rate was going to rise by 100 bp.
- the T-Bill yield was going to rise by 50 bp.
- the prime rate was going to rise by 75 bp.

If the investor's projections were correct, then Note B would be the best choice for the investor because it would soon offer a higher coupon rate than the alternatives. As an investor's projections change, so does the investor's preferences.

However, from the *issuer's* point of view, they would like to tie their FRN to whichever note will have the lowest coupon rate. Given the same projections, issuers would prefer to issue notes tied to the T-Bill yield, because they are projected to have the lowest coupon rate. As always, the objectives of the issuers and the objectives of the investor are diametrically opposed.

## The Reset Period

The reset period of an FRN is the amount of time it takes while the FRN's coupon rate is adjusted. Like the index rate and the spread relative to the index, the reset period is fixed when the FRN is originally issued. The commonly used reset periods are: daily, weekly, monthly, quarterly, semiannually, and annually.

The reset period used by a specific note has a direct impact on its value. At different times, either short reset periods or long reset periods are preferable. If an investor expected market interest rates to rise, then the investor would want the coupon rate to reset frequently, so that the investment would closely track the index rate.

However, if the investor expected market interest rates to fall, the investor would want a relatively long reset period so that the FRN earned an above-market rate of return for a longer period of time.

(Note that the reset period cannot exceed the maximum maturity outlined in the investor's investment policy statement.)

**Figure 2.4** *Rising Interest Rate Environment*

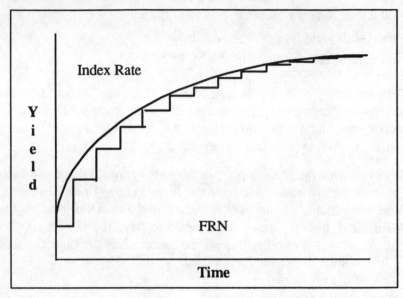

**Figure 2.5** *Falling Interest Rate Environment*

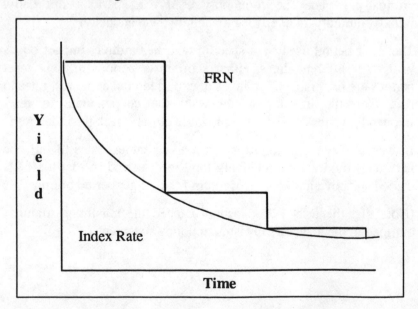

## *Floors, Caps, and Collars*

Although the coupon rates of all FRNs float in response to changes in market interest rates, they cannot float in an unlimited manner. Many FRN issues have a maximum coupon rate that they *can* pay and/or the minimum coupon rate that they *must* pay. Both the minimum and maximum coupon rates (if any) are fixed when the FRN is first issued.

The maximum coupon rate is referred to as the "cap rate," and the minimum rate is referred to as the "floor rate." "Caps" protect the issuers by limiting how high the coupon rates can go--regardless of how high the index rates go. "Floors" protect the investors by limiting how low the coupon rates can go--regardless of how low the index rates drop.

Consider what the coupon rate of an FRN would be if:

- the note's coupon was set at T-Bills plus 50 bp.
- the note had a 13% "cap."
- the note had a 7.5% "floor."
- the note had a daily reset.

**Figure 2.6** *FRN Yields with Cap and Floor*

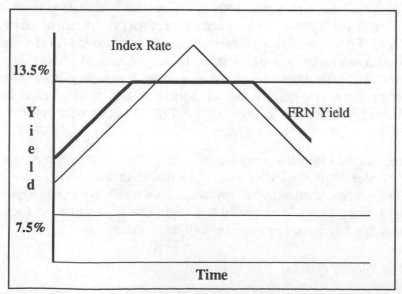

Note that when the T-Bill yield exceeds 12.5%, the FRN will be "capped out" at 13%. As the T-Bill yield rises above 12.5%, the 13% return that the FRN pays becomes less attractive and, as a result, the market value of the FRN declines, sometimes significantly below usual. For investors whose FRNs are "capped out," there are only two possible alternatives:

- a *decline* in the FRN's price if interest rates *rise*.
- a *decline* in the FRN's coupon rate if interest rates *fall*.

Admittedly, this is not an attractive set of alternatives. Because an FRN that is "capped out" is a lose-lose proposition, investors should sell FRNs well before they are "capped out." However, when the T-Bill rate drops below 7%, the FRN is "floored." For investors whose FRNs are "floored," there are only two possible alternatives:

- a *rising* FRN price if interest rates *fall*.
- a *rising* coupon rate if interest rates *rise*.

Because an FRN that is "floored" is a win-win proposition, investors should buy FRNs when they expect that they will become "floored."

### Spread over the Index

The spread that a particular FRN offers over its index rate is fixed at the time the FRN is first issued. However, the spread of newly issued FRNs over their respective indices changes as market conditions change. For example, in January, AA-rated FRNs tied to the T-Bill yield might be issued at a 35 bp spread. By July, if the balance between the number of borrowers and lenders changes, borrowers may have to offer a spread of 50 bp on new AA-rated FRNs.

Because the FRNs that were issued in July offer a higher spread over the index than the FRNs that were issued in January, they will always be more attractive to investors. As a result, we would expect the January FRNs to be priced at a slight discount, while the FRNs issued in July would be priced at a slight premium.

### The Spread Quote

Spreads are usually quoted in one of two ways: either as a fixed number of basis points, or as a fixed percentage of the index rate.

The alternative that is more attractive depends on whether the index rate rises or falls. Consider the following example:

Suppose there were two FRNs (A and B) that were identical in every way except that Note A's coupon rate was equal to the index plus 70 bp, and Note B's coupon rate was equal to 110% of the index rate.

If the index rate was currently 7%, both FRNs would offer a 7.70% coupon. However, as the index rate changed, the two notes would no longer offer the same return:

**Table 2.4** *FRNs with Different Spread Quotes*

|  | 7% | 5% | 9% |
|---|---|---|---|
| Note A (+70 bp) | 7.70% | 5.70% | 9.70% |
| Note B (+110%) | 7.70% | 5.50% | 9.90% |

Thus, if the index rate declines having the spread defined in basis points is the more attractive alternative. However, if the index rate increases, one would rather have their spread defined in terms of a percentage of the index rate.

## *Liquidity*

The liquidity of an FRN is determined primarily by

- the size of the issue (generally, the larger the issue, the more liquid it will be).
- the name recognition of the issuer (generally, the more recognizable the name of the issuer, the more liquid the issue).
- the issue's structure (generally, the less complicated the structure, the more liquid the issue).

Thus, a $200 million issue from IBM that is tied to six-month Libor with a six-month reset will be more liquid than a $25 million issue from a no-name issuer that is tied to the prime rate of an obscure bank.

In conclusion, the type of FRN that is most attractive depends on one's expectations about the direction of interest rates.

**Table 2.5 *FRN Summary***

| | Interest Rates Rise | Interest Rates Fall |
|---|---|---|
| Index | Libor or Prime | T-Bills or Prime |
| Reset Period | Short | Long |
| Caps/Floors | No Cap or High Cap | High Floor |
| Spread | Percentage of Index Rate | Index Rate + Spread (bp) |

# RIDING DOWN THE YIELD CURVE

One strategy that investors frequently employ is to buy longer-term assets and then sell them prior to their maturity. In other words, if an investor wanted to make a six-month investment, rather than buy a six-month instrument, the investor would buy a 1-year instrument and sell it in six months. The risk of using long-term assets to meet short-term liabilities is that if interest rates rise, the value of the security will decline (i.e., interest-rate risk). Although this risk certainly exists, it is mitigated whenever the yield curve experiences a sharp positive slope. Consider the following example:

Suppose an investor wants to make a 1-year investment when the yield curve resembles the following:

**Figure 2.7 *Riding Down the Yield Curve***

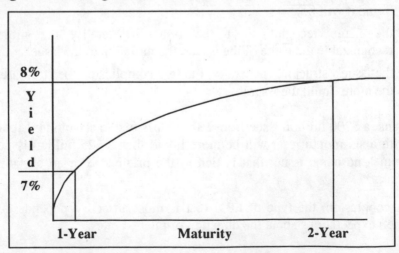

The investor could, of course, simply buy the 1-year Corporate Bond, which is currently yielding 7% (30/360). If the investor bought the 1-year bond and held it until it matured, the investor would have no interest-rate risk. However, the investor would also have no interest rate opportunity.

As an alternative to simply buying the 1-year bond, the investor could buy the 2-year bond and sell it in a year. The 2-year bond is currently yielding 8% (30/360). However, if the investor bought it and interest rates rose, when the investor sold the bond in a year he or she might take a loss. Fortunately, the investor's interest rate exposure can be easily quantified--as can the net advantage or disadvantage of buying the 2-year bond instead of the 1-year bond.

**Table 2.6** *The Net Return of a $5Million Investment in a 7% 1-Year Bond Compared to a $5Million Investment in an 8% 2-Year Bond Given Various Interest Rate Changes over the Holding Period (Ignoring Reinvestment Income)*

| Interest Rate Change | Interest Gain | Capital Gain or Loss | Net Gain or Loss |
|---|---|---|---|
| -300 bp | +$50,000 | +$200,000 | +$250,000 |
| -250 bp | +$50,000 | +$175,000 | +$225,000 |
| -200 bp | +$50,000 | +$150,000 | +$200,000 |
| -150 bp | +$50,000 | +$125,000 | +$175,000 |
| -100 bp | +$50,000 | +$100,000 | +$150,000 |
| -50 bp | +$50,000 | +$75,000 | +$125,000 |
| 0 | +$50,000 | +$50,000 | +$100,000 |
| +50 bp | +$50,000 | +$25,000 | +$75,000 |
| +100 bp | +$50,000 | 0 | +$50,000 |
| +150 bp | +$50,000 | -$25,000 | +$25,000 |
| +200 bp | +$50,000 | -$50,000 | 0 |
| +250 bp | +$50,000 | -$75,000 | -$25,000 |
| +300 bp | +$50,000 | -$100,000 | -$50,000 |

By investing $5,000,000 in the 2-year 8% bond instead of the 1-year 7% bond, the investor will earn an extra 1%, or $50,000, in interest income. In addition, the investor will have a capital gain or loss depending on what happens to market interest rates.

Note that if interest rates remain unchanged, the investor will have a capital gain simply because the 2-year note the investor bought is now a 1-year note. The investor will have traveled the positively sloped yield curve. If interest rates remain unchanged, the investor will be able to price the note to offer a 7% yield, although it pays an 8% coupon. In other words, the investor will be able to sell the note at a premium simply because the note is now closer to maturity.

If 1-year rates rise by 200 bp over the next year, from 7% to 9%, then the investor will sell the notes at a loss--but the capital loss will be offset by the additional income, resulting in no difference between the net return the investor receives from either the 2-year or 1-year note. Thus, if rates decline, stay the same, or rise by 200 bp or less, the investor nets a better "all in return" from the 2-year than from the 1-year note.

## SYNTHETIC MONEY MARKET INSTRUMENTS

In addition to the natural instruments described previously, very sophisticated investors can also create synthetic money market instruments by using futures, options, and options on futures. These instruments are discussed in later chapters.

# 3

# TAX-ADVANTAGED MONEY
# MARKET INSTRUMENTS

## INTRODUCTION

Tax-advantaged money market instruments have become
increasingly popular. Often, investors can earn a higher after-tax
return from tax-advantaged instruments than they can from taxable
money market instruments. Tax-advantaged money market
instruments fall into one of two categories: municipal securities or
equities.

### Municipal Securities

A municipal security is issued by a state or political subdivision of a
state. (Municipal securities are discussed in greater detail in Chapter
15.) The first question that needs to be answered regarding
short-term municipal investments is, "How will it be taxed?"
However, this is sometimes very difficult to answer. How a
municipal security is taxed depends on a variety of factors, including
the state in which the bond is issued.

- the state in which the investor resides.
- the type of municipal security.

In addition, if the investor is a corporation, the following factors can
also influence the tax status of a municipal security:

- The state in which the corporation is headquartered.
- The investor's balance sheet.
- Where the investor's parent company, if any, is incorporated and
  headquartered.

Whereas all of the various tax issues involved are beyond the scope of this text, it is imperative that investors verify the tax status of the particular municipal securities that they are considering prior to making any investments.

## THE VARIOUS TYPES OF MUNICIPALS

There are seven principal types of short-term municipal securities with which investors need to be familiar:

- Tax Anticipation Notes (TANs)
- Bond Anticipation Notes (BANs)
- Revenue Anticipation Notes (RANs)
- Short-term municipal leases
- Long-term municipal securities with short remaining lives
- Long-term municipal securities with embedded options
- Municipal low floaters

### Tax Anticipation Notes

Tax Anticipation Notes (TANs) are short-term notes that municipalities issue as a form of "bridge financing," usually until the next tax collection date. For example, suppose a city collects its property taxes in January and June. If this city runs out of cash in November, it may elect to issue a TAN in order to meet its expenses from November until January. These short-term notes would be secured by the January tax receipts. Thus, before the city could use the January tax receipts for any other purpose, it would first have to pay off the TANs.

One problem with TANs is that cities sometimes become too dependent on them. They are fine to bridge some short-term cash flow mismatches, but if a city starts to borrow regularly against its future tax revenue in order to meet its current operating expenses, sooner or later the city will find itself in a financial crisis. Thus, it is very important to monitor the credit quality of TANs.

## Bond Anticipation Notes

Bond Anticipation Notes (BANs) are short-term municipal notes that are secured by the sales proceeds of a future bond offering. In effect, a BAN is a borrowing that is secured by the proceeds of a future borrowing. There are two reasons why a municipal issuer would issue a BAN: the issuer either expects that market interest rates will decline, or that its credit quality will improve (or both).

For example, suppose that the State of New Jersey wants to borrow $250 million to build a new highway and wants to pay for this highway over a 20-year period. If interest rates are presently very high, 20-year municipal interest rates might be around 10%. If New Jersey elects to borrow the money it needs now, it will be stuck paying that high 10% rate for the next 20 years. However, if the Controller of the State of New Jersey thought that interest rates were going to decline over the next year, the Controller might elect to delay the borrowing for one year. However, in order to start construction immediately, the State of New Jersey would issue a 1-year $250 million BAN.

By issuing the BAN, the state gets the money it needs to start construction. The state also delays the issuance of its long-term debt for one year when, hopefully, interest rates will be lower. If 20-year rates drop by 150 bp over the next year, the city will save $3,750,000/year in interest expense every year for the next 20 years. Of course, in order for the original BANs to be paid off, the state will have to either issue the bonds in one year or be able to roll over its BANs for another year. The risk to investors is that the state will be unable to do either, and therefore will be unable to settle the original BANs in full and on time.

## Revenue Anticipation Notes

Revenue Anticipation Notes (RANs) are short-term notes that are secured by a revenue source other than taxes or a future bond issue. This category is a "catch all" for notes that are secured by other future revenue sources. Some of the types of future revenue sources that commonly secure RANs are federal grants, state revenue sharing programs, excise taxes, license fees, and proceeds of asset sales.

## Municipal Leases

One of the fastest growing segments of the municipal market is the Municipal Lease Market. Municipal leases are often used by politicians to overcome a classic "Catch 22." In many states and municipalities, the government is prohibited from incurring any debt that lasts longer than one year without first obtaining the voters' approval by a public referendum. This restriction, although necessary to control spendthrift politicians, can cause some unexpected problems. For example, consider a situation in which a city wants to buy two fire trucks for $200,000. If the city doesn't have $200,000 in cash, it will have to finance the purchase. Ideally, the city would like to pay for the fire trucks over a 5-year period. Here is where the city faces a "Catch 22": The city cannot borrow money for five years without obtaining prior voter approval, however, obtaining voter approval can be very time-consuming and expensive.

The solution to this dilemma is for the city to finance the fire trucks by a series of five, 1-year renewable leases. Because each lease only lasts for one year, and because the city is not obligated to renew the lease when it matures, there is no requirement for a voter referendum. Thus, the city accomplishes its objective of obtaining 5-year financing without having to obtain voter approval. In order to encourage the city to renew the lease, the lease normally requires a substantial down payment, which would be lost if the city elected not to renew. In addition, if the city completes the series of leases, it can usually purchase the equipment for $1. Municipal lease deals are usually structured either by the leasing divisions of larger manufacturers, or third-party intermediaries that purchase the equipment from smaller manufacturers and then lease it to municipal governments.

To provide lease investors with additional protection, many leases include a provision that states that if the city elects not to renew an equipment lease agreement, for whatever reason, the equipment manufacturer will repurchase the equipment for a price equal to the remaining balance on the lease. This is referred to as a "buy back" provision. Thus, if after the first year the city elects not to renew its fire truck lease, the investor's call "puts" the equipment back to the fire truck manufacturer.

**Figure 3.1** *Equipment Leasing Transaction from the Intermediary's Point of View*

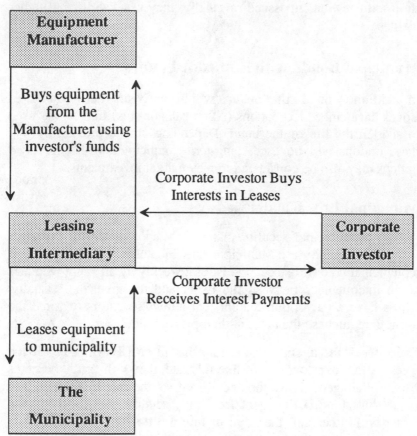

The market for leases is not as liquid as the market for the more traditional short-term securities, although liquidity has increased sharply in recent years. As a result of their relative lack of liquidity, leases often offer significantly higher yields than traditional instruments from the same city.

## Long-Term Municipals with Short Remaining Lives

Although most short-term investors focus on the instruments that are originally issued as short-term instruments, it is important to remember that every long-term Municipal Bond will eventually become a short-term instrument. Thus, every long-term bond will eventually become a money market instrument. Because a long-term bond with a short remaining life will usually be less liquid than a short-term instrument issued originally, they usually offer a higher yield.

## Municipal Bonds with Embedded Options

In addition to bonds that mature within one year, many Municipal Bonds have embedded options (either calls or puts) that can be used to shorten the life of the bond. Depending on the probability that these options will be used, long-term municipals with embedded options may also be considered money market investments.

## Municipal Low Floaters

A type of municipal security that is very appropriate for investors who value liquidity are Municipal Low Floaters (MLFs). A MLF is a municipal note whose coupon is reset weekly by an agent who acts as an intermediary between the issuer and the investors. Usually, MLFs have a put option feature that allows investors to force the agent to repurchase the notes at their proper value.

Every week the agent sets the rate that the MLF will pay for the week. If the investors do not like this rate, they will "put" the notes back to the agent. Thus, the agent must set the rate high enough to attract investors. If the agent frequently sets the rate too high, the issuer will either call the issue or hire a different agent. Thus, the agent is always between a "rock and a hard place."

# EQUITIES

The other type of tax-advantaged security that needs to be considered is equity. Obviously, not all types of equity are suitable investment vehicles for short-term portfolios (it would be very inappropriate to put growth stocks into a short-term portfolio). However, there are several types of equity that were specifically created to be included in short-term portfolios. In addition, there are several equity-related strategies that investors can implement in their short-term portfolios that offer very high potential returns-- particularly for corporate investors.

The reason equities are an attractive investment for corporate investors is that when one company invests in another company's equity, it is entitled to a 70% dividend exclusion on the dividends it receives. This means that the investing corporation has to pay Federal Income Tax on only 30% of the dividends it receives. Even if the investing corporation is in the maximum 34% tax bracket, its overall tax rate is just:

$$[(70\% * 0) + (30\% * 0.34)] = 10.2\%$$

Only two conditions must be met in order to claim this dividend exclusion:

- The investing corporation must be a Subchapter "C" corporation. Subchapter "S" corporations are not entitled to the dividend exclusion, because their income is passed through to their shareholders.

- The investing corporation must hold the investment for a minimum of 45 days (i.e, it can sell the equity on the 46th day after it is purchased).

## Adjustable Rate Preferred Stocks

One of the earliest types of equity created specifically to be suitable as a short-term corporate cash investment is the Adjustable Rate Preferred Stock (ARP). As the name implies, ARPs are preferred stocks whose dividend rate is adjusted periodically. However, instead of the dividend rate being adjusted to reflect changes in the company's earnings, as with common stocks, with ARPs the dividend rate is adjusted to reflect changes in market interest rates. The concept of ARPs is similar to that of FRNs. Because the dividend rate is allowed to float in response to changing market interest rates, the principal value should remain reasonably constant. However, as discovered in the chapter on FRNs, just because a security is designed to have minimal interest-rate risk, that does not mean that it is risk-free.

As with FRNs, ARPs are tied to an index rate, however, that index rate is not as simple. The index rate that most ARPs are tied to is referred to as the *basis rate*. The basis rate is defined as the highest yield offered by either the three-month T-Bill, 10-year T-Note, or 20-year T-Bond.

The advantage of having the index rate of an ARP set to the highest of these three rates is that the investor is largely protected against changes in the shape of the yield curve. Regardless of whether short-, intermediate, or long-term interest rates are the highest, the ARP's yield will be competitive.

## Advantages of Adjustable Rate Preferred Stocks

The advantages that ARPs offer corporate investors are:

- Liquidity, because equities can usually be bought or sold quickly and at a fair price.
- Low transaction costs, often as low as $0.03/share.
- Tax-advantaged income, because the dividends have a 70% dividend exclusion.
- Partial protection against changes in market interest rates, because the dividend rate adjusts.
- Partial protection against changes in the shape of the yield curve, because of the way the index is structured.

## Disadvantages of Adjustable Rate Preferred Stocks

Although ARPs have many features that make them attractive corporate investments, they also have two very significant risks: credit risk and bracket risk.

The credit risk is that the ARP's credit quality will be downgraded. Because the ARP's spread, relative to the basis rate, is fixed when the note is issued, any decline in the credit quality of the ARP will result in a loss in the ARP's market value. The market naturally expects a higher return from a BBB-rated issue than it does from a AA-rated issue. Because a particular ARP's spread, relative to the basis rate, does not adjust for changes in credit quality, the market value of the ARP will.

The bracket risk is that the ARP will be "capped out" at its maximum rate. As with FRNs, if an ARP is capped out, its market value will decline whenever interest rates rise--like a fixed-rate instrument.

For ARP investors, most of the early issuers were, unfortunately, money center banks. Soon after ARPs became popular, the market experienced what is now "affectionately" referred to as the Latin American Banking Crisis, as well as record-high interest rates. The combination of these events caused the credit rating of ARPs to be downgraded at the same time that they were capped out. Consequently, their market values dropped well below normal. As a result of their poor performance in the early 1980s, ARPs developed a bad reputation among cash managers.

Because ARPs were not selling, Wall Street investors "went back to the drawing board" and tried to redesign ARPs so that they would still offer the same benefits--but without the credit risk and bracket risk. As a result, several creative "offshoots" of ARPs have been introduced into the market.

## Collateralized Adjustable Rate Preferred Stocks

The first ARP alternative that was created was the Collateralized Adjustable Rate Preferred Stock (CARP). As its name implies, CARPs are ARPs that are secured with collateral. Their typical structure is illustrated in Figure 3.2.

**Figure 3.2** *Collateralized Adjustable Rate Preferred*

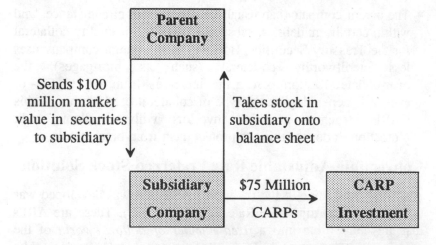

Within this structure, the parent company creates a subsidiary whose sole purpose is to hold high-quality collateral and issue ARPs that are secured by that collateral. Usually, the collateral is U.S. Treasury Securities, and there are four dollars of collateral for every three dollars of CARPs that are issued. The parent company takes the subsidiary's equity onto its own balance sheet. In effect, the parent company substitutes *X* dollar's worth of its subsidiary's stock for *X* dollar's worth of Treasury Securities on its balance sheet. Thus, the parent company's total assets are unaffected.

The major rating agencies have looked at the deal structure and given it their highest ratings, although the parent companies may be comparably weak. Many CARP issues have one or more special provisions that are designed to benefit either the issuer or the investor. For example:

■ The parent company is usually allowed to substitute the collateral that is held by the subsidiary. By allowing collateral substitutions, the parent company remains free to trade its entire portfolio of Treasury Securities.

■ If the value of the collateral should rise, the parent company can usually withdraw the surplus collateral--as long as the 4:3 coverage ratio is maintained. Similarly, if the value of the collateral drops, the parent company must usually transfer more collateral into the subsidiary or call the CARP issue.

■ The subsidiary's corporate charter usually prohibits the subsidiary from doing any business other than holding the collateral and issuing the CARPs.

■ The parent company can usually, under certain circumstances and within certain guidelines, substitute lower-credit-quality collateral for the Treasury Securities. However, if the parent company uses less creditworthy collateral (such as mortgages), the over-collateralization percentage increases from 4:3 to 5:3--or even 2:1, depending on the type of collateral used. Although this CARP structure provides investors with excellent credit protection, it does nothing to protect them from bracket risk.

## Convertible Adjustable Rate Preferred Stock Solution

A second alternative to the traditional ARP that was developed was the Convertible Adjustable Rate Preferred (CAP). These are ARPs that are convertible into a *fixed number of dollars' worth* of the company's common stock. It should be noted that CAPs are unlike most types of convertible securities in which the security is convertible into a *fixed number of shares of the issuer's common stock*. The reason that the conversion feature of CAPs is different is that CAPs are designed to protect the investor's principal, whereas most convertible securities are designed to allow the investors to profit from rises in the value of the common stock. For example, a CAP that is initially issued at $100 will be convertible into $100 worth of the issuer's common stock. If the issuer's common stock is selling for $20/share, an investor would receive five shares by converting. If the issuer's common stock is selling for $10/share, an investor would receive 10 shares by converting. In other words, CAP investors receive virtually as many shares of the company's common stock as needed in order to recoup their original investment. Once an investor has converted a CAP into $100 worth of the issuer's common stocks, the investor can sell the stock to recoup its $100 investment. Thus, if the credit quality of the CAP should decline, or if interest rates rise to the point where an investor is capped out, investors have an available escape route. Thus, CAPs protect investors from both credit risk and bracket risk.

Whereas CAPs are a very good deal for investors, issuers have been slow to embrace the concept. They have because they do not want to be in the position of having to issue additional common shares (or having to buy their own shares in the open market) at a time that may be disadvantageous to them. However, because issuers are finding it difficult to raise capital, CAPs may soon become more popular with them.

## Money Market Preferreds

An entirely different approach to solving the risk associated with ARPs was developed by Lehman Brothers, Inc.® Instead of providing credit enhancements like CARPs, or an escape route like CAPs, Lehman Brothers, Inc.® introduced the concept of Money Market Preferreds®(MMPs), which use a "Dutch Auction" process to mitigate the risk inherent in equities.

In the MMP market, an issuer, acting through an agent (usually an investment bank), offers investors the opportunity to bid for its MMP shares. Potential investors submit bids that include how many shares of the issuer's preferred they would like to buy and the minimum yield they require.

The agent collects all of the bids and ranks them in order from the lowest required yield to the highest. Bids are then filled in order, starting with the bid with the lowest required yield, until all of the available shares are assigned. The bid with the highest minimum yield that receives shares is referred to as the winning yield. *Every investor who successfully obtains shares in the auction receives this winning yield.* Thus, this auction is different from the T-Bill auction because every investor receives the same yield. For example, assume there were $50 million worth of shares available for auction and the bids listed in Table 3.1 were received.

**Table 3.1** *MMP Auction Bids*

| Bid | Size (in MMs) | Yield (%) | Bid | Size (in MMs) | Yield (%) |
|-----|---------------|-----------|-----|---------------|-----------|
| 1 | $0.200 | 5.78 | 15 | $1.000 | 6.11 |
| 2 | $3.000 | 5.81 | 16 | $3.000 | 6.11 |
| 3 | $0.100 | 5.83 | 17 | $0.200 | 6.12 |
| 4 | $0.400 | 5.83 | 18 | $6.000 | 6.15 |
| 5 | $0.500 | 5.84 | 19 | $0.300 | 6.17 |
| 6 | $0.700 | 5.91 | 20 | $0.500 | 6.18 |
| 7 | $2.000 | 5.92 | 21 | $2.000 | 6.21 |
| 8 | $5.000 | 5.95 | 22 | $2.500 | 6.21 |
| 9 | $0.300 | 5.97 | 23 | $4.000 | 6.25 |
| 10 | $5.500 | 5.99 | 24 | $0.300 | 6.25 |
| 11 | $4.000 | 6.01 | 25 | $0.200 | 6.28 |
| 12 | $8.000 | 6.05 | 26 | $0.100 | 6.35 |
| 13 | $0.200 | 6.05 | 27 | $0.200 | 6.75 |
| 14 | $10.000 | 6.05 | 28 | $10.000 | 7.01 |

In this auction, the bids would be filled starting with the $0.200 MM at 5.78%, and then moving progressively through the higher yields. The issuer would run out of shares just prior to filling bid #18 ($6 million at 6.15%). Only $5.9 million of this $6 million bid could be filled, because by this time, all of the available shares would have been allocated. Thus, the winning bid in this auction is 6.15%. All the investors who bid less than 6.15% would have their bids filled at a 6.15% yield. Those investors who bid more than 6.15% would be closed out of this auction.

Seven weeks from the day of this auction, the shares will be auctioned again. The shares are auctioned every seven weeks because that is the smallest number of whole weeks that includes more than 46 days. (The shares have to be held for at least 46 days in order to qualify for the dividend exclusion.)

In the next auction, the investors who currently have shares will have three alternatives:

- They can sell their shares in the next auction and get their cash back. All transactions in the auction are at value, so therefore the investor will have both bought and sold at value.

- They can enter "hold orders," meaning that their shares will not be part of the auction and will yield whatever rate is determined in the auction. However, a high number of hold orders tends to depress the winning yield. (In the preceding auction, if there were $15 million worth of hold orders, the winning bid would have been 6.05% instead of 6.15%.) Hold orders are very similar to non-competitive bids in the T-Bill auction.

- They can enter a sell order to sell their existing shares, and simultaneously enter another bid for shares at whatever yields they feel are attractive for the next seven weeks.

Investors in MMPs are exposed to two risks: credit risk and the risk that an auction will fail. Credit risk is the risk that the issuer will declare bankruptcy while you own its MMPs. Because MMPs are considered equity, they are very "junior" securities (often "senior" only to the issuer's common shares). If the issuer goes bankrupt, the probability that an investor will recover more than a few cents on the dollar is very small. (Of course, the probability that a highly rated issuer will go bankrupt is also very small.)

The second risk, the risk of a failed auction, is far more likely to occur. A failed auction occurs whenever there are not enough buyers to buy all of the shares that are offered for sale. In the event of a failed auction, usually the current investors continue to own the MMPs for another seven weeks, and the dividend rate is automatically set at a percentage of the composite AA-rated CP rate as published by the Federal Reserve Bank (110%-120% of this rate is very common).

If the second auction fails, the rate is usually raised to a higher percentage (150% of the AA-rated CP rate is typical). If the third auction fails, the issuer usually must call the issue. Auctions usually fail because some event has a negative impact on the issuer (such as credit downgrading, a takeover attempt, or the loss of a key contract).

### Money Market Preferreds Bidding Strategy

Investors who want to participate in this market need to formulate a bidding strategy that compliments their investment philosophy and complies with their investment policy guidelines. For example: If liquidity is especially important, investors should focus on those issues that offer both high-credit quality and little risk. Fortunately, for investors who buy MMPs, buying only high-credit-quality MMPs does not necessarily mean sacrificing return. This market is still inefficient and often high-credit-quality issues end up yielding more than low-credit-quality issues. (The yield of an MMP is often determined more by the aggressiveness with which the agents solicit bids than by the actual attractiveness of the specific issue.)

Investors who are willing to sacrifice liquidity in exchange for a high yield might want to seek those issues that are in danger of having failed auctions--or that have already experienced failed auctions. These issues offer an exceptionally high yield without necessarily having a high risk. For example, when Kroger, Inc.® was subject to a takeover bid, its auctions failed despite that both the current management and the aggressor had stated that they would call the company's MMPs. A Citicorp, Inc.® MMP issue recently offered a yield of over 12.5% on fears of bank failure.

Regardless of whether investors want to bid for conservative or aggressive issues, they will need to calculate the yield at which to bid. The simplest way to do that is to use this three-step process:

- Calculate how much interest you will receive from a traditional instrument with comparable credit risk on an after-tax basis.
- Convert the number of after-tax dollars you receive into a simple after-tax interest rate.
- Calculate the yield you would need to receive from an MMP in order to earn a higher after-tax return from the MMP than you would from the traditional instruments.

For example, if you concluded that an issue of CP (rated A-2+ and maturing in 45 days) offered a comparable degree of risk to a specific MMP issue, and the CP was yielding 8.78%, and you were in the 34% tax bracket, you would calculate the yield at which to bid as follows:

$$Interest\ Earned = \$1,000,000 * 0.0878 * 45 / 360$$

$$Discount = \$10,975$$

$$After\text{-}Tax\ Interest = \$10,975 * (1 - 0.34) = \$7,243.50$$

After-Tax Yield (annualized) of the CP on a Simple Interest Basis

$$(\$7,243.50 / \$989,025) * (365 / 45) * 100 = 5.94\%$$

Thus, an investment in an MMP issue with a comparable degree of risk must offer an after-tax return of at least 5.95% (on a simple interest basis) in order to be more attractive. The pre-tax yield that the issue must offer is therefore equal to:

$$5.95\% / [1\text{-}(Taxable\ Portion\ of\ Dividend * Tax\ Rate)]$$

$$5.95\% / [1 - (0.3 * 0.34)] = 6.63\%$$

Thus, an investor would have to bid 6.63% or higher in an MMP auction in order to net a return that is higher than the CP. If an investor bids 6.63% and is unsuccessful in securing shares, it does not matter, because the investor would then net a higher return by buying the CP.

## Money Market Preferreds Variations

Although we have been examining MMPs, realize that the same type of security goes by numerous other names and acronyms. (Lehman Brothers. Inc.® registered the term "Money Market Preferred" as a trademark.) For example, Solomon Brothers® refers to these securities as Dutch Auction Rate Securities® (DARTs)® and Smith Barney® refers to them as Short-Term Auction Rate Securities® (STARs)®. Note also that, in addition to the publicly traded issues, there are also a number of issues in the private placement market.

There are also several equity issues currently outstanding that look like MMPs, but are actually variations on the MMP concept. With some of these variations, the auction agent does not actually hold an auction. Instead, the auction agent sets the rate based on what seems to be a fair rate. This requires a delicate balance between the needs of the investors and the needs of the issuers. If investors think that the rate is too low, they will boycott the issue. If issuers think it is too high, they will boycott the auction agent.

## Typical Issuers and Investors

Because dividend payments are not tax-deductible and interest payments are, a dollar in interest expense usually costs an issuer less than a dollar in dividend payments. The exception, of course, is the company that does not pay taxes, either because it is not currently profitable or because it has tax-loss carry forwards. Thus, MMPs are more attractive to issuers that are *not* currently taxable. In addition, because MMPs are equity, they are very attractive to companies that need to maintain a certain debt-to-equity ratio, such as banks, insurance companies, and utilities. They offer them a way to raise equity without diluting their current holdings.

For issuers, MMPs are generally issued perpetually. This makes them attractive compared to Commercial Paper because CP has to be "rolled over" frequently. Although MMPs have to be reauctioned every seven weeks, in these auctions one investor sells the shares to another investor. The company itself is not the seller. As far as investors are concerned, the higher the investor's tax bracket the more attractive MMPs become as an investment alternative. In addition, the larger the investor's portfolio, the more attractive MMPs become from a diversification point of view.

## Why Money Market Preferreds Are Considered Equity

Money Market Preferreds are issued at value, the auction mechanism allows them to trade at value, and the rate they pay is reset frequently to reflect current interest rates. In short, MMPs come very close to the definition of debt. In fact, it took years to get a ruling for the Internal Revenue Service regarding the tax status of MMPs.

Finally, the IRS, in a private ruling, ruled that MMP-type securities were, in fact, equity. The rationale that the IRS used in reaching this decision was that:

- shares have no fixed maturity date.
- dividends have to be paid out of legal funds (generally, profits or retained earnings).

- investors cannot cause the issue to be called.
- issuer provides no guarantee that the investors will be able to sell at value.

## Market Outlook

Although MMPs were first issued less than 10 years ago, the market has grown to be a more than $10 billion market. The reason for the market's popularity is that MMPs are often a win-win situation. Because of the tax break that investors receive on dividends under our tax code, MMPs often cost issuers less than CP, yet offer investors a higher return. For example, compare the issuer's after-tax cost and the investor's after-tax return from both an issue of CP and an issue of MMP in the following:

**Figure 3.3** *Pre-Tax and Post-Tax Yield Comparison*

|  | Issuer with Tax Loss Carry Forward | Investor in a 34% Tax Bracket |
|---|---|---|
| CP at 8% | 8% | 5.28% |
| MMP at 7% | 7% | 6.29% |
|  | Issuer Saves 1% | Investor Earns an Extra 1% |

# DIVIDEND ROLLOVER PROGRAMS

Instead of simply buying and holding a portfolio of equities, there are several strategies investors can use to increase their potential return. One is to implement a dividend roll program. With a dividend roll program, an investor buys a stock just before it goes "ex-dividend." The investor collects the dividend, holds the stock for 46 days so that the dividend qualifies for the dividend exclusion, sells the stock, and then uses the proceeds to buy another issue that's about to go ex-dividend. Consider an oversimplified example to illustrate the benefits of implementing this strategy: Assume that there are two preferred stocks--Preferred A and Preferred B--and that both pay a $10 dividend and sell for $100 each. Preferred A goes ex-dividend on the 10th of March, June, September, and December. Preferred B goes ex-dividend on the 25th of April, July, October, and January.

On March 10th, if an investor bought Preferred A, the investor would receive the $2.50 dividend. On March 11th, the stock would probably start to trade for $97.50 (stocks generally drop in value by the amount of the dividend when they go ex-dividend). Over the next three months, the value of the dividend would grow until the stock was once again worth $100 and pays its next $2.50 dividend. Thus, assuming that interest rates are constant (for the sake of the example), the price path of Preferred A would be expected to follow:

**Figure 3.4** *Dividend Payout and Buildup*

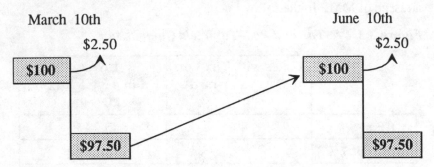

Instead of keeping the bond from one dividend payment to the next, if the investor sold Preferred A in 46 days (for $98.75) and bought Preferred B just before it went ex-dividend, the investor would collect another $2.50 dividend and sustain a $1.25 capital loss. If the investor continues this process and swaps money back and forth between the two stocks eight times per year, the investor will collect eight $2.50 dividends and sustain eight $1.25 capital losses.

Pre-Tax Dividend Income    8 * $2.50 = $20.00

Pre-Tax Capital Losses    8 * $1.25 = $10.00

On a pre-tax basis, the investor is no better off than if the investor had just owned one stock (i.e., a net $10.00). However, on an after-tax basis, it is substantially beneficial for the investor to implement a dividend roll program, as long as the investor has some capital gains that can be offset by the capital losses generated by this strategy.

**Figure 3.5** *Dividend Roll Programs*

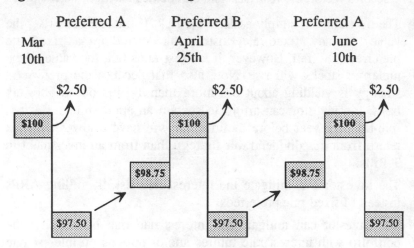

Pre-Tax Dividend Income    8 * $2.50 = $20.00
Pre-Tax Capital Losses    8 * $1.25 = $10.00

If the investor simply bought and held the one stock, the investor's after-tax return would be (assuming that there is a 34% tax rate):

$10.00 * (1 - 0.102) = $8.98 After-Tax Dividend Income

However, if the investor implemented the dividend roll program, the investor's return would be:

$20.00 * (1 - 0.102) = $17.96 After-Tax Dividend Income

$10.00 * (1 - 0.34) = $6.60 After-Tax Capital Loss

The net gain is $11.96, or a 33% increase over the buy and hold strategy--and a 120% higher return than the after-tax return on T-Bills.

Although the preceding example is illustrative, it is oversimplified. This example excluded transaction costs and assumed that market interest rates remain constant. Transaction costs need to be kept to a minimum. This strategy requires the execution of eight trades per year. Assuming that there is a commission of $0.03 per share, the total cost per share will be $0.24. Because this cost is tax-deductible, the after-tax impact of transaction costs is only $0.16, reducing the net cost per share to $11.80, from $11.96.

The second factor, interest-rate risk, can be dealt with three ways:

- The investor can simply assume the risk. If interest rates rise, the value of any fixed-rate instrument, including a fixed-rate preferred, will fall. However, if interest rates fall, the value of the preferred stocks will rise. Note also that because the preferred's strategy is yielding about 6% more than T-Bills on an after-tax basis, the investor can afford to sustain an approximate 8% loss (pre-tax) per year before the investor will have a lower after-tax return from this dividend roll strategy than from an investment in T-Bills.

- The investor can mitigate the interest-rate risk by rolling ARPs instead of fixed-rate preferreds.

- The investor can mitigate the interest-rate risk by hedging the portfolio with interest rate futures and/or options on interest rate futures (examined in a later chapter).

## DIVIDEND CAPTURE STRATEGY

Another strategy that investors can implement is a "dividend capture strategy." With this, the investor again buys a stock just before it goes ex-dividend, only instead of buying a preferred stock, the investor buys a common stock. Simultaneously, the investor sells an "in the money" call option that generates additional income and provides partial downside price protection. Because the call is "in the money," the stock will then get called away. Consider the following example:

Assume that XYZ, Inc. stock is currently selling for $58, that it pays a dividend of $5.20 per year, and that an investor can sell a 60-day call option with a strike price of $50 for $10. In a dividend capture strategy, the investor would buy the stock, collect a dividend payment, and "loose" the stock at the strike price to the option holder. The net cash flows would be:

- Buy the stock for $58, loose it for $50, netting an $8 capital loss, which costs $5.28 after tax.
- Collect a dividend payment of $1.30, which nets $1.17 after tax.
- Collect $10 of option premium, which nets $6.60 after tax.
- Spend $1 in transaction costs, which nets $0.66 after tax.

The net effect of these cash flows is a $1.83 after-tax gain on a $48 net investment over a 60-day period, which annualizes at a 23% after-tax rate of return.

(Note that in order to take dividend exclusion, options cannot be more than 15% "in the money," and if the strike price is less than 50, the option's term must be greater than 31 days and less than 180 days.)

Instead of using options on individual stocks, it is often more efficient to build a diversified portfolio of individual stocks and use options on stock index futures to generate the additional income and hedge the portfolio against price risk.

# 4

# MONEY MARKET MATHEMATICS

## INTRODUCTION

In order to manage a short-term portfolio successfully, it is essential
to have a thorough understanding of money market mathematics.
Most money market calculations, while not overly complex, are not
straight forward. Consider the following example:

Suppose that on March 1, 1990, an investor with approximately
$1,000,000 is offered the following investment opportunities and has
to determine which one offers the highest return:

- A six-month CD (compounded monthly) quoted at 8.11%
  (actual/actual).
- A six-month T-Bill quoted at an 8% discount (actual/360).
- A series of 182 overnight repos quoted at a 7.95% discount
  (actual/360).

Interestingly, the alternative with the highest *stated yield* (the CD in
this example) does not necessarily offer the highest return. The
reason for this is that the stated yields of different instruments are
calculated differently. Because of this, the yields of different money
market instruments are not always directly comparable. This chapter
examines how the stated yields of different money market
instruments are calculated and how they compare.

## VARIABLES IN MONEY MARKET CALCULATIONS

The stated yield of every money market instrument depends on three
variables:

- The type of "calendar" that the instrument uses.
- Whether the instrument is sold on a discounted or interest-bearing basis.
- How frequently the instrument "compounds."

## Different Instruments Use Different Calendars

Whereas the formula for simple interest is straight- forward:

Interest = Principal (P) * Rate (R) * Time (T)

the *time* element in this equation can be quoted in one of three different ways:

*30/360* or *Actual/360 (A/360)* or *Actual/Actual (A/A)*

Different money market instruments use different calendars -- and the type of calendar an instrument uses has a direct impact on its yield.

If an instrument uses a 30/360 calendar, every month is assumed to have 30 days and a year is assumed to have 360 days. Of course, since neither of these assumptions is very accurate, neither are the yield quotes based on this calendar. For example, if an investment ran from 4/1/1991 to 7/1/1991, the time component in the interest equation would be 90/360 if the instrument used a 30/360 calendar. Thus, $1,000,000 invested at 10% for this time period on a 30/360 calendar would earn:

P * R * T = $1,000,000 * 0.10 * 90/360 = $25,000.00

If an instrument uses an Actual/360 calendar, every month is assumed to have its actual number of days, although a year is assumed to have 360 days. (This makes even less sense than the 30/360 designation!) If the preceding investment used this designation, the amount of interest that the investment would earn over the same period would be:

P * R * T = $1,000,000 * 0.10 * 91/360 = $25,278.78

If the instrument uses an Actual/Actual calendar, both the months and years are quoted on an actual day basis. Thus, the amount of interest the preceding investment would earn on an Actual/Actual basis over the same period would be:

$$P * R * T = \$1,000,000 * 0.10 * 91/365 = \$24,931.51$$

Thus, the first step in calculating an investment's return correctly is to know what calendar designation it uses.

## Discount Basis versus an Interest-Bearing Basis

The *basis* that is used to calculate an instrument's interest has a significant impact on its stated return. Instruments that are sold on an *interest-bearing basis* are normally sold at par value, pay their investors interest--either periodically or at maturity--and are redeemed at par value when they mature. Instruments that are quoted on a *discounted basis* are sold at a discount, pay no interest, and are redeemed at par value when they mature.

As an illustration of the impact of these alternatives, calculate the return (expressed on a simple interest basis) of an interest-bearing instrument and a discount instrument that both offer the same stated return. For example, the amount of interest earned by

- investing $1,000,000 in a 10% interest-bearing instrument for one year, assuming that it is quoted on an actual/360 basis, and that interest is paid at maturity.
- investing in a $1,000,000 10% one year discount instrument assuming that it, too, is quoted on an actual/360 basis.

The *interest-bearing instrument* would earn:

$$\text{Interest} = \$1,000,000 * 0.10 * 365/360 = \$101,388.89$$

and its return (expressed on a simple interest basis) would be:

$$(\$101,388.89 / \$1,000,000) * 100 = 10.14\%$$

The *discount instrument*, would earn:

$$\text{Discount} = \$1,000,000 * 0.10 * 365/360 = \$101,388.89$$

and its return (expressed on a simple interest basis) would be:

$$(101,388.89 / \$898,611.11) * 100 = 11.28\%$$

Thus, whether an instrument's stated yield is quoted on an interest-bearing basis or a discounted basis has a significant impact on the investment's return.

## Different Compounding Frequencies

The third variable is the frequency with which the interest that is earned is compounded. Consider how different compounding frequencies influence the amount of interest you would accumulate over a 1-year period from a 10% interest-bearing instrument quoted on an Actual/Actual basis:

The formula for calculating the amount accumulated over time, for a given compounding frequency, is:

$$\text{Amount of Interest} = [PV(1 + i)^n] - PV$$

where:

$$PV = \text{Initial Investment}$$

$$i = \text{Interest Rate per Period}$$

$$n = \text{Number of Compounding Periods}$$

**Table 4.1** *Impact of Compounding Frequency*

| Compounding Frequency | Amount of Interest |
|---|---|
| No Compounding | $100,000.00 |
| Monthly Compounding | $104,713.07 |
| Weekly Compounding | $105,064.79 |
| Daily Compounding | $105,155.78 |
| Continuous Compounding | $105,170.92 |

## Comparing Yields

Because the yields of different instruments are quoted differently, it is impossible to compare the yields of different investments unless the method by which the yields were calculated is known. The easiest way to compare the different stated yields offered by different money market instruments is to convert every yield into a simple yield. Thus, to answer the question posed at the start of this chapter, regarding the most attractive investment alternative, all three yield quotes would have to be converted to a simple interest basis.

### Six-Month Certificate of Deposit (Compounded Monthly) Quoted at 8.11% (a/a)

Because CDs are interest-bearing instruments and because we know that the one yield in this section is quoted on an actual/actual basis, we can calculate the total amount that we would accumulate over six months by using the compound interest formula.

$$\text{Amount of Interest} = [PV(1 + i)^n] - PV$$

where:

$$PV = \$1,000,000$$
$$i = 8.11\% / 12 = 0.6758\% \text{ per month}$$
$$n = 6$$

Thus:

$$\text{Interest} = [\$1,000,000(1 + 0.006758)^6] - \$1,000,000$$
$$\text{Interest} = \$41,239.26$$

Expressed on an annual simple interest yield basis, the yield would be:

$$(\$41,239.29 / \$1,000,000) * 2 * 100 = 8.25\%$$

### Six-Month T-Bill Quoted at an 8% Discount (a/360)

For the T-Bill, the discount would be:

$$\$1,000,000 * 0.08 * (182 / 360) = \$40,444.44, \text{ or}$$

expressed on an annual simple interest yield basis is:

$$(\$40,444.44 / 959,555.56) * 2 * 100 = 8.43\%$$

### 182 Overnight Repos Quoted at a 7.95% Discount (a/360)

For the repo, the discount would be:

$$\$1,000,000 * 0.0795 * 1/360 = \$220.83$$

On a daily basis, the simple interest rate would be:

(220.83 / $999,779.17) * 100 = 0.0221%

However, this return is compounded daily for 182 days, resulting in interest income (on a $1 million investment) of:

$41,014.90 / $1,000,000) * 2 * 100 = 8.20%

Thus, of the three alternatives, the T-Bill is the most attractive on a pre-tax basis. (Investors who are subject to taxation would need to consider the impact of taxes, as well.)

# 5

# THE FEDERAL RESERVE BANK

## INTRODUCTION

All serious investors should understand how the Federal Reserve Bank (FED) influences the financial markets because the FED probably has more impact on the markets (over the short term) than any other organization or institution, including the White House and the Congress.

## OVERVIEW OF THE FEDERAL RESERVE BANK

The "Banking Crisis of 1907" resulted in a large number of bank failures and tremendous losses by depositors. Shortly thereafter, in an effort to limit both the number and the severity of future bank failures, Congress created the FED. The FED was charged with the responsibility of regulating the banking industry and acting as the primary bank of the United States.

The FED is controlled by a Board of Governors whose members are appointed by the President of the United States, with the consent of the Senate. Board members are appointed for 14-year terms so that they can (theoretically, at least) act in the best interest of the nation without fear of offending the politicians who appointed them. Not having to worry about being replaced provides the Board of Governors with a fair degree of independence.

One member of the Board of Governors is appointed to serve as Chairman (also by the President, with the consent of the Senate). The Chairman of the FED is often considered to be the second most powerful person in the country, next to the President. The Chairman is only appointed for a 4-year term and, thus, *does have to worry* about the possibility of being replaced. Thus, the Chairman is often more susceptible to political influence than the other board members.

The United States is divided into 12 regions, each of which has its own branch of the Federal Reserve Bank. The local banks are each controlled by a local Board of Governors, and are administered by a president and a staff. The reason for having 12 regional banks instead of just one is that the local FEDs can fine-tune the national FED policy to meet the specific needs and economic conditions of their respective regions.

The FED's internal structure is composed of numerous committees. The most well-known committee of the FED is the Federal Open Market Committee (FOMC). All of the members of the National Board of Governors, as well as the presidents of the 12 regional banks, serve on this committee. (Note that although all of the presidents of the regional banks serve on the FOMC, they only get to vote on a rotating basis.)

The FOMC meets approximately eight times a year to debate and decide the FED's economic objectives. The transcript of each FOMC meeting is distributed to the public after the following FOMC meeting. Thus, the public is always one meeting behind the FOMC.

# THE FEDERAL RESERVE BANK'S ECONOMIC PRIORITIES

Aside from serving as the Central Bank of the U.S., and as the principal regulator of the banking industry, the FED is also charged with two critically important economic responsibilities: to promote non-inflationary growth and, full employment. These goals are sometimes mutually exclusive, however, because promoting full employment causes inflation, and fighting inflation frequently results in unemployment. Because of this, the FED's Board of Governors needs to determine on a regular basis which of these goals is the higher priority.

For example, when Arthur Burns was the FED Chairman, he faced a unique challenge regarding the FED's goal of promoting full employment:

- First, the "Baby Boom Generation" was about to enter the work force, and because these were to be their first jobs, the business community generally exhausted the pool of experienced personnel before incurring the expense of training the inexperienced.

- Second, as a result of the Women's Liberation Movement, a large number of women ("Baby Boomers" and not) were seeking careers.

Thus, Arthur Burns faced the problem that two large groups of inexperienced workers were looking to enter the work force at the same time. The only way that enough jobs could be created to accommodate both of these groups was for the FED to stimulate the economy on a massive scale. Although it accomplished this, the high level of economic stimulation caused high inflation.

Later, when Paul Volcker became the FED Chairman, he changed the FED's priorities. By this time, both the groups had already been assimilated into the work force. Thus, promoting full employment was no longer the high priority it once was. Instead, Mr. Volcker was more concerned with controlling the inflation rate, which was approaching double digits (in terms of percent). The classic way of controlling inflation is to slow down the economy--which Mr. Volcker did intensely. Although his policies brought inflation under control, the price that the country paid was a severe recession and double-digit unemployment.

Having the power to put the country in a severe recession and throw millions of people out of work makes the FED a very powerful institution--and its Chairman a very powerful individual.


## HOW THE FED INFLUENCES THE ECONOMY

Once the FOMC of the FED sets its economic objectives, the FOMC, working with the professionals on the FED's staff and its trading desk, has to develop and implement strategies that are designed to achieve those objectives. The FED has several tools at its disposal that can be used to exert influence on the economy. These tools include increasing or decreasing the reserve requirement, discount rate, and money supply.

## Adjusting the Reserve Requirement

Every bank that is part of the Federal Reserve System has to maintain an account at its local Federal Reserve Bank. The balance of this non-interest-bearing account must equal a percentage of the deposits that it accepts from its customers. Thus, every time a bank accepts a new deposit, the amount that it must keep in its reserve account increases. For example, if the reserve requirement is 5%, any time that the bank accepts an additional $1 deposit from a customer, it must also add $0.05 to its reserve account, leaving it with $0.95 to lend.

Naturally, if the FED increases a bank's reserve requirement from 5% to 6%, the bank will have to maintain a larger reserve balance and have less money available for lending. Thus, by increasing the reserve requirement, the FED reduces the amount that the bank can lend to its customers. As the supply of lendable funds decreases, the cost of borrowing money (i.e., interest rates) increases. Thus, increasing the reserve requirement raises market interest rates and, in turn, depresses the economy. Because adjusting the reserve requirement can have a significant impact on interest rates and on the economy overall, it is an action that the FED takes only on rare occasions--when *drastic action* is required.

## Adjusting the Discount Rate

When a bank is more successful at making loans than it is at attracting deposits, it will frequently need to borrow money (or raise equity) in order to get the cash it needs to raise its reserve requirement. Banks can borrow the money they need in a variety of ways, including issuing bonds, commercial paper, time deposits or certificates of deposit, selling bankers' acceptances, borrowing from other banks (i.e., borrowing "Fed Funds"), or, as a last resort, borrowing from the FED itself.

Although it may sound illogical for a bank to borrow from the FED so that it can meet its reserve requirement *at* the FED, it is actually very common. When a bank borrows from the FED, it pays interest to the FED. The rate of interest that it pays is a discount rate, and borrowing from the FED is referred to as *borrowing at the discount window*. When the FED adjusts this rate, it influences the cost of funds of banks that borrow in this manner. Of course, if a bank's cost of funds rises, so will its loan rates. Discount-rate changes are relatively infrequent--and well-publicized--events.

One fact that confuses many investors is that banks often elect *not* to borrow at the discount window, despite that the discount rate is usually lower than the rates banks have to pay on their CDs, CP, repos and Fed Fund purchases. The reason that banks often elect to borrow in the public markets (although they pay a higher interest rate) is that banks that borrow at the discount window are considered "weak" by other banks, depositors, and the bank regulators. (From the banks' viewpoint, it is often better to pay a higher interest rate than to scare depositors and possibly trigger a FED audit by borrowing too often at the discount window.) In addition, banks that borrow too often at the discount window are generally prohibited by the FED from participating in "non-banking activities," such as travel services, brokerage services, and information services, which many banks count on for future growth.

## Adjusting the Money Supply

Whereas the FED adjusts both the reserve requirement and the discount rate when it needs to implement significant changes in the economy, most of the time the FED needs only to "fine-tune" the economy to achieve its economic objectives. Fine-tuning the economy is usually accomplished by making small adjustments to the money supply and/or amount of money in circulation.

The tools that the FED uses to make small changes to the money supply are referred to collectively as its *open-market operations.* In its open-market operations, the FED either buys, sells, repos, or reverse repos, Treasury Securities. The counterparts in these transactions are the primary dealers, which are those banks and securities dealers that do such a large volume of government securities transactions that they are authorized to trade directly with the FED.

Open-market operations can either be temporary or permanent, depending on whether the FED wants to cause a temporary or permanent adjustment to the money supply and/or amount of money in circulation. (The term "permanent," when applied to an open-market transaction, is relative, and means that the adjustment will last more than a few days.)

## Permanent Open-Market Operations

If the FED wants to *permanently increase* the money supply and the amount of money in circulation, it will buy U.S. Treasury Securities from its primary dealers. One of the advantages of the FED is that it does not necessarily need to have any "cash" to buy Treasury Securities. Instead, when the FED buys Treasury Securities from its dealers, it pays for them with a check that it draws on itself. Because the FED "clears" its own checks, they are, *by definition*, good, regardless of whether it has any money in its account. If the FED buys $100,000,000 worth of Treasury Securities from its primary dealers, it will pay for them by writing checks from its "magic checkbook." The dealers will deposit the checks and the FED will clear them. Thus, the net result is that the FED will now own $100,000,000 of U.S. Treasury Securities and the dealers will have $100,000,000 that didn't exist before this transaction. Thus, by buying these securities, the FED increases both the *money supply and the amount of money in circulation*. According to the law of supply and demand, if the supply of money goes up, the cost of money (i.e., interest rates) should go down--at least initially.

When the FED is buying Treasury Securities, the transactions are referred to either as *Bill Passes* or *Coupon Passes*, depending on whether the FED is buying T-Bills or long-term Coupon Bonds. If the FED wants to *permanently decrease* the money supply, it will sell Treasury Securities to its primary dealers. Unlike the FED, when the dealers buy securities they can't simply "create money" with which to pay for them. Dealers need to pay for the securities that they buy with cash. After they pay for them, the money is held at the FED and, thus, there is less money in circulation. (Note that the total supply of money has not changed, just the amount in circulation.) Again, because of the law of supply and demand, interest rates will rise.

## Temporary Open-Market Operations

The FED can also enter into transactions with its primary dealers that are designed to temporarily adjust the money supply and/or the amount in circulation. If the FED wants to *temporarily increase* the money supply, it will enter into repos with its dealers in which it lends money to them and holds Treasury Securities as collateral.

There are two sources of funds that the FED can use to implement these repos: its customers' funds and its "magic checkbook":

- If the FED uses its customers' funds (funds left on deposit at the FED by foreign governments), the transaction is referred to as a *Customer Repo*. The maximum size of a Customer Repo is approximately $3 billion. Whereas Customer Repos do increase the amount of money in circulation, they do not increase the total money supply. (The money that the FED lends to the dealers has already been in existence.)

- If the FED uses its "magic checkbook," the transaction is referred to as a *System Repo*. The maximum size of a System Repo is approximately $7 billion. System Repos, like the outright purchases of securities, increase both the amount of money in circulation *and* the money supply.

If the FED wants to *temporarily decrease* the money supply, it will borrow money from its dealers and allow them to hold securities as collateral. These transactions are referred to as *matched sales*. These transactions reduce the amount of money in circulation, but not the overall money supply.

## Economic Impact of Open-Market Operations

When the FED implements an *open-market operation,* it starts a series of actions that, hopefully, moves the economy closer to the FED's objectives. For example, when the FED sells securities to its primary dealers, the liquidity of the banks who are dealers (and the liquidity of the banks who lend to dealers) is reduced because the securities have to be paid for with cash. Because their liquidity is reduced, these banks need to borrow more money to meet their reserve requirements, and because of this, the Fed Funds' rate, as well as other short-term rates, tends to rise. As these rates rise, the alternative of borrowing at the discount window becomes more attractive. (Whereas a bank may be willing to pay a rate that is 50 bp higher than the discount rate to avoid the embarrassment of borrowing at the discount window, it may not be willing to pay a rate that is 150 bp more than the discount rate.) Thus, as interest rates rise, so does the amount of borrowing at the discount window.

If a bank needs to resort to borrowing at the discount window, it will try to pay the loan as soon as possible to reassure its depositors and the regulators that it is not a "problem bank." To pay the FED quickly, the bank will try to generate other funds by offering higher rates on its Time Deposits, Commercial Paper, and other investment options. In order to maintain its spread if the bank raises the rate that it offers investors, it also has to raise the rate that it charges borrowers. Thus, its mortgage rates, car loan rates, commercial loan rates, and so on, will also rise. When these rise, fewer people are able to buy houses and cars, and fewer businesses are able to expand, and, therefore, the economy slows down. The greater the increase in interest rates, the more depressed the economy becomes. When the economy slows down, businesses are forced to reduce their prices and limit wage increases, reducing the rate of inflation.

### *Frequency of Open-Market Operations*

Whereas the FED may only adjust the discount and reserve requirement rates occasionally, it uses one or more open-market operations several times per week. In addition to achieving its economic objectives, the FED also uses its open-market operations to adjust the money supply in order to mitigate the impact of "events" that influence the liquidity of the banking system. Two examples of these events are the monthly deposit of social security checks and the auctioning of government bonds. Usually, if the FED is going to implement any open-market operations, it does them at 11:40 A.M. EST.

## "FED-WATCHING"

Because the FED's policies and actions have a tremendous impact on interest rates, and thus on securities prices, researchers spend a lot of time and effort trying to anticipate what the FED will do. Monitoring the FED, commonly referred to as "FED-watching," is a very complicated activity.

In an effort to anticipate future significant FED actions, "FED-watchers" will:

- compare the objectives set by the FOMC to current market conditions.

- read and reread speeches made by FOMC members looking for changes of opinion and attitude.

- "handicap" the probability that the FED Chairman will be replaced.

# 6

# SAMPLE SHORT-TERM INVESTMENT POLICIES

## INTRODUCTION

The following section includes three investment policy statements. The first investment policy was written for the XYZ, Inc. This organization is a non-taxable, not-for-profit organization that had approximately $5,000,000 in surplus cash, a very low tolerance for risk, and one full-time cash manager with limited experience and expertise. Additionally, the organization expected to draw down most of its cash reserves over the next six months.

The second investment policy was written for PDQ, Inc., which is a hypothetical, for-profit, public corporation that had approximately $15,000,000 in surplus cash, a moderate tolerance for risk, one experienced senior cash manager, and one inexperienced assistant cash manager. The company did not anticipate needing to draw on its cash reserves.

The third investment policy was written for LMN, Inc., which is a hypothetical, for-profit, privately held corporation that had $370,000,000 in surplus cash, a relatively high tolerance for risk, one very experienced senior cash manager, two relatively experienced associate cash managers, and two cash management clerks. The company did not anticipate needing to draw on its cash reserves.

As you review the following three investment policies, note how the they reflect the different organizations' investment capabilities, investment goals, tolerance for risk, and investment expertise.

# XYZ, INC.  INVESTMENT POLICY

This policy is the short-term investment policy for XYZ, Inc.

## Primary Objective

The primary objective of XYZ, Inc. is to obtain the highest return possible, while assuming a very low level of risk.

## Minimum and Maximum Maturity

Because XYZ, Inc. expects to be drawing upon its cash reserves in the near future, the cash manager is instructed to

- maintain a cash reserve equal to the greater of 10% of the projected cash draw-down over the next six months, or $500,000. This reserve is to be invested exclusively in either overnight repurchase agreements, term repurchase agreements, or T-Bills whose maturity is equal to or less than seven business days.

- invest the remaining balance so that the aggregate maturities of the various investments provides sufficient cash flow to meet the cash draw-downs projected by the organization's treasurer. The cash manager, at their discretion, may decrease the aggregate maturity of the portfolio below this maximum.

## Approved Investment Vehicles, Credit Rating Requirements, and Diversification Requirements

The senior cash manager is instructed to ensure that the aggregate investments do not violate the policies and provisions as defined in the following table:

**Table 6.1** *Approved Investment Vehicles, Credit Rating Requirements, and Diversification Requirements*

| Investment Vehicle | Credit Rating Requirements | Diversification Requirements |
|---|---|---|
| T-Bill | -- | None |
| LTTB | -- | <$2,500,000 |

| Agency | AA+ | <$1,500,000 |
|--------|-----|-------------|
| Repo | AA | None |
| CP - direct | A1-P1 | $250,000/Issuer |
| CP - dealer | A1-P1 | $250,000/Issuer |
| CP - private | None | ------- |
| BA | "1" | $500,000/Institution |
| CD | AA | $1,000,000/Institution |
| TD | AAA | $1,000,000/Institution |

## Notes:

Instruments that are downgraded below the required ratings must be sold.

The portfolio's weighted average credit rating must be investment-grade.

No part of this portfolio can be invested in non-rated securities.

Under no circumstances can more than 5% of the portfolio be exposed to one issuer.

The cash manager is instructed to ensure that the aggregate investments do not violate the policies and provisions as defined in the preceding table.

## Personnel Responsibilities

The investment policy of XYZ, Inc. is determined by the Investment Policy Committee. This committee is composed of the treasurer, cash manager, vice president of operations, and controller. This committee meets at least once every six months to review and modify, if necessary, the organization's investment policy. In addition, any member of this committee may call a special meeting if that member deems it necessary. A transcript is kept for all meetings. Changes require the approval of three members of this committee, and memos that summarize these changes are sent to the chairman and president. The cash manager is authorized to enter any transaction that specifically and fully complies with the policies and provisions described in this investment policy without prior approval. Any transaction that *may* violate this investment policy must be approved by the exception procedure described in the following section.

## Procedure for Exceptions

*Prior to making any investment that may violate this investment policy,* the cash manager obtains the written approval of at least two members of the Investment Committee. All requests for exceptions are submitted on the *Exceptions Form.* It is the responsibility of the cash manager to maintain a copy of all the exception forms, regardless of whether they are approved or denied.

## Required Audit Procedures

Copies of this investment policy are sent to the outside auditors with instructions to draw up procedures to ensure compliance. In addition, the controller is instructed to develop monthly reporting procedures in order to monitor the portfolio and ensure compliance with this policy. To facilitate compliance, the cash manager is instructed to maintain the entire short-term portfolio on a spreadsheet that is updated daily. This spreadsheet incorporates the appropriate functions and macros to test the portfolio for compliance with the criteria outlined in this investment policy. In addition, the spreadsheet has a macro (one that cannot be disabled) that automatically notifies the controller of any violations.

## Required Criteria for Dealers and Custodians

The cash manager enters only into transactions with banks or securities dealers that are designated *primary dealers* by the Federal Reserve Bank. In addition, the cash manager is required to obtain competitive bids from a minimum of three banks and/or dealers prior to making any investment over $250,000.

# PDQ, INC. INVESTMENT POLICY

This is the short-term investment policy for PDQ, Inc.:

## Primary Objective

The primary objective of PDQ, Inc. is to earn the highest after-tax return possible, while maintaining a relatively low level of risk.

## Minimum and Maximum Maturity

Because PDQ, Inc. does not expect to have to draw upon its cash reserves, the maximum weighted average maturity of the portfolio is set by the Investment Policy Committee. Regardless of what the maximum weighted average maturity of the portfolio is, the senior cash manager is instructed to maintain a cash reserve equal to $250,000. This reserve is invested exclusively in either overnight repurchase agreements, term repurchase agreements, or T-Bills whose maturity is equal to or less than seven business days. The senior cash manager sets the weighted average maturity of the balance of the portfolio to any maturity within the limits established by the Investment Policy Committee.

## Approved Investment Vehicles, Credit Rating Requirements, and Diversification Requirements

The senior cash manager is instructed to ensure that the aggregate investments do not violate the policies and provisions as defined in the following table:

**Table 6.2** *Approved Investment Vehicles, Credit Rating Requirements, and Diversification Requirements*

| Investment Vehicle | Credit Rating Requirements | Diversification Requirements |
|---|---|---|
| T-Bill | -- | None |
| LTTB | -- | None |
| Agency | AA- | <$3,000,000 |
| Repo | AA | None |

| CP - direct | a1-p2/a2-p1 | $1,000,000/Issuer |
|---|---|---|
| CP - dealer | a1-p2/a2-p1 | $1,000,000/Issuer |
| CP - private | a1-p1 | $1,000,000/Issuer |
| BA | AA | $1,000,000/Institution |
| CD | A+ | $1,000,000/Institution |
| TD | AA | $1,000,000/Institution |
| FRN | A+ | $500,000/Issuer |
| TAN | "1" | $500,000/Issuer |
| RAN | "1" | $250,000/Issuer |
| BAN | "1" | $250,000/Issuer |
| MLF | AA | $500,000/Issuer |
| ML | AA | $500,000/Issuer |
| LTMB | AA+ | $500,000/Issuer |
| MMP | AA | $1,000,000/Issuer |

## *Notes:*

Instruments that are downgraded below the required ratings may be held or sold.

The weighted average credit quality of this portfolio must be investment-grade.

Up to 10% of this portfolio can be invested in non-rated securities.

Under no circumstances can more than 10% of the portfolio be exposed to one issuer.

## Personnel Responsibilities

The investment policy of PDQ, Inc. is under the direction of the Investment Policy Committee. This committee is composed of the treasurer, senior cash manager, assistant cash manager, vice president of operations, and controller. This committee meets at least once every six months to review and revise, if necessary, the organization's investment policy. In addition, any member of this committee may call a special meeting if that member deems it necessary. A transcript is kept for all meetings. Changes require the approval of both cash managers and two other members of this committee. Memos that summarize any changes are sent to the chairman, president, and chief financial officer. The senior cash manager is authorized to enter any transaction that specifically and fully complies with the policies and provisions described in this investment policy without prior approval. Any transaction that *may* violate this investment policy must be approved by the exception procedure described in the following section.

The assistant cash manager is authorized to enter any transaction that specifically and fully complies with the policies and provisions described in this investment policy, as long as the investment is not for more than $200,000.

## Procedure for Exceptions

*Prior to making any investment that may violate this investment policy,* the senior cash manager obtains the written approval of at least two other members of the Investment Committee. All requests for exceptions will be submitted on the *Exceptions Form*. It is the responsibility of the senior cash manager to maintain a copy of all exception forms, regardless of whether they are approved or denied.

## Required Audit Procedures

Copies of this investment policy are sent to the outside auditors with instructions to draw up procedures to ensure compliance. In addition, the controller is instructed to develop monthly reporting procedures to monitor the portfolio and ensure compliance. To facilitate compliance, the senior cash manager is instructed to maintain the entire short-term portfolio on a spreadsheet that is updated daily. This spreadsheet incorporates the appropriate functions and macros to test the portfolio for compliance with the criteria outlined in this investment policy. In addition, the spreadsheet has a macro (one that cannot be disabled) that automatically notifies the controller of any violations.

## Required Criteria for Dealers and Custodians

The cash managers can only enter transactions with banks or securities firms that are either primary dealers or on the approved list of secondary institutions prepared by the Investment Policy

Committee. In addition, the cash managers are required to obtain competitive bids from a minimum of two banks and/or dealers prior to making any investment over $250,000, and three banks and/or dealers prior to making any investment over $500,000.

# LMN, INC. INVESTMENT POLICY

This policy is the short-term investment policy for LMN, Inc.:

## Primary Objective

The primary objective of LMN, Inc. is to obtain the highest return possible in exchange for assuming a relatively high level of risk.

## Minimum and Maximum Maturity

Because LMN, Inc. does not expect to have to draw upon its cash reserves, the maximum weighted average maturity of the portfolio is set by the Investment Policy Committee. Regardless of what the maximum weighted average maturity of the portfolio is, the senior cash manager is instructed to maintain a cash reserve equal to $250,000. This reserve is invested exclusively in either overnight repurchase agreements, term repurchase agreements, or T-Bills whose maturity is equal to or less than seven business days. The senior cash manager sets the weighted average maturity of the balance of the portfolio to any maturity within the limits established by the Investment Policy Committee.

## Approved Investment Vehicles, Credit Rating Requirements, and Diversification Requirements

The senior cash manager is instructed to ensure that the aggregate investments do not violate the policies and provisions as defined in the following table:

**Table 6.3** *Approved Investment Vehicles, Credit Rating Require-ments, and Diversification Requirements*

| Investment Vehicle | Credit Rating Requirements | Diversification Requirements |
|:---:|:---:|:---:|
| T-Bill | -- | None |
| LTTB | -- | None |
| Agency | AA- | <$100,000,000 |
| Repo | AA | None |

| CP - direct | a2-p2 | $25,000,000/Issuer |
|---|---|---|
| CP - dealer | a1-p2/a2-p1 | $15,000,000/Issuer |
| CP - private | a1-p2/a2-p1 | $10,000,000/Issuer |
| BA | A | $25,000,000/Institution |
| CD | A+ | $10,000,000/Institution |
| TD | A+ | $5,000,000/Institution |
| FRN | A- | $5,000,000/Issuer |
| TAN | "2" | $2,500,000/Issuer |
| RAN | "1" | $1,000,000/Issuer |
| BAN | "1" | $1,000,000/Issuer |
| MLF | A- | $10,000,000/Issuer |
| ML | A | $5,000,000/Issuer |
| LTMB | A+ | $5,000,000/Issuer |
| MMP | A | $5,000,000/Issuer |
| ARP | A+ | $1,000,000/Issuer |
| DRP | A+ | $1,000,000/Issuer |
| DCP | A+ | $1,000,000/Issuer |

## Notes:

Instruments that are downgraded below the required ratings may be held or sold.

The weighted average credit rating of this portfolio must be at least one grade below investment-grade.

Up to 20% of this portfolio may be invested in non-rated securities.

Under no circumstances can more than 20% of the portfolio be exposed to one issuer.

## Personnel Responsibilities

The investment policy of LMN, Inc. is under the direction of the Investment Policy Committee. This committee is composed of the treasurer, senior cash manager, two associate cash managers, vice president of operations, controller, and assistant controller. This committee meets at least once every six months to review the organization's investment policy. In addition, any senior member of this committee may call a special meeting if that member deems it necessary. A transcript is kept for all meetings. Changes require the unanimous approval of the cash managers and three other members of this committee. Memos summarizing any approved changes are sent to the chairman, president, and chief financial officer. The senior cash manager is authorized to enter any transaction that specifically and fully complies with the policies and provisions described in this investment policy without prior approval. Any transaction that *may* violate this investment policy must be approved by the exception procedure described in the following section.

The associate cash managers are authorized to enter any transaction that specifically and fully complies with the policies and provisions described in this investment policy, as long as the investment is not for more than $200,000.

## Procedure for Exceptions

*Prior to making any investment that may violate this investment policy,* the senior cash manager obtains the written approval of at least two of the other members of the Investment Committee. All requests for exceptions are submitted on the *Exceptions Form.* It is the responsibility of the senior cash manager to maintain a copy of all the exception forms, regardless of whether they are approved or denied.

## Required Audit Procedures

Copies of this investment policy are sent to the outside auditors with instructions to draw up procedures to ensure compliance. In addition, the controller is instructed to develop monthly reporting procedures to monitor and ensure compliance. To facilitate compliance, the senior cash manager is instructed to maintain the entire short-term portfolio on a spreadsheet that is updated daily. This spreadsheet incorporates the appropriate functions and macros to test the portfolio for compliance with the criteria outlined in this investment policy. In addition, the spreadsheet has a macro (one that cannot be disabled) that automatically notifies the controller of any violations.

## Required Criteria for Dealers and Custodians

The cash managers can only enter transactions with banks or securities dealers that are either primary dealers or on the approved list of secondary institutions prepared by the Investment Policy Committee. They can also enter transactions in which the securities dealers are not on the approved list, as long as all transactions are done on a delivery vs. payment (DVP), basis with a primary dealer acting as the intermediary.

In addition, the cash managers are required to obtain competitive bids from a minimum of two banks and/or dealers prior to making any investment over $250,000, and three banks and/or dealers prior to making any investment over $500,000.

# PART II
# Fixed-Income Mathematics

# 7

# BOND PRICES AND ACCRUED INTEREST

## INTRODUCTION

The total cost of acquiring a bond, or the total proceeds from selling a bond, can be determined by solving the following equation, which consists of three components:

$$Total = MV + AI +/- TC$$

where

> MV= Market Value
> AI = Accrued Interest
> TC = Transaction Costs

(In this equation, the buyer of the bond would have the transaction charges added to the cost, whereas the seller would have the transactions costs subtracted from the proceeds.) The text of this chapter deals with determining the values of the three components in this equation.

## QUOTING BOND PRICES

Bond prices are generally quoted in points where each point is worth $10. Thus, a price quote of 92 is equal to $920 and a price of 106 is equal to $1,060. The way in which "partial points" are quoted depends on the type of bond being priced.

United States Treasury Bonds and Mortgage-Backed Pass Through Securities are generally quoted in points and 32nds of points. Thus, if a Treasury Bond had a price quote of 96-01, this would equate to a market price of 96 points and 1/32 of a point. To convert the points into dollars, multiply the price in points by $10.

$$(96 * \$10) + (1/32 * \$10) = \$960.3125$$

Using the same procedure, to convert a price quote of 102-20 into dollars:

$$(102 * \$10) + (20/32 * \$10) = \$1,026.25$$

For Treasury Bonds that are traded actively, the minimum price increment is sometimes reduced to a 64th of a point. A 64th of a point is generally signified by a plus (+) sign after the price quote. Thus, a price quote of 88-12+ is equal to a price of 88 points and 12 1/2 points.

$$(88* \$10) + (12.5/32 * \$10) = \$883.91$$

For Corporate, Municipal, and some U.S. Agency Bonds, the minimum increment for partial points is eighths of a point (reduced if possible). Thus, if the price of a Corporate Bond rose from 88 to 89 in a series of minimal price changes, its price would rise as follows:

**Table 7.1** *Corporate and Municipal Bond Prices*

| Quote in 8ths of a point | Normal Quote | Price |
|:---:|:---:|:---:|
| 88 | 88 | $880.00 |
| 88 1/8 | 88 1/8 | $881.25 |
| 88 2/8 | 88 1/4 | $882.50 |
| 88 3/8 | 88 3/8 | $883.75 |
| 88 4/8 | 88 1/2 | $885.00 |
| 88 5/8 | 88 5/8 | $886.25 |
| 88 6/8 | 88 3/4 | $887.50 |
| 88 7/8 | 88 7/8 | $888.75 |
| 89 | 89 | $890.00 |

The price or market value (MV) is the first component of the preceding equation.

# ACCRUED INTEREST

Bond interest is usually paid in arrears. This means that when an investor receives an interest payment, it is to compensate the investor for holding the bond from some point in the past to the present. In other words, the interest that is paid has already been earned; it is not paid in advance. For example, bonds issued in the U.S. generally pay interest twice a year. Treasury Bonds generally make their interest payments on the 15th day of the payment months, whereas Corporate Bonds generally pay their interest on the first day of the payment months. Thus, if an investor owned a Treasury Bond that pays interest in January and July, the investor would receive an interest check on the 15th of January (to compensate the investor for holding the bond from July 15th of the previous year through January 14th), and the 15th of July (to compensate the investor for holding the bond from January 15th through July 14th).

Suppose one investor buys the Treasury Bond from another investor in March. Because the seller has owned the bond from the last interest payment date (i.e., January 15th), the seller is entitled to the interest that the bond has *accrued* from January 15th (but has not yet paid). Usually, when an investor buys a bond, the buyer is required to pay the seller the interest that has accrued from the last interest payment date. The buyer is reimbursed for this interest on the next interest payment date because the buyer receives a full six-month interest payment, although the buyer has not owned the bond for a full six months. The following equation is used to calculate the amount of accrued interest to which the seller is entitled.

$$AI = \text{Bond's Face Value (FV)} * \text{Rate (R)} * \text{Time (T)}$$

The bond's *face value* is almost always $1,000 and represents the amount that the issuer borrowed (and therefore, the amount on which the issuer must pay interest).

The *rate* is equal to the amount of interest that the bond pays in **one** interest payment period, divided by the bond's face value.

The *time* factor is equal to the number of days of accrued interest to which the seller is entitled, divided by the number of days in the interest period.

The time factor is the most complicated component of this equation. To calculate the time factor, it is necessary to know four key dates:

- The last interest payment date (LIPD), which is the date when the bond last paid interest.

- The trade date (TD), which is the date when traders, acting on behalf of the buyer and seller, agree to a transaction.

- The settlement date (SD), which is the date when the bonds are delivered to the buyer and the money to pay for the bonds is delivered to the seller. (The various settlement options are examined in the following section.)

- The next interest payment date (NIPD), which is the next day when the bond will pay interest.

The number of days of accrued interest to which the seller is entitled is equal to the number of days *between* the LIPD and the SD. (To calculate the number of days *between* the two dates, the LIPD is counted but the SD is not.) In order to calculate the number of days between the LIPD and the SD, it is necessary to determine exactly when the trade will settle.

When a bond trade settles depends on which settlement option is used. The decision about which settlement option to use is determined by the traders at the time they agree to the trade. The five most common settlement options are:

- Same-Day Settlement. The trade settles the same day as the trade date.

- Next-Day Settlement. The trade settles on the first *business* day after the trade day (most Treasury Bond transactions settle "next day").

- Skip-Day Settlement. The trade settles on the second *business* day after the trade date.

- Regular Way Settlement. The trade settles on the fifth *business* day after the trade date (most Corporate Bonds and Municipal Bonds settle "regular way").

- Seller's Option or Buyer's Option. The trade settles within 60 *calendar* days of the trade date.

Fortunately, there is no need to consult a calendar to determine the number of days between two dates. The HP-12C calculator (as well as many others) has a built-in function that automatically calculates the number of days between two dates. To use this function:

■ Key in the first date. In this text we will use the default date format of *mm.ddyyyy*. Thus, the date March 13, 1990 would be entered as 3.131990 and the date November 5, 1990 would be entered as 11.051990. (Refer to your manual for information on alternative date formats.)

■ Press the [ENTER] key.

■ Key in the second date.

■ Then press the [g] key and the [ΔDYS] key to display the number of days between the two dates (on a 365-day basis).

■ If, *and only if*, the financial instrument uses a 360-day year (i.e., a Corporate or Municipal Bond), then press the [X><Y] key. This converts the number of days between two dates from a 365-day basis to a 360-day basis.

Perhaps the best way to understand all of this together is to study some sample problems:

## *Problem One*: **Purchase of a Treasury Bond**

Calculate the total number of dollars that a buyer would have to pay in order to acquire a 10% January, 1999, U.S. Treasury Bond that was purchased for 92.12 points on Thursday, April 6, 1990, for next-day settlement, if the commission is $5 per bond.

$$\text{Total Cost} = MV + AI + TC$$

MV = 92.12 points, or

$$(92 * \$10) + (12/32 * \$10) = \$923.75$$

$$AI = FV * R * T$$

$$AI = \$1,000 * 0.05 * (\text{LIPD to SD} / \text{LIPD to NIPD})$$

Because this bond is a Treasury Bond, it pays its interest on the 15th of the payment months. In addition, because this bond matures in January and the maturity date is also an interest payment date, we know that this bond pays interest in January and July.
Thus,

- the LIPD is January 15, 1990,
- the NIPD is July 15, 1990,
- the SD is equal to the first business day after the TD. Because the TD is Thursday, April 6th, this trade settles on April 7th.

Substituting these values into the AI equation:

$$AI = \$,1000 * 0.05 * Time$$

$$AI = \$50 * (1.151990 \text{ to } 4.071990 / 1.151990 \text{ to } 7.151990)$$

$$AI = \$50 * (82 / 181) = \$22.65$$

(Note that the six-month period from January 15th to July 15th only includes 181 days. Thus, investors earn more interest per day during the period from January to June than they do during the period from June to January, which has 184 days.)

Thus,

$$Total\ Cost = MV + AI + TC$$

$$Total\ Cost = \$923.75 + \$22.65 + \$5 = \$951.40$$

## *Problem Two:* **Sale of a Treasury Bond**

Calculate the sales proceeds that a seller would receive from selling a 12% April, 2020, U.S. Treasury Bond on Friday, July 6, 1991, for next-day settlement at a price of 102.24 points, if the commission is $10.

$$The\ Total\ Sale\ Price\ (SP) = P + AI - TC$$

(Note that in a sale, the transaction costs are subtracted from the sales proceeds.)

$$MV = 102.24 = (102 * \$10) + (24/32 * \$10) = \$1,027.50$$

$$AI = F * R * T$$

$$AI = \$1,000 * 0.06 * (LIPD \text{ to } SD / LIPD \text{ to } NIPD)$$

Because this bond is a Treasury Bond, it will pay interest on the 15th of the payment months. In addition, because it matures in April and the maturity date is also an interest payment date, we know that this bond pays interest in April and October. Thus,

- the LIPD is April 15, 1990,
- the NIPD is October 15, 1990,
- the SD is equal to the first business day after the TD. Because the TD is Friday, July 6, this trade settles on the next *business* day, which is Monday, July 9.

Substituting these values into the AI equation:

$$AI = FV * R * T$$

$$AI = \$1,000 * 0.05 * T$$

$$AI = \$50 * (4.151990 \text{ to } 7.091990 / 4.151990 \text{ to } 10.151990)$$

$$AI = \$50 * (88 / 183) = \$22.65$$

$$\text{Total Sales Proceeds} = MV + AI - TC$$

$$\text{Sales Proceeds} = \$1,027.50 + \$27.87 - \$10 = \$1,045.37$$

## *Problem Three:* Purchase of a Corporate Bond

Calculate the total price that a buyer would have to pay in order to acquire an 11% April, 2002, IBM Bond at a price of 102 1/2 points, if it were purchased on Friday, July 20 and paid a $7.50 commission.

$$\text{Total Cost} = MV + AI + TC$$

where

$$MV = 102 \ 1/2 = (102 * \$10) + (1/2 * \$10) = \$1,025.00$$

$$\text{and } AI = FV * R * T$$

$$\$1,000 * 0.055 * (\text{LIPD to SD} / 180)$$

Because this is a Corporate Bond, its accrued interest needs to be calculated on a 30/360 basis. This means that we are to assume that every month has 30 days regardless of how many days it actually has. Because every month is assumed to have 30 days, one year must have 360 days (30 * 12).

The bond matures in April, so we know that the bond pays interest on April 1st and October 1st. Because the TD is Friday, July 20, and the transaction settles regular way, we know that the SD is five business days later, or July 27th. Thus,

- the LIPD = 4.011990.
- the SD = 7.271990.
- the number of days from one interest payment date to the next is always 180.

Thus,

$$AI = \$1,000 * 0.05 * (4.011990 \text{ to } 7.271990 / 180)$$

$$AI = \$50 * (117/ 180) = \$35.44$$

$$\text{Total Cost} = MV + AI + TC$$

$$\text{Total Cost} = \$1,025 + \$35.44 + \$7.50 = \$1,067.94$$

## *Problem Four:* Sale of a Corporate Bond

Calculate the sales proceeds that a seller would receive from selling an 8% March, 2000 GM Bond at a price of 70 1/8 points on Thursday, July 3, if the commission is $15.

$$\text{Total Sale Proceeds} = MV + AI - TC$$

$$MV = 70 \ 1/8 = (70 * \$10) + (1/8 * \$10) = \$701.25$$

$$AI = FV * R * T$$

$$AI = \$1,000 * 0.04 * (LIPD \text{ to } SD / 180)$$

In this problem the TD is Thursday, July 3. Because Friday is a legal holiday, it is not a business day. Thus, the SD, in order to be five business days later, must be Friday, July 11.

$$AI = \$40 * (3.011990 \text{ to } 7.111990 / 180)$$

$$AI = \$40 * (132 / 180) = \$29.33$$

$$\text{Total Sales Proceeds} = MV + AI - TC$$

$$\text{Total Sales Proceeds} = \$701.25 + \$29.33 - \$15 = \$715.50$$

# 8

# TIME-VALUE CALCULATIONS

## INTRODUCTION

Every investment can be broken down into a series of cashflows: one or more cashflows that the investor makes, and one or more cashflows that the investor receives. An investment's *return* is measured by the internal rate of return of these various cashflows. Because of this, the objective of most investment analysis is to predict the *size, direction, timing,* and *certainty* of an investment's future cashflows. Because the impact of the *size* and *direction* of the cashflows on the investment's overall return is obvious, we limit our examination to the impact of *timing* and *certainty* of the cashflows on the investments overall return.

## TIMING OF THE CASHFLOWS

The timing of a cashflow is extremely important because it has a direct impact on the value of a specific cashflow to the investor. The sooner a cashflow is received by the investor, the sooner it can be reinvested, and the more reinvestment income ($I_r$) it can earn. The more ($I_r$) an investor earns, the greater the investor's overall return-- all other factors being equal.

Similarly, the longer an investor can delay making a payment, the less expensive that payment becomes. The funds that will eventually be used to make the payment can be invested until the payment is actually made, again, increasing the investor's ($I_r$). For example, given a 10% interest rate, $100 now is worth the same as $110 one year from now. Assuming that there is no credit risk, a sensible investor with no immediate need for funds would have no preference when offered the choice of receiving (or paying) $100 now or $110 in one year. The present $100 is worth the same as $110 in one year, regardless of whether the funds are being received or paid out.

The relationship between the value of a dollar now (i.e., its present value [PV]) and its value at some future time (i.e., its future value [FV]) can be expressed by the following formula:

$$FV = PV(1 + i)^n$$

where:

FV = value of the dollars in the future
PV = value of a dollar now
i   = interest rate per compounding period
n   = number of compounding periods

This equation can also be restated in order to determine how much a cashflow that will be received at some future time is worth today:

$$PV = FV / (1 + i)^n$$

or, alternatively, what interest rate is required in order to grow a certain number of dollars now into a certain number of dollars at some future time:

$$i = (FV/PV)^{1/n} - 1$$

While the preceding equations are certainly useful, they deal only with one cashflow in each direction. Of course, most investments are composed of more than two cashflows. For example:

Investing in a 10-year Eurobond will have a total of 11 cashflows:

- one cashflow "out" when the investor purchases the bond
- ten cashflows "in" as the investor receives the annual interest payments and the principal payment.

Issuing a 10-year Eurobond will have the same 11 cashflows, however, from the issuer's viewpoint, there is one cashflow "in" and 10 cashflows "out."

Investing in a 30-year Treasury Bond will have 61 cashflows:

- one cashflow "out" when the investor purchases the bond
- 60 cashflows "in" as the investor receives the semiannual interest payments and the principal payment.

The relationship between the purchase price of a bond investment and all of its subsequent cashflows can be expressed mathematically by the following formula:

$$PV = \frac{CF_1}{(1+Y)^1} + \frac{CF_2}{(1+Y)^2} + ... + \frac{CF_n}{(1+Y)^n}$$

or, expressed in mathematical notation:

$$PV = \sum_{n=1} \frac{CF_n}{(1+Y)^n}$$

where:

PV = present value
CF(n) = value of each cashflow
i = interest rate per period
n = period number

This equation can be solved very easily by using the financial functions built into any reasonable sophisticated financial calculator. (We will use the old reliable Hewlett Packard HP-12C® calculator in our examples.) Which of the calculator's financial functions you employ to solve a specific financial problem depends on the size and the direction of the investment's cashflows. The financial functions that are most commonly employed are referred to as *basic financial registers,* and are identified in Table 8.1.

The value of any of the five basic financial registers can be determined as long as the value of the other four is known, or can be determined (see examples that follow). These basic financial function keys can be used to solve problems as long as the *intermediate cashflows* (cashflows other than the first or last) are all:

- the same size.
- paid or received at equal intervals.
- flow in one direction (either paid or received).

Consider the following examples:

**Table 8.1** *The HP-12C Basic Financial Registers*

| Function | Purpose |
|----------|---------|
| n | Equal to the number of compounding periods over the term of the investment. |
| i | Equal to the interest rate per period. The interest rate can be positive or negative. |
| PV | Equal to the value of the investment presently. Dollars paid are entered as a negative number, while dollars received are entered as a positive number. |
| PMT | Equal to the periodic payments made to, or by, the investor. Dollars paid are entered as a negative, while dollars received are entered as a positive. The calculator can be programmed to solve the calculation assuming that the payments are made or received at either the beginning or end of the compounding period. |
| FV | Equal to the future value of the investment. Dollars paid are entered as a negative number, while dollars received are entered as a positive number. |
| CHS | Used to change a positive number to a negative, and vice versa. |

1. What would $1,000 be worth if it were invested for 10 years, assuming that there is an 8% interest rate and annual compounding?

**Table 8.2** *Solution to Problem 8.1*

| Keystrokes | Purpose |
|------------|---------|
| [CLX] | Clears display. |
| 1,000 [CHS] [PV] | Changes the sign of the $1,000 purchase price to a negative number (because it is paid out) and then enters it as the present value. |

| 10 [n] | Enters 10 as the number of compounding periods. |
|--------|--------------------------------------------------|
| 8 [i] | Enters 8 as the interest rate per period. |
| 0 [PMT] | Enters 0 for the payments because there are no intermediate payments. |
| FV | Solves for the future value, which is $2,158.92 |

(Note that the *order* in which the four known variables are entered is irrelevant.)

2. What would $1,000 be worth if it were invested for 10 years, assuming that there is an 8% interest rate and semiannual compounding?

To solve this, only the values of $i$ and $n$ need to be changed in order to reflect that the interest is now compounded semiannually. Because the interest is compounded semiannually, the value of $i$ changes to 4% and the value of $n$ becomes 20. These are the only two variables that need to be changed.

**Table 8.3** *Solution to Problem 2*

| Keystrokes | Purpose |
|------------|---------|
| 4 [i] | Changes the value of $i$ to 4. |
| 20 [n] | Changes the value of $n$ to 20. |
| FV | Solves for the future value, which is $2,191.12 |

3. What would $1,000 be worth if it were invested for 10 years, assuming that there is an 8% interest rate and monthly compounding?

To solve this, the values of $i$ and $n$ need to be changed in order to reflect that the interest is now compounded monthly. The HP-12C has a convenient way of converting annual interest rates and compounding periods into their monthly equivalents. This conversion is accomplished by simply pressing the blue key [g] prior to the basic financial function key. For example, in order to convert an 8% annual rate and 10 years into their monthly equivalents, the keystrokes would be as follows:

**Table 8.4** *Solution to Problem 3*

| Keystrokes | Purpose |
|---|---|
| 8 [g] [12/] | Converts the 8% annual interest payments into monthly interest payments and enters the monthly interest rate as $i$. |
| 10 [g] [12x] | Converts the 10 annual compounding periods into monthly compounding periods and enters the number of periods as $n$. |
| FV | Solves for the future value, which is $2,219.64 |

It should be noted that as the compounding frequency increases, so docs the FV of the investment, which is logical, because as the compounding frequency increases, so does the amount of interest that can be earned by reinvesting the cashflows.

# CALCULATING THE INTERNAL RATE OF RETURN WHEN THE INTERMEDIATE PAYMENTS ARE EQUAL

Whereas the preceding examples have no intermediate cashflows, the HP-12C makes solving problems with intermediate cashflows easy. As mentioned previously, the size and direction of the intermediate cashflows are incorporated into the calculation by using the payment [PMT] key. Before this key is used, however, the calculator must be informed whether the payments occur at the beginning or the end of the compounding periods. If the payments occur at the end of the periods, then press [g] [END] prior to entering the payment. If the payments occur at the beginning of the periods, press [g] [BEG] prior to entering the payment. (If the calculator is set to begin, a small **BEGIN** indicator will be visible in the display window.)

For example, what would 10 cashflows of $50 each be worth, given that i = 5% per period, and that the cashflows are received at the end of each period?

**Table 8.5** *Solution to Problem 4*

| Keystrokes | Purpose |
|---|---|
| [CLX] | Clears display. |
| 10 [n] | Enters 10 as the value of *n*. |
| 5 [i] | Enters 5 as the value of *i*. |
| [g] [END] | Sets payments to END. |
| 50 PMT | Enters 50 as the PMT. |
| 0 FV | Enters 0 as the FV. |

Pressing [PV] calculates a present value of -$386.09. In other words, $389.09 is a fair price to pay for 10 $50 payments, assuming that the interest rate per period is 5% and that the payments are received at the end of the periods.

As another example, what would 10 cashflows of $50 each be worth, given that i = 5% per period, and that the cashflows are received at the beginning of each period?

**Table 8.6** *Solution to Problem 5*

| Keystrokes | Purpose |
|---|---|
| [g] [BEG] | Sets PMT to Beginning. |
| [CLX] | Clears display. |
| 10 [n] | Enters 10 as the value of *n*. |
| 5 [i] | Enters 5 as the value of *i*. |
| 50 PMT | Enters 50 as the PMT. |
| 0 FV | Enters 0 as the FV. |

Pressing [PV] calculates a present value of -$405.39. Because the cashflows are received at the beginning of the period and can be reinvested for a longer period of time, the value of the future payments is higher.

As another example, what interest rate would result in the accumulation of $80,000 at the end of 20 years, assuming that the initial investment was $35,000, and that an additional $10,00 were added to the account at the end of each year?

**Table 8.7** *Solution to Problem 6*

| Keystrokes | Purpose |
|---|---|
| [CLX] | Clears display. |
| [g] End | Sets payment to End. |
| 20 [n] | Enters 20 as the number of periods. |
| 35,000 [CHS] [PV] | Enters a -35,000 as the PV. |
| 1,000 [CHS] [PMT] | Enters a -1,000 as the PMT. |
| 80,000 [FV] | Enters 80,000 as the FV. |

Pressing [i] calculates an interest rate of 2.29% per period. Because there are two periods to a year, the annualized return is 4.57% (2.29% * 2).

# CALCULATING THE INTERNAL RATE OF RETURN WHEN THE INTERMEDIATE PAYMENTS ARE UNEQUAL

The basic financial function keys cannot accommodate unequal intermediate payments. To calculate the internal rate of return (IRR) for a payment stream with unequal intermediate payments, the following four functions are used:

**Table 8.8** *Unequal Cashflow Function Keys*

| Functions | Purpose |
|---|---|
| $CF_o$ | Enters the initial cashflow. |
| CFj | Enters subsequent cashflows. |
| Nj | Enters repetitive cashflows. |
| IRR | Calculates the IRR. |

For example, suppose an investment was expected to generate the following cashflows:

**Table 8.9 *Periodic Cashflows***

| CF | Amount | CF | Amount | CF | Amount |
|----|--------|----|--------|----|--------|
| 1 | -120,000 | 7 | +10,000 | 13 | +12,500 |
| 2 | -10,000 | 8 | +10,000 | 14 | +12,500 |
| 3 | +15,000 | 9 | +10,000 | 15 | +12,500 |
| 4 | +15,000 | 10 | +10,000 | 16 | +12,500 |
| 5 | +15,000 | 11 | +17,500 | 17 | +12,500 |
| 6 | +15,000 | 12 | +17,500 | 18 | +12,500 |

**Table 8.10 *Keystrokes to Calculate the IRR***

| Keystrokes | Purpose |
|------------|---------|
| 120,000 [CHS] [g] [CF$_o$] | Enters a negative $120,000 as the initial cashflow. |
| 10,000 [CHS] [g] [CFj] | Enters a negative $10,000 as the second cashflow. |
| 15,000 [CFj] | Enters $15,000 as the third cashflow. |
| 4 [g] [Nj] | Informs the calculator that the $15,000 cashflow is repeated four times. |
| 10,000 [g] [CFj] | Enters $10,000 as the seventh cashflow. |
| 4 [g] [Nj] | Informs the calculator that the $10,000 cashflow is repeated four times. |
| 17,500 [CHS] [g] [CFj] | Enters $17,500 as the eleventh cashflow. |
| 2 [g] [Nj] | Informs the calculator that the $17,500 cashflow is repeated two times. |

| 12,500 [g] [CFj] | Enters $12,500 as the thirteenth cashflow. |
|---|---|
| 6 [g] [Nj] | Informs the calculator that the $12,500 is repeated six times. |
| [F] [IRR] | Calculates the IRR, which is 5.68%. |

To calculate the IRR of the cashflows in Table 8.9, enter the keystrokes presented in Table 8.10.

It may take time for the calculator to generate an answer to a difficult problem, because it solves the problem by a trial-and-error process. If the problem is very complicated, the calculator may display an **ERROR 3** message, which indicates that either the problem is beyond the calculator's capability or that the problem has multiple answers. Multiple answers, and thus **ERROR 3** messages, often result when the intermediate cashflows change directions. The procedure for resolving an **ERROR 3** is described in the calculator's manual.

## ADDITIONAL SAMPLE PROBLEMS

1.  What is the value of $10,000,000 in 15 years, if it is invested at 7.5%, assuming that there is monthly compounding?

2.  How much would have to be invested now in order to accumulate $4,500,000 in 10 years, assuming that you could earn a 10% return and had semiannual compounding?

3.  If you had $10,000 in a savings account and were going to contribute an additional $1,000 per year, how many years would it take to accumulate $500,000, assuming that there is semiannual compounding, and that the payments are to be made at the end of the period?

4.  What is the IRR of the following series of cashflows? (Note that the following series of cashflows have unequal intermediate payments.)

**Table 8.11** *Cashflow Series*

| Series 1 | Series 2 | Series 3 |
|----------|----------|----------|
| $-100,000 | $-57,000 | $-100,000 |
| $10,000 | $10,000 | $20,000 |
| $15,000 | $12,500 | $20,000 |
| $15,000 | $12,500 | $-10,000 |
| $15,000 | $14,000 | $30,000 |
| $20,000 | $14,500 | $30,000 |
| $20,000 | $15,000 | $30,000 |
| $20,000 | $15,000 | $30,000 |
| $20,000 | $15,000 | $30,000 |

## *Answers:*

**Table 8.12** *Answer to Additional Problem 1*

| Set Function | Equal to: |
|--------------|-----------|
| n | 15 [g] [12X] |
| i | 7.5  [g] [12/] |
| PV | 10,000,000  [CHS] |
| PMT | 0 |
| FV | $30,694,517.27 |

**Table 8.13** *Answer to Additional Problem 2*

| Set Function | Equal to: |
|--------------|-----------|
| n | 20 |
| i | 5 |
| PMT | 0 |
| FV | $4,500,000 |
| PV | $-1,696,002.67 |

**Table 8.14** *Answer to Additional Problem 3*

| Set Function | Equal to: |
|:---:|:---:|
| i | 6 |
| PV | $-10,000 |
| FV | $500,000 |
| PMT | [g] [END] $1,000 [CHS] |
| n | 51 periods, or 25.5 years |

*Answer to Problems 4 - Series One*:

100,000 [CHS] [g] [CFo]
10,000  [g] [CFj]
15,000  [g] [CFj]
3 [g] [Nj]
20,000[g]  [CFj]
4 [g] [Nj]
[F] [IRR] =  6.49

*Answer to Problems 4 - Series Two*:

57,000 [CHS] [g] [CFo]
10,000 [g] [CFj]
12,500 [g] [CFj]
2 [g] [Nj]
14,000 [g] [CFj]
14,500 [g] [CFj]
15,000 [g] [CFj]
3 [g] [Nj]
[F] [IRR] = 15.79

*Answer to Problems 4 - Series Three*:

100,000 [CHS] [g] [CFo]
20,000 [g] [CFj]
2 [g] [Nj]
10,000 [CHS] [g] [CFj]
30,000 [g] [CFj]
5 [g] [Nj]
[F] [IRR] =  12.89

# 9

# YIELD TO MATURITY

## INTRODUCTION

The definition of yield to maturity (YTM) is that it is the interest rate that, when used to discount the future cash flows, will result in the sum of the present value of the future cash flows equaling the purchase price of the bond. In other words, it is the interest rate that relates the bond's purchase price to its future cash flows. Perhaps the best way to think of a bond's YTM is as its internal rate of return (IRR). The YTM is the most commonly quoted and widely used measure of return presently. Almost all bonds are traded on a YTM basis. Newspapers and quote services quote the YTM when they want to describe a bond's yield.

## DISADVANTAGES OF YIELD TO MATURITY

Whereas the YTM is the most widely used yield measure, it is *not* a very accurate measure of a bond's true return. For our purposes, we define an investment's *true return* as the IRR that relates the investor's buying power at the investment's inception to the investor's buying power at some specific time in the future. Whereas the YTM may accurately measure the IRR of a bond's cash flows, it does not accurately measure a bond's return.

There are many reasons that the YTM is often a dreadful measure of return. First, inherent in the YTM calculation is the assumption that each cash flow (i.e., each interest payment) will be reinvested at a YTM that is identical to the YTM at which the bond was originally purchased. Thus, if a bond offered a 9% YTM on the day that it was purchased, it is assured that each interest payment will be reinvested at the same rate. Of course, in order to actually earn a 9% YTM, every cash flow would have to be reinvested at 9%.

To be able to reinvest each cash flow at an identical YTM, the traditional yield curve (YTM vs. maturity) would have to be both perfectly flat and remain unchanged over the life of the investment. In other words, the yield curve would have to resemble the following curve over the entire investment period:

**Figure 9.1** *Flat Yield Curve*

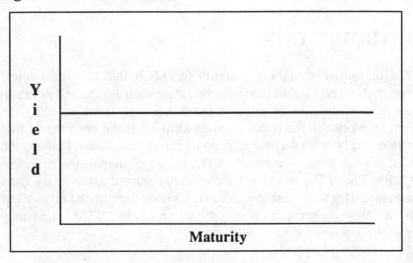

Assuming that the yield curve is going to remain flat and fixed is, of course, unrealistic for two reasons:

- Market interest rates, and thus reinvestment rates, are constantly changing. Because of this, it is unreasonable to assume that the reinvestment rate will remain constant.

- The yield curve is usually not flat. Even if interest rates were to remain constant, each coupon would be reinvested for a different term and, thus, at a different rate. (For a calculation that assumes a more accurate reinvestment rate, see Chapter 10. For an examination on the shape of the yield curve, see Chapter 19.)

The second reason that the YTM is often a poor measure of a bond's true return is taxes. Whereas taxes certainly have a negative impact on the true return that some investors receive from their bonds, the YTM calculation neither acknowledges nor includes a provision for taxes in the calculation. (For a calculation that includes a provision for taxes, see Chapter 10.)

Third, the YTM is a poor measure of true return because of inflation. Whereas inflation has a negative impact on the true return that most investors receive from their bonds, the YTM calculation neither acknowledges nor includes a provision for inflation in the calculation. (For a calculation that includes a provision for inflation, see Chapter 10.)

Fourth, the YTM is a poor measure of true return because the calculation includes no provision for credit risk. Whereas defaults and delays have a negative impact on an investor's real return over time, the YTM calculation neither acknowledges nor offers any way to include a provision for credit risk in the calculation. (To include a provision for credit risk, see Chapter 16.)

Fifth, the YTM is a poor measure because the calculation includes no provision for currency risk. Whereas currency values can fluctuate wildly, the YTM calculation neither acknowledges nor offers any way to include a provision for currency risk in the calculation. (To include a provision for currency risk, see Chapter 25.)

## CALCULATION OF YIELD TO MATURITY

As defined previously, the YTM is the yield that will cause the following equation to be true. The bond's market value (MV), including accrued interest, is:

$$MV = \frac{\phantom{xxxx}}{(1+y)^1} + \frac{\phantom{xxxx}}{(1+y)^2} + ... + \frac{\phantom{xxxx}}{(1+y)^n}$$

where

$CF_{(x)}$ = periodic cashflow(s)

$y$ = YTM per period

To solve this equation, insert a guess for a value of $y$ and solve for the purchase price. If the resulting market value is below the bond's actual market value, then the value of $y$ is too high. If it is above, then the value of $y$ is too low. By trial and error, the true value of $y$ can be determined. (The process of making a series of guesses in order to determine the true value of *y* is called *iteration.*) This process of making progressively better guesses is how the HP-12C calculates a bond's YTM.

For U.S. Government Bonds (or any other bond using an actual/actual calendar), the **YTM** function is pre-programmed into the calculator:

■ Enter the annual coupon as a percentage of the value and press [PMT]. Thus, if the bond had a 10% coupon, it would be entered simply as "10."

■ Enter the bond's price as a percentage of the value and press [PV]. Thus, a bond priced at 92.08 points would be entered as 92.25 [($922.50/$1,000)*100)].

■ Enter the settlement date and press [Enter].

■ Enter the maturity date and press [F] [YTM].

For U.S. Treasury Bonds, the **PRICE** function is also pre-programmed into the calculator. To utilize it:

■ Enter the annual coupon as a percentage of the value and press [PMT].

■ Enter the bond's YTM and press [i].

■ Enter the settlement date and press [Enter].

■ Enter the maturity date and press [F] [PRICE].

■ Press X><Y to calculate the accrued interest.

■ Press [+] to determine the bond's total purchase price (excluding transaction costs).

Although the only bond functions that are pre-programmed into the HP-12C are based on an actual/actual calendar, the HP-12C can still be used to calculate the yield and price of bonds that are based on a 30/360 calendar by entering a program into the calculator and then using the program to solve for the bond's price and yield.

**Table 9.1** *30/360 Bond Yield Program*

| Step | Keystrokes | Display |
|------|------------|---------|
| 1 | [F] [P/R] | |
| 2 | [F] CLEAR [PRGM] | 00- |

| 3 | [F] CLEAR [FIN] | 01- 42 34 |
| 4 | [G] [BEG] | 02- 43   7 |
| 5 | [RCL] 2 | 03- 45   2 |
| 6 | 2 | 04-      2 |
| 7 | [/] (i.e., divide) | 05-     10 |
| 8 | [PMT] | 06-     14 |
| 9 | [STO] 6 | 07- 44   6 |
| 10 | [RCL] 5 | 08- 45   5 |
| 11 | [+] | 09-     40 |
| 12 | [FV] | 10-     15 |
| 13 | [RCL] 3 | 11- 45   3 |
| 14 | [RCL] 4 | 12- 45   4 |
| 15 | [g] [ΔDYS] | 13- 43 26 |
| 16 | [R↓] | 14-     33 |
| 17 | 1 | 15-      1 |
| 18 | 8 | 16-      8 |
| 19 | 0 | 17-      0 |
| 20 | [/] (i.e, divide) | 18-     10 |
| 21 | [n] | 19-     11 |
| 22 | [g] [FRAC] | 20- 43 24 |
| 23 | 1 | 21-     ·1 |
| 24 | [X><Y] | 22-     34 |
| 25 | [-] | 23-     30 |
| 26 | [RCL] 6 | 24- 45   6 |
| 27 | [x] | 25-     20 |
| 28 | [RCL] 0 | 26- 45   0 |
| 29 | [g] [x = 0] | 27- 43 35 |
| 30 | [g] [GTO] 39 | 28-43,33 39 |
| 31 | 2 | 29-      2 |
| 32 | [/] (i.e., divide) | 30-     10 |

| 33 | [i] | 31- 12 |
|----|-----|---------|
| 34 | [PV] | 32- 13 |
| 35 | [CHS] | 33- 16 |
| 36 | [X><Y] | 34- 34 |
| 37 | [-] | 35- 30 |
| 38 | [g] [LSTx] | 36- 43 36 |
| 39 | [X><Y] | 37- 34 |
| 40 | [g] [GTO] 00 | 38-43,33 00 |
| 41 | [R ] | 39- 33 |
| 42 | [RCL] 1 | 40- 45 1 |
| 43 | [+] | 41- 40 |
| 44 | [CHS] | 42- 16 |
| 45 | [PV] | 43- 13 |
| 46 | [i] | 44- 12 |
| 47 | 2 | 45- 2 |
| 48 | [x] (i.e., multiply) | 46- 20 |
| 49 | [F] [P/R] |  |

The following are operating instructions for the program:

- Press [STO] [EEX] to activate the program (when activated, the "c" indicator will be displayed).
- Enter the annual coupon and press [STO] 2.
- Enter the settlement date and press [STO] 3.
- Enter the maturity date and press [STO] 4.
- Enter the redemption value as a percentage of the value and press [STO] 5.

Then, to determine the YTM:

- Press 0 [STO] 0.
- Enter the price as a percentage of the value and press [STO] 1.
- Press [R/S] to calculate the YTM.

Or, to determine the Price:

- Enter the YTM as a percentage of the value and press [STO] 0.
- Press [R/S] to obtain the price as a percentage of the value.
- Press [X><Y] to display accrued interest.

## SAMPLE PROBLEMS

1. What is the YTM of a 5% U.S. T-Bond priced at 89-08 points that settles on June 15, 1990, and matures on Sept. 30, 2003?

2. What is the market price of a 10% U.S. T-Bond that settles on July 20, 1991, matures on Aug. 1, 1999, and offers an 8.65% YTM?

3. What is the total purchase price of 1,000 of the bonds in problem-2 if the commission were $1.50 per bond?

4. What is the YTM of an IBM 11% bond priced at 88 1/8th points that settles on December 5, 1992 and matures on December 1, 2010?

5. What is the price of a GM 8% bond that settles on July 12, 1992, matures on June 15, 1999, and is priced to offer a 10.35% YTM?

6. If you were to sell 100 of these GM Bonds and paid a commission of $1/bond, what would your sale proceeds be?

**Table 9.2** *Answer to Problem One*

| Step | Purpose |
|---|---|
| [CLX] | Clears display |
| [f] [FIN] | Clears the financial registers |
| 5 [PMT] | Enters the annual coupon |
| 89.25 [PV] | Enters the purchase price |
| 6.151990 [ENTER] | Enters the settlement date |
| 9.302003 [f] [YTM] | Enters the maturity date and displays that the YTM is 6.20% |

**Table 9.3** *Answer to Problem Two*

| Step | Purpose |
|------|---------|
| [CLX] | Clears display |
| [f] [FIN] | Clears the financial registers |
| 8.65 [i] | Enters the YTM |
| 10 [PMT] | Enters the annual coupon |
| 7.201991 [ENTER] | Enters the settlement date |
| 8.011999 [f] [PRICE] | Enters the maturity date and displays that the PRICE is 107.70 points |
| [X><Y] | Displays accrued interest |
| [+] | Displays that the total of the price plus the accrued interest is 112.36% |
| 0.36 * 0.32 = .1152 | Determines that the total proceeds in points and 32nds is 112.11+. |

### Answer to Problem Three

A price of 112.36% translates into a price of 112.11+% when it is quoted in 32nds. In dollars, a price of 112.11+ points would equal $1,123.59375 and, thus, 1,000 bonds would cost:

$$1,000 * (1,123.59375 + \$1.50) = \$1,125,097.50$$

### Answer to Problem Four

First enter the 30/360 program and then complete the following steps:

**Table 9.4** *Steps for Problem Four*

| Step | Purpose |
|------|---------|
| [CLX] | Clears display |
| [f] [REG] | Clears registers |
| [STO] [EEX] | Activates program |
| 11 [STO] 2 | Stores coupon in Register 2 |

| | |
|---|---|
| 12.051992 [STO] 3 | Stores settle date in Register 3 |
| 12.012010 [STO] 4 | Stores maturity date in Register 4 |
| 100 [STO] 5 | Stores redemption value in Register 5 |
| 0 [STO] 0 | Stores 0 in Register 0 |
| 88.125 [STO] 1 | Stores the price in Register 1 |
| [R/S] | Calculates that the YTM is 12.69% |

### Answer to Problem Five

First, enter the 30/360 program and then complete the following steps:

**Table 9.5** *Steps for Problem Five*

| Step | Purpose |
|---|---|
| [CLX] | Clears display |
| [f] [REG] | Clears registers |
| [STO] [EEX] | Activates program |
| 8 [STO] 2 | Stores coupon in Register 2 |
| 7.121990 [STO] 3 | Stores settle date in Register 3 |
| 12.012010 [STO] 4 | Stores maturity date in Register 4 |
| 100 [STO] 5 | Stores redemption value in Register 5 |
| 10.35 [STO] 0 | Stores the YTM |
| [R/S] | Determines that the price is 80.17 points. |
| [X><Y] | Determines accrued interest |
| [+] | Determines that the total price is 81.09 points |

### Answer to Problem Six

A price of 81.09 points translates into a price of $810.90 per bond. Thus, for 100 bonds, the after-commission sale proceeds would equal:

$$($810.90 * 100) - $100 = $80,990$$

# 10

## ADVANCED YIELDS

## INTRODUCTION

As examined in the preceding chapter, the YTM provides a poor measure of a bond's true return because it does not incorporate the impacts of various reinvestment rates, taxes, inflation, credit risk, and currency risk on the bond's return. Fortunately, there are other, more sophisticated, yield measures that incorporate these factors and, thus, are better at predicting a bond's true return.

## REALIZED COMPOUND YIELD

The Realized Compound Yield (RCY) is the IRR that relates the purchase price of the bond to the total dollar return (T$R) that a bond generates over a specific investment horizon. (The T$R is equal to the sum of the principal [P], interest [I], and interest on interest [IOI] generated over the investment period.)

### Advantages of Using Realized Compound Yield

Whereas the YTM calculation assumes that every cash flow is reinvested at the same YTM as the original investment, the RCY calculation allows investors to use alternative, and hopefully more realistic, reinvestment rate(s). The reinvestment rate(s) that an investor plugs into an RCY calculation depends on

- how, specifically, the investor expects interest payments to be reinvested.
- the investor's expectations regarding future interest rates.
- the current shape of the yield curve (s).

For example, if a group of investors expect to reinvest their interest payments in a money market fund, it is sensible for them to assume that their reinvestment rate will equal whatever money market rates are projected to be. However, if those same investors expect to reinvest their interest payments in 10-year Treasury Bonds, they should assume that their reinvestment rate will equal whatever the 10-year Treasury Bond is projected to yield.

The accuracy of the RCY calculation depends on the accuracy of the reinvestment rate(s) used in the calculation. Because it is very doubtful that the investor's reinvestment rate assumptions will be precise, it is also very doubtful that the RCY calculation will be precise. Although the RCY calculation is imprecise, it is usually far more accurate, and more useful, than the YTM calculation.

For example, investors often mistakenly make decisions regarding the relative attractiveness of two bonds by comparing their respective YTMs (i.e., all other factors being equal, the bond with the higher YTM is regarded as more attractive). However, if the investors are going to reinvest the interest payments, they should base their decisions on the bonds' RCYs instead of their YTMs. The reason is that sometimes the bond with the lower YTM will have the higher RCY. Because the RCY provides a more meaningful measure of return, investors who reinvest their interest payments should seek to maximize their RCYs--not their YTMs.

## Limitations of Realized Compound Yield

Because the RCY calculation makes no provision for taxes or inflation, it is only applicable to investments and/or accounts that are both tax exempt and immune from inflation. For example, one type of account for which the RCY is an especially suitable measure of return is Defined Benefit (DB) Plans. As their name implies, DB Plans provide a specific benefit (i.e., $100,000/year for 20 years). Because the plan's sponsor is only obligated to provide the plan's beneficiaries with a *fixed number of dollars*, inflation has no impact on the sponsor.

Further, because DB Plans are "qualified plans," investments within DB Plans are entirely free from taxes (at least currently). Although DB Plans may seem like a very narrow market niche, there is presently over two trillion dollars of assets in DB Plans, making them the largest pool of investable assets in the world.

## Calculation of Realized Compound Yield

The formula for the RCY is:

$$RCY(\%) = k[(T\$R/PP)^{1/n} - 1] * 100$$

where

| | |
|---|---|
| k | = the number of compounding periods per year. |
| T$R | = total dollar return. |
| PP | = the bond's market price (including accrued interest, if any). |
| n | = number of compounding periods. |

Because the purchase price, total number of compounding periods, and number of compounding periods are all known, the only variable that needs to be estimated to solve this equation is the bond's T$R. There are numerous ways to estimate a bond's T$R and, in turn, its RCY. These methods range from being very simple to extraordinarily complex, with the complex methods being the most accurate. Several alternate methods of estimating the T$R and the RCY of a bond are examined in the next section.

## Simple Methods of Estimating Total Dollar Return and Realized Compound Yield

If an investor is willing to assume a constant reinvestment rate over the entire investment period, the RCY calculation can be performed on the HP-12C by estimating the total dollar return (T$R), the RCY per period, and the annual RCY.

### *Step One:*

The T$R of a given bond over a given period is equal to the sum of its three components:

Principal (P) + Interest (I) + Interest on Interest (IOI)

| | |
|---|---|
| P | = the bond's redemption value. |
| I | = the sum of the bond's coupons. |
| IOI | = the interest earned by reinvesting the bond's interest payments |

The sum of the *I* and the *IOI* can be calculated by and solving for the future value (FV).

The FV, in turn, is equal to the sum of the *I* and the *IOI* components. The size of each component can be easily calculated by subtracting the interest component from the total.

**Table 10.1** *Summing I Plus IOI*

| Setting | Equals |
|---------|--------|
| n | The number of compounding periods from the payment date *prior to* the settlement date, to the maturity date. |
| i | The reinvestment rate per period. |
| PMT | The interest payment per period (set PMT to "End"). |
| PV | Zero. |

To calculate the T$R, add the *P* to the sum of the *I* and *IOI*.

### Step Two:

Once the T$R is determined, the *RCY per period* can be calculated by the following steps and solving for the periodic interest rate (*i*). The value of *i* is equal to the RCY per period.

**Table 10.2** *Calculating "i"*

| Setting | Equals |
|---------|--------|
| FV | The T$R. |
| PMT | Zero. |
| n | The number of periods, including partial periods, from the settlement date to the maturity date. |
| PV | The purchase price plus accrued interest. |

### Step Three:

Multiply *i* by the number of payments per year in order to annualize the return.

## Sample Calculations of Realized Compound Yield

Problem One - What RCY can a non-taxable investor expect to receive from an 8% 10-year U.S. Treasury Bond priced at 80 points, if the investor expects to be able to reinvest the interest payments at 8.5%?

### Step One: Determining the T$R

T$R = (P + I + IOI)
P = $1,000
I + IOI =
    n = 20
    i = (8.5 / 2) = 4.25%
    PV = 0
    PMT = $40.00 (80 / 2)
    Solving for FV = I + IOI = $1,222.50
Thus, T$R = $1,000 + $1,222.50 = $2,222.50

### Step Two:  Determining the RCY Per Period

n = 20
PV = -$800
PMT = 0
FV = $2,222.50
i = 5.24% = RCY per period

### Step Three:  Annualizing the RCY

5.24 * 2 = 10.48% per year

Problem Two - What RCY can an investor expect to receive from an 11% U.S. Treasury Bond of January, 2005, if the bond is purchased for 101.16 points to settle on August 21, 1990, and expects to be able to reinvest at 10%?

### Step One:  Determining the T$R

T$R = (P + I + IOI)
P = $1,000
I + IOI =

n = number of periods from the payment date prior to the
settlement date (July 15, 1990) to the maturity date
(January 15, 2005), or 29 periods
i = 5% (10% / 2)
PV = 0
PMT = $55 ($110 Interest / 2)
Solving for FV = $3,427.75

Thus, T$R = $1,000 + $3,427.75 = $4,427.75

## Step Two: Determining the RCY Per Period

n = number of periods from:
    the settlement date (August 21, 1990)
    to the maturity date (January 15, 2005)
  from August 21, 1990 to January 15, 1991
    = 147/184 = 0.7989 periods
  from January 15, 1991 to January 15, 2005
    = 28 periods
 Total = 28.7989 periods

PV = purchase price and accrued interest
    Purchase price = $1,015
    Accrued interest = P * R * T
    Time = July 15, 1990 to August 21, 1990
    Accrued interest = $1,000 * 0.055 * 37/184 =
    $11.06
    Total = -$1,026.06

PMT = 0
FV = $4,427.75
Solving for i = 5.21% RCY per period

## Step Three: Annualizing the RCY

    5.21 * 2 = 10.42%

Problem Three - What RCY can an investor expect to receive from
the 8% September, 2005, Treasury Bond if the bond is purchased to
settle on Wednesday, November 3, 1991, for 102.08 points,
assuming a 7.5% reinvestment rate?

## *Step One: Determining the T$R*

T$R = (P + I + IOI)
P = $1,000
I + IOI =
    n = number of periods from:
        the payment date prior to the settlement
        date (September 15, 1990)
        to the maturity date (September 15, 2005),
        or 30 periods
        i = 3.75% (7.5% / 2)
        PV = 0
        PMT = $40 ($80 Interest / 2)
        Solving for FV = $2,151.97
Thus, T$R = $1,000 + $2,151.97 = $3,151.97

## *Step Two: Determining the RCY Per Period*

n = number of periods from:
    the settlement date (November 3, 1990)
    to the maturity date (September 15, 2005)
    from November 3, 1990 to March 15, 1991
    = 132/181 = 0.7293 periods
    from January 15, 1991 to January 15, 2005
    = 29 periods
    Total = 29.7293 periods
PV = Purchase price and accrued interest
    Purchase price = $1,022.50
    Accrued interest = P * R * T
    Time = Sept. 15, 1990 to Nov. 3, 1990
    Accrued interest = $1,000 * 0.04 * 49/181 = $10.83
    Total = -$1,033.33
PMT = 0
FV = $2,151.97
Solving for i = 2.5% RCY per period

## *Step Three: Annualizing the RCY*

2.5 * 2 = 5%

In the above example, the reinvestment rate was assumed to remain constant over the life of the investment. Naturally, this assumption can be changed to more accurately reflect the investor's expectations about future interest rates. Some of the more commonly used reinvestment rates are

- the prevailing rates in the current yield curve.
- the forward rates--which can be calculated from the current yield curve (see Chapter 20).
- the rates projected by a favorite economist or economic model.

Naturally, for difficult problems, it often makes sense to use a spreadsheet to perform the RCY calculations. A spreadsheet is used to solve the following two problems: one where the reinvestment rate is held constant, and one where the reinvestment rate periodically increases for the first five years.

**Table 10.3 *RCY Calculation of a 10-Year 10% Treasury Bond Priced at 80 Points, Assuming That There Is an 8% Reinvestment Rate***

| Period | CashFlow | Number Of Dollars Reinvested | Interest on Interest |
|--------|----------|------------------------------|----------------------|
| 1 | $50 | -- | -- |
| 2 | $50 | $50 | $2 |
| 3 | $50 | $102 | $4.08 |
| 4 | $50 | $156.08 | $6.24 |
| 5 | $50 | $212.32 | $8.49 |
| 6 | $50 | $270.82 | $10.83 |
| 7 | $50 | $331.65 | $13.27 |
| 8 | $50 | $394.91 | $15.80 |
| 9 | $50 | $460.71 | $18.43 |
| 10 | $50 | $529.14 | $21.17 |
| 11 | $50 | $600.31 | $24.01 |
| 12 | $50 | $674.32 | $26.97 |
| 13 | $50 | $751.29 | $30.05 |
| 14 | $50 | $831.34 | $33.25 |

| 15 | $50 | $914.60 | $36.58 |
| 16 | $50 | $1,001.18 | $40.05 |
| 17 | $50 | $1,091.23 | $43.65 |
| 18 | $50 | $1,184.88 | $47.40 |
| 19 | $50 | $1,282.27 | $51.29 |
| 20 | $1,050 | $1,383.56 | $55.34 |

For the above bond,

IOI = $488.90 (the sum of the last column)
P = $1,000
I = $1,000

Thus, the T$R = ($1,000 + $1,000 + $488.90) =

$2,488.90

To solve for the RCY per period

n = 20
PV = $-800
FV = $2,488.90
PMT = 0
Solving for i, RCY = 5.84%

To annualize the RCY = 5.84% * 2 = 11.68%

**Table 10.4** *RCY Calculation of a 10% 10-Year U.S. T-Bond Priced at 80 Points, Assuming That There Is a Reinvestment Rate of 8% That Increases 1/4% per Period for the First Five Years*

| Period | CashFlow | Number of Dollars Reinvested | Interest on Interest |
|--------|----------|------------------------------|----------------------|
| 1 | $50 | -- | -- |
| 2 | $50 | $50 | $2.13 |
| 3 | $50 | $102.13 | $4.60 |
| 4 | $50 | $156.72 | $7.44 |
| 5 | $50 | $214.16 | $10.71 |

| 6 | $50 | $274.87 | $14.43 |
|---|---|---|---|
| 7 | $50 | $339.30 | $18.66 |
| 8 | $50 | $407.97 | $23.46 |
| 9 | $50 | $481.42 | $28.89 |
| 10 | $50 | $560.31 | $35.02 |
| 11 | $50 | $645.33 | $40.33 |
| 12 | $50 | $735.66 | $45.98 |
| 13 | $50 | $831.64 | $51.98 |
| 14 | $50 | $933.62 | $58.35 |
| 15 | $50 | $1,041.97 | $65.12 |
| 16 | $50 | $1,157.09 | $72.32 |
| 17 | $50 | $1,279.41 | $79.96 |
| 18 | $50 | $1,409.37 | $88.09 |
| 19 | $50 | $1,547.46 | $96.72 |
| 20 | $1,050 | $1,694.18 | $105.89 |

In the following table,

IOI = $850.06 (the sum of the last column)
P = $1,000
I = $1,000

Thus, the T$R = ($1,000 + $1,000 + $850.06) = $2,850.06

To solve for the RCY per period:

n = 20
PV = $-800
FV = $2,850.06
PMT = 0
Solving for i, RCY = 6.59%

To annualize the RCY,

6.59% * 2 = 13.2%

## Improving the Accuracy of the Realized Compound Yield

Whereas the preceding calculations are fairly easy to perform, their accuracy is limited by the accuracy of the assumption regarding the reinvestment rate. To improve the accuracy of the assumed reinvestment rate(s), many market proponents would suggest that each cash flow be reinvested at the projected forward spot rate(s)-- which can be, in turn, be derived from the traditional yield curve (see Chapter 19 - Yield Curve Analysis).

# NET REALIZED COMPOUND YIELD

The Net Realized Compound Yield (NRCY) is the IRR that relates the purchase price of the bond to the *after-tax* total dollar return (T$R$_T$) that a bond generates over a specific investment period. (The T$R$_T$ is the sum of the after-tax principal (P$_T$), the after-tax interest (I$_T$), and the after-tax interest on interest (IOI$_T$) generated over the investment period.)

## Advantage(s) of the NRCY

Whereas the RCY calculation examined previously makes no provision for taxes, the NRCY calculation does. Including the impact of taxes into the return measure is often important because taxes influence the returns of different bonds in different ways. Even when the bonds are the same type (i.e., all Treasuries or all Corporates), taxes still influence the yields of different bonds to different degrees. Determining the true impact of taxes on a bond's real return is somewhat complex.

Many individuals make the mistake of simply multiplying the pre-tax return (either the YTM or RCY) by the inverse of the tax rate in order to determine the after-tax return. However, this is mathematically incorrect. For example, a bond that had an 8% RCY and was taxed at a 40% rate *would not* necessarily have a 4.8% (8% * (1 - 0.4)) after-tax return. The reason that the impact of taxes is complex is that taxes influence each of three components of a bond's T$R (i.e., P + I + IOI) differently. For example, taxes play an important role in reducing the IOI component. Thus, the larger the relative size of a given bond's IOI component, the more its yield will be influenced by taxes.

## Limitation(s) of the NRCY

Because the NRCY calculation makes no provision for inflation, it is only applicable to investments and/or accounts that are immune from inflation. For example, life insurance companies are largely immune from the impact of inflation because their liabilities are fixed. They may have to pay Mr. Jones' beneficiary $1,000,000 when Mr. Jones dies, but what that amount buys is the beneficiary's concern.

# CALCULATING THE NRCY

The formula for the NRCY is:

$$NRCY(\%) = k\{[(T\$R_T/PP)^{1/n})-1] * 100\}$$

where

    k      = the number of compounding periods per year.

    $T\$R_T$    = total *after-tax* dollar return.

    PP      = purchase price (including accrued interest).

    n      = number of compounding periods.

Because the purchase price, the number of compounding periods, and the number of compounding periods per year are all known, only the $T\$R_T$ must be calculated. Like the T$R, there are numerous ways to calculate the $T\$R_T$ and, in turn, the NRCY. These methods range from being simple to being complex, with precision often being directly related to complexity.

## Simple Method of Calculating Net Realized Compound Yield

If one is willing to assume both a *constant reinvestment rate* and a *constant tax rate*, the $T\$R_T$ can be performed on the HP-12C by estimating the after-tax total dollar return ($T\$R_T$), determining the NRCY per period, and determining the annual NRCY.

## Step One:

The T$R$_T$ of a given bond over a given period is equal to the sum of its three components:

After-Tax Principal ($P_T$) + After-Tax Interest ($I_T$) + After-Tax
Interest on Interest ($IOI_T$).

- The $P_T$ equals the bond's redemption value minus any capital gains tax.
- The $I_T$ equals the sum of the bond's coupons times the inverse of the tax rate.
- The $IOI_T$ equals the interest earned by reinvesting the after-tax intermittent cash flows at the after-tax reinvestment rate (reinvestment rate times the inverse of the tax rate).

The sum of the $I_T$ and the $IOI_T$ can be calculated by

**Table 10.5** *Calculating I $_T$ + IOI$_T$*

| Setting | Equals |
|---------|--------|
| n | The number of compounding periods, from the payment date *prior to* the settlement date, to the maturity date. |
| i | The reinvestment rate per period multiplied by (1 - the tax rate). |
| PMT | The interest payment per period multiplied by (1 - the tax rate). |
| PV | Zero. |

and solving for the future value (FV). The FV is equal to the sum of the $I_T$ and the $IOI_T$. The size of each component can be easily calculated by subtracting the $I_T$ from the total.

To calculate the T$R$_T$, add the $P_T$ to the sum of the $I_T$ + $IOI_T$.

## Step Two:

Once the T$R$_T$ is determined, the *NRCY per period* can be calculated by

**Table 10.6** *Calculating the NRCY Per Period*

| Setting | Equals |
|---------|--------|
| FV | The T$R. |
| PMT | Zero. |
| n | The number of periods from the settlement date to the maturity date. |
| PV | The purchase price plus accrued interest. |

and solving for the periodic interest rate (i). The value of *i* is equal to the NRCY per period.

### Step Three:

Multiply *i* by the number of payments per year in order to annualize the return.

## Sample Calculations of Net Realized Compound Yield

What NRCY can an investor expect to receive from an 8% 10-year U.S. Treasury Bond priced at 80 points if the investor is in the 40% tax bracket and expects to reinvest the coupons received at 8.5%?

*Step One*: Determining the T$R$_T$

$$T\$R_T = (P_T + I_T + IOL_T)$$
$$P_T = \$1,000 - (\$200 * 0.40) = \$920$$
$$(I_T + IOL_T) =$$
$$n = 20$$
$$i = [8.5 * (1 - 0.4)] / 2 = 2.55\%$$
$$PV = 0$$
$$PMT = (80 * (1 - 0.4)) / 2 = \$24$$
Solving for $FV = I + IOI = \$616.17$
Thus, $T\$R_T = \$920 + \$616.17 = \$1,536.17$

*Step Two*: Determining the NRCY per period

$$n = 20$$
$$PV = -\$800$$
$$PMT = 0$$
$$FV = \$1,536.17$$
$$i = 3.31\% = NRCY \text{ per period}$$

*Step Three*: Annualizing the NRCY

3.31% * 2 = 6.62% per year

What NRCY can an investor expect to receive from an 11% U.S. Treasury Bond of January, 2005, if they purchase the bond for 101.16 points to settle on August 21, 1990, expect to reinvest at 10%, and are subject to 28% taxes on both interest and capital gains?

*Step One*: Determining the T$R$_T$

$T\$R_T = (P_T + I_T + IOI_T)$
$P_T = \$1,000$
$(I_T + IOI_T) =$
    n = number of periods from:
        the payment date prior to the settlement
        date (August 21, 1990) to the maturity date
        (January 15, 2005), or 29 Periods
    i = 3.60% = (10 * (1 - 0.28)) / 2
    PV = 0
    PMT = $39.60 = [$110 * (1 - 0.28)] / 2
    Solving for FV = $1,967.79
Thus, $T\$R_T = \$1,000 + \$1,967.79 = \$2,967.79$

*Step Two*: Determining the NRCY per period

n = number of periods from:
    the settlement date (August 21, 1990)
    to the maturity date (January 15, 2005)
    from August 21, 1990 to January 15, 1991
    = 147/184 = 0.7989 periods
    from January 15, 1991 to January 15, 2005
    = 28 periods
    Total = 28.7989 periods

PV = Purchase price and accrued interest
    Purchase price = $1,015
    Accrued interest = P * R * T
    Time = July 15, 1990 to August 21, 1990
    Accrued interest = $1,000 * 0.055 * 37/184
    = $11.06
    Total = -1,206.06

PMT = 0
FV = $2,967.79
Solving for i, the NRCY per period = 3.76%

*Step Three*: Annualizing the NRCY

3.76% * 2 = 7.52%

The NRCY can also be calculated via a spreadsheet:

**Table 10.7 *NRCY Calculation of a 10% 10-Year Bond Priced at 80 Points, Assuming That There Is a 50% Tax Rate and an 8% RIR.***

| Period | Cashflow | After-tax Cashflow | Dollars Reinvested | IOI | After-tax IOI |
|--------|----------|--------------------|--------------------|----|---------------|
| 1 | $50 | $25 | -- | -- | -- |
| 2 | $50 | $25 | $25 | $1.00 | $0.50 |
| 3 | $50 | $25 | $50.50 | $2.02 | $1.01 |
| 4 | $50 | $25 | $76.51 | $3.06 | $1.53 |
| 5 | $50 | $25 | $103.04 | $4.12 | $2.06 |
| 6 | $50 | $25 | $130.10 | $5.20 | $2.60 |
| 7 | $50 | $25 | $157.70 | $6.31 | $3.15 |
| 8 | $50 | $25 | $185.86 | $7.43 | $3.72 |
| 9 | $50 | $25 | $214.57 | $8.58 | $4.29 |
| 10 | $50 | $25 | $243.87 | $9.75 | $4.88 |
| 11 | $50 | $25 | $273.74 | $10.95 | $5.47 |
| 12 | $50 | $25 | $304.22 | $12.17 | $6.08 |
| 13 | $50 | $25 | $335.30 | $13.41 | $6.71 |
| 14 | $50 | $25 | $367.01 | $14.68 | $7.34 |
| 15 | $50 | $25 | $399.35 | $15.97 | $7.99 |
| 16 | $50 | $25 | $432.34 | $17.29 | $8.65 |
| 17 | $50 | $25 | $465.98 | $18.64 | $9.32 |
| 18 | $50 | $25 | $500.30 | $20.01 | $10.01 |
| 19 | $50 | $25 | $535.31 | $21.41 | $10.71 |
| 20 | $50 | $25 | $571.01 | $22.84 | $11.42 |

$P_T = \$1,000 - (\$200 * 0.5) = \$900$

$L_T = \$1,000 - (\$1,000 * 0.5) = \$500$

$IOL_T = \$107.43$

Thus, $T\$R_T = \$900 + \$500 + \$107.43 = \$1,507.43$

To calculate the NRCY:

    n= 20
    PV = -$800
    FV = $1,507.43
    PMT = 0
    Solving for i = 3.22%

To annualize the NRCY, 3.22% * 2 = 6.44%

## SAMPLE PROBLEMS

Calculate the NRCY of the following U.S. Treasury Bonds:

**Table 10.8** *Sample Problem Data*

|  | Bond # 1 | Bond # 2 | Bond # 3 |
|---|---|---|---|
| Coupon | 8.55% | 9.35% | 12.85% |
| Settlement Date | 9/30/91 | 8/15/92 | 10/1/90 |
| Maturity Date | 9/30/10 | 2/15/05 | 1/1/20 |
| Price | 88.16 | 107.08 | 60.24 |
| Reinvestment Rate | 7.05 | 6.65 | 10.85 |
| Capital Gains Tax | 35% | 35% | 15% |
| Income Tax | 35% | 45% | 50% |

Bond # 1

$P_T = \$1,000 - (115 * 0.35) = \$959.75$

$(I_T + IOL_T) =$

> n = 19 years, or 38 periods
> i = (7.05% * (1 - 0.35)) / 2 = 2.29%
> PV = 0
> PMT = ($85.50 * (1 - 0.35)) / 2 = $27.79
> Solving for FV = $1,655.35

Thus, the T$R = $959.75 + $1,655.35 = $2,615.10

Calculating the NRCY Per Period:

> n = 38
> PV = $885
> FV = $2,615.10
> PMT = 0
> Solving for i = 2.89%

Annualized NRCY = 2.89% * 2 = 5.78%

Bond # 2

$P_T = \$1000 - (0 * .35) = \$1,000$

$(I_T + IOL_T) =$

> n = 12.5 years, or 25 periods
> i = (6.65% * (1 - 0.45)) / 2 = 1.83%
> PV = 0
> PMT = ($93.50 * (1 - 0.45)) / 2 = $25.71
> Solving for FV = $805.86

Thus, the T$R = $1,000 + $805.86 = $1,805.86

Calculating the NRCY Per Period:

> n = 25
> PV = $1,072.50
> FV = $1,805.86
> PMT = 0
> Solving for i = 2.11%

Annualized NRCY = 2.11% * 2 = 4.22%

Bond # 3

$P_T = \$1,000 - (392.50 * 0.15) = \$941.13$

$(I_T + IOI_T) =$

n = 29.25 years, or 58.5 periods
i = (10.85% * (1 - 0.50)) / 2 = $2.71
PV = 0
PMT = ($128.50 * (1 - 0.50)) / 2 = $32.13
Solving for FV = $4,405.27

Thus, the T$R = $941.13 + $4,405.27 = $5,346.40

Calculating the NRCY Per Period:

n = 58.5
PV = P + accrued interest
PV = $607.25 + (P * R * T)
PV = $607.25 + (1,000 * 0.06425 * 92/184)
PV = $639.38
FV = $1,805.86
PMT = 0
Solving for i = 1.79%

Annualized NRCY = 1.79% * 2 = 3.58%

Net-Net Realized Compound Yield

The Net-Net Realized Compound Yield (NNRCY) is equal to the NRCY (adjusted for credit and currency risk) minus the inflation rate (either actual or projected). It is the return earned by investors whose return is influenced by both taxes and inflation. When the reinvestment is low and both the tax rate and inflation rate are high, the NNRCY can actually become *negative*, meaning that the investor who buys the bond will lose buying power over time. Whenever the NNRCY becomes negative, investors should either invest in a different vehicle or sell the bond.

# 11

# DURATION

## INTRODUCTION

Duration analysis is one of the most useful analytical tools that market participants have at their disposal. Duration analysis can be applied in many ways, including

- determining when, during a bond's life, its RCY will equal its YTM.
- predicting how the value of a bond, or bond portfolio, will change in response to a change in market interest rates.
- allowing short-term liabilities to be funded with long-term assets, without incurring significant interest-rate risk.
- establishing and maintaining valid hedges.
- creating meaningful yield curves.

## UNDERSTANDING DURATION

As examined in Chapter 10, a bond's *T$R* is composed of three components $(P + I + IOI)$. Each of these components is impacted differently when market interest rates change. For example, let's evaluate the influence that a change in market interest rates would have on the $P$, $I$, & IOI components of a 10%, 10-year U.S. Treasury Bond priced at par.

Assuming that market interest rates remain constant and each cashflow is reinvested at the same YTM at which the bond was originally purchased, the values of the three components of the bond's T$R would be:

$$(P + I + IOI) = (\$1,000 + \$1,000 + \$653.30) = \$2,653.30$$

These values are often referred to as the various component's *expected values* and are given the following notation: $P_E$, $I_E$, $IOI_E$, and $T\$R_E$. As discussed in the previous chapter, the $T\$R_E$ can easily be calculated at any point along the bond's life. For this bond, the $T\$R_E$ over time would be:

**Figure 11.1** *$T\$R_E$ of a 10-Year, 10% Bond Priced at Par*

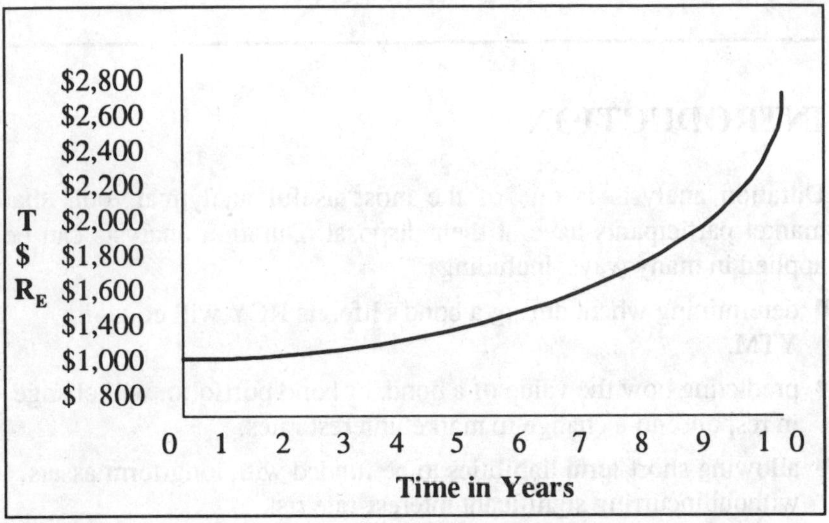

Of course, the *actual T\$R* (notational defined as $T\$R_A$) of this bond will only follow the path in the above figure if the yield curve remains both fixed and flat over the entire term of the bond's life. (The yield curve would have to remain both fixed and flat in order for each coupon payment to also be reinvested at a 10% YTM.) Of course, it is unrealistic to expect the yield curve to remain fixed and flat and so the $T\$R_A$ will be different than the $T\$R_E$.

To examine this difference, assume that immediately after the above bond was purchased, the yield curve rises from a flat 10% to a flat 12% (i.e., it experiences a parallel shift of +200 bp). What impact will this have on the bond's $T\$R_A$ and its various components?

An instantaneous rise in market interest rates to 12% will, of course, cause the bond's market value to decline. As a result, the $P_A$ component will initially decline by $114.70 to a price of $885.30. Whereas the value of the bond initially drops by $114.70, this decline is, of course, just temporary. As the bond approaches maturity, its value acretes towards par.

The $I_A$ component is unaffected.

The $IOI_A$ component will initially be unaffected by the change in market interest rates because there are no cashflows to reinvest for the first six months. However, once there are cashflows to be reinvested, the $IOI_A$ component will grow faster than originally expected, because the cashflows can now be reinvested at 12% instead of 10%.

Thus, the two impacts that this increase in market interest rates has on the various components of this bond's return are:

- an immediate and sharp decline in the value of $P_A$--which is mitigated over time.

- a delayed and progressive increase in the $IOI_A$ component --which accelerates over time.

Over the short term, the *cumulative* impact of a +200 bp increase in market interest rates from 10% to 12% is that the $T\$R_A$ of the investment is reduced because the $\Delta P_A$ is greater than $\Delta IOI_A$. In other words, the $T\$R_A$ is *less than* the $T\$R_E$). As time passes, however, the negative impact that the $\Delta P_A$ has on the $T\$R_A$ becomes less significant, and the positive impact that the $\Delta IOI_A$ has on the $T\$R_A$ becomes more significant. Thus, over the long term, the $\Delta IOI_A$ becomes greater than $\Delta P_A$, and the $T\$R_A$ is greater than the $T\$R_E$.

**Figure 11.2** *T\$R_E versus the T\$R_A for a 10% 10-Year Bond at Par after a +200 bp Market Interest Rate Increase*

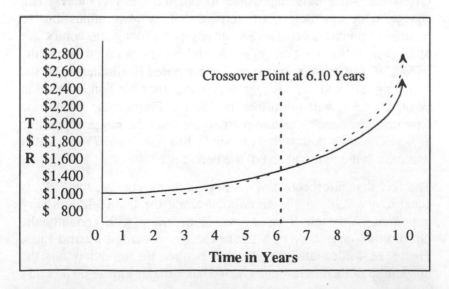

Because over the short term $\Delta P_A$ is greater than $\Delta IOI_A$ and over the long term $\Delta IOI_A$ is greater than $\Delta P_A$, there *must* be some time during a bond's life where $\Delta P_A = \Delta IOI_A$ (the crossover point in the preceding chart). When the $\Delta P_A$ is equal to the $\Delta IOI_A$, they will offset each other exactly. Thus, at this point along the bond's life, the $T\$R_A$ must equal the $T\$R_E$. This point where the $T\$R_A$ is equal to the T\$R$_E$ is referred to as the bond's *duration point*.

Thus, at the bond's duration point, the:

$$(P_A + I_A + IOI_A) = (P_E + I_E + IOI_E)$$

$$\text{and thus } T\$R_E = T\$R_A$$

$$\text{and thus YTM} = \text{RCY}$$

For this bond, the duration point is approximately 6.54 years, and thus at 6.54 years, the investor's RCY is equal to the bond's original YTM, regardless of the interest rate change. The reason that the RCY equals the YTM is that at the bond's duration point, any $\Delta P_A$ will be offset by an equal, yet opposite, $\Delta IOI_A$. If the bond's duration point is 6.54 years, then regardless of whether market interest rates increase or decline, after 6.54 years have passed the bond's RCY will equal the YTM the bond originally offered. (Note this is true only if we have one initial, instantaneous, interest rate change -- we will address a more realistic scenario in the future.)

Of course, since it is impossible to predict a future interest rate change with any degree of certainly, it is also impossible to accurately predict a bond's $T\$R_A$ at any point along the bond's life other than at its duration point. At the bond's duration point, the impact of any change in market interest rates is eliminated by the offsetting $\Delta P_A$ and the $\Delta IOI_A$. Prior to and after the bond's duration point, the $\Delta P_A$ will not offset the $\Delta IOI_A$. Further, the greater the time from the bond's duration point, the greater the range of possible $T\$R_A$s. Thus, the points along a bond's life where the $T\$R_A$ is most uncertain is the start and end of the bond's life.

The fact that, irrespective of an interest rate's change, the $T\$R_A$ is equal to the $T\$R_E$ at the same point along the bond's life, is very important. Although it is impossible to know with certainty the direction or magnitude of a future change in market interest rates, Figure 11.4 illustrates clearly that neither the direction nor the magnitude of the interest rate change has a major impact on a bond's

$T\$R_A$, as long as the bond is held until its duration point. At the duration point, regardless of the direction or magnitude of the interest rate change, the $T\$R_A$ will approximately equal the T$RE.

**Figure 11.3**  *Point Where the $T\$R_E$ Equals the $T\$R_A$ for Various Interest Rate Changes*

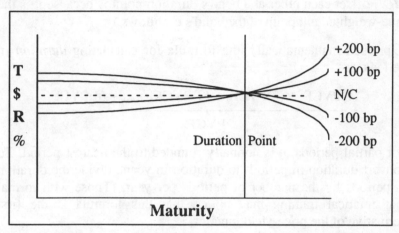

Thus, although it is impossible to predict the actual values of $P_A$ + $IOI_A$, it is possible to know that the sum of $P_A$ and $IOI_A$ will equal the sum of $P_E$ and $IOI_E$. Since a change in market interest rates will not impact the $I$ component, the $I_A$ will equal the $I_E$.

Because at the bond's duration point any $\Delta P_A$ will be offset by an equal yet opposite $\Delta IOI_A$, the actual pre-tax, pre-inflation yield that the bond earns (i.e., the bond's RCY) will equal the bond's original YTM. Thus, the YTM is "misnamed." The YTM should really be called "YTD" (Yield to the Bond's Duration Point) because the duration point is the only point along a bond's life where it is reasonably assured that it will actually earn the YTM that it offered when purchased.

**Table 11.1** *Relationship between RCY and YTM*

|  | Market Interest Rates Rise | Market Interest Rates Fall |
|---|---|---|
| Pre-duration point | RCY<YTM | RCY>YTM |
| At the duration point | RCY=YTM | RCY=YTM |
| Post-duration point | RCY>YTM | RCY<YTM |

## CALCULATION OF DURATION

Duration can be defined several ways, but perhaps the best way is to define it as the midpoint of the present values of the bond's time-weighted cashflows. (In fact, the reason that the $\Delta P_A$ and the $\Delta IOI_A$ offset each other at a bond's duration point is because it is the time-weighted midpoint of the bond's cashflows.)

Expressed mathematically, the formula for calculating *duration* in periods is:

$$\frac{(1)PVCF_1 + (2)PVCF_2 + (3)PVCF_3 + ... + (n)PVCF_n}{PVCF_T}$$

For partial periods, n is normally rounded to the nearest period. To convert duration in periods to duration in years, divide the duration in periods by the number of periods per year. (Those with formal mathematical training may notice that this formula is the first derivative of the price-yield function.)

Manually, a bond's duration can be calculated by a five-step process:

- Calculate the PV of each cashflow, to account for the delay in receiving the cashflow.
- Multiply the PV of each cashflow by its period number, to weight the cashflow for when it is received.
- Add the time-weighted PVs.
- Divide the sum by the market value of the bond, including any accrued interest.
- Divide the answer of the previous step by the number of periods per year in order to annualize the answer. The unit for the answer is *years*.

As an illustration, consider the spreadsheet in Table 11.2. The sum of the last column is $9,765.41. This sum is divided by the market value of the bond ($800) in order to calculate the duration in periods (12.21 years). When this sum is divided by the number of periods per year, the duration per year can be calculated (6.10 years).

**Table 11.2** *Duration Calculation for a 10-Year, 10% U.S.*
*Treasury Bond Priced at 80 Points*

| Period | Cashflow | PV of Cashflow | Column 1 * 3 |
|--------|----------|----------------|--------------|
| 1 | $50 | $46.79 | $46.79 |
| 2 | $50 | $43.78 | $87.56 |
| 3 | $50 | $40.96 | $122.89 |
| 4 | $50 | $38.33 | $153.32 |
| 5 | $50 | $35.87 | $179.33 |
| 6 | $50 | $33.56 | $201.37 |
| 7 | $50 | $31.40 | $219.83 |
| 8 | $50 | $29.38 | $235.08 |
| 9 | $50 | $27.50 | $247.46 |
| 10 | $50 | $25.73 | $257.28 |
| 11 | $50 | $24.07 | $264.82 |
| 12 | $50 | $22.53 | $270.32 |
| 13 | $50 | $21.08 | $274.02 |
| 14 | $50 | $19.72 | $276.13 |
| 15 | $50 | $18.46 | $276.84 |
| 16 | $50 | $17.27 | $276.31 |
| 17 | $50 | $16.16 | $274.71 |
| 18 | $50 | $15.12 | $272.17 |
| 19 | $50 | $14.15 | $268.82 |
| 20 | $1,050 | $278.02 | $5,560.36 |

As an alternative to using a spreadsheet, there are many bond math packages available commercially, or you can use the following program with your HP-12C.

**Table 11.3** *Duration Program for the HP-12C*

| Step | Keystrokes | Display |
|------|------------|---------|
| 1 | [f] [P/R] | |
| 2 | [f] [PRGM] | 00- |
| 3 | [RCL] [FV] | 01- 45 15 |
| 4 | [STO] 2 | 02- 44  2 |
| 5 | [RCL] [n] | 03- 45 11 |
| 6 | [x] (i.e., times) | 04-    20 |
| 7 | [FV] | 05-    15 |
| 8 | [PV] | 06-    13 |
| 9 | [RCL] [n] | 07- 45 11 |
| 10 | [CHS] | 08-    16 |
| 11 | [RCL] [PMT] | 09- 45 14 |
| 12 | [x] (i.e., times) | 10-    20 |
| 13 | [FV] | 11-    15 |
| 14 | [PV] | 12-    13 |
| 15 | [RCL] [i] | 13- 45 12 |
| 16 | [/] (i.e., .divide) | 14-    10 |
| 17 | 1 | 15-     1 |
| 18 | 0 | 16-     0 |
| 19 | 0 | 17-     0 |
| 20 | [STO] 1 | 18- 44  1 |
| 21 | [x] (i.e., times) | 19-    20 |
| 22 | [+] | 20-    40 |
| 23 | [RCL] 2 | 21- 45  2 |
| 24 | FV | 22-    15 |
| 25 | PV | 23-    13 |
| 26 | [/] (i.e., divide) | 24-    10 |
| 27 | 1 | 25-     1 |
| 28 | [RCL] [i] | 26- 45 12 |

| 29 | [RCL] 1 | 27- 45 | 1 |
|----|---------|--------|---|
| 30 | [/] (i.e., divide) | 28- | 10 |
| 31 | [+] | 29- | 40 |
| 32 | [/] (i.e., divide) | 30- | 10 |
| 33 | [f] [P/R] | | |

In order to utilize this program,

- enter the number of payments and press [n].
- enter the bond's price in dollars (including accrued interest) and press [PV].
- enter the periodic payment in dollars and press [PMT].
- enter the bond's redemption value in dollars and press [FV].
- solve for *i* by pressing [i].
- press [R/S] to display the bond's modified duration in periods (explained later).
- press [X><Y] to display duration in periods.

For example, for the preceding 10-year, 10% U.S. Treasury Bond priced at 80, the calculation would be as follows:

**Table 11.4** *Duration Calculation*

| Keystrokes | Purpose |
|------------|---------|
| [CLX] | Clears display. |
| [f] [FIN] | Clears financial registers. |
| 20 [n] | Enters 20 periods. |
| -800 [PV] | Enters PV. |
| 1,000 [FV] | Enters FV. |
| 50 [PMT] | Enters PMT. |
| [i] | Solves for i (6.87%). |
| [R/S] | Calculates that the MD is 11.42 periods. |
| [X><Y] | Calculates that the duration is 12.21 periods, or 6.10 years. |

# FACTORS THAT INFLUENCE DURATION

By examining the formula for duration and how it is calculated, it is apparent that there are three factors that directly influence a bond's duration: coupon, maturity, and YTM.

## The Bond's Coupon

All other factors being equal, the lower a bond's coupon, the higher its duration. This is logical because the lower the coupon, the more significant the principal payment becomes compared to the bond's coupon payments. As the coupon gets smaller, the midpoint of the present values of the bond's time-weighted cashflows gets closer to the bond's maturity date. If a fulcrum were placed under the bond's time-weighted cashflows, it would have to be shifted to the right in order to "balance" the cashflows if the coupon became smaller. Carrying this logic further, the type of bond with the lowest coupon bond is, of course, a Zero Coupon Bond (ZCB). In order for the fulcrum under a Zero Coupon Bond's cashflow to balance, it would have to be directly under the bond's only cashflow. Thus, the duration of a ZCB is equal to its maturity. This is the reason that, at maturity, a ZCB's RCY is equal to its YTM.

## Maturity of a Bond

All other factors being equal, the longer a bond's maturity, the higher its duration. As the payment series becomes longer, the fulcrum has to shift to the right in order to balance the time-weighted cashflows.

## Yield to Maturity of a Bond

All other factors being equal, the higher a bond's YTM, the lower its duration (again, as long as all other factors are equal). In the duration calculation, all of the bond's cashflows are discounted by the bond's YTM in order to determine their PVs. However, because this discounting is done on a compounded basis, not all of the bond's cashflows are affected equally by a change in the discount rate. The longer it is until a cashflow is received, the greater the number of compounding periods, and thus, the greater the impact a change in market interest rates will have on the cashflow's PV. Thus, a change in the discount rate has a greater effect on the PV of the later cashflows than it does on the PV of the earlier cashflows. Because an increase in market interest rates will reduce the PVs of future cashflows on a compounded basis, the relationship between interest rates and duration is usually inverse. (Note that there are some exceptions to this rule, primarily, deep-discount, long-term bonds.)

Previously, we calculated the duration of our 10-year, 10% to be 6.54 years. If market interest rates were to rise 200 bp so that the bond now offered a 12% YTM, its duration would decline from 6.54 to 6.10 years. Thus, as market interest rates rise, the bond's duration decreases.

# USING DURATION TO PREDICT VOLATILITY

One purpose of duration is to predict a bond's interest-rate volatility. The higher the bond's duration, the higher its interest-rate volatility. Thus, for a given change in market interest rates, the higher the bond's duration, the greater the change in the bond's market value (expressed either in dollars or percentage points). This relationship between a bond's duration and its volatility can be calculated by the following equations:

$$\text{Modified Duration} = \frac{\text{Duration}}{[1 + (\text{YTM} / \text{number of payments per year})]}$$

$$\Delta \text{ in the Bond's Price (\%)} = -MD * \Delta \text{ in Market Interest Rates (\%)}$$

For example, suppose a bond has:

- a market value of $987.50
- a duration of 6.85 years
- and offers a 9.65% YTM.

What will happen to the bond's price if interest rates rise 150 bp?

To answer can be calculated by the following three steps:

(1). Calculate the bond's MD:

$$MD = 6.85 / (1 + (0.0965 / 2)) = 6.53$$

(2). Calculate the bond's volatility in (%)

$$\text{Volatility} = -6.53 * (150 / 100) = -9.80\%$$

(3). Calculate the bond's approximate new value

$$\text{Bond's Price} = \$987.50 - (987.50 * 0.098) = \$890.73$$

As another example, calculate the price of the following bond after a 100 bp decline in market interest rates. The bond has a market value of $1,002.50, a duration of 4.35 years, and offers an 8.35% YTM.

$$(1). \text{ MD} = 4.35 / (1 + (0.0835 / 2)) = +4.17$$

$$(2). \text{ Volatility} = -4.17 * (-100 / 100) = +4.17\%$$

$$(3). \text{ Bond Price} = \$1,002.50 + (1,002.50*0.0417) = +\$1,044.30$$

Alternatively, the modified duration can be calculated by the same HP-12C program used to calculate duration. Because modified duration is used more commonly than duration, the program calculates modified duration first.

## Using Duration to Predict "Dollar Volatility"

Sometimes it is more useful to compute the change in a bond's price in *dollars* instead of *percentage points*. By rearranging the preceding equations, the following formula can be derived:

Price Change of a Bond ($) = Bond's Current Market Value * Bond's MD * Change in Market Interest Rates (in bps)

For example, if a bond had a current market value of $985, a MD of 6.34, and market interest rates changed by 25 bp, the bond's price would change by:

$$\text{Change Bond's Price } (\$) = \$985 * 6.34 * 0.0025 = \$15.61$$

Often the volatility of different instruments is compared by comparing the price change that would result from a 1-bp change in market interest rates, often referred to as the *value of an .01*. For example, consider the following two bonds:

- Bond #1 is priced at $987.50, and has a MD of 6.35
- Bond #2 is priced at $1,002.50, and has a MD of 4.17

The value of an .01 for Bond #1 =

$$6.35 * \$987.50 * 0.0001 = \$0.6270 \text{ or } 63 \text{ cents}$$

The value of an .01 for Bond #2 =

$$4.17 * \$1,002.50 * 0.0001 = \$0.4180 \text{ or } 42 \text{ cents}$$

Thus, Bond #1 is 1½ times as volatile as Bond #2 (0.6270/0.4180 = 1.5). For a given interest rate change, the value of Bond #1 will change by $1.50 every time the value of Bond #2 changes by $1.00.

## Volatility of Bond Portfolios

Duration can also be used to calculate the volatility of an entire bond portfolio. Because duration and modified duration are "additive functions," the duration or modified duration of an entire portfolio can be calculated by taking the weighted average of the individual bonds in the portfolio. Once the weighted average modified duration of a portfolio has been calculated, only the market value of the portfolio is needed in order to calculate the portfolio's dollar volatility. For example, if a portfolio has a market value of $54,897,567.78, and a weighted average modified duration of 5.56, the value of an .01 for the portfolio would be:

Value of an .01 for a Portfolio = Value of the Portfolio * Weighted Average MD of the Portfolio * the Change in Market Interest Rates.

$$\$54,897,567.78 * 5.56 * 0.0001 = \$30,523.05$$

Thus, every time market interest rates go up or down by 1 bp, the value of the portfolio will change by $30,523.05.

Thus, all of the coupons, maturities, prices, and yields of all of the bonds that compose a portfolio can be simplified to a single "volatility number": the value of an .01 for the portfolio. The portfolio's volatility can then be used in a variety of different situations, including:

- using long-term assets to meet short-term liabilities.
- immunizing a portfolio against changes in market interest rates.
- establishing valid hedges for fixed-income portfolios.
- creating yield curves that illustrate accurately the relationship between risk and reward.

## Using Long-Term Assets to Fund Short-Term Liabilities

Suppose an investor wants to set up an account and an investment program *now* that will allow the investor to pay a $1 million liability that becomes due in exactly five years (in other words, the investor wants to fund a $1,000,000 5-year liability today). The investor's objectives related to this funding are twofold:

- The investor wants a guarantee that they will not have to put up any additional funds.
- The investor wants to fund the liability at the lowest possible cost.

There is a vast number of ways in which this liability can be funded. Perhaps the simplest way would be to buy 5-year U.S. Government Zero Coupon Bonds (ZCBs). Treasury Zeros would eliminate both credit risk and interest-rate risk. The cost of the ZCBs necessary to fund this liability can easily be determined from the yield curve. If the current yield curve was the curve illustrated in Figure 11.4.

**Figure 11.4  *Representative Yield Curve***

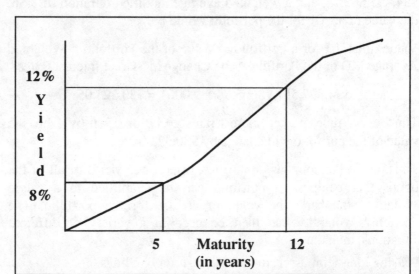

Because 5-year ZCBs are yielding 8%, the cost of funding the liability with the 5-year ZCBs is:

$$PV = FV / (1 + i)^n = \$1,000,000 / (1 + 0.04)^{10} = \$675,564.17$$

Whereas funding the liability with ZCBs absolutely eliminates both credit risk and interest-rate risk, it is also extremely expensive because it only offers an 8% return. The low yield increases the cost of funding the liability.

As an alternative, assume that there is also a 15-year Treasury Bond with a 5-year duration that offers a 12% YTM. (In order to have a duration this short, the bond would have to have a very high coupon). If the liability were funded with this bond, the higher yield it offers would reduce the cost of funding the liability.

The problem with using a 15-year bond to fund a 5-year liability is that if interest rates rise, the value of the bonds will decline. Thus, when the bonds are sold in five years to raise the cash necessary to meet the liability, the $T\$R_A$ may be less than 12% $T\$R_E$, and thus the $P_A + I_A + IOI_A$ may equal less than \$1,000,000. However, if the 15-year bond had a 5-year duration, this bond could be used to fund the liability *without being exposed to interest-rate risk*. Because the bond would be sold at its duration point, the bond's $T\$R_A$ would equal the YTM that the bond offered when originally bought. The reason for this is that at the bond's duration point:

$$\Delta P_A = \Delta IOI_A, \text{ and thus, the } T\$R_A = T\$R_E, \text{ and thus}$$

$$(P_A + I_A + IOI_A) = (P_E + I_E + IOI_E)$$

Although the three components of return may change, the net effect is that their total remains unchanged. At the 5-year point, any loss on the $P_A$ will be offset by an increase in the $IOI_A$ and vice versa.

Because the yield at the 5-year point will equal the original YTM, the discount of the liability can be determined by the original YTM of the 15-year bond in order to determine how many of the 5-year bonds will have to be bought in order to fund the liability.

$$PV = FV / (1 + i)^n = \$1,000,000 / (1 + 0.06)^{10} = \$558,394.78$$

Because the 15-year bond offers a higher YTM than the 5-year ZCB, it will take a smaller investment now--\$558,394.78--in order to accumulate \$1,000,000 in five years. Thus, if these bonds were selling at par, 559 of them would be needed to fund the liability. However, if the bonds were selling for \$895 each, then 624 bonds (\$558,394.78 / \$895) would be needed. Regardless of whether the bonds are selling at par, the net result is that the cost of funding the liability with the 12% bonds instead of 8% bonds results in a savings of approximately $117,169.39 ($675,564.17 - $558,394.78).

Carrying this analysis further, an investor seeking to fund this 5-year liability should consider every bond (or combination of bonds) that has a 5-year duration (or weighted average duration), and that meets the investor's credit and other criteria in order to fund the bond(s) that offer the highest yield (and thus, the lowest funding cost).

By matching the duration of the asset to the duration of the liability, the investor can use longer-term--and generally higher yielding--assets to fund the shorter-term liabilities, without being exposed to interest-rate risk. Portfolios that use long-term assets that meet short-term liabilities with the same duration are often referred to as *immunized portfolios,* because they are "immunized" against interest-rate risk.

## Using Duration Analysis to Create Valid Hedges

In a perfect hedge, the amount lost on a position should be offset exactly by an equal profit on the hedge, and vice versa. For a bond portfolio, the amount that the portfolio will lose if interest rates rise by 1 bp (the value of an .01) will equal:

Portfolio's Market Value * The Portfolio's MD * 0.0001

For a hedge to be valid, it must have the same volatility, or "value of an .01." Generally, because the size of the portfolio is known, and the volatility and hedging vehicle can be calculated, one can readily determine what quantity of the hedging vehicle is required in order to create a valid hedge.

Investors often enter into "naive" hedges believing, for example, that to hedge a $10,000,000 U.S. Government Bond portfolio requires $10,000,000 (face value) of T-Bond future's contracts when, in fact, the future's contract (i.e., the hedging vehicle) may have very different volatilities.

# LIMITATIONS OF DURATION ANALYSIS

## The Passage of Time

Whereas duration analysis is extremely useful, it does have limitations. The first limitation is that it is accurate only over a *short period of time*. The reason for this limitation is that, as time passes, the durations of both assets and liabilities get shorter. This is reasonable because of the way that duration is calculated. As time passes, there are fewer cashflows remaining, so that the sum of the time-weighted present values of the cashflows declines.

The path by which a bond's duration declines as time passes is dependent on the type of bond being considered. For example, the duration of ZCBs decline in a *linear* manner because their duration equals their maturity. Thus, every day that passes shortens the bond's maturity by one day - and its duration by one day. The path by which the duration of a coupon bond declines is more complex. Usually, for coupon bonds, the rate of decline of the bond's duration accelerates in an ever-increasing manner.

Note also that this decay path is not completely "smooth." The actual payment of a coupon payment will sometimes result in small upward spikes in the curve. Thus, the loss of a very short-term coupon has the effect of temporarily increasing a bond's duration. The fact that the duration of a bond changes as time passes has important ramifications for both immunized portfolios and hedges.

**Figure 11.5** *Duration Path of Different Types of Bonds*

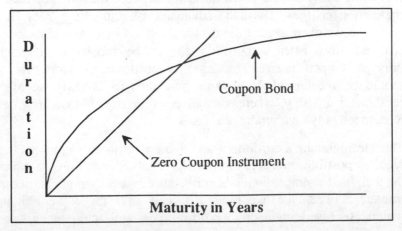

## Passage of Time and Immunized Portfolios

For example, when immunized portfolios are first established, the weighted average durations of the assets and liabilities are equal--and thus the portfolio is not exposed to interest rate risk. As time passes, the weighted average durations of both the assets and the liabilities decline. However, they usually do not decline at the same rate.

The rate at which the weighted average duration of the liabilities declines as time passes is often linear. However, the rate at which the weighted average duration of the assets declines as time passes often starts out very slowly and then increases at an ever-increasing rate (illustrated previously). As a result of this unequal "rate of decay" in the weighted average durations of the assets and the liabilities, the two values become increasingly unequal or "unbalanced." When the portfolio becomes unbalanced, the portfolio is no longer immunized against changes in interest rates.

To correct this tendency of the weighted average durations to become unbalanced over time, an immunized portfolio needs to be periodically "rebalanced." Rebalancing is generally accomplished by swapping portfolio assets to adjust the portfolio's weighted average duration and/or using derivative instruments to alter the portfolio's weighted average duration until it again matches the weighted average duration of the liabilities.

## Rebalancing an Immunized Portfolio

Ideally, immunized portfolios would be rebalanced every day. However, every time a portfolio is rebalanced, the investor incurs transaction charges. Thus, the advantage of remaining "balanced" has to be weighed against the disadvantage of incurring transaction charges. How often a portfolio should be rebalanced depends principally upon its size. The larger the portfolio, the more often it should be rebalanced. Very large portfolios (>100MM) are often rebalanced monthly, whereas small portfolios (<25MM) are often rebalanced only on a semiannual basis.

Thus, immunizing a portfolio is an ongoing, semi-active process that requires portfolio managers to initially establish positions in which the weighted average durations are balanced--and then maintain that balance between the two moving targets over the entire holding period. Because immunizing a portfolio is a semi-active process and has some associated costs, the preceding example somewhat exaggerated the savings offered by immunization.

### *Passage of Time and Interest Rate Hedges*

In addition to rebalancing immunized portfolios, portfolio managers must also rebalance their interest rate hedges. As time passes, the volatility of the vehicle being hedged, as well as the vehicle being used as the hedge, will change. Periodically, the hedge needs to be rebalanced so that its volatility equals the volatility of the portfolio being hedged. Specific examples of hedges and the art of rebalancing hedges are provided in the chapters on derivative instruments.

## Duration and Yield Curve Shifts

The second limitation of duration analysis is that it provides an accurate measure of a bond's volatility in response to changes in market interest rates if, and only if, the change in market interest rates is equal at all points along the yield curve. In other words, the shift in the yield curve must be *parallel*. The further that the change in the shape of the yield curve deviates from being parallel, the less accurate duration becomes as a measure of volatility--and the less useful it becomes in immunizing portfolios and validating hedges.

**Figure 11.6  *Parallel Versus Non-Parallel Yield Curve Shifts***

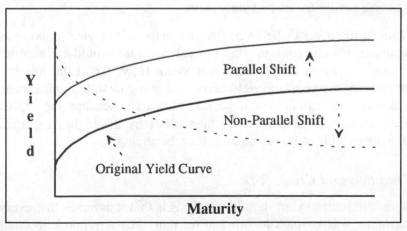

However, not all immunized portfolios or hedges are equally exposed to the risk that the yield curve will shift in a non-parallel manner. The better the "match" between the timing of the cashflows generated by the portfolio and the timing of the cashflows necessary to meet the liabilities, the lower the investor's exposure to the risk that the shape of the yield curve will change. To illustrate this concept, consider the below simple example:

Suppose an investor was going to construct an immunized portfolio with a weighted average MD of eight years in order to fund a liability that becomes due in eight years. The investor has to decide to use one of the two portfolios below to fund the liability.

Portfolio A is composed of equal dollar amounts of two bonds:

- Bond #1 has an MD of 7.5 years
- Bond #2 has an MD of 8.5 years

Portfolio B is also composed of equal dollar amounts of two bonds:

- Bond #3 has an MD of 4 years
- Bond #4 has an MD of 12 years

Whereas both portfolios have a weighted average MD of eight years, the second portfolio is *more* exposed to changes in the shape of the yield curve because the cashflows of the bonds have a wider dispersion around the timing of the liability. Whereas the second portfolio has a greater cashflow mismatch, and thus greater yield curve risk, its advantage is that it will usually offer a higher yield (given a positively-shaped yield curve).

Thus, if the investor believed that the shape of the yield curve was going to remain constant, the second portfolio would be a better choice because it offers the higher yield. However, if the investor thought the shape of the yield curve was going to shift significantly, the second portfolio would be less attractive, because the higher yield would probably be more than offset by the higher expenses associated with an increased need for rebalancing.

## *Duration and Credit Risk*

The third limitation of duration analysis is that it assumes that every cashflow will be paid in full and on time. For any portfolio other than one composed exclusively of Treasury Bonds, this assumption is often erroneous. Defaults change the volatility of a portfolio (as measured by the value of an .01) by reducing its size, and altering its weighted average MD.

Although it is impossible to predict accurately the impact that credit defaults will have on a small portfolio, it is possible to predict the impact of defaults on large, well-diversified portfolios by using statistical techniques. Once a portfolio's likely default rate has been determined, it is fairly easy to incorporate that rate into the portfolio's weighted average duration calculation.

## Duration and Interest Rate Changes

The fourth limitation of duration analysis is that it is accurate only for small changes in market interest rates. Because a bond's duration is a function of its YTM, as market interest rates change, so does the bond's YTM, and as its YTM changes, so does its duration. For very small changes in market interest rates, the change in the bond's duration is negligible and often ignored. However, for large changes in market interest rates, the change in duration is large enough to result in distorted volatility measures and unbalanced hedges. Fortunately, there is a way to account for how changes in market interest rates will influence the duration of a bond or bond portfolio (see Chapter 12).

# 12

# CONVEXITY

## INTRODUCTION

In the previous chapter, duration and modified duration were used to approximate how the value of a bond would change in response to an instantaneous change in market interest rates. We determined that for a 10-year, 10% bond priced at $800, the modified duration was 5.71% - and the value of an .01 was $0.46. Thus, for every 1% change in market interest rates, we would expect that the bond's price would change by 5.71% - and for every basis point change in market interest rates, we would expect that the value of the bond would change by $0.46.

By employing the analysis and techniques discussed in the last chapter we can approximate what the price of this bond will be after a +/- 50, +/- 100, +/- 150, and +/- 300 bps change in market interest rates. The projected bond prices can be determined by multiplying the price of the bond by the bond's modified duration and by the change in market interest rates (See Table 12.1). If we then plot the change in market interest rates against the bond's projected price, and connect the data points, the result would be a straight line (See Figure 12.1). Thus, we can say that duration is a *linear function*. Because duration is the first derivative of the price-yield function, it will be linear because simple first-derivative functions are always linear.

## DEFINITION OF CONVEXITY

However, in the market, the actual price of this bond does **not** follow a linear path as interest rates change. Instead, the observed price path of this bond as interest rates change is a curved line (See Figure 12.1). How can the variation between the linear path predicted by duration and the curved path observed in the market be explained?

**Table 12.1** *Duration Predicted Price Change*

| Initial Bond Price | Times Modified Duration | Times Interest Rate Change | Projected Change in Bond's Price | Predicted New Price of Bond |
|---|---|---|---|---|
| $800 | 5.71 | -300 bp | $137.04 | $937.04 |
| $800 | 5.71 | -150 bp | $68.52 | $868.52 |
| $800 | 5.71 | -100 bp | $45.68 | $845.68 |
| $800 | 5.71 | -50 bp | $22.84 | $822.84 |
| $800 | 5.71 | 0 bp | 0 | $800.00 |
| $800 | 5.71 | 50 bp | -$22.84 | $777.16 |
| $800 | 5.71 | 100 bp | -$45.68 | $754.32 |
| $800 | 5.71 | 150 bp | -$68.52 | $731.48 |
| $800 | 5.71 | 300 bp | -$137.04 | $662.96 |

**Figure 12.1** *Price Yield Function Predicted by Duration Versus the Actual Price Path*

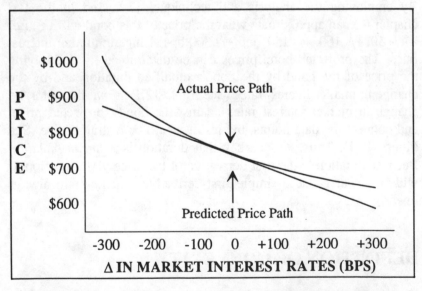

The explanation for this discrepancy is, actually, relatively simple. In the previous chapter we noted that, as market interest rates change, so does a bond's duration and MD. There are three reasons why the MD of a bond changes when market interest rates change:

- In the duration calculation each cashflow is discounted by the bond's YTM. As market interest rates change, so does the bond's YTM. Since the bond's YTM changes, so does its duration.

- In the duration calculation the sum of the time-weighted cashflows is divided by the market value of the bond. As the bond's YTM changes, so does the bond's market value. Since the bond's market value changes, so does its duration.

- In the MD calculation, the duration is divided by (1 + the YTM / # of payments per year). As market interest rates change, so does the bond's YTM. Since the bond's YTM changes, so does its MD.

As market interest rates change, the *collective* impact of the above influences on the bond's modified duration are such that *when market interest rates decline, the MD of this bond increases - and when market interest rates increase, the MD of the bond declines.* Fortunately for investors, the relationship between the change in market interest rates and the change in this bond's modified duration works to their advantage. When market interest rates decline, investors want the volatility of their bonds to increase because a higher volatility increases the bond's price appreciation for a given rise in market interest rates. However, when market interest rates rise, investors want the volatility of their bonds to decrease because a lower volatility results in a smaller price decline for a given decline in market interest rates (see Table 12.2).

For this bond, the change in the bond's MD in response to a change in market interest rates works to the benefit of investors regardless of whether market interest rates increase or decrease. As a result of the change in modified duration and volatility, the actual relationship between price and yield is *convex* when viewed from below - hence the name *convexity*. Since the investor is helped regardless of whether interest rates increase or decrease, this type of convexity is referred to as *positive convexity*.

Mathematically, *convexity* is defined as the change in the bond's duration in response to a change in market interest rates.

$$\text{Convexity} = \frac{\Delta \text{ Duration}}{\Delta \text{ Interest Rates}}$$

**Table 12.2** *The Impact of Convexity on the MD and Projected Prices of an 10% 10 Year Bond Priced at $800.*

| Interest Rate Change | Bond's Initial MD | Bond's Adjusted MD | Duration Predicted Price | Actually Observed Price | Convex. ($) |
|---|---|---|---|---|---|
| -300 bp | 5.71 | 6.13 | $937.04 | $955.30 | $137.04 |
| -150 bp | 5.71 | 5.92 | $868.52 | $872.78 | $68.52 |
| -100 bp | 5.71 | 5.85 | $845.68 | $847.48 | $45.68 |
| -50 bp | 5.71 | 5.78 | $822.84 | $823.19 | $22.84 |
| 0 bp | 5.71 | 5.71 | $800.00 | $800.00 | 0 |
| 50 bp | 5.71 | 5.64 | $777.16 | $777.49 | -$22.84 |
| 100 bp | 5.71 | 5.58 | $754.32 | $755.56 | -$45.68 |
| 150 bp | 5.71 | 5.51 | $731.48 | $735.32 | -$68.52 |
| 300 bp | 5.71 | 5.31 | $662.96 | $678.04 | -$137.04 |

# CALCULATING CONVEXITY

Because convexity measures the rate of change in a bond's duration, and since duration is itself the first derivative of the price yield function, convexity is actually the second derivative of the price-yield function.

The formula for calculating convexity *in periods* is:

$$\frac{(1)(2)PVCF_1 + (2)(3)PVCF_2 + \ldots + (n)(n+1)PVCF_n}{(1 + YTM)^2 * PVCF_T}$$

and convexity *in years* is:

$$\text{Convexity (in Years)} = \frac{\text{Convexity in Periods}}{(\text{Interest Rate Change})^2}$$

Note that the calculation is very similar to the duration calculation discussed in the last chapter.

**Table 12.3** *Example Convexity Calculation of a 10-Year, 10% U.S. Treasury Bond Priced at 80 Points*

| Period Number | Cashflow | PV Cashflow | Column 1 * (Column 1+1) * Column 3 |
|---|---|---|---|
| 1 | $50 | $46.79 | $93.57 |
| 2 | $50 | $43.78 | $262.67 |
| 3 | $50 | $40.96 | $491.57 |
| 4 | $50 | $38.33 | $766.61 |
| 5 | $50 | $35.87 | $1,076.00 |
| 6 | $50 | $33.56 | $1,409.56 |
| 7 | $50 | $31.40 | $1,758.60 |
| 8 | $50 | $29.38 | $2,115.71 |
| 9 | $50 | $27.50 | $2,474.63 |
| 10 | $50 | $25.73 | $2,830.12 |
| 11 | $50 | $24.07 | $3,177.83 |
| 12 | $50 | $22.53 | $3,514.19 |
| 13 | $50 | $21.08 | $3,836.33 |
| 14 | $50 | $19.72 | $4,141.98 |
| 15 | $50 | $18.46 | $4,429.39 |
| 16 | $50 | $17.27 | $4,697.27 |
| 17 | $50 | $16.16 | $4,944.73 |
| 18 | $50 | $15.12 | $5,171.20 |
| 19 | $50 | $14.15 | $5,376.42 |
| 20 | $1,050 | $278.02 | $116,767.61 |

In the above table, the sum of the last column is $169,336 which becomes the numerator in our equation.

The convexity *in periods* is equal to:

$$169,336 / (1 + 0.0687)^2 * 800 = 185.33 \text{ Periods}$$

The convexity *in years* is equal to: $185.33 / 2^2 = 46.33$

Once a bond's convexity, in years, is calculated - it can be used to calculate the change in a bond's price (in percent) that will result from a change in market interest rates as a result of the bond's convexity. The formula for calculating this change is:

Change in a bond's price (%) =

$$(0.5 * \text{Convexity} * \text{Yield Change in bp}^2) * 100$$

In this calculation the convexity of the 10-year, 10% bond priced at $800 was equal to 46.33. If market interest rates were to rise 3% (from 13.74% to 16.74%), then the impact of convexity on the bond's price would be:

Change in a bond's price (%) =

$$(0.5 * 46.33 * 0.03^2) * 100 = 2.08\%$$

*Note that since the yield change is squared, regardless of whether the yield change is positive or negative, the net effect is a positive change in the value of the bond.*

$$2.08\% \text{ of } \$800 = \$16.68$$

In Table 12.2 we compared the actual price of a bond after an interest rate change to the price predicted by duration. We determined that the value of our $800 bond would actually *decline* to $678.04 if interest rates were to rise by 3%. However, *duration analysis by itself* predicted that the price would drop to $662.96. The error of the duration calculation, in dollars, is $15.08. However, if we add the impact of convexity to the duration prediction, the error is only:

$$\$678.04 - (662.96 + 16.68) = -\$1.60$$

Thus, using both convexity and duration to predict the response of a bond's price to an instantaneous change in market interest rates provides a more accurate answer than using duration alone. (The remaining error is the result of the change in convexity as interest rates change).

Note that for very small changes in market interest rates the impact of convexity is so low it's negligible. For example if market interest rates were to change by 5 bp, the impact of convexity would be:

Convexity = $(0.5 * 46.33 * 0.0005^2) = 0.00000579 = 0.000579\%$

As another example, if market interest rates changed by +/- 100 points, the resulting change in the value of the 10-year, 10% bond priced at $800 would be projected to be:

**Table 12.4** *Combination of Duration and Convexity*

|  | Market Interest Rates Rise by 100 bp | Market Interest Rates Fall by 100 bp |
|---|---|---|
| Duration Impact | -$45.68 | +$45.68 |
| Convexity Impact | + 1.85 | +$ 1.85 |
| Total Dollar Change | -$43.83 | +$47.53 |

## CONVEXITY AND ZERO COUPON BONDS

Zero coupon bonds (ZCBs) are a special case that is worth exploring. Since ZCBs have only one incoming cashflow, the convexity formula reduces to:

$$\text{Convexity}_{ZCB} = n(n + 1) / (1 + y)^2$$

For example, a 15-year ZCB that is priced to offer a 10% return (calculated as if it compounded semiannually) will have the following convexity:

$$\text{Convexity}_{ZCB} = n(n + 1) / (1 + y)^2$$

$$= 30(30 + 1) / (1+.05)^2$$

$$= 843.54 \text{ periods}$$

$$843.54 / 2^2 = 210.88 \text{ years}$$

*Generally, ZCBs have the least convexity for bonds with the same duration, and the most convexity for bonds with the same maturity.*

## VALUING CONVEXITY

Just like duration, credit rating, and liquidity, a bond's convexity is another "characteristic" of a bond that investors have to take into account when valuing the bond and evaluating the relative attractiveness of the bond against other available issues. Because positive convexity benefits investors - regardless of whether interest rates rise or fall - bonds with high positive convexities are often sought out and bid up in the market. As a result, they often also offer lower yields than comparable bonds that have lower positive convexities - or negative convexities (discussed below). Dealing with the trade-off between yield and convexity is one of the more difficult challenges facing bond investors.

Part of the problem investors face when trying to deal with this trade is trying to quantify the benefit that convexity provides. While having an investment with a high positive convexity means better price performance in response to a change in market interest rates, having an investment with a high positive convexity provides no benefit to the investor if market interest rates do not change. Thus, the first step to quantifying the benefit of positive convexity is to make an assumption about the future volatility of market interest rates.

If an investor expects that market interest rates will be very volatile, the investor might be willing to make a significant yield sacrifice in order to "buy convexity." However, if the investor expects market interest rates to remain relatively constant, the investor may not be willing to sacrifice any yield in order to "buy convexity."

**Figure 12.2** *Price Path of High Convexity vs. Low Convexity Bond*

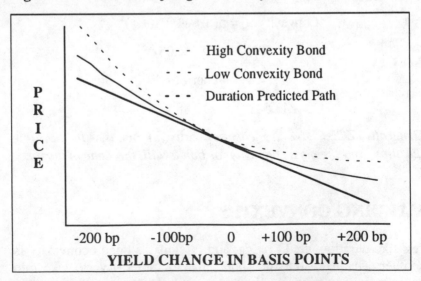

The "value" that convexity offers can be evaluated in a variety of ways. For example, suppose we have two bonds that have the following characteristics:

**Table 12.5 *Representative Bond Characteristics***

|  | Bond A | Bond B |
|---|---|---|
| Yield | 8.65 | 8.55 |
| Modified Duration | 6.51 | 6.51 |
| Convexity | 22.85 | 68.73 |
| Price | Par | Par |

The principal differences between the two bonds is that Bond A offers a 10 bp higher yield than Bond B, but has a significantly lower convexity. For various time frames, investors can calculate how much market interest rates would have to change within a given time frame in order for the bond with better price performance to offer the same total return as the bond that offers the higher yield.

For example: if the investor's time frame is six months, the bond with the higher yield will offer the investor an extra 10 basis points in return over that six month time frame. In dollars, that difference is:

$$\$1000 * .0005 = \$0.50 \text{ per Bond}$$

Thus, the break-even interest rate change would be whatever change would result in the *difference* between the two bond's convexities providing an extra \$.50 price move in the bond with the higher convexity.

The difference in the convexities is: 68.75 - 22.85 = 45.90

Thus the required change in market interest rates is:

$$(.5 * 45.90 * Yield^2) * 100 = \text{change in percent}$$
$$(.5 * 45.90 * Yield^2) * 100 = (\$.50 / \$1000) * 100$$
$$(.5 * 45.90 * Yield^2) * 100 = .05\%$$
$$(.5 * 45.90 * Yield^2) = .0005$$
$$22.95 * Yield^2 = .0005$$
$$Yield^2 = .00002179$$
$$Yield = .004667$$
$$47 \text{ basis points}$$

Thus, if the investor expects market interest rates to change by less that 47 basis points, the bond with the higher yield should offer the higher overall return. However, if interest rates change by more than 47 basis points, in either direction, then the bond with the lower yield but the higher convexity should offer the higher return.

## NEGATIVE CONVEXITY

Thus far, this chapter has focused exclusively on positive convexity (i.e., the type of convexity that helps the investor). Every bond that does *not* have an embedded option of one type or another (call options, sinking funds, and so on) has positive convexity to one degree or another. However, there are many financial instruments in the market that have embedded options. These embedded options can impact the convexity of the instrument in such a way that the overall instrument ends up with negative convexity for certain interest rate changes.

Negative convexity results when the duration of the instrument gets longer as market interest rates increase - and shorter as interest rates fall. Thus, negative convexity works against the investor regardless of which way interest rates change. The price path of a bond with negative convexity would resemble the path in Figure 12.3.

**Figure 12.3** *Negative Convexity Price Path*

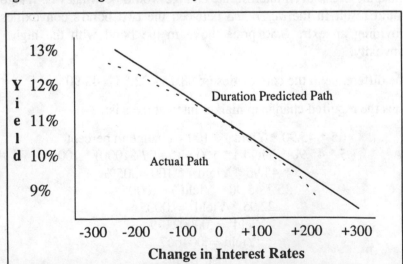

## Callable Bonds

A callable bond can have *negative convexity* because the embedded call option gives the bond's issuer the right to shorten the bond's maturity. If the bond's maturity is shortened, its duration is also shortened. Thus, the probability that the bond will be called will impact its duration.

Fur example, suppose we have an 10%, 30-year bond that is currently selling at par and is callable in 10 years. If the bond is not called, its duration, as of today, is 9.94 years. However, if the bond is called, then its duration, as of today, is 6.54 years.

If the probability that the bond will be called is zero (which it would be if market interest rates were significantly above the coupon), the bond's duration would be 9.94 years. However, if the probability that the bond would be called was 100% (which it would be if market interest rates were substantially below the bond's coupon), the bond 's duration would be 6.54 years. Naturally, a 50/50% probability of being called would result in a duration of 8.24 years. Thus, as interest rates rise, the effective duration of the bond increases.

## Mortgage Backed Securities

Mortgage Pass-Through Securities often exhibit negative convexity because of the homeowner's right to prepay or refinance their mortgage at any time. When interest rates fall, homeowners refinance their mortgages and pay off their existing mortgages (i.e., those in the pass-through pool). As the number of mortgages in the pool that are paid off increases, the duration of the pool decreases. Thus, just when the investor would like the security to have a long duration because interest rates are falling, the duration of the security decreases. Of course, if interest rates are rising and the investor wants the duration to be short, fewer people will refinance, causing the effective duration to increase.

# PART III

## Types of
## Fixed-Income Securities

# 13

## U.S. TREASURY BONDS

### INTRODUCTION

Because of its habitual budget deficits, the United States has become the largest borrower in the world. The market for Treasury Bonds is currently a multi-trillion dollar market with a daily trading volume of approximately $150 billion. Because the U.S. is expected to continue to have more than $100 billion dollar deficits for the foreseeable future, the size of this market, and the average daily trading volume, will certainly increase.

Although the Congress sets the overall debt limit, it is the responsibility of the Treasury Department to decide what types of securities to issue. Although the U.S. Government borrows in both public and private markets, we limit our examination to securities issued in public markets.

### ADVANTAGES OF TREASURY BONDS

The first advantage of Treasury Securities is that they have no credit risk, which means that because the U.S. Government will not fail, it is unlikely that it will default on its obligations. Of course, this does not mean that buying and holding Treasuries until they mature is risk-free. Although investors in Treasury Securities are assured of receiving both their interest and principal in full and on time, there is no guarantee what those dollars will be worth, because although the government can print enough dollars to meet its obligations, the more dollars it prints, the less each dollar is worth.

Second, Treasury Securities are very liquid. Although the Treasury market is very large, it is composed of relatively few bond issues and, thus, the size of each issue tends to be very large. Generally, the larger the size of the issue, the more liquid it is. The combination of the large market size, large issue size, and the active level of trading results in very narrow bid-ask spreads--usually 1/8th of a point or less. Narrow bid-ask spreads make is easier to generate short-term trading profits in this market.

Third, Treasury Securities are exempt from state and city taxes. For investors in high-tax states, this is a significant advantage that Treasury Securities offer compared to Corporate Bonds.

Fourth, Treasury Securities offer excellent call protection. Most Treasury Securities cannot be called. Even those issues that can be called can only be called five years before there scheduled maturity.

Fifth, Treasury Securities are held in "book entry" form, which means there are no actual paper securities issued. Thus, there are no securities to keep track of and safeguard, and no coupons to clip. Instead, Treasury Securities are held in electronic form at a bank or brokerage firm.

Sixth, Treasury Securities have some special provisions. For example, some have a provision that makes them valuable for estate tax purposes. These securities are referred to as *Flower Bonds,* and the advantage that they offer is that regardless of their current market value, they are worth their full face value when they are used to pay estate taxes. Thus, if they can be purchased at a discount, there is an immediate arbitrage profit available to investors who are trying to settle an estate.

# DISADVANTAGES OF TREASURY BONDS

The first disadvantage of Treasury Bonds is that they offer a relatively low yield. This is the tradeoff for the advantages listed above.

The second disadvantage of Treasury Bonds is that the market is reasonably efficient, making it very difficult to find situations in which Treasury Bonds are significantly mispriced. Sophisticated investors can exploit mispriced securities in order to profit. (Of course, less sophisticated investors view the efficiency of the Treasury Bond market as an advantage.

The third disadvantage of Treasury Bonds are subject to Federal Income Tax and Capital Gains Tax.

# INITIAL DISTRIBUTION OF T-BONDS

The process by which Treasury Bonds are distributed is very similar to that used for distributing T-Bills. The Treasury Department similarly uses the Federal Reserve Bank as its distribution agent. The current auction schedule is listed in the following table:

**Table 13.1** *Auction Schedule for Treasury Securities*

| Security | Auction Schedule |
|---|---|
| 2-year notes | Every month |
| 3-year notes | Second month of quarter |
| 10 and 30-year bonds | Second month of quarter |
| 4 and 7-year notes | Third month of quarter |
| 5-year notes | As required |

Investors bid for new T-Bonds on a yield-to-maturity basis (bid to two decimal places). As in T-Bill auctions, investors can bid either competitively or non-competitively. The primary dealers are expected to bid in every auction and to maintain an active secondary market. Their level of activity is monitored closely by the FED, and if it drops too low, they can lose their "primary dealer" status.

# SECONDARY MARKET FOR T-BONDS

In the secondary market, the most recently issued bond of each maturity is referred to as the "on the run" issue, and are the most actively traded issues. To enhance the liquidity of their positions, many dealers swap into the new bonds each time that they are issued. Dealers who trade Treasuries can make money from

- the bid-ask spread they earn by making a market.
- trading both long and short positions.
- the "carry." A dealer's inventory will often generate more in interest than the cost of financing the position with repurchase agreements (see Chapter 3).

## ZERO COUPON BONDS

Zero Coupon Bonds (ZCBs) are different from traditional bonds in that they make no periodic interest payments. Instead, ZCBs are issued at a discount and pay their face value when they mature. The investor's return is the difference between the purchase price and either the maturity value--or the resale value. Because ZCBs have only two cash flows, they are simpler to price and analyze than traditional bonds. For example, a 10-year ZCB priced to offer an 8% return would be priced at $456.39

$$PV = FV/(1 + i)^n \quad PV = \$1,000/(1 + 0.04)^{20} = \$456.39$$

Note that the procedure that most dealers use when calculating the price of ZCBs is to assume semiannual compounding so that the yields are more comparable to traditional bonds that pay interest semiannually. Because ZCBs do not pay interest, the imputed interest compounds internally (unlike traditional bonds with which the interest has to be reinvested in order to compound). Because the interest compounds internally, the path that ZCBs track as they approach maturity is convex. The graph in Figure 13.1 assumes that interest rates are constant. The market price will deviate from the path if interest rates should change.

**Figure 13.1** *Price Path of a 10-Year Zero Coupon Bond*

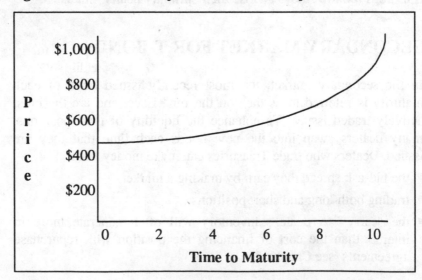

## Creation of Zero Coupon Bonds

Zero Coupon Bonds can be created one of two ways: either by starting with traditional bonds and selling each cash flow separately (referred to as *stripping*), or by issuing ZCBs from the start (referred to as *original-issue* discounts).

Whereas original-issue discounts are straight-forward, stripped ZCBs are not. The best way to understand stripping is to work through a simple example: The bonds to be used are 20 newly issued, 30-year 10% coupon U.S. Treasury Bonds priced at value. Because the bonds are priced at value, they can be purchased for $20,000 (20 * $1,000), plus accrued interest (if any).

Because these bonds are bought at value, all of the bonds' 60 cash flows are purchased at a 10% annual discount rate (see Chapter 8 for a complete discussion). However, just because these 60 cash flows are purchased as a package does not mean that they have to be sold that way. If each cash flow were sold separately, the available cash flows would be as follows:

- 59 cash flows of $1,000 each (created by combining the $50 semiannual interest payments from each of the 20 bonds).
- One cash flow of $20,000 ($1,000 maturity value * 20 bonds) at the end of 30 years.

Because the cash flows were purchased at a 10% discount does not mean that they would have to be resold at the same discount. Instead, each cash flow can be priced at a rate appropriate for its maturity. For example, if 6-month instruments were yielding 6% and the 6-month interest payment would be priced at

$$PV = \$1,000 / (1 + 0.03)^1 = \$970.87$$

although it was purchased for:

$$PV = \$1,000 / (1 + 0.05)^1 = \$952.38$$

depending on where the ZCB Yield Curve is relative to the Coupon Bond Yield Curve, stripping Coupon Bonds into ZCBs can be very profitable (see Chapter 19 for a more complete discussion of the spot yield curve, versus the ZCB curve, versus the coupon curve).

Prior to 1982, ZCBs were created by separating coupons from bonds and trading them separately. However, because coupons were bearer instruments, and were very small and therefore easy to lose, stripping actual coupons was never very popular. In 1982 Merrill Lynch® started trading Treasury Receipts. Each receipt was a surrogate for a specific cash flow from a portfolio of Government Bonds that were held in a trust account. Treasury Receipts offered the advantages of easy safekeeping and greater flexibility regarding the denominations available to investors.

Shortly after Merrill Lynch® introduced its Treasury Receipts (called TIGRS®), other investment banking firms soon followed: Solomon Brothers® introduced CATS® and Lehman Brothers® introduced LYONS®. The U.S. Treasury got into the act in 1985 by stripping its own bonds, which are now quoted in the Government Bond section of the paper.

## Advantages of Zero Coupon Bonds

The first advantage that ZCBs offer is convenience, because there are no cash flows to reinvest. If an investor has relatively few dollars to invest, the small periodic cash flows from a traditional bond can be annoying. There are few, if any, investment vehicles that investors can use to reinvest small coupon payments and earn high returns. This makes ZCBs one of the most popular investment choices for IRA accounts, small pension accounts, and small savings accounts.

They also offer the advantage of "locking in a YTM"--provided the ZCBs are held to maturity. In other words, the RCY of a ZCB equals its YTM, again provided that the bond is held to maturity. Thus, if an investor believes that market interest rates will fall, the investor may choose to lock in the current YTM by purchasing ZCBs.

Finally, the yield that ZCBs offer is generally higher than that of comparable coupon bonds with the same maturity. This higher yield is, of course, a reflection of the fact that ZCBs have a higher volatility than other Coupon Bonds with the same maturity. However, ZCBs generally have the lowest yield of any bond with the same duration, reflecting that they generally have shorter maturities than other bonds with the same duration (assuming that the yield curve has its normal positive slope).

## Disadvantages of Zero Coupon Bonds

The first disadvantage of ZCBs is that volatility is a "double-edged sword." Whereas owning high-volatility bonds will boost the total return when interest rates fall, it will also cause large losses when interest rates rise. From a "percentage" viewpoint, the longer the ZCBs maturity, the higher its duration, and the greater its volatility. However, on a "dollar" basis, ZCBs with the greatest volatility are the bonds with an intermediate maturity. The reason that the bonds with an intermediate maturity show the greatest dollar volatility is that short-term bonds generally have small discounts and, thus, small price changes to changes in yield. Long-term bonds have long compounding periods to make up any change in the discount rate so that the dollar change can be relatively small.

The second disadvantage of ZCBs is that they have greater credit risk than coupon bonds. Because ZCBs have no periodic cash flows, investors can lose both their principal and accumulated interest if the issuer should go bankrupt.

Third, ZCBs can generate tax liabilities without generating the income with which to pay the taxes. (This drawback only applies to taxable accounts.) A taxable investor must have income from another source to cover tax liabilities. A further complication is that ZCBs can be subject to different methods of computing the annual tax liability depending on when the bonds were originally issued. There are various tax treatments for ZCBs, because every time that the law was changed, the ZCBs that were outstanding were "grandfathered" under the previous tax act.

For most ZCBs, investors are taxed annually on the normal appreciation from their original purchase price as ordinary income. If the bonds are sold prior to maturity, and are sold at a price that is not on the normal appreciation curve, the difference between the sale price and the normal appreciation curve is treated as a capital gain/loss in the year that the sale occurs.

For example, if an investor bought the preceding 10-year, 10% ZCBs when they were issued and wanted to sell them three years later, their accreted value would be:

$$PV = \$1,000 \, (1 + 0.05)^{14} = \$505.07$$

The difference between $505.07 and $456.39 would be subject to income tax. If the sale price were lower than $505.07, the difference would be a capital loss. If the sale price were higher, the difference would be subject to capital gains tax.

## Applications of Zero Coupon Bonds

The most common use of ZCBs is to match future cash flows with future liabilities. For example, a family that was planning for a child's college education could purchase ZCBs whose maturity matches the expected tuition dates. Similarly, on a larger scale, ZCBs can be purchased to meet the pension liabilities of a defined benefit plan. They can also be used as trading vehicles. Because of their high durations and volatility, they are great for investors who are prohibited from using derivative instruments to "play" the interest rate moves.

# TARGETED INVESTOR NOTES

Some Treasury Bonds are designed specifically for foreign investors. These securities, referred to as Targeted Investor Notes (TINs), have five important differences from other Treasury Bonds:

- Consistent with Euromarket practices, TINs have annual coupons.
- To provide investors with anonymity, TINs are registered in the name of a foreign financial institution that certifies that the "beneficial owner" is a U.S. alien.
- There are no non-competitive bids in TIN auctions.
- Consistent with Euromarket practices, the yield is calculated on a 30/360 basis, instead of an actual/actual basis.
- Although TINs are not relatively liquid, they can be irrevocably exchanged into "Traditional Treasuries" to enhance their liquidity.

# FUTURE OF THE TREASURY MARKET

The size of this market will continue to increase because of our unrelenting budget deficits. Whereas politicians are arguing over who will do the most to decrease the *rate of increase* in the federal deficit, no one is talking about reducing the actual size of the deficit--much less about generating a budget surplus.

The interest bill on the debt is now estimated to be hundreds of billions of dollars per year. Whereas our national debt was only 2% of the GNP during World War II, it is now 6% of the GNP and rising. Unless the budget imbalances are soon corrected, the U.S. will find itself in an irreversible quagmire.

# 14

# U.S. GOVERNMENT AGENCY BONDS

## INTRODUCTION

Many investors find it difficult to understand why the Federal Government would permit several of its Agencies to issue their own Bonds. After all, the greater the number of issuers, the lower the liquidity of each issue. The lower the liquidity of each issue, the higher the government's (therefore the taxpayer's!) interest expense. Since the Federal Government has either a direct and/or a moral obligation to back the securities issued by the various Federal Agencies, having multiple issuers would not seem to make sense from a *financial* viewpoint.

However, from a *political* viewpoint, having the various Federal Agencies issue their own bonds makes perfect sense. The advantage that politicians receive from allowing agencies to issue their own debt is *off-balance sheet financing* for the Federal Government. By creating agencies and having them issue their own bonds, politicians can finance the services that their constituents want without raising taxes and increasing the size of the *reported* Federal deficit. The size of the actual Federal deficit is, of course, increased every time a Federal Agency issues debt.

## CREDIT QUALITY OF AGENCY BONDS

Since all Federal Agency Bonds are backed either by the full faith and credit of the Federal Government or by the moral guarantee of the Federal Government, Agency Bonds are usually perceived as having little or no credit risk. Occasionally, that perception changes as specific sections of the economy become especially weak.

For example, from 1982 to 1984 the U.S. farming industry was under extreme financial pressures. These pressures resulted in a record number of farm failures. This high failure rate, especially among family farmers, resulted in a very high default rate on the loans made to these farmers by the Federal Farm Credit Bank. The default rate became so high that by 1984 some investors started questioning whether or not the Federal Farm Credit Bank would fail. As a result of this uncertainty, the market value of the Federal Farm Credit Bank's bonds declined in the open market. Fortunately, the combination of a new management team and an upturn in farm prices and productivity was able to restore investor confidence.

As another example, in 1988 the Federal Housing Administration (FHA) was plagued by a series of scandals that had an adverse impact on the level of investor's confidence in the Agency. As investor's confidence declined, so did the market value of the agency's bonds.

Because of these occasional lapses in investor confidence, as well as their lower liquidity, Agency Bonds offer a higher yield than comparable Treasury Bonds. Like Treasury Bonds, most Agency Bonds are exempt from state and local taxes. But unlike Treasury Bonds, they are priced and traded on a 30/360 basis, instead of on an actual/actual basis.

## THE FEDERAL FINANCING BANK

Although the Federal Government has dozens of agencies, most do not "tap" the credit markets directly. Instead, they sell their bonds to another agency known as the Federal Financing Bank (FFB). The FFB, in turn, obtains its funds by issuing securities and borrowing from the Treasury. The advantages of this approach are that the calendar is not crowded with dozens of small issuers trying to borrow directly, and the cost of borrowing for the smaller agencies (which would have the most illiquid securities) is substantially reduced.

# THE SELF-ISSUING AGENCIES

Whereas small agencies use the FFB to obtain their funding, several of the larger agencies tap the credit markets directly. These agencies include the:

- Student Loan Marketing Association
- Federal Home Loan Banks
- Federal Farm Credit System.
- Federal National Mortgage Association
- Government National Mortgage Association
- Federal Home Loan Mortgage Corporation

## Student Loan Marketing Association

The Student Loan Marketing Association (SLMA), which is widely known as *Sallie Mae,* is a private stockholder-owned corporation that is sponsored by the Federal Government. Its purpose is to raise money that it then funnels into a variety of student loan programs. The securities that it issues are "silently" guaranteed by the Federal Government.

Because most of the loans that Sallie Mae makes are floating-rate loans, it usually either issues floating-rate debt or fixed-rate debt and then swaps fixed rate liabilities for floating rate liabilities (see Chapter 22) in order to match its assets and liabilities. Sallie Mae is widely regarded as one of the most innovative Federal Agencies with regards to its financing. It is often the first Federal Agency to implement the use of innovative deal structures and vehicles in order to lower its cost of funding.

## Federal Home Loan Banks

The 12 regional Federal Home Loan Banks are controlled by the Federal Government and are nominally owned by the savings and loan institutions that are members of the Federal Home Loan Bank System. The purpose of these banks is to lend money to S&Ls that have temporary cashflow or funding problems. These banks raise their funds by issuing securities with maturities of one to 10 years directly to the public. To reduce their offering expenses, the banks borrow collectively by what are referred to as Federal Home Loan Consolidated Bonds. Whereas these bonds are not backed by the full faith and credit of the U.S. Government, it is inconceivable that the Federal Government would allow a Federal Home Loan Bank to fail. As evidence of its support, to date the Federal Government has committed over $500 billion to bailing out the S&L Industry.

## Federal Farm Credit System

The Federal Farm Credit System is also controlled by the Federal Government, and is nominally owned by the 37 different Farm Banks that make up the system. This system includes the Federal Land Banks, the Bank for Cooperatives, and the Federal Intermediate Credit Banks.

The purpose of these banks is to provide funding for loans to farmers and cooperatives. Again, the securities issued by the Federal Farm System are not direct obligations of the Treasury, but have a strong implied guarantee.

The other three issuers, the Federal National Mortgage Association, the Government National Mortgage Association, and the Federal Home Loan Mortgage Corporation, are examined in Chapter 17.

# 15

## MUNICIPAL BONDS

## INTRODUCTION

Municipal Bonds are issued by states and political subdivisions of states (including counties, cities, municipalities, and regional authorities). The proceeds from these bond sales are used to finance the construction, maintenance, and operation of a wide variety of public facilities and services, including airports, sewer systems, waste management facilities, roadways, bridges, government offices, public power facilities, recreation facilities and parks, housing facilities, hospitals, and educational institutions. In addition, some Municipal Bonds are used to finance certain private industrial projects.

## THE MUNICIPAL BOND MARKET

The Municipal Bond market is a very large and fragmented market. On both a dollar-volume basis and a number-of-issues-outstanding basis, the Municipal Bond market is far larger than the Corporate Bond market. At any time, there are usually well over one million Municipal Bond issues outstanding. Because Municipal Bonds are used to finance everything from firehouses to massive power complexes, the size of Municipal Bond issues ranges from being very small (a few hundred thousand dollars) to enormous (several billion dollars). Although it is the multibillion dollar issues that make the news, the vast majority of municipal issues are relatively small and interesting only to "local" investors. (For example, very few investors in New York City have the desire to own bonds that were issued to finance the construction of an elementary school in Mason, Ohio.)

There are three principal reasons that investors tend to be biased toward "local" Municipal Bond issues:

- Few investors (or brokers) in New York have ready access to the data that would be necessary to properly analyze the bonds issued by Mason, Ohio.

- Investors in New York receive less favorable tax treatment from Ohio Municipal Bonds than they do from New York Municipal Bonds. The reason for this is that the tax treatment of Municipal Bonds depends on *both* the state of residence of the investor and the location of the issuer (examined later in more detail).

- Investors prefer buying bonds from issuers with whom they are familiar.

## Municipal Bond Dealers

Unlike the Government and Corporate Bond markets, the Municipal Bond market is not dominated by a few large securities firms. Instead, because of their high overheads, large securities firms tend to only be interested in the larger Municipal bond issues. They literally cannot afford to get involved with small issues. This lack of interest by the larger securities firms in the smaller Municipal Bond issues leaves a wide-open market for smaller, regional Municipal Bond firms. These smaller regional dealers usually restrict themselves to underwriting and making a market in issues with strong local interest.

## Increasing Volatility of the Municipal Bond Market

Whereas the Municipal Bond market used to be a reasonably "sedate" market, four factors have combined to increase the degree of risk, reward, and sophistication in this market:

- As interest rates have become more volatile, so have Municipal Bond prices.

- The volume of low-quality municipal debt has increased substantially.

- Municipal deal structures have become more innovative and complex, making analysis more difficult and complex.

- The market for municipal derivatives has experienced tremendous growth.

The higher the degree of risk, the greater the expertise required to properly manage the risk. Even the smallest dealers have had to improve their analytical capabilities and have had to learn how to hedge the interest rate risk and credit risk of their portfolios.

# TAX TREATMENT OF MUNICIPAL BONDS

There is a lot of confusion regarding the taxation of Municipal Bonds. The provisions in the past few Tax Acts have managed to confuse even the most seasoned Municipal Bond investors. Hopefully, this section will clarify some of the confusing issues.

The first step to understanding Municipal Bond taxation is to realize that capital gains are taxed differently from interest income. Capital gains, which result from selling a Municipal Bond for more than its purchase price (or buying a Municipal Bond at less than the price at which it was shorted), are usually fully taxable. The tax advantages that Municipal Bonds offer apply exclusively to the tax treatment of the bond's *interest income,* not its capital gains.

For U.S. investors, the principal attraction of Municipal Bonds is that the interest income *can be* exempt from federal, state, and local income taxes. However, different investors who own the same Municipal Bond issue are often subject to different tax liabilities. Just as U.S. Treasury Securities are exempt from state and local taxation, Municipal Securities are usually exempt from Federal Income Taxes (due to the so-called "reciprocality rule"). In addition to this federal tax exemption, many states also exempt Municipal Bond interest income from taxation *provided* the investor is a legal resident of the state, *and* the bond is issued by an issuer from within the state.

Most cities also exempt Municipal Bond interest income from income tax and/or personal property tax, as long as the same two conditions are met. Thus, a New York City resident who purchases a bond issued by a New York County will have no federal, state, or city income tax liability. However, if the same bond were purchased by a New Jersey resident, the investor would only receive a federal tax exemption. The interest income would be subject to state--and possibly city--income tax. (Bonds that are issued by U.S. territories [Puerto Rico, Guam, and American Samoa] have an automatic federal, state, and local tax exemption, regardless of the investor's state of residence.)

## Taxable Municipal Bonds

Whereas the interest from most Municipal Bonds is exempt from Federal Income Tax, there are two notable exceptions: bonds issued to exploit interest arbitrage possibilities, and "excess" Industrial Development Bonds.

## Exploiting Arbitrage Possibilities

Because of the tax advantages that Municipal Bonds offer, they can be issued with coupons that are sharply lower than Corporate Bonds and Treasury Bonds with comparable ratings and maturities. For example, for an investor in the following income tax brackets:

- federal--33%
- state--6%
- city--3%

the following three bonds would offer the same YTM. (Note that as examined in Chapter 10, the bonds would probably offer different realized compound yields.)

**Table 15.1** *Bonds with the Same After-Tax YTM*

| Type of Bond | Yield |
|--------------|-------|
| Corporate | 13.79% |
| Treasury | 8.79% |
| Municipal | 8.00% |

It did not take long for municipalities to figure out that they could issue Municipal Bonds with a low coupon, use the proceeds to buy Treasury Bonds with an identical maturity *but* a higher coupon. Since the municipality is not taxed on the interest it receives from the Treasury Bonds, the municipality earns the "spread" between the two yields as a risk-free profit. Thus, it became common for municipalities to issue bonds purportedly to build schools, roads, and other public facilities that they had no real intention of actually building.

Instead, the sale proceeds from the Municipal Bond offerings were simply invested in Treasury Securities so that the municipality could earn the spread. The U.S. Congress, understandably, felt that this practice was an abuse of the tax-advantaged status that Municipal Bonds offer, and outlawed the practice in the Tax Reform Act of 1986. Today, If the proceeds of a Municipal Bond offering are not used for the purpose for which they were intended within a reasonable period of time (usually two years), the bond's federal tax exemption may be denied retroactively to when the bond was originally issued.

## Industrial Development Bonds

### *History of the IDB Market*

Another abusive practice that was curtailed by the Tax Acts of 1984 and 1986 was that of allowing states to issue an excessive amount of Industrial Development Bonds (IDBs). An IDB is a Municipal Bond *issued on behalf of* a Corporate Issuer.

Since an IDB is technically a Municipal Bond, it offers investors the same tax advantages as other Municipal Issues. However, since the bonds are issued on behalf of a corporate issuer, only that corporate issuer has the responsibility for making the interest and principal payments in full and on time. Thus, although a municipality is technically the issuer (making the interest on the bonds tax free to qualified investors), the municipality has no financial obligation to investors. The investors must instead rely solely on the credit quality of the underlying corporation. Thus, if the State of New Jersey issued an IDB on behalf of IBM, Inc., only IBM, Inc. would be responsible for servicing the debt.

The incentive for municipalities to issue IDBs on behalf of a corporation is that by allowing the corporation to obtain financing at the very favorable municipal interest rates, the corporation is more likely to either relocate to, or expand within, the municipality's jurisdiction. For example, almost every State tries to encourage businesses to either relocate to, or expand within, their state in order to stimulate economic growth and provide jobs for the State's residents. States frequently offer tax incentives, lower utility rates, employee training programs, and other incentives to corporations as they compete with other states for the jobs and other economic benefits that the corporations can provide.

However, while many of these enticements are very expensive for a state to offer, IDB financing is an enticement that a state can offer that doesn't really cost the state very much. (After all, the cost of an IDB is actually borne by the federal government which loses the income taxes on what would otherwise have been a taxable corporate bond issue.) Since IDB financing is both a very powerful enticement from the corporation's point of view and a very low cost enticement from the state's point of view, prior to the Tax Acts of 1984 and 1986 offering IDB financing to corporations was both very popular and very prevalent.

Unfortunately for municipalities, Congress never intended for IDBs to be a "free-for-all" for States and corporations. Instead, they were originally created so that municipalities would have a tool that would allow them to attract and promote the development of critical industries in distressed areas. The Tax Acts of 1984 and 1986 effectively limited the volume of tax-advantaged IDBs that can be issued within a state. Presently, the total dollar volume of IDBs that a state can issue is limited by a formula that is tied to the state's population. Because the number of tax-advantaged IDBs that a state can issue is limited, the right to issue IDBs has become more valuable. Each state is free to decide which companies can issue IDBs and which companies cannot--(hence, the dramatic increase in lobbying at the state level).

Note that States are free to issue more IDBs than the Congressional formula allows, but the bonds will *not* receive a Federal Income Tax exemption. Investors who want tax-free income should check the tax status of an IDB prior to making an investment.

## Categories of Industrial Development Bonds

There are three different categories or types of IDBs. These categories differ with regards to the maximum size of the issue, and how the sales proceeds can be utilized.

- *Type-1*. There is no limit on the size of a Type-1 IDB issue, however, the trade-off is that the proceeds can be used only for "true" public projects such as convention facilities, airports, wharfs, sewer systems, and other public works projects.

- *Type-2.* Type-2 IDB issues are limited in size to $1,000,000, they can be used by any corporation as long as the proceeds are used to acquire real estate or a depreciable asset. In other words the proceeds cannot be used to purchase services or be used as working capital.

- *Type-3.* Type-3 IDB issues are limited in size to $10,000,000, but can be used for any purpose. They are only available to a company that has not borrowed more than the IDBs' issue size in the last three years, and agrees not to borrow more than the IDBs' issue size for the next three years.

# CATEGORIES OF MUNICIPAL BONDS

Municipal Bonds are divided into two broad categories: General Obligation Bonds and Revenue Bonds. The difference between the two types of bonds is the source of the funds that are used to service the bond issues.

## General Obligation Bonds

General Obligation Bonds (GOs) are backed by the *full faith and credit* of the issuer. This means that the issuer is legally obligated to use every source of revenue that it has at its disposal to meet its principal and interest payments in full and on time. If it becomes necessary for the issuer to impose or raise a sales tax, property tax, or personal income tax in order to meet the payment schedule on its GO Bonds, the issuer must do so.

Because of the naturally tendency of politicians to "spend now and pay later," most states, counties, and local governments have wisely enacted statutory or constitutional limitations on the dollar volume of GO Bonds that can be issued. Otherwise, politicians would inevitably create so much GO debt that the tax rates required to service the accumulated debt would become intolerable. The high tax rates required to service the high debt load would force many businesses and individuals to leave the municipality. Of course, when businesses and individuals leave a municipality, it increases the tax burden on those left behind--encouraging even more businesses and individuals to leave. The end result of this "downward spiral" is, of course, default.

## Revenue Bonds

By contrast, Revenue Bonds are backed solely by the revenue generated by a specific project. If the revenue is sufficient to service the debt, the bond-holders will get paid. If the revenue is not sufficient, the issue will go into default. The bond-holders have no claim against the general taxing power of any governmental body. Predictably, GOs and Revenue Bonds are analyzed differently.

# THE FUTURE OF THE MUNICIPAL BOND MARKET

It is no secret that many of the public facilities in the U.S. (the bridges, roads, sewers, ports, etc.) are generally in poor condition. Whereas opinions vary, depending on the source, it seems apparent that a significant percentage of our bridges are, or will become, unsafe within the next decade. There has been only one major airport project started within the last decade (and likely will not be completed until at least 1995). There is also a critical shortage of waste treatment plants and roadway improvements.

In the face of this overwhelming and growing need, the amount of federal funds available for such purposes are being decreased (on a relative basis) because of other spending priorities and the pressures of the Federal budget deficit. It seems inevitable that a growing percentage of the costs of developing and maintaining the infrastructure of the U.S. will fall upon the states and cities. The question is not whether there will be a dramatic increase in the number of Municipal Bond issues and the size of the Municipal Bond Market, but when it will occur. Given this information, the future of the Municipal Bond business should be very bright.

# MUNICIPAL BOND UNDERWRITING

Municipal Bonds are underwritten in one of two ways: either on a *competitive basis* or on a *negotiated basis*. The choice of which underwriting method to use is largely a function of state law.

## Competitive Underwriting

As the name implies, in a competitive underwriting, various securities firms compete for the right to underwrite a specific bond issue. Bond issuers generally solicit bids from potential underwriters by placing "request for bids" advertisements in Municipal Bond publications such as *The Blue List*®, and by putting the word out to underwriters that have expressed interest in working with the issuer in the past. The issuer then provides the potential underwriters with additional information, including the purpose for which the funds will be used, the amount of money the issuer wants to borrow, the maturity (or maturities) that the investor desires, the maximum interest rate that the issuer is willing to pay, and so on.

Armed with the necessary information, the underwriters then prepare their bids, seal them, and submit them to the issuer at a designated time and place. (Sometimes, a single firm will submit a bid, and other times--particularly when the size of the offering is relatively large--a group of firms will collectively submit a bid.) The bids are submitted in terms of "the average cost of funds to the issuer," and the bid that results in the lowest "net cost of funds" to the issuer wins. The winning underwriter(s) then purchase the bonds in accordance with the terms outlined in their bid and then try to sell them to investors at a profit.

Often, the competition between underwriters is intense, particularly for those issues that are either relatively large or are issued by prestigious issuers, such as state governments or large cities. Sometimes, the competition is so fierce that the winner actually turns out to be the loser when, in order to win the auction, an underwriter bids too aggressively and ends up not being able to resell the bonds to investors at a profit. Other times, the issuer's terms are unacceptable, and the issuer receives no bids. When this happens the issuer can either change the terms it deems to be acceptable or cancel the offering. Generally, most GO Bonds are underwritten competitively.

## Negotiated Underwritings

Instead of the competitive process, sometimes an issuer simply negotiates directly with an underwriter. Most Revenue Bonds are underwritten by the negotiated process. Whereas a negotiated underwriting may not always result in the lowest cost of funds for the issuer, they are certainly simpler for the issuer to arrange. (In addition, the politicians who have the power to select underwriters for the issuer's bond offerings often aggressively seek campaign contributions from the underwriters they select.)

# CREDIT ANALYSIS OF MUNICIPALS

Determining the credit quality of most Municipal Bonds is difficult, because only a small percentage of all Municipal Bonds (usually the larger issues) are rated by one or more of the recognized rating companies. Two of the implications of this lack of readily available credit ratings are that

- Municipal Bond issues with identical credit characteristics often trade at sharply different prices/yields.
- Non-rated bond issues tend to have price movements that are larger, and less predictable, than comparable issues that are rated.

Because relatively few Municipal Bond issues are rated by the traditional rating agencies, Municipal Bond investors must often rely on their own research capabilities and/or the capabilities of their brokers. The factors that need to be analyzed vary, depending on the type of bond being analyzed and the purpose for which the sales proceeds will be used.

## Analyzing General Obligation Bonds

Because GO Bonds are backed by the full faith and credit of the issuer, GO Bond analysis examines the major factors that influence the issuer's ability to meet its obligations.

### *Stability and Diversity of the Issuer's Economic Base*

Many areas of the country are largely dependent on a single industry, and if that industry goes into a protracted and severe recession, the "ripples" often have devastating effects on the region's entire economy (as the people of Houston, Dallas, Detroit, and New York have recently discovered). For this reason, Municipal Bonds that can be jeopardized by a downward turn in a single industry are considered more risky and, therefore, less attractive than those issues that are issued by regions that have a well-diversified economy. Issuers from one-industry regions often have to offer a higher interest rate to entice investors and underwriters.

## Existing Debt Burden of the Issuer

Like individuals, a region's ability to service additional debt depends on the region's existing debt. Issuers that are already deeply in debt may have great difficulty generating the additional cash flow needed to make principal and interest payments on time. A region's existing debt level can be measured on both a relative and absolute basis by examining the region's debt on a *per capita* basis, as a percentage of the region's property value, and as a percentage of the region's personal income. This analysis should be performed using the region's existing debt level, as well as the region's projected debt level. As always, this analysis should be performed periodically so that the region's debt trend can also be determined and monitored.

## Existing Tax Burden of the Region

Because GOs are backed by general tax revenues, an important factor to consider is the region's ability and willingness to bear the additional tax burden that may be necessary to service the additional debt. There are several ways of gauging a region's ability to pay. First, the lower the existing tax rates, the easier it is for the region to bear the burden of additional taxes. It should be remembered that a new bond issue that dramatically increases a region's tax burden has a detrimental effect on the credit quality of any previously issued, still outstanding, GO Bond issues.

When considering a region's current tax burden, all taxes applied at the regional level have to be considered. For example, if a state were going to issue GO Bonds, the analysis would have to include the state's individual and corporate income tax rates, sales tax rates, personal property tax rates, school tax rates, and licensing fees.

If the various state taxes are already high, the state would have great difficulty increasing taxes further, increasing the probability that the credit quality of that state's bonds would decline in the future. However, a state or city that had relatively low taxes would probably be able to increase taxes sufficiently to service its debt.

## Use of Proceeds

One sign of an issuer who's credit strength is deteriorating is an issuer who issues bonds to raise funds to fund an operating deficit. Bond proceeds that are converted into assets such as schools, roads, and parks can be considered investments. Bond proceeds that are used to meet operating expenses are simply a cloud over the state's economic future.

## Reputation of the Issuer's Political Leadership

Bond issues from states and cities with strong leaders are more likely to perform well than issues from states and cities with inept or corrupt management. Likewise, bonds from states and cities that have a high number of political patronage jobs (like New York and Louisiana) are tougher to sell than bonds from states with fewer patronage jobs.

## Breadth and Depth of the Issuer's Management and Control Systems

As creditors of the issuer, investors should examine the steps that the issuer takes to avoid unpleasant credit surprises, including cost-control mechanisms, record keeping and audit procedures, budgetary controls, accounting policies, and unfunded pension/post-retirement liabilities.

## Trend of Property Values

One of the most important indicators of how well a region is doing is the rate of increase or decrease in property values. Again, both the short-term and long-term trends need to be analyzed.

## Issuer's Anticipated Future Financing Needs

Investors also need to be aware of issuers that will need to raise additional large sums of financing in the future. The greater the issuer's future need to borrow funds, the greater the probability that the credit quality of the issuer's debt will decline. Bond analysis must be an on-going process. The economic strength of a region can change suddenly and dramatically. Those who do not monitor their investments closely will sustain the inevitable consequences.

## Analyzing Revenue Bonds

Revenue Bonds are usually backed solely by the revenue of the projects that they finance. Thus, although they are indirectly dependent on the economic strength of the regions that they serve, they primarily depend on the relative success or failure of a specific project. The analysis of a Revenue Bond starts with a review of the "feasibility study" for the project. The feasibility study is basically a business plan for the project, and the information and type of projections that it contains varies depending on the type of project being financed. Regardless of what type of project is being financed, the feasibility study should attempt to answer the following basic questions:

- Is there a real and sufficient demand for the services that the project is financing?

- Is there sufficient financing to complete the project, including a reserve for the inevitable unexpected contingencies?

- Will the project generate enough surplus cash flow to meet the debt service, even if the project is not as successful as projected?

- Is there a valid legal opinion and appropriate loan agreement to protect the bondholders?

Once these general questions are answered, the investor or analyst can then focus on the questions that relate to the specific project being financed. The following are some of the questions that investors should ask before investing in certain categories of bonds.

### *Public Power Bonds*

- Is the future demand for power going to increase as some are projecting, or will conservation and higher fuel prices combine to curtail power usage?

- If the issuer has a construction program, is it on schedule and within budget?

- What is the issuer's current and projected fuel mix?

- Will the regulators allow the issuer to have the rate increases that it will need to meet the debt service?

- How good, or bad, is the company's management team?

### Public Housing Bonds

- What type of housing will be built with the bond proceeds?
- Is the neighborhood where the housing is being built improving or declining?
- What rights will the tenants have after government rent subsidies (if any) expire?
- If the project is dependent on government assistance or financing, is the aid package guaranteed?

### Public Hospital Bonds

- Is there sufficient demand for the hospital's services?
- Will the insurance companies and the government set their reimbursement schedules at rates that will allow the hospital to meet its debt service?
- Does the hospital offer the ancillary services (drug and alcohol treatment centers, allergy clinics, sports medicine, specialty surgical procedures, and so on) that generate high cash flow and high profitability?

## MUNICIPAL BOND INSURANCE

To provide investors with an extra level of protection, many issuers now have their bonds insured by an insurance company or guaranteed by a letter of credit. In the event that the bonds go into default, the insurance company pays off the bondholders. The three biggest insurers currently are the American Municipal Bond Insurance Corporation (AMBIC), the Municipal Bond Insurance Corporation (MBIC), and the Financial Guarantee Insurance Corporation (FGIC). The insurance reassures investors in two ways: the insurance coverage itself, and the guarantee that the insurers maintain strict underwriting standards. Clearly, they only want to insure bonds that do not need insurance. Thus, bonds that are insured have been examined by some of the sharpest Municipal Bond analysts, and have been found to be safe.

# 16

## CORPORATE BONDS

---

## INTRODUCTION

A Corporate Bond is evidence of a loan from an investor to a corporation. Instead of borrowing money from investors one at a time, corporations issue bonds to borrow from numerous investors simultaneously. This way, the company does not have to negotiate loan terms and conditions separately with thousands of investors. Instead, the company prepares one master loan document (referred to as the bond's *indenture*) and offers investors the opportunity to loan the company money on a "take it or leave it" basis under the terms spelled out in the indenture. The indenture specifies not only the interest rate that the bonds will pay, but also all the restrictions that the company agrees to adhere to as conditions for obtaining the loan. These conditions are referred to as the loan's "covenants."

In practice, when a company is drafting its bond indenture, the company (or more likely its investment banking firm) will solicit input from a large number of potential investors in order to determine the lowest possible yield and the most lenient covenants that they will accept. However, once the indenture is finalized, it is offered as a "take it or leave it" proposition. Corporate Bonds are almost always issued in $1,000 denominations, and in the U.S. the convention is for semiannual interest payments (the convention in Europe is for annual payments).

## EVALUATING CORPORATE BONDS

Evaluating Corporate Bonds is more complicated than evaluating Treasury Bonds. Corporate Bonds have more variables that need to be considered and analyzed than Treasury Bonds. Whereas the value of a Treasury Bond is largely a function of the bond's duration, coupon, and maturity, the value of a Corporate Bond also depends on the bond's seniority, credit rating, loan covenants, early redemption provisions, and relative liquidity.

# SENIORITY OF CORPORATE BONDS

Unlike Treasury Bonds, which all have the same credit strength, various issues of Corporate Bonds from the same issuer have different "seniorities." The seniority of an issuer's bond issues determines the order in which they will be paid off in the event that the issuer defaults or encounters severe cashflow problems. Theoretically, when an issuer defaults, its most senior bond issue is paid off first, and then the others are paid in descending order. Generally, the order of seniority for Corporate Bonds is:

- Escrowed Bonds
- Mortgage Bonds
- Equipment Trust Certificates
- Collateral Trust Bonds
- Senior Debentures
- Subordinated Debentures
- Convertible Bonds
- Income Bonds

## Escrowed Bonds

Escrowed Bonds are bonds that are secured not only by the full faith and credit of the issuer, but also by an irrevocable trust containing sufficient Treasury Securities to meet all of the principal and interest payments remaining on the corporate issue. In order to create an Escrowed Bond, a corporation places the Treasury Bonds into an irrevocable trust that prohibits the trust's assets from being used for any purpose other than servicing the Corporate Bond issue. By escrowing an outstanding bond issue, a corporation effectively removes it from its balance sheet. (Note that an issuer will only escrow a bond issue when it cannot be called, because calling a bond issue is certainly easier and cheaper.)

Escrowing outstanding bond issues is sensible when market interest rates are very high. When market interest rates are high, Treasury Bonds can be purchased cheaply. Because of this, the issuer can collateralize its outstanding bonds for a price that is substantially less than the face value of the outstanding issue. For example, if a corporation originally issued a $100 million 30-year, 8% Corporate Bond, and 10 years later interest rates had risen to the point where new 20-year Treasury Bonds were yielding 12%, then the Corporate Bonds could be escrowed for a cost of $8,000,000 (annual interest expense), divided by $120 (interest per bond). This means that 66,667 bonds would be needed to generate enough interest to meet the interest payments. In addition, an additional 33,333 of 20-year ZCBs would be needed to retire the remaining principal when the bond matures.

Using the above data, the approximate cost of escrowing the $100 million face amount of the 30-year, 8% Corporate Bond issue with a 20-year remaining life is:

- The cost of buying 66,667 of the 20-year, 12% Treasury Bonds to escrow all of the interest payments, and $66,667,000 of the final principal payment would cost 66,667 * $1,000 = $66,667,000, assuming the bond is selling at par.

- The cost of buying 33,333 20-year ZCBs to escrow the remaining final principal payment would be 33,333 * $97.22 = $3,240,707, assuming the bonds were priced to offer a 12% YTM.

Thus, the issuer can effectively remove a $100 million liability from its balance sheet for a cost of $69,907,707, increasing its book value by $30,092,293.

Because Escrowed Bonds are fully secured with Treasury Bonds and are largely free from credit risk, they are priced to offer a very low yield. Often, the yield that they offer is just a few basis points higher, on an after-tax basis, than Treasury Bonds with comparable durations.

## Mortgage Bonds

Mortgage Bonds are Corporate Bonds that are secured by the full faith and credit of the issuer, and by a lien against some real property owned by the issuer. If the company fails to make its interest and principal payments in full and on time, the bondholders can, theoretically, force the corporation into involuntary bankruptcy, seize the property, and sell it in order to recoup their investments. Because real estate generally has a long history of relative price stability and predictable long-term appreciation, it is considered excellent collateral. Thus, Mortgage Bonds are considered second only to Escrowed Bonds in quality. In many cases, there are several issues of Mortgage Bonds secured by a single piece of property. This is especially true when that property's value has risen significantly over the years. In this case, the different classes of bonds will be referred to as First Mortgage Bonds, Second Mortgage Bonds, Third Mortgage Bonds, and so on. If the property has to be sold, the holders of the First Mortgage Bonds should be paid off first, then the others, in descending order.

## Equipment Trust Certificates

Equipment Trust Certificates are Corporate Bonds that are secured by the full capabilities and credit of the issuer, and by a lien against some equipment the issuer owns. The types of equipment that are typically financed by Equipment Trust Certificates include aircraft, railroad cars, and truck fleets. Any equipment that can quickly be resold is suitable as collateral for Equipment Trust Certificates.

## Collateral Trust Certificates

Collateral Trust Certificates are Corporate Bonds that are secured by the full capabilities and credit of the issuing company, and by a lien against some collateral--usually securities--that the company owns. Issuers frequently use Collateral Trust Certificates to turn illiquid equity positions in their subsidiaries into cash. Consider the following example:

**Figure 16.1** *Collateral Trust Certificates*

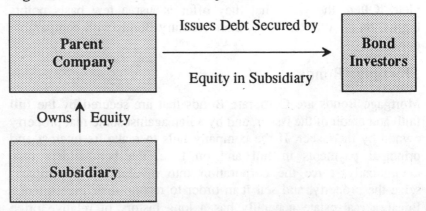

## Senior Debentures

Senior Debentures are Corporate Bonds that are backed solely by the full capabilities and credit of the issuing company, and not by liens against any other assets. If a company issues more than one debenture issue, the most senior issue is referred to as the Senior Debenture.

## Subordinated Debentures

Subordinated Debentures are Corporate Bonds that are backed solely by the full capabilities and credit of the issuing company, and are junior to the Senior Debentures. If an issue has more than one Subordinated Debenture, the senior issue is referred to as the Senior Subordinated Debenture. If the issuer defaults on its debentures, the bondholders can force the company into bankruptcy to try to recoup their investment.

## Convertible Bonds

Convertible Bonds (CBs) are Corporate Bonds that can be converted into a fixed number of shares of the company's common stock and are discussed below.

## Income Bonds

Income Bonds are a special type of Corporate Bond that only require the issuer to make interest and principal payments if the issuer can afford to make them. To prevent issuers from abusing its Income Bond investors, the indentures of Income Bonds usually prohibit the paying of dividends to the common shareholders and the paying of bonuses to company executives--unless the issuer is meeting its obligations on its Income Bonds.

Income Bonds are divided into two categories: cumulative and non-cumulative. If an Income Bond is *cumulative*, any missed interest payments accrue against the issuer and must be paid off before dividends or bonuses can be paid. If an Income Bond is *non-cumulative*, any interest payments that are missed are simply forgotten. Because the issuers of Income Bonds are not under obligation to make timely payments of principal and interest, investors have no right to force a company into bankruptcy because it misses payments on its Income Bonds.

## Limitations of Seniority

Whereas determining and enforcing the seniority of debt instruments would seem very simple, bankruptcy court judges have been known to disregard seniority issues and valid property liens completely when deciding a bankruptcy case. For example, when Eastern Airlines® fell behind on its financial obligations, its creditors took it to bankruptcy court and demanded that the assets that were pledged as security for their loans be turned over to them (a reasonable request under the circumstances). The bankruptcy judge, however, decided to ignore the loan agreements and bond indentures, and permitted Eastern® to keep flying. By allowing them to continue flying, the bankruptcy court also allowed them to squander many tens of millions of dollars that rightfully belonged to the creditors.

## LOAN COVENANTS

As mentioned previously, a Corporate Bond's covenants are the restrictions that the issuer agrees to abide by in exchange for obtaining the loan from the investors. These covenants are detailed in the bond's indenture, but they are often written in such obscure "legalese" that they are difficult for non-lawyers (and sometimes lawyers) to understand. Although there are thousands of different covenants that can be included in an indenture, we only mention the five most common with which investors should be familiar:

- Minimum amount of over-collateralization
- Additional debt limitations
- "Poison puts"
- Negative pledges
- Asset transfer restrictions

## Minimum Amount of Over-collateralization

For the various types of Corporate Bonds that are secured by assets, regardless of whether the assets are real estate, equipment, or securities, the bond's indenture will usually specify the amount (in dollars and/or percentages) that the bonds are to be over-collateralized. For example, the indenture of an Equipment Trust Certificate might specify that the "fair market value of the equipment should exceed the face value of the bonds by 30% at all times." Whereas this covenant is designed to protect investors, it can sometimes work to their disadvantage. For example, the indenture may specify that if the value of the collateral declines below the minimum value specified in the indenture, the bonds must be called--even if the investors would prefer that they not be called.

## Debt Limitations

Many bond indentures include limitations on the types and amounts of additional debt that the company may incur. This covenant is designed to protect the investor from the risk that the issuer will borrow additional funds and, in the process, jeopardize the issuer's ability to service its previous debt. This covenant may:

- only limit the amount of debt that can be issued that is senior to the issue in question.
- only limit the amount of *funded debt,* i.e., debt with a maturity longer than one year.
- only limit the amount of debt that can be issued without placing any limits on the amount of preferred stock that can be issued.
- only limit the amount of debt that the actual issuer can issue without placing any limitations on either the parent or subsidiary (companies) to issue additional debt.

Thus, the *exact wording* of this covenant is critical.

## "Poison Puts"

Usually, when a company is taken over and the acquirer uses debt to finance the acquisition, the debt-to-equity ratio of the company increases--often substantially. When the issuer's debt-to-equity level increases, the credit rating and the market value of the issuer's existing bonds decline. To protect investors against this risk, some bonds include "poison put" provisions that require the company to redeem the bonds under favorable terms in the event of a takeover or "change of control."

Of course, this type of poison put provision makes acquiring a company more expensive. How a poison put provision actually defines a "change of control" is critical in determining when and how the poison put is activated. (Note also that some poison puts are only activated if management opposes the takeover.)

## Negative Pledge

Negative pledges are also designed to protect investors, particularly those who purchase *unsecured* debt. A negative pledge of assets provision states that bonds that are currently unsecured by liens against any specific assets will become secured if the issuer issues additional debt. The types and amounts of additional debt that are needed to trigger this clause is also specified.

## Asset Transfer Restrictions

Many bond indentures attempt to limit the issuer's ability to transfer corporate assets to parent companies or subsidiaries. Even if the issuer is asset-rich presently, the value of corporate assets can fall both quickly and sharply. Thus, limiting the transfer of corporate assets can become important in the future, even if it seems unnecessary now.

## The Value of Covenants

The question of how much yield an investor should sacrifice to obtain favorable covenants is not a question that is easily answered. How much a covenant is worth can only be determined within the context of a specific investor buying a specific bond at a specific time and under specific market conditions. Whereas analyzing the specific covenants of a bond offering is both a time-consuming and difficult process, it is an essential part of determining a bond's true value. Understanding the "fine print" in a bond indenture is part of what separates the professionals from the amateurs.

# BONDS THAT CAN BE CALLED, PUTABLE, AND SINKING-FUND BONDS

Whereas almost every Corporate Bond has a scheduled maturity date, many also include one or more provisions that can shorten the bond's actual life.

# Bonds That Can Be Called

## Call Provisions

If a bond has call provisions, the issuer has an *embedded* option that allows the issuer to accelerate the bond's maturity. However, all embedded call options are not created equal. Callable bonds differ with regards to:

- the period of *call protection*. Most callable bonds offer investors some period of time before the bonds can be called. Depending upon the issue, this period is usually between five and ten years.

- whether the call is *continuous or discrete*. Once the period of call protection expires, some callable bonds can be called at any time the issuer chooses. This type of embedded call is referred to as a continuous option. More typical however is the discrete call in which the issuer has one opportunity to call the bond. The date the issuer must elect to either call, or not call, the bond is referred to as the *call date*. (As a compromise between these two alternatives, some callable bonds give the issuer a number of discrete calls. For example, allowing the issuer to call the bond on the same day each year for a ten-year period would be ten discrete calls.) Naturally, a continuous call is usually more valuable to the issuer than a series of discrete calls; which are, in turn, usually more valuable than a single discrete call.

- whether or not the issuer can make *partial calls*. While most calls require the issuer to either call--or not call--the entire issue, some embedded calls give the issuer the right to call only a portion of the issue.

## When Issuers Call bonds

There are two reasons why issuers call their bonds. First, some issuers will call their bonds if they no longer need the money and want to strengthen their balance sheets. More typically, however, are the issuers who will call their bonds in order to refinance their debt at a lower rate. In other words, when market interest rates decline, they will call their bonds and issue new bonds that pay a lower interest rate. Note, that an issuer will only refinance an outstanding bond issue by calling the outstanding issue and issuing a new bond issue if the interest savings more than exceeds the cost of executing the call and issuing the new debt.

### *Impacts of a Call on Bondholders*

When a bond issue is callable, it adversely impacts the bondholders in three ways:

- They lose a bond that offered an above-market yield and are forced to reinvest their funds at the lower current rate--costing them both interest and interest on interest.

- It makes their cashflow schedule uncertain. Many investors implement strategies that are dependent upon having a predictable cashflow schedule. When bonds are called, the investor's projected cashflow schedule is disturbed, and the investor's strategy becomes less effective.

- An embedded call limits the capital appreciation potential of the bond because bonds that can be called usually have "negative convexity."

### *Compensating Investors for Imbedded Calls*

Because bonds that can be called have the above disadvantages, investors have to be compensated for those disadvantages. Generally there are two ways that investors are compensated for granting issuers the right to call their bond issues.

- Callable bonds offer a higher return than comparable non-callable bonds. How much additional yield an investor should receive for granting the issuer the right to call the bond can be calculated via the statistical methods discussed in Chapter 23.

- As a consolation to bondholders who actually have their bonds called in the early part of the call period, most issuers pay a small premium for early calls. For example, many bond issues pay $1,030 for a bond if it is called in the first year of the call period, $1,020 for a bond called in the second year of the call period, $1,010 for a bond called in the third year, and $1,000 thereafter.

## Putable Bonds

If a bond has put provisions, the investor has an *embedded* option that allows the investor to accelerate the bond's maturity. For example, a 20-year bond may be putable any time after five years. Investors will elect to use their option when interest rates rise so that they can get their capital back and reinvest it at a higher rate. Puts are almost always at par value.

Because the issuer has, in effect, sold the investor an option, the investor needs to pay for the option. The way that investors pay for embedded put options is by accepting a lower yield than they would receive from non-putable bonds with comparable maturities and credit ratings.

## Sinking-Fund Bonds

A *sinking-fund provision* requires the issuer to retire a portion of a bond issue prior to its stated maturity date. This provision, which is included in the bond's indenture, is designed to force the issuer to periodically retire portions of its debt so that the entire bond issue does not become due at one time. For example, a $100 million, 10%, 20-year bond may require the issuer to retire $5 million/year at the start of years 11 through 20--leaving only $50 million to be retired at the end of 20 years.

Most sinking-fund provisions allow the issuer to either buy back the bonds in the open market or issue a series of random calls in order to obtain the bonds. If interest rates are high and the bonds are selling at a discount, the issuer will attempt to buy the bonds in the open market. If interest rates are high and the bonds are selling at a premium, the issuer will call the bonds instead. The fact that 50% of this issue will be retired prior to the bond's maturity should be considered when calculating the bond's YTM, average life, and duration. To get accurate measures of these characteristics, it is necessary to calculate the weighted average YTM, average life, and duration using the projected maturities of each issue.

# LIQUIDITY

As long as interest rates and markets continue to be volatile, investors will continue to value liquidity. Therefore, the higher a bond's liquidity, the lower its yield (all other factors being equal). A bond's liquidity is, in turn, influenced by the:

- size of the bond issue. Generally, the larger the bond issue, the more liquid the issue.

- name recognition of the issuer. Generally, the higher the name recognition of the issuer, the more liquid the issue.

- bond's credit rating. Generally, the higher the bond's credit rating, the more liquid the issue.

- bond's coupon. Generally, the closer the bond's coupon is to prevailing interest rates, the more liquid the issue.

# CREDIT RATING

The larger bond issues are analyzed and rated by the major rating agencies. The ratings range from "AAA" to "D." Issues rated BBB+, or higher, are considered to be "investment-grade"--meaning that they are acceptable investments for commercial banks under current banking regulations. Those bonds with lower credit ratings are considered high-yield bonds--or junk bonds--depending on your view point.

When one of the major rating agencies reviews the credit rating of a bond issue, it usually places the issue on its "watch list" and indicates whether the issue is being reviewed for a possible rating increase or decrease. As soon as the news is released, the bond's price responds accordingly. If, and when, the issue's credit rating is changed, the bond's market price will change for a second time. Thus, the bond's price will respond to both the expectation of an interest rate change and the actual rating change. The coupon bond research departments of securities firms justify their existence, in part, by trying to out-guess and second guess the rating agencies in order to profit from the rating changes.

## High-Yield Bonds

The high-yield bond market is currently a $250+ billion dollar market and, as such, is too big for many Corporate Bond investors to ignore. While this market use to be relatively obscure, the dramatic increase in the use of high-yield bonds to finance takeovers coupled with the recent defaults of several highly visible junk bond issues, has made high-yield bonds a front-page news item for investors, as well as for the public at large.

The original sales pitch for high-yield bonds presented by Drexel Burnham Lambert, Inc.,® and copied by every other firm in the business, was that although high-yield bonds posed greater credit risks than investment-grade bonds, the extra yield that they offered more than compensated investors for the additional risk. Thus, as long as investors build a well-diversified portfolio of high-yield bonds, the investors' net returns should exceed the return available from a high-quality portfolio.

As the size of this market has grown, dealers have expanded their commitments and increased their high-yield analytic and research capabilities. Whereas high-yield bonds are Corporate Bonds, they behave differently, and are analyzed differently, than other Corporate Bonds. For example:

- Determining the credit quality of a high-yield issue is more difficult than determining the credit quality of a high-quality While the credit quality of a high-quality issue is largely determined by the company's financial ratios and other readily quantifiable benchmarks, the credit quality of a high-yield issue often hinges on more subjective items like the issuer's strategic plan, the quality of its management, the loyalty of its customers, etc. In addition, the credit quality of high-yield issues needs to be reevaluated more frequently.

- A change in the rating of a high-yield bond has a much greater effect on the bond's price than a change in the rating of an investment-grade bond. Whereas a high-quality bond's market value might change by a few points in response to a rating change, a high-yield bond's market value might change by 20 points or more.

- Unlike high-quality Corporate Bonds, high-yield Corporate Bonds have low covariance with Treasury Bonds (see Chapter 28).

- The bid-ask spreads for high-yield bonds can be very high, resulting in high trading costs and a lack of liquidity.

## *Categories of High-Yield Bonds*

High-yield bonds generally fall into one of three categories: Rising Stars, Fallen Angels, and "DBs."

- *Rising Stars* is the slang expression for small companies that borrow capital for expansion. Because the borrower is small and generally has a weak balance sheet, its bonds do not qualify for an investment-grade rating. The risk of Rising Stars is that, because the issuer is a growing company and will probably need additional capital in the future, there is often little chance that the company's debt-to-equity ratio will improve substantially, even if the company is successful. Thus, there is little chance that the bonds will be upgraded.

- *Fallen Angels* is the slang expression for large companies that have "fallen" on hard times. When a company suffers serious setbacks, the company's bonds are downgraded from investment-grade. The question with Fallen Angels is, has the company taken the drastic action that is often necessary to correct business problems?

- *DBs* is the slang expression for divisional buy-outs. Divisional buy-outs have the advantage of having established and highly motivated management teams in place. In addition, they are not usually burdened with business setbacks. All that usually changes in a DB is the capital structure. The principal question with DBs is, will the new capital structure allow a division enough cashflow to operate properly and service the debt, or is the debt too high?

## CONVERTIBLE BONDS

A Convertible Bond is a Corporate Bond that can be converted into a fixed number of shares of the company's common stock, usually at the time of the investor's choice. For example, if XYZ, Inc.'s common stock were selling for $8/share, XYZ, Inc. might issue a debenture that can be converted into 100 shares of the company's common stock. Because the bond is convertible into stock, the bond's value will be equal to *the value of the option to convert the bond into stock* plus *the value of the bond's income stream.*

Naturally, the higher the market value of the stock, the greater the value of the option. Initially, the option to convert a $1,000 bond into 100 shares of stock, when the stock only has a market value of $8, will not be very valuable. However, as the value of the stock rises, so will the value of the option (see Chapter 23). The value of the income stream of a Convertible Bond is determined by the usual factors: duration, yield, credit quality, as well as others.

## Convertible Bonds versus the Underlying Stock

Whenever an investor is considering investing in a Convertible Bond, this question has to be asked, "Is it better to buy the Convertible Bond or the underlying stock?" To determine the answer, investors use two tools: the bond's *conversion premium* and its *workout period.*

A Convertible Bond's conversion premium is a measure of how much the investor is *overpaying* for the equity component of the bond.

The formula for the conversion premium is:

$$\frac{(\text{Bond's MV - Bond's Conversion Value})}{\text{Bond's Conversion Value}} * 100$$

For the preceding bond, the conversion calculation would be:

$$\frac{\$1,000 - (100 \text{ shares} * \$8/\text{share})}{(100 \text{ shares} * \$8/\text{share})} * 100 = 25\%$$

The lower a bond's conversion premium, the more attractive the Convertible Bond becomes - relative to owning the stock directly. Many investors prefer to buy the stock directly if the conversion premium exceeds 20%.

The workout period, on the other hand, is a measure of how long it will take the investor to recoup the conversion premium.

The formula for the workout period is:

$$\frac{\text{Conversion Premium (\$)}}{\text{Annual Income From Bond - Annual Income From Stock}}$$

In the preceding example, the stock paid no dividend and, thus, the workout period is:

$$\frac{(\$1,000 - (100 * \$8))}{(\$80 - \$0)} = 2.5 \text{ years}$$

However, if the stock paid a $0.14 dividend per year, the workout period would be:

$$\frac{(\$1,000 - (100 * \$8))}{(\$80 - ((\$1,000/\$8)*\$0.14))} = 3.2 \text{ Years}$$

(Note that in the denominator we assume that we are buying $1,000 worth of stock since the bond costs $1,000.) The lower the workout period, the more attractive the bond is compared to owning the stock directly. Convertible Bond investors often seek out bonds with workout periods of two years or less.

(Note that whereas the conversion premium and workout period are useful tools, each Convertible Bond must be evaluated individually.)

## The Advantages and Disadvantages That Convertible Bonds Offer Issuers

### The Advantages

- Allows the issuer to incur a lower interest expense. (In the case of issuers with poor credit quality often providing a conversion feature is the only way they can borrow money at any rate.
- Because Convertible Bonds are usually converted into equity (eventually), they provide issuers with a cheap way for companies to issue equity at a premium. Further, when investors convert their Convertible Bonds into equity, the issuer's debt-to-equity ratio improves.

### The Disadvantages

- Issuing a Convertible Bond may dilute the value of the company's equity and earnings per share on a fully diluted basis.
- Issuing a Convertible Bond will weaken the issuer's balance sheet.

## The Advantages and Disadvantages That Convertible Bonds Offer Investors

Convertible Bonds have sharply different performance characteristics than the underlying common stock. Relative to the common stock, the Convertible Bond generally offers a higher current yield, less intermediate price volatility, and a more stable return over time.

The disadvantages of Convertible Bonds for investors are that they will appreciate less than the underlying common stock in a bull market, and that almost all Convertible Bonds can be called. By calling a Convertible Bond that is selling at a premium, the issuer effectively forces investors to convert their bonds into equity. Consider the following example:

Suppose that the value of XYZ, Inc.'s stock rises to $15/share. In this case, the value of the Convertible Bond would be equal to at least $1,500, because it can be converted into 100 shares of the common stock, plus the bond would have additional value because it also generates $80 of interest income per year. If we assume that the bond is worth an extra $250 because it generates an income stream, the bond would be selling in the open market for $1,750. If an investor believed that the market value of XYZ's stock was going to rise, the investor might buy some of these bonds for $1,750.

If, however, the bond is called, the investor is faced with the choice of turning the bond in to the issuer and receiving $1,000 in cash, or converting the bond into equity and losing $250 in the process (a $1,750 bond that would convert into $1,500 worth of stock). Thus, the embedded call options in Convertible Bonds can be detrimental to investors in two ways:

- Like all call options, they can cause the bond to have negative convexity.

- If the bond is a Convertible bond, an embedded call option can also cause investors to lose whatever conversion premium is built into the bond's market value.

# 17

# MORTGAGE PASS-THROUGHS

## INTRODUCTION

One of the major trends of the financial services area is *securitization* (the process of converting financial assets that are not liquid into liquid securities). Assets are securitized by placing the non-liquid assets into an irrevocable trust account and then issuing securities that are secured by the trust. Although the underlying assets technically remain non-liquid, the securities that are secured by them can be traded freely.

Commercial banks, savings and loan institutions, insurance companies, mortgage bankers, finance companies, leasing companies, and other financial services firms, benefit from an increase in the liquidity of the financial assets that they either create or purchase. By converting their non-liquid assets into liquid securities, the financial services firms obtain the following benefits:

- The securities can be sold quickly if the institution needs to raise capital.
- The securities can be exchanged for other assets whose risk/reward profile is better suited to the institution's objectives.
- The securities are often easier to manage and hedge.

Almost any reasonably homogeneous pool of financial assets can be securitized. Lately, boat loans, car loans, credit card receivables, fixed-rate residential mortgages, floating-rate residential mortgages, as well as some commercial mortgages, have been securitized.

Whereas securitization certainly benefits the financial institutions that originate and own massive quantities of non-liquid assets, the creation of liquid securities from non-liquid assets also benefits investors. Investors benefit because the new varieties of securities that are created possess risk/reward profiles that are different from those of more traditional securities. The risk/reward profiles of these new securities may make them more desirable than traditional securities.

However, because the securities created by the securitization process possess different risk/reward profiles, it is important for investors to take time to understand them completely before investing in them. Because more fixed-rate and adjustable-rate mort- gages have been securitized than other types of assets, it is sensible to use mortgages to illustrate the securitization process. It should be noted that many of the concepts covered in this chapter apply to other types of financial assets, as well.

# FIXED-RATE MORTGAGES

In order to understand the securities that are created by securitizing fixed-rate residential mortgages, it is essential to first understand the fixed-rate residential mortgages themselves. The value of an individual fixed-rate residential mortgage to an investor is determined primarily by the mortgage's nine major characteristics:

- Payment Frequency
- Term
- Amortization Schedule
- Interest Rate
- Prepayment Provisions and Penalties
- Assumability Provisions
- Seniority
- Credit Quality
- Payment Structure

## Payment Frequency

The frequency with which the borrower makes mortgage payments has a direct impact on the value of the mortgage because of the time value of money. In the past, when the U.S. was primarily an "agrarian society," most mortgages required the borrower to make either quarterly or annual payments. Currently, however, the most popular payment frequency for residential mortgages is monthly, although biweekly mortgages are becoming more common as borrowers realize how much interest they can save by increasing the frequency of their mortgage payments (see Tables 17.1-17.3).

## Term

The term of the mortgage will also affect its value to an investor because mortgages with the same face value, but different terms, will have different cash flow schedules and durations. The terms of residential mortgages range typically from five to 40 years--with 30- and 15-year mortgages currently being the most popular. (Generally, the more popular the mortgage's term, the easier it is to securitize.)

The trend has recently been toward shorter mortgages because the public has realized that the monthly payment for a $100,000, fully amortizing 15-year mortgage, is not that much higher than the monthly payment for a $100,000, fully amortizing 30-year mortgage (see Tables 17.1 - 17.3).

## Amortization Schedule

Because a mortgage's cash flows are determined by its amortization schedule, this schedule also influences the mortgage's value. The amortization schedule is the schedule by which the mortgage's principal balance is paid. Most residential mortgages are fully amortizing, meaning that the entire principal balance of the loan is paid over the term of the mortgage.

Mortgages that are not fully amortizing have a remaining balance that becomes due and payable at the end of the mortgage's term. This remaining balance is often referred to as the mortgage's "balloon payment." A mortgage that is less than fully amortizing will, of course, have lower monthly payments than a fully amortizing mortgage because less principal will have to be paid each month.

However, borrowers who choose a partially amortizing mortgage will have to either pay off or refinance the "balloon payment" when the mortgage becomes due. If no principal is amortized over the life of the mortgage, the mortgage is referred to as an *interest-only* mortgage (see Tables 17.1 - 17.3). Almost all residential mortgages issued in the U.S. are fully amortizing.

## Interest Rate

The mortgage's interest rate also has an impact on its value. The interest rate on a fixed-rate mortgage is determined by the prevailing level of market interest rates when the mortgage is originated, the credit quality of the borrower, the relationship between the value of the property and the size of the mortgage, and the type of lender making the mortgage loan, as well as numerous other variables. The following tables illustrate the payments of $100,000 mortgages under various interest rate, payment frequency, term, and amortization assumptions. (Note that the following tables assume that the payments are made at the end of the month.)

**Table 17.1** *Payments for a $100,000 6% Mortgage*

|  | 15 years | | 30 years | |
|---|---|---|---|---|
|  | Monthly | Biweekly | Monthly | Biweekly |
| 0% Amortization | $500.00 | $230.77 | $500.00 | $230.77 |
| 50% Amortization | $691.93 | $309.96 | $549.78 | $253.68 |
| 100% Amortization | $843.86 | $389.15 | $599.55 | $276.58 |

**Table 17.2** *Payments for a $100,000 10% Mortgage*

|  | 15 years | | 30 years | |
|---|---|---|---|---|
|  | Monthly | Biweekly | Monthly | Biweekly |
| 0% Amortization | $833.33 | $384.62 | $833.33 | $384.62 |
| 50% Amortization | $953.97 | $440.05 | $855.45 | $394.75 |
| 100% Amortization | $1074.61 | $495.49 | $877.57 | $404.89 |

**Table 17.3** *Payments for a $100,000 14% Mortgage*

|  | 15 years | | 30 years | |
|---|---|---|---|---|
|  | Monthly | Biweekly | Monthly | Biweekly |
| 0% Amortization | $1166.67 | $538.46 | $1166.67 | $538.46 |
| 50% Amortization | $1249.20 | $576.27 | $1175.77 | $542.61 |
| 100% Amortization | $1331.74 | $614.09 | $1184.87 | $546.75 |

## Prepayment Provisions and Penalties

The value of a mortgage to an investor also depends on the mortgage's prepayment provisions and penalties. Most residential mortgages offer the borrower the option of prepaying the mortgage at any time, without any penalty whatever. In effect, the borrower has an "immediate put option" that can be exercised any time during the mortgage's term. (As we shall see in a later section, the value of this option is a critical factor in determining the value of a mortgage.)

Borrowers generally exercise this option when market interest rates drop and they want to refinance their mortgages at a lower rate (or when they simply want to pay off their mortgages). Whereas most smaller residential mortgages do not have prepayment penalties, some large mortgages (those greater than $500,000) do have prepayment penalties that are defined either as a fixed number of extra payments or as a fixed percentage of the remaining balance. Often, the prepayment penalty, if any, is tied to a sliding scale based on the remaining life of the mortgage.

## Assumability

Another factor that can affect the value of a mortgage is whether the mortgage is "assumable." An assumable mortgage is one that can be transferred from the original borrower to another qualified borrower during its term. In effect, the right to transfer the mortgage to another borrower is an option, just like the option to prepay. The option of being able to transfer a mortgage to another borrower becomes very valuable to the original borrower when market interest rates rise sharply. For example, if a homeowner were selling a house and could offer a potential buyer the right to assume an existing 8% mortgage--when a new mortgage would cost the buyer 16%--the seller would be offering the buyer something of tremendous value.

Residential mortgages that are insured by the Federal Housing Administration (FHA) and the Veterans Administration (VA) are assumable. Most private mortgages issued directly by banks, savings and loan institutions, and mortgage companies, are *not* assumable and, thus, any remaining balance becomes due when the home is sold.

## Seniority

A single piece of property can secure several mortgages. When this happens, the mortgages are ranked in order of their "seniority." The most senior mortgage is referred to as the first mortgage, the next senior mortgage is referred to as the second mortgage, and on down the line. Theoretically, if the borrower defaults and the property must be sold to repay the mortgage lenders, the sale proceeds should first be used to retire the first mortgage, then the second mortgage, etc., until the proceeds are exhausted. Thus, a first mortgage is considered more secure than a second mortgage, and a second mortgage is more secure than a third mortgage. However, bankruptcy court judges often disregard the seniority of mortgages when they are dividing up the proceeds of a property sale. This makes it unwise for investors to rely too strongly on a mortgage's seniority as a source of credit protection.

## Credit Quality

The less likely it is that a mortgage will default, the more attractive it will be to investors. In addition to the mortgage's seniority, there are a variety of factors that directly or indirectly influence the credit quality of a specific mortgage, including

- the size of the mortgage in relation to the value of the property.

- whether the value of the property is increasing or decreasing.

- the financial condition and credit rating of the borrower.

- whether the borrower suffers any untimely financial hardships resulting from unemployment, death in the family, disability, or divorce.

## Payment Structure

Another factor that determines the value of a mortgage is its payment structure. Most fixed-rate mortgages require the borrower to make consistent payments throughout the term of the mortgage. However, although the payments may be constant, the percentage of each payment that is principal and the percentage that is interest changes each month.

During the early years of a fixed-rate mortgage, almost all of the monthly payment is interest. As time passes, the percentage of each payment that is principal increases as illustrated in the following chart:

**Figure 17.1** *Paydown Path of Mortgage*

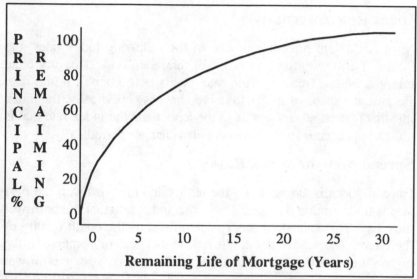

(Many homeowners are horrified to find that after making five years of mortgage payments on a 30-year, $100,000 11% mortgage, they still owe $97,164.94.)

The reason that the percentage of the payment that is interest and the percentage that is principal is important is because only the interest is subject to taxation for taxable investors.

# ADJUSTABLE-RATE MORTGAGES

The interest rate that the borrower pays on an adjustable-rate mortgage (ARM) is tied to the specific index rate in the mortgage contract. Because the index rate changes over time, so does the borrower's periodic mortgage payment. Whereas all ARMs are alike insofar as the interest rate that the borrower pays is periodically adjusted, ARMs differ from each other in several important ways, including the

- index to which they are tied.
- spread of the mortgage to the index rate.
- reset period.
- interest rate caps.

## Index Rate Alternatives

Most ARMs are priced from one of the following index rates: the 90-day T-Bill rate, the 1-year T-Bill rate, the 2-year Treasury Note rate, the 5-year Treasury Note rate, or a specific bank's prime rate. Because the shape of the yield curve changes periodically, the index rate that is most advantageous to the lender and the index rate that is most advantageous to the borrower also changes periodically.

## Spread over the Index Rate

Once an index is agreed to by the lender and the borrower, the next step is to determine the spread over that index rate that the borrower must pay. This spread is usually determined by the credit quality of the issuer. The higher the credit risk (either real or perceived), the higher the spread. For example, whereas a very strong borrower might negotiate a rate of "two points over the 1-year T-Bill rate," a borrower with a weaker credit rating might have to pay a spread of four points over the same index. Initially at least, an ARM should cost a borrower less than a fixed-rate mortgage, because a lender assumes less interest-rate risk with an ARM than it does with a fixed-rate mortgage.

## Reset Period

The reset period is the period between the dates when an ARM's interest rate is adjusted. Reset periods range typically from a period as short as three months to five years--with 1- and 3-year reset periods being the most common.

## Interest Rate Caps

To protect borrowers from sudden large increases in their mortgage payments if index rates should experience sharp increases, most residential ARM contracts have limitations on *how quickly* the borrower's mortgage interest rate can increase and by *how much*.

To ensure that the interest rate does not increase too quickly, most ARMs have limitations on how much the interest rate can increase within a certain period of time, regardless of how much the index rate increases within the same period. For example, if the ARM had a 1% *annual* cap, and the index rate went up by 3% within one year, the interest rate that the borrower would have to pay would only go up by 1%. If the index rate remained at 3% more than the initial rate, the ARM's interest rate would increase by another 1% the following year, and the final 1% in the third year.

To limit the maximum rate that the borrower will have to pay over the life of the mortgage, most ARMs have lifetime caps. For example, a mortgage with a 5% lifetime cap that was issued with an original interest rate of 8% would never have an interest rate above 13%, regardless of how high the mortgage's index rate might rise. In practice, the two caps are generally quoted together, with the periodic cap being quoted first. The most common types of adjustable-rate mortgages right now are what are referred to as 1-5s and 2-6s. A 1-5 cap means that the mortgage's interest rate cannot increase by more than 1% on each reset date, and cannot increase by more than 5% over the life of the mortgage. A 2-6 cap means that the mortgage's interest rate cannot increase by more than 2% on each reset date, and cannot increase by more than 6% over the life of the mortgage.

Assume that you had an ARM at 2 points over the 1-year T-Bill rate that had a 1-5 cap and an annual reset. On the day you received your mortgage commitment, if the 1-year Treasury Bill is yielding 8.6%, your mortgage rate would originally be fixed at 10.6%. One year later, if the 1-year T-Bill rate were 10%, your mortgage rate would be adjusted to 11.6% instead of 12%, because your mortgage's interest rate cannot increase by more than 1% per reset date. Your mortgage would be *capped out*.

When a mortgage is capped out, the "small print" in the contract usually specifies one of two treatments for the difference between what the lender is entitled to and what the borrower actually pays (0.4% in this example). In some mortgages the difference is simply forgotten, and the lender/investor can never collect it; in others, the difference *is added to the principal balance of the mortgage*. This second alternative is referred to as *negative amortization*. If an ARM has a negative amortization provision and market interest rates rise sufficiently, it is possible for the mortgage's principal balance to actually increase over time. Thus, lenders, borrowers, and investors must make sure that they thoroughly understand the cap provisions of an ARM. (Note that mortgages that have negative amortization provisions often have lower spreads, and so there is something of a drawback for both participants to consider.)

## Graduated Pay Mortgages

It is important not to confuse an ARM with a graduated pay mortgage (GPM). A GPM is a fixed-rate mortgage in which the payments start out low but increase according to a predetermined schedule. In other words, unlike an ARM, whereas the payments may not all be equal, they are all known in advance.

# MORTGAGE-BACKED SECURITIES

Until the early 1960s, mortgage loans were considered relatively non-liquid assets by the institutions that originated them. When a bank, a savings and loan institution, or a mortgage banker made a mortgage loan, it listed the loan as an asset and, with rare exception, held the loan until it either was paid off, went into default, or matured. When (and if) the lender received its capital, it would lend it again. Mortgage issuers saw the advantages of increasing the liquidity of their mortgage assets, regardless of whether they wanted to sell them. For mortgage issuers that wanted to sell all or a portion of their mortgage portfolios, making mortgages more liquid could

- reduce their exposure to credit risk. By selling its mortgages, the original lender could transfer the credit risk to the buyer, assuming that the mortgages were sold on a "non-recourse" basis.

- reduce their exposure to interest-rate risk. Most mortgage lenders obtain the money that they need for mortgage loans by borrowing in the short-term market. This practice exposes lenders to a classic asset-liability mismatch. For example, assume that a S&L borrows money at 7% by issuing 1-year CDs--and then issues 30-year fixed-rate mortgages at 11%. Initially, the S&L will earn a 4% spread. However, when the CDs become due, if the S&L must offer 13% in order to secure funding again, it will find itself in the unenviable position of borrowing at 13% and lending at 11%--and be on its way out of business. By selling the mortgages, the issuer can eliminate both an asset (the mortgage) and the need for a liability (the CDs) from its balance sheet, and thus the possibility of an asset-liability mismatch.

■ generate additional fees. By selling mortgages, lenders can "recycle" their capital. The proceeds that they receive from selling a portion of their existing mortgage portfolio can be lent to new borrowers. Because of the fees that lenders collect when they originate mortgages (points, application fees, and so on), many mortgage issuers can make *more* money by originating and selling mortgages than by holding them and trying to earn a spread between their cost of funds and the mortgages' interest rate. Issuers that elect to concentrate on mortgage originations can have more predictable earnings.

■ increase their "servicing" business. When mortgage issuers sell mortgages from their portfolios to investors, they can insist on retaining the responsibility for "servicing the mortgages." Servicing the mortgages entails collecting and accounting for the mortgage payments, preparing client statements, and executing foreclosure proceedings. For providing these services, the mortgage issuer receives a fee from the investors, who buy the mortgages but have neither the resources nor the inclination to service them. Given a sufficient volume of mortgages to service, this business can be quite profitable. (Issuers that do not want to service mortgages will still try to retain the *right* to service them, because this right can be sold to another institution and, thus, has real value.)

■ reduce their reserve requirements and improve their debt-to-equity ratios. Most mortgage issuers are regulated companies (banks and S&Ls) that must maintain a reserve account against their deposits. When an institution sells a portion of its mortgage portfolio, it reduces its requirement for deposits and therefore its reserve requirement. Further, by selling some of its mortgages, the institution can often reduce the amount of money that it needs to borrow and thereby reduce its debt-to-equity ratio. Given the increased regulatory scrutiny to which financial institutions are being subjected, reducing its reserve requirements and debt-to-equity ratio are objectives that appeal to many institutions.

- increase their overall return. By carefully selecting which mortgages to sell and when, the issuing institutions can try to enhance the overall performance of their mortgage program.

For mortgage issuers that do not necessarily want to reduce the size of their mortgage portfolios, increasing the liquidity of their mortgages can still offer the following benefits:

- Permit easy geographical diversification. Regional institutions can sell some of the mortgages that they originate locally and buy mortgages originated in other parts of the country, in order to diversify their portfolios and reduce the risk that their portfolio will be severely affected by a local recession.

- Permit easy swaps between fixed- and floating-assets. By converting mortgages into liquid securities, mortgage issuers have more flexibility to give their customers the type of mortgages they want--fixed- or floating- rate--regardless of which type of mortgages they want to hold in their portfolios. They can issue fixed-rate mortgages and swap them with another institution for floating-rate mortgages, and vice versa.

- Permit the institution to elect whether the sale is to be treated as an actual sale or a financing for tax purposes and, thus, do a better job of tax management.

Making mortgages liquid can also benefit *borrowers*. As the risk level for the lenders declines, they should be able to lower the rates that they charge borrowers. Also, as the mortgage business becomes less risky, more institutions should be attracted to the business of increasing the availability of mortgage loans.

*Investors* can also benefit from having a liquid market for mortgages because mortgages offer both high credit quality and relatively high yields.

Finally, having a liquid market for mortgages benefits the entire public. The lower mortgage interest rates that result from the reduced level of lender risk allows more Americans to qualify for mortgages. The greater the number of Americans that qualify for mortgages, the greater the number of homes, condominiums, and cooperatives that have to be built to accommodate them. The construction of new homes tends to be very stimulative to the economy. In addition to the construction industry, landscapers, furniture manufacturers and retailers, carpet manufacturers, and others, all benefit from lower mortgage rates. Thus, making mortgages liquid benefits lenders, borrowers, investors, and the whole economy.

# OBSTACLES TO CREATING A LIQUID MARKET FOR MORTGAGES

It is obvious from the preceding information that making mortgages liquid could benefit a tremendous number of people. Although the benefits of creating a liquid market for mortgages are undoubtedly substantial, from a practical perspective, there are a number of obstacles to creating a liquid market for individual mortgages. Some of these obstacles include

- their large size. The median size of the first mortgages originated in the U.S. presently is over $100,000. Although this presents no problem to institutional investors, few individual investors have both the ability and willingness to invest $100,000 into a single instrument. Thus, the large size of mortgages tends to limit the number of potential investors.

- their relative complexity. Mortgages are more complex than other investment vehicles. Consider an investor who purchases a typical 30-year, 11% fixed-rate fully amortizing $100,000 mortgage. This investor would have to receive and track 360 separate monthly payments instead of the 60 semiannual payments that a traditional 30-year bond would generate. The investor would also have to assume additional accounting responsibilities for tax purposes. Whereas the size of each monthly payment would remain the same because the mortgage has a fixed rate, the percentage of the payment that is principal and the percentage that is interest would be different every month.

- their tax treatment. Although an investor who buys a mortgage would receive the same payment each month, in the early years most of the payments would be interest, and in the later years most of the payments would be principal. However, the interest is taxable and, thus, the tax liability of mortgages is "front-loaded." Because the tax liability is front-loaded, mortgages may have NRCYs and NNRCYs that are lower than might be expected.

- their credit risk and the high cost of assessing it. The credit risk inherent in a specific mortgage is very difficult, time-consuming, and expensive to assess. To accurately assess the credit risk inherent in a mortgage, an investor may need to

  - have the property appraised.
  - have the property tested for toxic waste or other environmental damage.
  - secure a credit report on the borrower.
  - make sure that the homeowner has sufficient life, property, and casualty insurance.
  - secure and verify the borrower's employment history.
  - secure title insurance.

- their prepayment risk. Perhaps the biggest impediment to creating a liquid market for residential mortgages is that the borrower almost always has the right, but not the obligation, to prepay the mortgage without penalty. The fact that the borrower has this option always works to the detriment of the investor, regardless of which way market interest rates move.

As market interest rates fall, mortgages, like any fixed-rate instrument, become more valuable. For mortgage investors, however, just when an investment is really becoming worthwhile, the borrower may elect to refinance the mortgage--and thus return the investor's funds.

For example, consider an investor who purchases a 14% fixed-rate mortgage when market interest rates are reasonably high. A few years later, if market interest rates drop to 8%, the investor will likely want to keep the investment. (Who wouldn't want an investment that pays 14% when the alternative is to earn 8%?) However, just as the mortgage investment becomes really worthwhile, the homeowner will likely refinance his home and pay off the investor's mortgage--leaving the investor with no choice but to reinvest the funds at the available lower rate. *Thus, mortgages experience negative convexity when market interest rates decline.*

(Note, however, that refinancing is not free. The appraisal fees, points, legal costs, etc., all have to be paid by the borrower. Because of these costs, market interest rates usually have to decline approximately 200 bp below the mortgage's current rate before it is sensible for the borrower to refinance.)

On the other hand, if market interest rates rise, any fixed-rate investment--including a mortgage--becomes less worthwhile. However, if interest rates rise, the borrower will not want to refinance, leaving the investor with a lesser rate of return for an extended period of time.

For example, if an investor purchased a fixed-rate mortgage when interest rates were 9% and subsequently rose to 14%, the mortgage would become an unattractive investment, because the homeowner would probably not be interested in refinancing. Also, if the mortgage is assumable, it may not even be paid off if the homeowner moves. Thus, *when market interest rates rise, mortgages experience negative convexity.*

Because of these impediments, few investors are interested in buying individual mortgages, and a liquid market for them has never developed.

## OVERCOMING THE IMPEDIMENTS OF INDIVIDUAL MORTGAGES

For a liquid market for mortgages to develop, the impediments listed previously need to be overcome. One method of overcoming some of them is for a well-financed intermediary to

- purchase individual mortgages from the mortgage issuers.
- collect them into pools.
- insure the mortgages against credit risk.
- place the mortgage pools into trust accounts.
- sell undivided interests in these mortgage pools to investors.

An an illustration of how having an intermediary structure can help overcome some of the impediments of this transaction, consider the following simple example:

Assume that there are 10 homeowners, each of whom secures a 30-year, 11% fixed-rate fully amortizing $100,000 mortgage from their local bank. The bank then immediately sells the mortgages to the intermediary at full face value, but retains the right to service them in exchange for a fee equal to 1/2% of the remaining principal per year. The intermediary puts the mortgages into a trust account after taking a 1/4% fee to cover its costs.

**Figure 17.2** *Creation of Pass-Throughs*

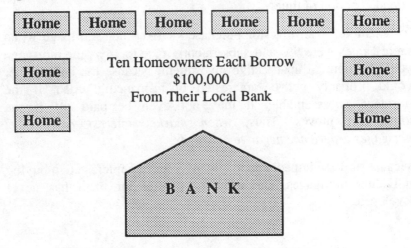

Ten Homeowners Each Borrow $100,000 From Their Local Bank

The Bank Sells the Mortgages to an Intermediary That Usually Insures Them. The Intermediary Then Places the Mortgages into a Trust Account

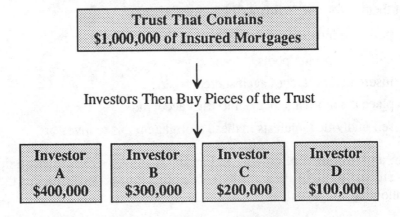

The intermediary then sells undivided interests to only four investors who buy 40%, 30%, 20%, and 10% of the pool, respectively. (Undivided interest means that if you buy 40% of this pool, you are not buying four of the 10 mortgages in the pool; instead, you are buying 40% of every mortgage in the pool.)

Each month, the S&L receives three types of cash flows from the homeowners: the regularly scheduled interest payment, the regularly scheduled principal payment, and any unscheduled principal prepayments (either partial or complete prepayments).

The principal payments are passed through to the investors in their entirety. The S&L and the intermediary subtract their fees from the interest payments and pass the balance on to the investors. Because the principal is passed through to the investors, these undivided interests in pools of mortgages are referred to as *pass-through securities* or *participation certificates*.

To illustrate the impact of this, assume that one of the mortgages is paid off in its entirety. In this case, $100,000 of principal will be sent to the bank, which will pass it on to the intermediary, and then on to the investors on a proportional basis. After the principal is distributed, the investors will have the following remaining balances:

**Table 17.4** *Investors' Balances after Prepayments*

| Investor | Previous Balance | New Balance |
|----------|------------------|-------------|
| A | $400,000 | $360,000 |
| B | $300,000 | $270,000 |
| C | $200,000 | $180,000 |
| D | $100,000 | $90,000 |

Thus, participation certificates are self-liquidating because the principal is returned to the investors each month when the mortgages are paid and/or prepaid, rather than when the investment matures. Further, as principal is paid, the investors' monthly interest payments also decline. If we consider the five impediments that were originally mentioned, the problems that participation certificates solve are the credit problem and the size problem.

## Credit Problem of Individual Mortgages

Assuming that the financial intermediary has the capability of absorbing any losses incurred on the underlying mortgages, the investors can look to the intermediary for credit protection instead of doing a thorough credit analysis of the underlying mortgages. In effect, the credit risk becomes the intermediary's problem, not the investor's problem.

If the intermediary does not have the financial resources to provide an unqualified credit guarantee, then some other method is needed to enhance the credit quality of the certificates to the point where the investors feel that they do not need to analyze the credit quality of the underlying mortgages. Some of the methods used to provide additional credit protection for participation certificates include

- over-collateralizing the certificates.
- having recourse (full or limited) to the mortgage issuer.
- obtaining an explicit or implicit government guarantee.
- securing a letter of credit, financial bond, buy-back agreement, or other financial guarantee from a third party.

## Size Problem of Individual Mortgages

From a theoretical viewpoint, an undivided interest in a pool of mortgages can be any size (there is no minimum). However, from a practical viewpoint, because each undivided interest has to be administered, most participation certificates are originally sold in minimum denominations of $25,000. Investors who want to make smaller investments can either buy older participation certificates in which a substantial portion of the principal has already been prepaid, or invest in participation certificates indirectly by choosing one of the numerous mutual funds or unit investment trusts that invests in pass-through securities. Because the minimum investment for many mutual funds is only $250, it is affordable by almost every investor.

# UNSOLVED PROBLEMS OF MORTGAGES

## Complexity Problem of Individual Mortgages

Because participation certificates are "conduits" for the payments flowing from underlying mortgages, pass-through securities have all of the complexity of underlying mortgages.

## Tax Problem of Individual Mortgages

Because participation certificates are conduits, and the early cash flows of the underlying mortgages are primarily interest, the early payments received by investors in participation certificates are primarily interest. Thus, the tax burden of a participation certificate is incurred in the early years, and this has a detrimental effect on the investment's NRCY and NNRCY.

## Prepayment Risk Problem of Individual Mortgages

Any prepayments are simply passed through to the owners of the participation certificates and, thus, these investors are exposed to the same prepayment risks as investors who purchase individual mortgages. Although participation certificates only overcome two of the five major impediments of creating a liquid market for mortgages, that was enough to allow a multihundred billion dollar market to develop.

## Intermediaries

Now that we know which obstacles participation certificates overcome, and which they do not, we should turn our attention to the major intermediaries that create participation certificates. The intermediaries who create participation certificates fall into one of two broad categories: those sponsored (to some degree) by the government, and those who are private.

### Government National Mortgage Association

Probably the best-known intermediary is the Government National Mortgage Association (GNMA), commonly known as "Ginnie Mae." GNMA is a government agency that buys FHA- and VA-insured mortgages from qualified mortgage issuers, packages them into pools, and then sells participation certificates to the public.

They are considered the safest participation certificate from a credit risk viewpoint because the timely payments of both the principal and interest are backed explicitly by the full capabilities and credit of the U.S. Government. Of course, because GNMAs are backed by the Government, they offer the lowest yield of any participation certificate.

The Government issues approximately $60 billion of new GNMAs per year. At press time, there is a huge backlog of mortgages that are waiting to be securitized. (The fact that a huge number of additional securities will be hitting the market has depressed existing GNMA prices, and has increased the yield spread between Treasury Bonds and GNMAs.)

### *Federal National Mortgage Association*

The second best-known intermediary is the Federal National Mortgage Association (FNMA), which is commonly referred to as "Fannie Mae." The FNMA is a publicly held, government-sponsored corporation. This means that although anyone can buy stock in it, the ultimate control of the corporation remains with the government. The FNMA generally buys traditional mortgages (i.e., mortgages that are not insured by either the FHA or VA) from commercial banks. Like GNMA, FNMA also guarantees the investors who buy its participation certificates that they will receive both their principal and interest in full and on time. The FNMA's credit strength, and thus, the value of its credit guarantee, comes from

- the equity that it has raised from the public.
- its line of credit with the U.S. Treasury.
- its implied U.S. Government guarantee.
- its limited recourse to mortgage issuers.

Because FNMA participation certificates do not have an explicit government guarantee, they generally yield slightly more than GNMA certificates.

The normal cash flow cycle for an FNMA certificate is as follows:

- The homeowner pays the S&L on the first of the month. (Most mortgages are written so that the money is due on the first of the month.)
- The S&L remits the payment to the FNMA on the 18th of the month.

- The FNMA remits the payments to investors on the 25th of the month.

Thus, FNMAs have a 25-day delay period.

## Federal Home Loan Mortgage Corporation

The Federal Home Loan Mortgage Corporation (FHLMC), commonly known as "Freddie Mac," also buys conventional mortgages from issuers. However, unlike the FNMA, the FHLMC generally buys its mortgages from savings and loan institutions instead of commercial banks. It guarantees the timely payment of interest and the ultimate payment of principal, and the sources of its credit strength are similar to those of the FNMA's credit strength.

The FHLMC has a 45-day delay. It takes 45 days from the due date for the money to actually make it all the way through the system, and for the owners of the pass-throughs, or participation certificates, to get paid.

## Private Intermediaries

Mortgage issuers do not have to use the government-sponsored intermediaries in order to package their mortgages into participation certificates. Instead, they can either act as their own intermediaries or hire a private financial services firm to package their mortgages for them. There are several reasons that a mortgage issuer would elect *not* to use a government-sponsored intermediary:

- First, the mortgage issuer may be able to package its mortgages itself (or hire a financial services firm) at a lower "all in" cost than the fees charged by the government-affiliated agencies.
- Second, the mortgages that the issuer wants to sell may not meet the specifications of the government intermediaries. For example:
  - Because the government agencies are designed to benefit lower- and middle-class taxpayers, there are limitations on the size of the mortgage that an agency will buy ($187,500 for GNMA). Mortgages larger than $187,500 (so-called "jumbo" loans) must be packaged by private intermediaries if they are to be sold.
  - The mortgages may not have the appropriate documentation. The government intermediaries can be very "fussy" about the paperwork.

- The mortgages may not qualify. The property may not have the value-to-loan ratio that the agencies require, or the borrower may have insufficient income.
- The government agencies may have a backlog of work and may be unable to package the mortgages within a time period acceptable to the issuer.

Because private issuers do not have explicit or implicit government credit guarantees, they must use the alternative methods of credit enhancement. The most commonly employed method of credit enhancement is over-collateralizing the participation certificates. Thus, the issuer might secure $100 million of participation certificates with $120 million (face value) of mortgages. Thus, more than $20 million of the mortgages would have to go into default before the investors' principal would be at risk.

Additionally, many participation certificates come with additional credit enhancements, such as letters of credit or financial performance bonds. The terms of these financial guarantees vary widely from issue to issue. Some offer complete protection whereas others offer only limited protection, or protection only under certain circumstances. Investors would be wise to review the "fine print" before making investment decisions.

## THE RELATIVE ATTRACTIVENESS OF PARTICIPATION CERTIFICATES

Like any other fixed-rate investment, the market price of a participation certificate will either trade at a premium or a discount value depending on whether the certificate's coupon is below or above (respectively) the current market interest rates. For example, suppose that an investor is interested in a GNMA participation certificate. The only six investment alternatives available are summarized in the following table:

**Table 17.5** *Characteristics of Example Pools*

| Coupon | Price | Yield | Speed | Location |
|--------|-------|-------|-------|----------|
| 8% | 87.16 | 10.55% | 121% FHA | Hartsville |
| 8% | 89.08 | 10.21% | 87% FHA | Cincinnati |
| 10% | 100.16 | 9.98% | 53% FHA | Dayton |
| 10% | 99.12 | 10.05% | 115% FHA | Phoenix |
| 12% | 104.12 | 10.35% | 265% FHA | Houston |
| 12% | 105.02 | 10.18% | 112% FHA | Atlanta |

How should the investor make the decision about which participation certificate to buy? That depends on two factors: the pool's yield and speed. The yields of the various participation certificates (using standard practices which are examined below) are given in the preceding table. The speeds of the various certificates will take more explanation.

Different pools of mortgages will experience different prepayment rates that are based on a variety of factors:

- The relationship between market interest rates and the coupons on the mortgages. The higher the mortgage's coupon relative to current market interest rates, the greater the incentive to pay off or refinance the mortgages.

- The percentage of homeowners in the pool who move (and pay off their existing mortgages) because they are "trading up" to a larger home. The stronger the national and regional economies are, the greater the percentage of homeowners who will be willing and able to purchase larger homes.

- The percentage of homeowners in the pool who cannot afford to keep their homes because of unemployment, death, disability, and divorce. The number of homeowners who lose their homes will, in turn, depend on the strength of the regional and national economies, as well as the current demographic and social trends.

- Whether regional property values are increasing or decreasing. If they are decreasing, it may be impossible for homeowners to refinance their mortgages even if market interest rates decrease. For example, suppose a homeowner buys a $150,000 home with a $30,000 down payment and a $120,000 mortgage. If property values decline 25%, the home will only be worth $112,500, making it impossible to secure a new $120,000 mortgage on the same property.

- Whether the mortgage is assumable. Assumable mortgages are paid off less frequently than non-assumable mortgages when market interest rates rise, because they have a separate value from the property itself.

- The age of the mortgages. Because of both personal and financial reasons, few homeowners move within the first two years of acquiring a new home. The most common years when people move are between five and seven years after they buy a home.

- The incidence of non-economic prepayments. Because mortgage interest is generally tax-deductible, borrowers who are financially able to pay off their mortgages are often better off investing the money in a tax-advantaged investment vehicle and earning a spread between the after-tax income on the investment and the after-tax cost of the mortgage. Despite the possibility of earning this spread, some borrowers get great personal satisfaction from paying off the mortgage, and thus, may elect to pay it off despite the possibility of earning a spread. The number of non-economic prepayments is determined by:
  - the size of the spread that can be earned.
  - the "values" that the borrowers have in the region from which the mortgages originate.
  - the size of the mortgages in the pool (neither very small nor very large mortgages have significant non-economic prepayments).

- Seasonal factors. Because most people prefer to move in the summer, the prepayment speed of participation certificates rises in the summer and falls in the winter.

- The size of the mortgages. As the average size of the mortgages in the pool increases, so does the incentive to refinance if market interest rates decline. The reason that the incentive to refinance is greater for large mortgages than for small mortgages is that the savings generated by refinancing--relative to the costs of refinancing--are greater for larger mortgages. Consider the payback period (in months) of two different-sized, 30-year fixed-rate mortgages if they are refinanced from 12% to 9%. The below calculation assumes the refinancing cost is $2,000 in fixed costs, plus one point. (Note, for the sake of simplicity, Table 17.6 ignores the impact of taxes and interest on interest.)

**Table 17.6** *Payback Period Calculation*

|  | Monthly Savings | Refinancing Costs | Payback Period |
|---|---|---|---|
| **$50,000** | $112.00 | $2,500.00 | 22.32 Months |
| **$250,000** | $559.98 | $4,500.00 | 8.04 Months |

- How over-collateralized the participation certificate is, and whether the surplus interest and principal payments are used to accelerate the prepayment of the participation certificates, or are accumulated in the trust account.

- The homogeneity of the mortgage pool. Mortgage pools vary widely regarding to the homogeneity of the mortgages that compose them. Some pools are composed of mortgages that have similar coupons, maturities, and sizes, and are originated in the same region of the country. Other pools are diversified regarding these criteria.

The degree of diversity of the mortgages within a pool will have a definite impact on the prepayment speed of the pool. Consider the following examples:

Suppose that there are two pools of mortgages, Pool A and Pool B. Pool A is composed exclusively of mortgages from northern New Jersey, whereas Pool B is composed of mortgages from around the country. If northern New Jersey should go into a deep recession, the speed of Pool A might increase sharply, whereas Pool B might be largely unaffected.

Suppose that we have two other pools, Pool C and Pool D. Pool C is composed exclusively of mortgages with 11% coupons, whereas Pool D is composed of equal portions of mortgages with 12% and 10% coupons. If market interest rates decline to the 10% level, the speed of Pool D will increase, because some of the 12% mortgages will be refinanced. Pool C will probably not be significantly influenced because saving 1% is usually not enough of an incentive to refinance.

However, if market interest rates decline to 9%, Pool C will experience a dramatic increase in speed, whereas the speed of Pool D may actually decline, because after the 12% mortgages are refinanced, only the 10% mortgages will remain.

It should also be noted that because the economic, social, and demographic trends are all constantly changing, so does the probability that a given mortgage, with a given size and property-loan ratio, in a given region of the country, will be paid off or refinanced within a given time period. Thus, historical data about the prepayment speed of a pool of mortgages is of limited use when it comes to predicting the future prepayment speed. *To successfully invest in mortgage pools, some predictions about the future prepayment speed of specific mortgage pools must be made.*

To try to predict the future prepayment speed of various mortgage pools, investors and dealers have developed very sophisticated economic models that process an incredible amount of economic data. Several firms, most notably Citicorp, Inc.®, have a strategic advantage in this market, because they originate and service millions of mortgages all over the country. Because Citicorp, Inc.® is servicing these mortgages, it is in an excellent position to collect and analyze prepayment data in order to predict the future prepayment speeds of various mortgage pools and participation certificates.

## QUOTING PREPAYMENT SPEED

Because the prepayment speed of a participation certificate is so important, several methods have been developed for quoting this speed. The first method is referred to as the Federal Housing Administration (FHA) method, and is based on data collected by that organization over the past 17 years. According to the FHA's data, the average life of a pool of mortgages is currently about nine years. Thus, investors who buy a participation certificate backed by a typical pool of mortgages can expect to receive approximately 50% of their principal back in nine years. A mortgage pool whose speed is equal to the FHA average is described as a 100% FHA pool. Consider the following:

A pool whose speed was twice as fast as the FHA average (i.e., where 50% of the mortgage's principal was paid back in 4.5 years) would be described as a 200% FHA pool. A pool with no prepayments would be described as a 0% FHA pool. A pool whose speed was halfway between a 100% and a 50% FHA pool would be described as a 50% FHA pool.

Note that as the speed of the pool becomes faster, the shape of the path moves from being concave to convex when viewed from beneath.

**Figure 17.3** *Various Prepayment Speeds*

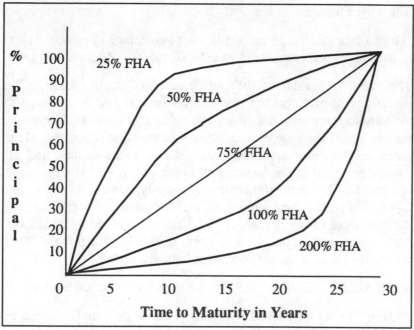

Once the speed of the pool is determined and its path plotted, it is relatively easy to estimate how much principal remains outstanding at any point along the life of the pool. Once the outstanding principal is determined, the monthly interest, and thus the total monthly cash flow, can also be determined.

Two other methods of quoting speed are the Public Securities Association (PSA) method and the Constant Prepayment Rate (CPR) method. Under the PSA method, the prepayment speed is assumed to escalate for the first six years and then remain fixed thereafter. The CPR method assumes no prepayment for the first 12 years, and then 100% prepayment. (There is also a modified CPR method that projects prepayment speed using the previous year's data.) Most bond software packages readily convert a speed quote determined using one method into a speed quote determined using another.

# DETERMINING THE PURCHASE PRICE OF A PARTICIPATION CERTIFICATE

The price of a participation certificate can be calculated by the following formula:

(Initial face amount of the certificate * Percentage of principal that has not yet been repaid * Agreed upon price) + Accrued interest

The initial face value of the certificate is, of course, known. The percentage of principal that has not yet been repaid is provided by the various intermediaries in a publication that they distribute after each month's mortgage payments are collected and processed. These remaining balances are commonly referred to as factors, and are usually provided to the hundred millionth of a point. The price that is agreed to by both participants is usually quoted in points and 32nds of a point. The accrued interest due the seller is calculated in the traditional manner. Thus, if an investor purchased a 9% $25,000 participation certificate with a factor of 0.897556 for a price of 92.16 points, the price of the security, in dollars, would be:

$25,000 * 0.897556 * 0.925 = $20,755.98 + accrued interest

Although mortgage backed pass through securities can be purchased any business day, they usually only settle one day a month because the remaining factors have to be released by the intermediaries before settlement can occur.

# YIELD CALCULATION CONSIDERATIONS

In the section on prepayment speed, we examined how, given the pool's speed, we could calculate the monthly cash flows that a pool of mortgages would generate. If we compare the total dollar return (T$R) of a $100,000 investment in 30-year 11% Treasury Bonds to the T$R of a $100,000 investment in a pool of 11% fixed-rate, 30-year mortgages, the cash flow patterns would be as follows (assuming that there is an 8% reinvestment rate):

**Table 17.7**  *Bond Versus Mortgage Investment*

|  | P | I | IOI | Total |
|---|---|---|---|---|
| **Bond** | $1,000 | $3,300 | $9,789 | $14,089 |
| **Mortgage** | $1,000 | $2,397 | $10,688 | $14,085 |

By examining the preceding table, some observations become apparent

- The T$R of the two investments is nearly identical.
- The P components of the two investments are equal.
- The I component of the Treasury Bond exceeds that of the mortgage pass-through because the pass-through security is a self-liquidating investment.
- The IOI component of the mortgage pass-through exceeds that of the Treasury Bond because the pass-through has monthly compounding, and because the principal of the pass-through can be reinvested.

Because the IOI component of the mortgage pass-through makes up a substantially higher percentage of the investment's T$R than the IOI component of the Treasury Bond, and because the IOI component is the least certain of the three components of return, the return from the mortgage pass-through is much less predictable than the return from the Treasury Bonds. Part of the reason that pass-throughs offer a higher yield than Treasuries is to compensate investors for this uncertainty.

## DOLLAR ROLLS

An inventory of participation certificates will typically be financed by executing transactions that are referred to as *dollar rolls*. As with repurchase agreements, in a dollar roll, securities are delivered to a lender in order to secure a loan and then, when the loan is paid off, securities are returned to the borrower. However, although dollar rolls have the same basic structure as repos, they are different from repos in three important ways:

- First, unlike repos, dollar rolls are generally not over-collateralized. Borrowers generally post a dollar of collateral (market value) for each dollar that they borrow.

- Second, in a dollar roll, the person who holds the securities as collateral is entitled to the interest and principal that the securities pay while they hold them. In a repo, the registered owner is still entitled to the interest payments, although the securities are being held by the lender. Because the monthly interest payment from a participation certificate is so high, the lender would be overcompensated if it kept all of the interest and bought and sold the securities at the same price. To bring the lender's return into line with its relatively low level of risk in this transaction, the lender frequently sells the securities back to the borrower at a lower price than it originally paid for them.

- Third, in a repo, the securities that are returned to the borrower are generally the same securities that are lent. In a dollar roll, the securities that the lender returns to the borrower must be very similar and, thus, lenders have the opportunity to upgrade their portfolios by entering into dollar rolls.

## SPECIAL RESERVIST CLAUSES

A special provision in the laws that apply to the activation of military reservists limits the interest rate that lenders can charge them on mortgages to 6%. The question is, if this rate is reduced to 6%, what impact, if any, does this have on the investors who own participation certificates?

The answer is that this provision has no impact on investors. If the intermediary is GNMA, the mortgage issuer is responsible for making up the difference between the 6% that the reservist pays and the mortgage's actual coupon. The reason that the issuer is liable is that GNMA is considered a conduit for the sale of mortgages by issuers, not an issuer itself. In the case of FNMAs and FHLMCs, the difference is made up by the intermediary, because these intermediaries actually purchase the underlying mortgages and are therefore considered the issuers of record.

# FUTURE OF THE SECURITIZATION BUSINESS

There will be no shortage of opportunities to securitize pools of mortgages in the future. There are several reasons for this.

Mortgages generally make up the largest percentage of the liquid assets that are held by the savings and loan institutions. Given that many of these institutions are seeking to raise capital, there should be no shortage of offerings stemming from the savings and loan industry.

- Many commercial banks need to increase their capital (as a percentage of assets) in order to comply with new international banking standards. In addition to mortgage backed securities, these institutions will probably increase their offerings of securities backed by charge cards, car loans, boat loans, and so on.

- The Resolution Trust Corporation will need to dispose of approximately 100 billion dollars worth of mortgages (as well as billions of dollars worth of other assets). Many of these will be disposed of as mortgage-backed securities.

Undoubtedly, there will continue to be a number of exciting developments in this field.

# 18

# COLLATERALIZED MORTGAGE OBLIGATIONS

## INTRODUCTION

In the previous chapter, participation certificates were shown to overcome two of the five major obstacles (credit risk and size of investment) that had impeded the development of a liquid secondary market for individual mortgages. Although participation certificates did not overcome all five obstacles to liquidity, they did overcome enough of the obstacles to allow a multihundred billion dollar market for participation certificates to develop. Although participation certificates were, and still are, a great success story, many investors have elected to avoid them because they believe that the three remaining obstacles (prepayment, accounting, and taxation) outweighed the benefits that participation certificates offered.

Because of the tremendous number of mortgages that mortgage issuers had accumulated in their portfolios, and because of the tremendous amount of pressure that they felt to sell those mortgages, the issuers quickly issued hundreds of billions of dollars of participation certificates and, in doing so, quickly saturated the market. As the participation certificate market became saturated, mortgage issuers realized that in order to expand the secondary market for mortgages even further, they were going to have to "go back to the drawing board" and design new types of mortgage-backed securities that appealed to new categories of investors.

These "second generation" mortgage-backed securities are collectively referred to as Collateralized Mortgage Obligations (CMOs), and are defined as Corporate Bonds that are secured, directly or indirectly, by mortgage loans. The mortgage loans that secure CMOs can either be a pool of individual loans or a participation certificate(s). The main difference between partici-

259

pation certificates and CMOs is that instead of investors purchasing an undivided interest in a pool of mortgages, they buy traditional bonds that are, in turn, secured by a pool of mortgages.

# HOW CMOS OVERCOME THE OBSTACLES TO LIQUIDITY OF MORTGAGES

## Credit Obstacle of Individual Mortgages

The credit problem of investing in individual mortgages is solved the same way for CMOs as it is for mortgage pass-throughs. A financial intermediary, either private or government-sponsored, usually guarantees the underlying mortgages, largely eliminating the credit risk inherient in the underlying mortgages.

## Tax Obstacle of Individual Mortgages

As with traditional bonds, most CMOs pay interest on a straight semiannual basis. The interest payments are not front-loaded, and so neither is the investor's tax liability. Thus, CMOs have a tax advantage relative to both individual mortgages and participation securities.

## Accounting Obstacle of Individual Mortgages

As with traditional bonds, the principal of CMOs is returned in one payment when the bond is called. Because there are no intermittent principal cash flows, the accounting treatment of CMOs is much simpler than that of either individual mortgages or participation certificates

## Prepayment Obstacle of Individual Mortgages

Although CMOs are structured as traditional semiannual bonds, the mortgages that secure them will still experience both the usual pay-down of principal and principal prepayments. Thus, any CMO structure must be designed to accommodate this paydown of principal.

## Size Obstacle of Individual Mortgages

As with traditional bonds, CMOs are sold in $1,000 denominations and, thus, are within the reach of nearly every investor.

# STRUCTURING COLLATERALIZED MORTGAGE OBLIGATIONS

The simplest CMO structure is to place the collateral into a trust account and then issue one class of bonds that are secured by the trust. With a single-class CMO, when principal comes into the trust account, either as a result of the regular pay-down of the underlying mortgages or from prepayments, that principal is used to call as many of the CMOs as possible. These calls are generally random, and are done in concordance with the semiannual payment.

For example, suppose $1,000,000 (face value) of mortgages were placed in a trust account and 1,000 bonds were issued, secured by the account. During the first six months of the CMOs life, if $15,670 of principal came into the trust, the issuer could then call 15 bonds when it paid its first interest payment. During the next six months, if an additional $18,700 of principal was collected, after one year an additional 19 bonds could be called.

Given the speed of the underlying mortgage pools, the expected maturities and expected average life of the whole CMO can be easily estimated. Although the expected average life of the entire CMO is easy to determine, it is often of little practical value to investors because

- knowing the expected average life of the whole CMO tells investors little about the expected life of the specific bonds that they own. The bonds that they own may be the first or last bonds called. (Note that if an investor buys an entire CMO issue, then statistically, the average life of the individual bonds will equal the average life of the whole issue.)
- the speed on the underlying mortgages will probably change over time, and as it does, the expected average life of the whole CMO will change, as well.

Thus, whereas this simple CMO structure overcomes four of the five obstacles to the creation of a liquid market for mortgages that we identified in the previous chapter (i.e., credit, size, tax, and accounting), the fifth problem--prepayment--is actually aggravated by this structure. Thus, this structure appeals to investors who are concerned about the accounting and tax obstacles of mortgage investments, but not about prepayment risk.

Because this CMO structure overcomes more of the obstacles to liquidity than participation certificates, investors are willing to accept a lower yield from these CMOs than they are from participation certificates. Thus, an issuer that elects to issue CMOs instead of participation certificates can often earn a higher spread between the collateral and the bonds than it can between the collateral and the participation certificates.

Because this structure exacerbates the prepayment problem, it has limited appeal. Therefore, most issuers elect to do some additional financial engineering in order to overcome the prepayment obstacle. The most common way of overcoming the prepayment obstacle of CMOs is to divide the bonds into classes and assign each class of bonds a different priority with regard to being called. (These classes are often referred to as *tranches*--from the French word for "slice.")

For example, if the preceding CMO was divided into five equal tranches, its structure might resemble the following:

**Table 18.1** *Tranche Structure*

| Tranche | A | B | C | D | E |
|---|---|---|---|---|---|
| Size (000s) | $200 | $200 | $200 | $200 | $200 |
| Coupon (%) | 8 | 8.5 | 9 | 9.5 | 10 |
| Average Maturity (Years) | 1.4 | 4.5 | 8.1 | 13.4 | 20.1 |
| Expected Maturity (Years) | 3 | 6.1 | 10.5 | 16.5 | 26.1 |
| Maximum Maturity (Years) | 15 | 18.2 | 22.4 | 27.3 | 30 |

Given the speed of the underlying pool, we can calculate

- when the last bond in each tranche should be called (i.e., the tranche's expected maturity).
- the expected average life of the bonds in each tranche. (Note that because the prepayment curve is not linear, the average life is not simply the tranche's midpoint.)

For example, if the underlying mortgage pool had a 100% FHA speed, the expected maturity and average life of each tranche could be determined by simply examining the prepayment curve of the pool. Because different tranches will have different expected average lives and expected maturities, investors can chose the tranche whose characteristics best match their objectives. The expected average life is only an *estimate* of a specific bond's maturity because

- a specific bond within a tranche can be the first or last one called. Thus, there is still a lot of variability regarding the maturity of a specific bond.
- the prepayment speed of the underlying mortgages will change and, as it does, so will the expected average lives of the tranches and the individual bonds.

**Figure 18.1**  *Life of Various Tranches*

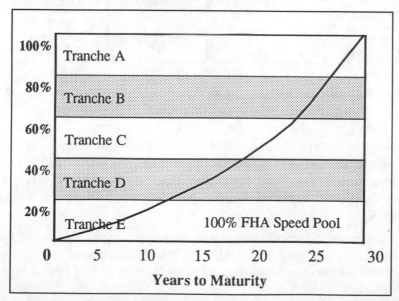

## Altering the Expected Average Life and Maturity of a CMO's Tranches

The expected average life and maturity of tranches can also be altered in order to meet the needs of either the investors or issuers. Some of the popular methods of altering the average life of a tranche(s) are

- changing the underlying collateral. The simplest way of increasing or decreasing the average life and expected maturity of all of the tranches of a CMO is to use a faster or slower pool of mortgages (or participation certificates) as the underlying collateral. However, any collateral substitutions need to be done before the CMOs are offered for final sale.

- changing the size of the tranches. By changing the size of the tranches, the expected average life can be changed. For example, suppose that in the preceding example, the size of Tranche A was reduced by 50%, and the size of Tranche B was increased by 50%. The average, expected, and maximum would become:

**Table 18.2** *Impact of Changing Tranche Size*

| Tranche | Average Maturity (years) | Expected Maturity (years) | Maximum Maturity (years) |
|---------|--------------------------|---------------------------|--------------------------|
| A | 0.8 | 2 | 10.2 |
| B | 3.5 | 6.1 | 18.2 |

Note that by reducing the size of the first tranche, both its average life and expected maturity are shortened. However, whereas the average life of the second tranche is also shortened, its expected maturity remains unchanged. Later tranches are unaffected by changing the sizes of the first two tranches in this manner. Similarly, if the sizes of two later tranches were changed, it would have no impact on the expected average life or maturities of the earlier tranches.

- changing the number of tranches. As with changing the size of the tranches, changing the number of tranches can also increase or decrease the expected average life and/or maturity of one or more tranches.

- making the last tranche or tranche(s) Zero Coupon tranches. If the last tranche is composed of ZCBs, commonly referred to as Z-bonds, the interest that would have been paid on these bonds is "freed up," and can be used to accelerate the call schedule of the bonds in Tranche A.

For example, suppose that in the preceding example, the last tranche (Tranche E) was a Zero Coupon tranche. If the last tranche is a Z-Bond, then the money that would have been used to make interest payments on the Tranche E bonds can instead be used to call the Tranche A bonds faster than anticipated. Thus, the bonds in Tranche A will all be called before $200,000 of principal is actually paid by the borrowers. Because the bonds in Tranche A are retired faster, the holders of Tranche A bonds receive interest payments for a shorter period of time. The interest that they would have received can therefore be used to retire the Tranche B bonds faster. Similarly, the shortening of the average life of the Tranche B bonds results in interest savings that can be used, in turn, to shorten the life of the Tranche C bonds and then, in turn, the Tranche D bonds. Finally, the interest savings on the Tranche D bonds can be used to make up the discounts on the Tranche E Z-Bonds.

Making sure that enough interest is saved over the lives of the earlier tranches to make up the discount on the Z-Bonds requires knowledgeable maneuvers, particularly when the speed of the underlying mortgages can change.

- changing the amount of over-collateralization. In order to provide CMO investors with credit protection, most CMOs are over-collateralized. Thus, $100 million in CMOs might be secured with $110 million of mortgages or $110 million of participation certificates. Depending on how the CMO is structured, the surplus interest and principal can either be used to accelerate the call schedule of the CMOs, or it can accumulate in the trust and be reinvested until the CMO is terminated. By altering the percentage of the surplus that is accumulated and the percentage that is used to accelerate the life of the bonds, the expected average life and expected maturity of the tranches can be altered.

By working with the preceding factors, the average life of either some, or all of, the tranches can be adjusted to create securities that have the average lives desired by the issuers and/or investors. Although these steps can adjust the average life of the tranches, there will still be some degree of uncertainty as to the bond's average life and maturity because the speed of the underlying mortgages can change, and because the bonds in each tranche are usually called in random order. For those investors who require a greater degree of certainty regarding the maturity of their bonds, more financial engineering is required.

We can take the preceding CMO structure one step further by subdividing a regular tranche into two sub-tranches in which one has a more reliable and predictable average life and expected maturity than the regular tranche, and the other has a more variable average life and expected maturity than the regular tranche.

For example, we could take Tranche C in the preceding example and divide it into two sub-tranches: Sub-tranche $C_1$ and Sub-tranche $C_2$. By splitting the volatility of Tranche C unequally between the two sub-tranches, we can create a very *predictable* sub-tranche and a very *volatile* sub-tranche.

The volatility of the regular tranche is divided unequally by accelerating or delaying the call schedule of the $C_2$ bonds, so that the call schedule of the $C_1$ bonds can remain constant despite changes in the speed of the underlying mortgages. For example,

- if the speed of the underlying mortgages is faster than expected, the call schedule of the $C_2$ bonds will be delayed so that the average life of the $C_1$ bonds can remain unchanged.

- if the speed of the underlying mortgages is slower than expected, the call schedule of the $C_2$ bonds will be accelerated so that the average life of the $C_1$ bonds can remain unchanged.

However, there are limits to how much the speed of the underlying mortgages can change before the average life of the $C_1$ bonds will be influenced because there are limits to how much volatility the call schedule of the $C_2$ bonds can absorb. In order to absorb additional volatility, some CMOs use the surplus account in the trust to provide or capture the cash flows that are necessary to keep the average life and expected maturity of the $C_1$ bonds from deviating from their expected values.

The highly predictable $C_1$ bonds are commonly referred to either as Planned Amortization Certificates (PACs) or Targeted Amortization Certificates (TACs), depending on how much volatility the structure of the CMO can absorb. The tranches that have the highly variable average lives are referred to as "companion tranches."

Thus, by careful design, a CMO can be created that includes a tranche that offers both the average life that the investor wants and a high degree of certainty that the average life will be maintained despite changes in the speed of the underlying mortgages (i.e., low variability). By eliminating the last obstacle, *every investor is a potential source of liquidity for mortgage issuers.*

## SETTING THE INITIAL YIELDS OF CMOS

When investment bankers structure CMO offerings, they try to balance the demands of the issuers against the demands of the investors. The issuers, understandably, want to maximize the return that they earn on the CMOs that they issue. The larger the difference between the number of dollars that the collateral generates and the number of dollars that the issuer has to pay to the bondholders, the more the issuer earns. In other words, in this example, the greater the number of dollars that are left in the trust after that last bond has been called, the greater the issuer's return.

The remaining value of the trust after all of the bonds have been called are referred to as the trust's *residual value* or, more simply, its residual. In order to maximize the value of the residual, the issuers and their agents employ very sophisticated computer-based "optimization software." The investors, on the other hand, want the bonds issued as part of CMO offerings to have attractive investment characteristics (attractive average lives, minimal variability, minimal credit risk, and high coupons).

Because the average life of a CMO can be adjusted by financial engineering, an investor can request that an investment banking firm create an investment with an average maturity that it wants, but is not readily available in the market. For example, a portfolio manager that needed a specific maturity in order to complete a committed portfolio would probably accept a lower yield in exchange for obtaining a bond with the maturity that it needed. In exchange for obtaining a specific average life, the investor might be asked to sacrifice some return. Thus, issuers, by designing their CMOs to meet the specific needs of an investor, can increase the return on their offerings and make their CMOs a win-win situation.

Because the variability of a CMO's maturity can be adjusted by financial engineering, an investor can select the variability that it wants. Again, generally, the lower the variability, the lower the coupon. For example, PACs always yield less than their companion tranches. Thus, investors face a clear trade-off between yield and variability.

# RESIDUALS

As mentioned previously, the residual value of a CMO is equal to the surplus cash flow remaining in the trust after all of the bonds have been called. For a deal to be profitable for the issuer, the proceeds of the bond sale, plus the value of the residual, must exceed the cost of the collateral and all other costs, expenses, and overhead.

Issuers go to great lengths to maximize the residual value of their CMO deals. They frequently employ sophisticated optimization techniques and complicated financial models in order to design the structure that maximizes their return. Some of the factors that influence the value of the residual are included in Table 18.3.

**Table 18.3** *Influencing the Value of the Residual*

| Factors Influencing the Value of the Residual | Direction of Factor | Value of Residual |
|---|---|---|
| The Collateral / CMO Yield Spread | Increases | Increases |
| Prepayment Speed of Pool | Increases | Decreases |
| Percentage of Over-Collateralization | Increases | Increases |
| Number of Defaults | Increases | Decreases |
| Reinvestment Rate | Increases | Increases |
| Percentage of Defaults Covered by Insurance | Increases | Increases |
| Percentage of Surplus Principal Used for Prepayments | Increases | Decreases |
| Percentage of Surplus Interest Used for Prepayments | Increases | Decreases |

Whereas the reason that most of these factors have the impact that they do is obvious, one of them requires additional explanation: the prepayment speed of a pool. Usually, the longer a tranche exists, the longer the period of time that the issuer earns the spread between the yield generated by the collateral and the yield paid on the bond.

When homeowners pay down (or pay off) their mortgages and the principal is used to call the bonds in a CMO offering, the investors' cash flow ceases (so does the issuers'). The issuer no longer receives any interest on the principal and so cannot make a spread. For this reason, issuers prefer to use mortgages whose speed is expected to decline as collateral for their CMOs.

When the speed of the underlying mortgages changes, so will the average life of the bonds. As the average life of the bonds changes, so does the value of the residual. In fact, because of the way CMOs are structured, even a small change in the average life of the bonds can have a very significant impact on the value of the residual. Thus, residuals tend to be very volatile instruments. Despite their high volatility, there is now a well-developed market for residuals, and there are even mutual funds that invest primarily in residuals. Thus, issuers can sell their CMOs and residuals simultaneously and make their profit immediately, rather than waiting for the mortgages to run their course.

## FLOATING-RATE TRANCHES

Although this chapter has focused on fixed-rate CMOs, there is also a very large market for floating-rate CMOs and floating-rate tranches. There are two ways to create floating-rate tranches. First, to simply use floating-rate mortgages as collateral for the issue, and then every tranche can be a floating-rate tranche. For example, if a trust account had $1,000,000 of ARMs that were yielding the 1-year T-Bill rate plus 200 bp, the tranches in Table 18.4 could be created.

In addition, floating-rate tranches can be created from fixed-rate tranches by dividing the fixed-rate tranches into floating-rate tranches and reverse floating-rate tranches. Consider the following example following Table 18.4:

**Table 18.4** *Hypothetical Floating Rate Tranches*

| Tranche | Yield Formula |
|---------|---------------|
| ARM-T1 | 1-year T-Bill +  25 bp |
| ARM-T2 | 1-year T-Bill +  50 bp |
| ARM-T3 | 1-year T-Bill + 100 bp |
| ARM-T4 | 1-year T-Bill + 125 bp |
| ARM-T5 | 1-year T-Bill + 175 bp |

Suppose that an issuer is about to create a CMO and one of the tranches is a $200,000 9% tranche with a 10-year expected average life. If the 1-year T-Bill rate were 8%, then this tranche could be divided into two $100,000 tranches, Sub-tranche A and Sub-tranche B, and the yield formula for each tranche would be:

**Table 18.5** *Floater and Reverse Floater Formulas*

| Tranche | Yield Formula |
|---------|---------------|
| Sub-tranche A | 1-year T-Bill Rate + 100 bp |
| Sub-tranche B | 18% - (1-year T-Bill Rate + 100 bp) |

Initially, both tranches would yield 9%. As the T-Bill rate changes, so would the yield on the two tranches. If the T-Bill rate rose to 10%, then Sub-tranche A would yield 11%, while Sub-tranche B would yield 7%. Because of the way that the yield formulas are defined, although the two yields would change, they would always average 9%.

# INTEREST ONLY / PRINCIPAL ONLY BONDS

There is another way to turn the cash flows derived from a pool of mortgages into bonds. Instead of issuing traditional bonds that are secured by the mortgages, an issuer can elect to issue bonds that are backed exclusively by either the principal cash flows or the interest cash flows coming from the collateral. Bonds that are secured by the principal cash flows are referred to as *Principal Only Bonds* (POs), and bonds that are secured by the interest payments are referred to as

*Interest Only Bonds* (IOs). Generally, both types of bonds are issued as ZCBs. Consider the following simple example:

Suppose that an issuer had a $1,000,000 pool of mortgages and wanted to issue two bonds: a PO Bond and an IO Bond. Suppose also that both bonds were sold for $500,000 each. The portfolio manager who purchased the PO Bond would receive 100% of the principal that came from the trust account, whereas the portfolio manager who purchased the IO Bond would receive 100% of the interest.

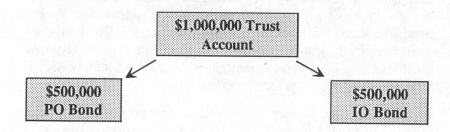

## PO Bonds

The portfolio manager who purchases the PO Bond knows that the bond will double in value. Because there are $1,000,000 worth of mortgages in the pool and, eventually, all of the mortgages will be paid off, the manger who buys the PO Bond will eventually receive $1,000,000. The question with POs, of course, is how long will it take to double the investment. Doubling an investment in one year provides a terrific annualized rate of return. Conversely, doubling an investment in 30 years provides a horrible rate of return. It should be remembered also that the first $500,000 that the PO Bond investor receives represents the return of the investor's capital.

Naturally, PO Bond investors hope that the underlying mortgages will be paid off quickly and, thus, that their annualized rate of return will be higher. PO Bond investors are aided by a decline in interest rates in two ways: First, as interest rates decline, refinancing becomes a more attractive alternative for homeowners, increasing the probability that the mortgages will be paid off. Second, as interest rates decline, the yield on the PO Bond becomes comparatively more attractive. Thus, when investors are seeking attractive PO Bond opportunities, they look for bonds secured by mortgage pools that are likely to experience increases in prepayment speeds.

## IO Bonds

Initially, the portfolio manager who purchases the IO Bond will receive more than a 20% rate of return. After all, the IO Bond receives all of the interest coming from the trust account (initially 10.25% on $1,000,000). Of course, the IO Bond only continues to receive interest as long as the principal remains outstanding. As the mortgages are paid down, the interest flow declines, and when the last mortgage payment is made, the cash flow stops. Like the PO Bond, the first $500,000 of interest that the IO Bond investor receives is really just the return of the investor's capital. Thus, IO Bond investors hope that the mortgages are paid off slowly so that they receive interest for a longer period of time.

Because one of the primary factors determining prepayment speed is the level of market interest rates, IO Bond investors actually hope that market interest rates will increase. Within certain limitations, as market interest rates rise, the value of IO Bonds also rises. Thus, IO Bonds can be, under certain circumstances, an effective vehicle for hedging traditional bond portfolios.

## Evaluating IO and PO Bonds

In reality, IO Bonds and PO Bonds will not be equally valuable. Depending on the projected speed of the mortgages and the projected principle and interest cash flows, either the PO Bond or the IO Bond may be more valuable. (Like all fixed-income investments, the value of these bonds is equal to the present value of their projected future cash flows.)

Because PO and IO Bonds are not equally valuable, they are not sold for the same price. Instead, the difference in their values can be accommodated in one of two ways:

- They can be sold at different prices as long as the sum plus the value of the residual exceeds the cost of the collateral and expenses. (Otherwise, the issuer would not be able to make a profit on the transaction.)

- The split between them may be less than complete. For example, if the PO side were considered more valuable than the IO side, Bond A might receive 95% of the principal, whereas Bond B might receive 100% of the interest and 5% of the principal.

## PO and IO Bond Tranches

Principal Only and Interest Only Bonds can also be divided into tranches. Establishing IO/PO tranches can be a win-win situation. The issuers can earn a higher spread and the investors can buy bonds whose characteristics match their needs.

Tranches can be established on a time or dollar basis. Time tranches are divided on a time basis wherein the investors receive either all of the interest, or all of the principal, that comes from the trust between two specific dates. Dollar tranches are divided on a dollar basis, meaning that the first tranche receives a certain amount of dollars, then the next tranche receives a certain amount of dollars, and so on. (Because the total amount of interest that will be recieved is not known, there may not be any interest left for Tranche IO-5.)

**Table 18.6** *Time Tranche Structure*

| Tranche | Time (years) | Tranche | Time (years) |
|---------|--------------|---------|--------------|
| PO-1 | < 6 | IO-1 | < 2 |
| PO-2 | 6 - 10 | IO-2 | 3 - 6 |
| PO-3 | 11 - 14 | IO-3 | 7 - 11 |
| PO-4 | 15 - 20 | IO-4 | 12 - 17 |
| PO-5 | 20 - 30 | IO-5 | 18 - 20 |

**Table 18.7** *Dollar Tranche Structure*

| Tranche | Amount | Tranche | Amount |
|---------|--------|---------|--------|
| PO-1 | $200,000 | IO-1 | $200,000 |
| PO-2 | $200,000 | IO-2 | $200,000 |
| PO-3 | $200,000 | IO-3 | $200,000 |
| PO-4 | $200,000 | IO-4 | $200,000 |
| PO-5 | $200,000 | IO-5 | ? |

# COMPARISON WITH MANUFACTURING

Collateralized mortgage obligations are probably best thought of as a "manufactured product." Starting with basic materials (i.e., a pool of mortgages), financial engineers proceed to manufacture bonds that are designed to meet specific objectives. Ideally, the process is an all around win situation in which the mortgage issuers, homeowners, investors, and the whole economy, benefit.

# PART IV
## Derivative Instruments

# 19

# YIELD CURVE ANALYSIS

## INTRODUCTION

The relationship between yield to maturity is expressed graphically by the traditional yield curve,. The study of this and other yield curves is referred to as "yield curve analysis," and is an important component of fixed income research. While some market participants believe that much can be learned from analyzing yield curves, others disagree. Both points of view are presented in this chapter.

Proponents of yield curve analysis argue that it is useful in determining:

- the optimum mixture of maturities to be included in a bond offering.
- the "market's consensus" with regard to the future level of interest rates.
- the "fair" market value of a bond.
- whether a particular bond offers an attractive risk/reward ratio.

Detractors of yield curve analysis argue that yield curve analysis is largely a waste of time. Before the pros and cons can be determined, however, the relationship between risk and reward must be understood. Although there are many ways to explore this relationship, there is no single best way.

## THE TRADITIONAL YIELD CURVE

Perhaps the most common way of exploring the relationship between risk and reward is with the traditional yield curve, which is created by plotting the Yield Term Maturity (YTMs) of similar bonds (same type of issuer, same credit quality, and so on) against their maturities, and then drawing the best line (determined via regression analysis) through the resultant data points.

**Figure 19.1** *Fitting a Yield Curve to the Data*

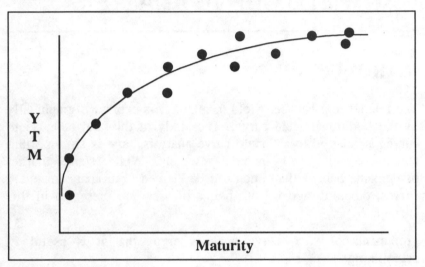

In the United States, the most commonly examined yield curve is the U.S. Treasury Bond Yield Curve. This yield curve is interesting not only to those who participate in the Treasury Bond market, but also to anyone who invests in any fixed-income instrument, because almost all American dollar fixed-income instruments are priced off of the Treasury Bond Yield Curve.

The U.S. Treasury Bond Yield Curve changes every time the YTM of any U.S. Treasury Bond changes. Yield curves can undergo two types of changes: parallel and non-parallel shifts. Parallel shifts occur when the yield curve shifts up or down (i.e., when market interest rates increase or decrease) without a change in the basic shape of the yield curve. Non-parallel shifts occur when short-term rates move up and long-term rates move down, and vice versa.

If short-term rates are lower than long-term rates, the yield curve is said to have a positive slope. If the relationship between short-term and long-term rates is reversed, the yield curve is said to have a negative slope. If short-term and long-term rates are the same, the yield curve will be flat.

# EXPLAINING THE SHAPE OF THE TREASURY YIELD CURVE

Over the years, many theories have been proposed to explain why and how the slope of the yield curve changes. Three common theories are the Future Expectations Theory, Liquidity Theory, and Preferred Habitat Theory.

## Future Expectations Theory

Perhaps the most widely accepted theory among investors is the Future Expectations Theory. According to this theory, if the market consensus is that interest rates will go up, the yield curve will have a positive slope. The reason for the positive slope is that if investors expect rates to rise, they will prefer to keep the maturities of their investments very short and wait until rates are higher before making long-term investments. Because the majority of investors prefer to make short-term investments, the law of supply and demand will push the yield of short-term paper down, and the yield of long-term paper up.

Using the same logic, when presented with an inverted yield curve, proponents of the Futures Expectation Theory would argue that the market consensus would be that interest rates would decline. Because market rates would be expected to decline, investors would favor long-term securities where they could lock in the current high returns for a longer period of time. As a result of investors expectations, short-term rates would rise due to a dearth of demand--while long-term rates would decline because of the increase in demand. A flat yield curve would indicate to proponents of this theory that investors expected no significant change in interest rates, and thus were ambivalent about the choice between short-term and long-term instruments.

Whereas this theory is logical and intellectually appealing, there are two significant disadvantages. First, there has not been a good historical correlation between the shape of the yield curve and the actual direction of future interest rate movements. Second, the yield curve is positively sloped about 80% of the time. Thus, in order for this theory to be valid, the market consensus opinion would have to be that market interest rates will rise 80% of the time. Because there is no rational reason that investors should expect interest rates to rise, nor any research to support this claim, it is evident that other factors--besides the market's consensus about future interest rates--have a significant impact on the shape of the yield curve.

## Liquidity Theory

The Liquidity Theory states that investors will sacrifice yield in order to obtain liquidity. Short-term instruments are generally more liquid than long-term instruments because they have two sources of liquidity (i.e., their rapid maturity and their secondary market), whereas long-term instruments are less liquid because they have only the secondary market to provide liquidity. Thus, according to this theory, short-term instruments should generally yield less than comparable long-term instruments. If this is true, the preference that investors have for the liquidity of short-term instruments should tend to exacerbate positively sloped yield curves and mitigate negatively sloped yield curves.

Further, if the market's consensus was that interest rates would remain flat, proponents of the Liquidity Theory argue that the yield curve would still have a positive slope because of the higher liquidity offered by short-term instruments. Only when the market's consensus was that interest rates would decline slightly would we expect to find a flat yield curve. Thus, this theory (when combined with the Futures Expectations Theory) does provide a logical and plausible explanation why the yield curve would mainly have a positive slope. Unfortunately, this theory provides no way to quantify how many basis points of yield investors are willing to sacrifice in order to increase the liquidity of their portfolios. In other words, there is no way to differentiate the impact that the market's consensus about future interest rates has on the shape of the yield curve from the impact that the investor's preference for more liquid investments has. Further, whereas it is reasonable to assume that at different times investors would be willing to sacrifice a different number of basis points in order to increase the liquidity of their portfolio, this theory provides no way to quantify how the price of liquidity changes over time.

Finally, this theory provides no plausible explanation for the irregularly shaped and humped yield curves that are sometimes observed in the market. Because neither the Future Expectations

Theory nor the Liquidity Preference Theory--nor the combination of the two--can adequately explain these unusual yield curves, there must be some other factor(s) involved in determining shapes of yield curves.

## Preferred Habitat Theory

The Preferred Habitat Theory states that, at different times, different types of investors will have a preference for investments with different maturities, because their needs and objectives will change. For example, as the average age of our population increases and the number of deaths per thousand increases, life insurance companies will develop a preference for short-term instruments because of their increased need for liquidity.

As another example, as 5-year interest rate swaps have become more popular, so have 5-year Treasury Bonds, because these can be used to hedge mismatched swap positions. Therefore, as the swap market continues to grow, it should have an increasing degree of impact on the yield of 5-year Treasury Bonds. The disadvantage of this theory is that any security that becomes mispriced because of an imbalance in supply and demand can be created synthetically via the derivatives market, thereby not explaining large humps in the yield curve.

Whereas all of these theories probably have an impact on the shape of the traditional yield curve, they are not the only theories. It is doubtful that there will be one theory (or even a collection of theories) that adequately explains the shape of the traditional yield curve.

# CONSTRUCTING THE TRADITIONAL YIELD CURVE

One of the principal disadvantages of the traditional Treasury Bond Yield Curve is that it is difficult to construct and also inaccurate. Whereas the Treasury Bond Market is composed of a fairly limited number of very liquid issues that are free of credit risk, the market is *not homogeneous*. The reason for this is that different Treasury Bonds have different coupons. Because a bond's coupon directly influences its value, when the data points are plotted, the resulting line is somewhat jagged. For example, two Treasury Bonds with nearly identical maturities, but very different coupons, would offer different YTMs.

Normally, the Treasury Bond Yield Curve is expressed as a smooth line. In order to convert the actual jagged data points into a smooth line, a variety of statistical and mathematical techniques, including regression techniques, are used. These statistical techniques generate the smooth line which best fits the data points. However, different market participants, using somewhat different statistical techniques, will generate yield curves with different shapes. In addition, if the data is subjected to too much "smoothing," investment opportunities may be overlooked.

Another way of looking at this is that yield curves are most illustrative when the data points are homogeneous--except the one being plotted. The bonds that are plotted in the traditional yield curve differ in two ways--coupon size and maturity--so therefore the curve is not smooth unless it is subjected to statistical techniques. Thus, yield curves can have a "bias" depending on which techniques are used to construct them. This bias naturally influences the accuracy of any analysis performed on a traditional yield curve. Even the most careful analysis will be limited in producing accurate results if it is based on biased or misleading data.

## THE SPOT YIELD CURVE

In addition to construction biases, traditional yield curves have a second drawback that limits their accuracy and, thus, their usefulness. Whereas traditional yield curves plot the YTMs against the maturities of the various Treasury issues, the YTM does not represent the true yield for a specific maturity. Instead, it is the "weighted average composite yield" of all the individual yields the investor receives on all the bond's individual cash flows. For example, suppose a 5-year Eurobond offers a 9% YTM. This does not mean that the 5-year yield is actually 9%, as would be indicated by a traditional yield curve. Instead, since Eurobonds have annual payments, this amount represents the weighted average yield of the bond's cash flows for years one through five. (Eurobonds generally only pay interest once per year.)

If the current Eurobond yield curve has a positive slope, we know that the early cash flows have true yields that are less than 9%. Therefore, in order for the weighted average yield of the bond's cash flows to be equal to 9%, the yields of the later cash flow must be greater. The question is, how much greater? Fortunately, there is a fairly simple way that one can calculate the true yield, also known as the "spot yield," for a specific maturity--assuming one has already constructed the traditional yield curve.

Consider the following:

We know from our discussion of YTM that the following equation is true:

$$\text{Bond Price} = \frac{CF(1)}{(1+y)^1} + \frac{CF(2)}{(1+y)^2} + \ldots + \frac{CF(n)}{(1+y)^n}$$

where,

$y$ = the bond's YTM per period
$CF(x)$ = the bond's cash flow

We also know that by definition:

$$\text{Bond Price} = \frac{CF(1)}{(1+y_1)^1} + \frac{CF(2)}{(1+y_2)^2} + \ldots + \frac{CF(n)}{(1+y_n)^n}$$

where,

$y_1$ = spot yield for cash flow #1 $\qquad$ $y_2$ = spot yield for cash flow #2
$y_n$ = spot yield for cash flow n $\qquad$ $CF(x)$ =the bond's cash flows

thus,

$$\frac{CF(1)}{(1+y)^1} + \frac{CF(2)}{(1+y)^2} + \ldots + \frac{CF(n)}{(1+y)^n} = \frac{CF(1)}{(1+y_1)^1} + \frac{CF(2)}{(1+y_2)^2} + \ldots + \frac{CF(3)}{(1+y_n)^n}$$

Since both of the equations are equal to the bond's price, they must also be equal to each other.

Thus, the sum of the periodic cashflows discounted by the bond's YTM is equal to the sum of the periodic cashflows discounted by their respective spot rates, and both of these sums are, in turn, equal to the bond's price. It is because of this relationship that we can readily determine the Spot Rate Yield Curve. Assuming that the following market data is accurate, let's determine the spot rates for each maturity.

**Table 19.1 *Traditional Yield Curve***

| Years to Maturity | Yield to Maturity | Coupon Rate | Price of Bond |
|---|---|---|---|
| 1 | 5.45% | 5.45% | $1,000 |
| 2 | 6.75% | 6.75% | $1,000 |
| 3 | 7.75% | 7.75% | $1,000 |
| 4 | 8.45% | 8.45% | $1,000 |
| 5 | 9.00% | 9.00% | $1,000 |

At the 1-year point, we know that the following equation must be true:

$$\frac{CF(1)}{(1+y)^1} = \frac{CF(1)}{(1+y_1)^1}$$

where,

$y$ = the YTM of the 1-year bond
$y_1$ = the spot yield at the 1-year point
$CF(1)$ = the cash flow at the 1-year point

From the preceding equation, it is obvious that the YTM and the spot yield must be identical for a bond with just one cash flow. Now that we know the 1-year spot rate, we can determine the 2-year spot rate by solving the following equation, which we know to be true for a 2-year bond:

$$\$1,000 = \frac{CF(1)}{(1+y_1)^1} + \frac{CF(2)}{(1+y_2)^2}$$

where,

$y_1$ = 1-year spot rate (equal to the 1-year YTM)
$y_2$ = 2-year spot rate
$CF(1)$ = cash flow #1 of a 2-year bond
$CF(2)$ = cash flow #2 of a 2-year bond

This equation has four variables. The values of the two cash flows can be calculated from the bond's coupon. The 1-year spot rate was calculated above, leaving only the 2-year spot rate as an unknown.

$$\$1000 = \frac{CF(1)}{(1+y_1)^1} + \frac{CF(2)}{(1+y_2)^2} = \frac{\$67.50}{(1+0.0545)^1} + \frac{\$1,067.50}{(1+y_2)^2}$$

$$\$1,000 = \$64.01 + \$1,067.50 / (1+y_2)^2$$
$$\$935.99 = \$1,067 / (1+y_2)^2$$
$$\$935.99 \times (1+y_2)^2 = \$1,067$$
$$(1+y_2)^2 = 1.14$$
$$1+y_2 = (1.14)^{1/2}$$
$$1+y_2 = 1.0679$$
$$y_2 = 0.0679$$
$$6.79\%$$

With the 2-year spot rate determined, it is now possible to determine the 3-year spot rate by expanding the preceding equation to include the third cash flow. For example:

$$\$1,000 = \frac{CF(1)}{(1+y_1)^1} + \frac{CF(2)}{(1+y_2)^2} + \frac{CF(3)}{(1+y_3)^3}$$

where,

$y_1 =$ 1-year spot rate (equal to the 1-year YTM)
$y_2 =$ 2-year spot rate (equal to the 2-year spot rate)
$y_3 =$ 3-year spot rate
$CF(1) =$ cash flow #1 of the 3-year bond
$CF(2) =$ cash flow #2 of the 3-year bond
$CF(3) =$ cash flow #3 of the 3-year bond

Of the six variables in the preceding equation, three are determined by examining the traditional yield curve, two were solved previously, and one is determined by solving the following equation:

$$\$1,000 = \frac{\$77.50}{(1 + .0545)^1} + \frac{\$77.50}{(1 + .0679)^2} + \frac{\$1,077.50}{(1 + y_3)^3}$$

$$\$1,000 = \$73.49 + \$67.96 + \$1,077.50 / (1 + y_3)^3$$
$$\$858.55 = \$1,077.50 / (1 + y_3)^3$$
$$(1 + y_3)^3 = 1.255$$
$$1 + y_3 = (1.255)^{1/3}$$
$$1 + y_3 = 1.0786$$
$$y_3 = 0.0786$$
$$7.86\%$$

Once the 3-year rate is determined, we can use this same method to determine the 4-year rate and the 5-year spot rate. Note that the spot rate yield curve, which is often referred to as "the term structure of interest rates," is higher than the traditional yield curve that utilizes composite yields. This makes sense because the 5-year spot rate is the true 5-year rate, whereas the traditional yield curve 5-year rate is a composite of the 1-year spot rate through the 5-year spot rate. (If the yield curve were inverted, the spot curve would be below the traditional yield curve for the same reason.)

## Spot Rates and Zero Coupon Bonds

The closest approximation of the term-structure of interest rates or the Spot Rate Yield Curve that exists is the Treasury Zero Coupon Bond (ZCB) Yield Curve. ZCBs have only one cash flow and thus are, in effect, spot payments that have specific maturity. Because ZCBs all have the same coupon, they theoretically have only one variable: their maturity. Because ZCBs are so homogeneous, a ZCB Yield Curve is less jagged than a yield curve composed of bonds with various coupons.

Because for ZCBs the traditional yield curve and the Spot Rate Yield Curve are the same, the ZCB Yield Curve tends to be a very close approximation of the term-structure of interest rates generated in the previous section. However, it is important to note that the ZCB Yield Curve is not an exact replication of the term-structure of interest rates. There are three major reasons for this: ZCBs are created in a variety of ways, have relatively high dealer spreads, and are very difficult to arbitrage.

## Zero Coupon Bonds Created in a Variety of Ways

Zero Coupon Bonds were first created by brokerage firms that placed traditional Treasury Bonds into an irrevocable trust, and then sold off each of the cash flows separately. Later, they were created and sold by the Treasury itself. Although investors incur only a minor amount of extra risk by investing in ZCBs that are created by brokerage firms (as opposed to those that are issued directly by the Treasury), ZCBs that are created by brokerage firms yield slightly more than those issued directly by the Treasury. Thus, yield curves that include both types of ZCBs may deviate sightly from the actual term-structure of interest rates.

## Relatively High Spreads

Because the durations of ZCBs are higher than coupon bonds with comparable maturities, they tend to be relatively volatile. Because of their proportion- ally higher volatility, dealers take a proportionally larger risk making a market in ZCBs than they do making a market in Treasury Bonds with comparable maturities. To compensate for this higher level of risk, dealers who make a market in ZCBs tend to post a higher spread on them (measured in percentage terms) than they do on traditional Treasury Bonds. The high spreads may inject construction errors that could, in turn, cause the ZCB curve to deviate from the term-structure of interest rates.

### *Lack of Arbitrage*

Whereas Coupon Bonds can easily be stripped into ZCBs by placing the bonds into trust and selling off the individual cash flows, ZCBs cannot easily be reconstituted into Coupon Bonds. Often, one or more of the ZCBs that would be needed to reconstitute the ZCB(s) into a Coupon Bond is simply not available in the market at a fair price. Further, operationally, there is no efficient mechanism to reconstitute Coupon Bonds out of their individual cash flows. As a result, if the ZCBs are trading at a higher yield (i.e., lower price) than they should be, it is not practical to buy them, combine them into a Coupon Bond, and then sell the Coupon Bond at a higher price. The inability to arbitrage ZCBs into Coupon Bonds eliminates one of the forces that would tend to push the ZCB Yield Curve toward the term-structure of interest rates.

For some applications, the ZCB Yield Curve serves as an acceptable surrogate for the Spot Rate Yield Curve. However, for most applications involving large sums of money, it would be unwise to assume that the ZCB Yield Curve and the term-structure of interest rates are identical.

## MEASURING RISK VERSUS RETURN

Whereas the term-structure of interest rates can offer market participants some unique market insights, it cannot provide much information about the dynamics of risk and reward. The reason for this is that the two variables that determine the Spot Rate Yield Curve (i.e., the spot yields and the maturities) are often poor surrogates for risk and reward.

As discussed in the chapter on yields, the YTM is rarely the best measure of return. Instead the RCY, NRCY, and NNRCY often provide better measures of return. As also stated, either duration or modified duration usually provide a better measure of risk than maturity. The distinction becomes important when the yield curve is used to assess the relative attractiveness of different issues.

# APPLICATIONS OF YIELD CURVE ANALYSIS

As noted previously in this section, the relationship between yield and maturity is used in a variety of different ways. Some of these applications include:

- determining the optimum mixture of maturities to issue at any time.
- determining the market's consensus about the future level of interest rates.
- valuing fixed-income securities and fixed-income derivative instruments.
- identifying securities that are either under- or overvalued.

## Determining the Optimum Mixture of Bonds to Issue or Call

Assume that a company that purchases and leases commercial real estate will generate $30,000,000 per year of surplus cash flow for the next 20 years. The company would like to issue bonds in order to raise funds to purchase additional real estate. It wants this new debt to be serviced exclusively by the surplus cash flow from existing leases. Because the company knows how much money it has to spend in order to service its debt, its primary consideration is, under current market conditions, what is the maximum amount of debt that can be serviced by $30,000,000 per year for the next 20 years?

With the traditional yield curve, it is possible to create the Spot Rate Yield Curve. From this curve, it is possible to create numerous combinations of bond issues that can be serviced by the company's lease income. However, there is one, and only one, combination of maturities that will allow the company to maximize the number of dollars it can borrow. This unique combination of maturities is determined by a mathematical process called *optimization*.

As another example, assume that the Controller of the Port Authority of New York and New Jersey is considering a proposal to build a new toll bridge. Based on estimates of the daily volume of cars that will use the bridge, as well as the average toll that can be charged, it is estimated that $130,000,000 per year will be collected. After operating expenses, it is estimated that there will be $80,000,000 of cash flow per year. Given the project's cash flow, the yield curve, the time frame in which the bridge must be paid (assume 30 years in this example), and the appropriate optimization calculations, the maximum amount that can be borrowed in the bond market and serviced by the cash flow can be calculated. If the cost of the bridge is less than this amount, the project is feasible; if not, it is *infeasible* (unless a subsidy can be obtained from another source).

## Determining the Market's Consensus about Future Interest Rates

It is reasonable to assume that sensible investors seeking a 2-year investment would not care whether they made:

- a straight 2-year investment,
- two consecutive 1-year investments,
- four consecutive 6-month investments,
- a 1-year investment followed by two consecutive 6-month investments, or
- any other combination of investments whose combined length was two years.

Because the maturity of all the alternatives is the same, sensible investors would:

- select the combination of maturities that offers the highest yield.
- arbitrage any significant yield imbalance between the various alternatives (see Chapter 20 for examples of arbitrage possibilities).

Because the return investors receive is a direct function of the actual cash flows the investors receive, the appropriate yield curve to use to calculate the implied forward rate is also the Spot Rate Yield Curve.

## Evaluating Securities to Be Issued

When securities are issued, the coupon is usually fixed several days prior to the actual offering. However, market interest rates may either rise or fall between the time the coupon is set and the time the bonds are actually issued. As a result, the price of the bonds must be adjusted to be either higher or lower so that the bonds will offer a competitive return at the exact time they are issued. If the return is too low, the investors will balk at purchasing the issue, and if the yield is too high, the issuer will balk at having to overpay.

Because we know that a bond constitutes a series of cash flows--and we know how to determine the value of any cash flow at any moment--we can determine the value of the bond by simply adding together the value of its cash flows. To evaluate the cash flows, we would discount each of them by their respective spot rates.

## *Evaluating Securities*

Many market participants believe that by plotting the traditional yield curve and then looking for bonds whose data points are either above or below the curve, they can identify bonds that are inexpensive or expensive, respectively, relative to the market. Bonds that are inexpensive may be attractive to buy, whereas bonds that are expensive may be attractive to sell or short. It is important to note that there is more to doing this type of analysis than simply drawing a curve and looking for points that are off the curve. It is essential to have a thorough understanding of the bond market being analyzed in order to avoid making errors and drawing erroneous conclusions. For example, just because a bond's data point is off the curve, that does not necessarily mean that the bond is mispriced. There is often an alternative explanation for the locations of the bond's data point.

For example, in the case of the U.S. Treasury Market:

- the bond's duration may be very different from its neighbors on the yield curve, justifying its position.
- the bond may be one of the issues that is convertible into ZCBs, making it more attractive than its neighbors.
- the issue may be unusually large, making it especially liquid--or unusually small, making it not especially liquid.

Thus, when a bond's data point deviates from the yield curve, there may be a reason other than the security being mispriced in the market. Complicating this analysis further is the fact that the statistical smoothing that turns a jagged curve into a smooth curve often hides mispriced securities. Part of the problem technicians face when constructing the traditional yield curve is how much smoothing to do. If the yield curve is not smoothed at all, it is sometimes too jagged to provide insight into the relationship between yield and maturity. However, if the yield curve is smoothed too much, mispriced bonds will be undetected.

In addition to looking for data points that are off the yield curve, an analyst examining the traditional yield curve might also look for the places along the curve where the slope changes sharply. A changing slope can indicate a change in the relationship between risk and reward. For example, the point where the slope of a positive yield curve flattens out may represent the point beyond which the investor receives little extra return for assuming additional risk. Consider a yield curve on which the slope is high until the seventh year--and relatively flat thereafter. Some market participants looking at a yield curve like this would conclude that it makes no sense to buy bonds with maturities longer than seven years because they offer higher risk (i.e., volatility) without a higher yield. Although the logic of this type of yield curve analysis is appealing, many progressive analysts believe that to look for bonds that offer yields above or below the traditional yield curve--or to look for points where the slope of the traditional yield curve changes--is the right analysis applied to the wrong curve.

The reason for this is that the analysis attempts to draw conclusions about the relative risk and reward of the various Treasury issues, despite that the traditional yield curve is based on poor surrogates for risk and reward: Maturity is used as a measure of risk and YTM as a measure of reward. As we have already noted, however, YTM is a poor indicator of a bond's total return. Also, risk is not just a function of maturity, but also a function of the bond's coupon and yield. Because the traditional yield curve only focuses on one component of risk, an increasing number of market participants believe that when it is used, any conclusions drawn about the relative risk of different Treasury issues must be considered uncertain.

Perhaps a better application of this analysis would be to examine a yield curve constructed by plotting either the RCY, NRCY, and/or NNRCY (whatever is appropriate for the investor) against either the bond's duration or modified duration. The RCY, NRCY, and NNRCY are more accurate estimates of return, whereas duration and modified duration are more accurate measures of risk.

# 20

# INTEREST RATE FORWARDS

## INTRODUCTION

The most basic of all interest rate derivative instruments is the interest rate forward, often referred to as a forward rate agreement (FRA). An interest rate forward or FRA is simply an agreement between two parties in which one party agrees to lend another party a certain sum of money for a certain period of time at some point in the future at an interest rate that is agreed upon in advance.

Consider the following question: What will 6-month interest rates be 6-months from now? If 1,000 investors were asked this question, they might possibly give 1,000 different answers. Each answer would have some probability of being correct since no one can know for certain what 6-month interest rates will be six month from now. However, suppose these same investors were asked a slightly different question; namely, if you had to agree to an interest rate today, what would you agree to receive or pay on a six-month loan, six months from now? Unlike the first question, given the same data, the various investors could probably agree on an answer to this second question.

## DETERMINING A FORWARD RATE

Suppose a client wants to borrow $1,000,000 from a lender for 6-month months but wants the transaction to commence in 6-months and also wants to the lender to quote the rate on the loan today. To accommodate the client and still protect itself, the lender needs to determine the lowest interest rate that allows the lender to

- cover the cost of "hedging" the transaction against liquidity risk.
- cover the cost of hedging the transaction against interest-rate risk.
- cover its overhead, as well as any transaction costs.

- compensate itself for the credit risk involved in the transaction.
- make a profit.

Fortunately, structuring a transaction to meet all of these objectives is relatively simple.

## Hedging Liquidity Risk

The first risk the dealer is exposed to, and therefore needs to "hedge" against, is liquidity risk. For example, if a lender enters into a contractual obligation to provide a client with $1,000,000 in 6-months, the lender has to be sure that it will have $1,000,000 available to lend to the client in 6-months. Because the lender can not be sure what the future holds, the only way it can be sure of having the $1,000,000 it promised to lend to its client in 6-months is to set the money aside today and "store" it until it lends it to its client. (The money that the lender sets aside can either be part of its own capital or money that the lender itself borrows in the open market.

**Figure 20.1** *Hedging Liquidity Risk*

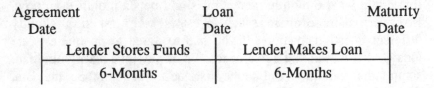

## Hedging Interest Rate Risk

The second risk is interest rate risk. In an FRA, the lender is contractually obligated to provide the loan to the client at a specific interest rate, regardless of what happens to market interest rates. Thus, the dealer must protect itself against the risk that interest rates will rise between the day it agrees to provide the loan and the day it actually makes the loan. In order to protect itself against interest rate risk, the dealer should:

- Arrange a fixed-rate loan for itself in the open market that matures on the same day that the client's loan matures.
- Store the funds by investing the borrowed funds in a risk-free, fixed-rate investment until the first day of the client's loan.

- Lend the funds to the client on the designated date for the designated term.

**Figure 20.2** *Hedging Interest Rate Risk*

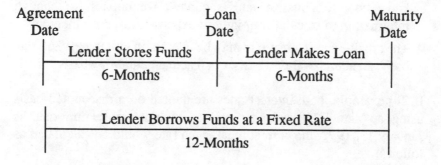

Because the lender is borrowing for a fixed term and at a fixed rate, it knows how many dollars of interest it will pay on its 1-year loan. The lender also knows how much interest it will earn by storing the money for 6-months by investing it in a fixed rate risk free investment. Therefore, in order for the dealer to break even on this transaction, the amount of interest that it must receive from the client must equal the amount it pays on its loan *minus* the interest it receives by storing the funds until they are needed. *Thus the interest that the lender receives from the investment plus the interest the lender receives from the loan must equal the interest the lender pays on the one year loan.*

For example, suppose the dealer was able to borrow for a year at 9%, and able to invest for 6-months at 8%. After examining Figure 20.2 an investor might conclude that the break-even rate that the lender needs to charge the client is 10%; after all, 8% for six months plus 10% for six months should equal 9% annually. However, the investor would be *wrong!* There are five factors which complicate the calculation of the break even interest rate.

- The dealer can compound the interest it earns in the first six-month period.

- The two six-month periods will likely have a different number of days (because not all months have the same number of days).

- The dealer does not need to borrow $1,000,000 today in order to have $1,000,000 available it in six months. The money that is being borrowed presently can be invested for six months, at the end of which time the dealer will need the money to lend.

- The interest rates quoted previously (8% and 9%) may be quoted on either a discounted or interest-bearing basis. Because we don't know how the interest rate is quoted, we don't have enough information to calculate our interest expense or interest income.

- The break-even interest rate may be quoted on either a 30/360-day basis, an actual/360-day basis, or an actual/actual-day basis.

If, for example, both interest rates are quoted on a discounted basis using an actual/360 calendar and the initial transaction date is January 15, 1991, the correct break-even rate would be calculated as follows:

Jan. 15, 1991            July 15, 1991            Jan. 15 1992

| Lender Stores Funds | Lender Makes Loan |
|---|---|
| 6-Months @ 8.00% Actual/360 | 6-Months |

| Lender Borrows Funds at a Fixed Rate |
|---|
| 12-Months @ 9.00% Actual/360 |

Step one is to determine how much the lender needs to borrow in order to have the $1,000,000 it needs to lend to the client in six months (i.e., on July 15, 1991). In other words, the lender must borrow just enough so that the amount it borrows - plus the interest it earns by investing from Jan. 15th to July 15th - will equal $1,000,000.

$$\text{Thus, } P + I = \$1,000,000 \text{ in six months.}$$

This equation, in its current form, can't be solved, because it has an infinite number of possible solutions. In order to solve it, one of the variables needs to be restated in terms of the other variable. Since $I = (P \times R \times T)$, $(P \times R \times T)$ can be substituted for I in the equation,

$$P + (P \times R \times T) = \$1,000,000 \text{ in six months}$$

This equation can be solved by inserting the 8% interest rate and the time from January 15, 1991, to July 15, 1991, on an actual/360 basis and solving for P:

$$P + (P \times 0.08 \times 181/360) = \$1,000,000$$
$$P + (0.0402P) = \$1,000,000$$
$$1.0402P = \$1,000,000$$
$$P = \$961,333$$

P is determined to be \$961,333. Thus, the dealer must borrow \$961,333 presently in order to have the \$1,000,000 it promised to lend the client on July 15, 1991.

*Step Two:* Determine the dealer's interest expense on its 1-year loan.

If the dealer borrows \$961,333 for one year at a 9% interest rate (actual/360), its interest expense will be

$$(P \times R \times T) = (\$961,333 \times 0.09 \times 365/360) = \$87,722$$

*Step Three:* Determine how much interest the dealer must receive from the client to break even. This number is equal to the difference between its interest expense (on its loan) and interest income (on its investment):

Loan Interest - Investment Interest = Client Interest

Substituting actual figures,

$$\$87,722 - \$38,667 = \$49,056$$

*Step Four:* Convert the amount the dealer receives from the client into a break-even interest rate.

To convert \$49,056 into an interest rate (again expressed on an actual/360 basis), we divide by \$1,000,000 and then annualize it:

$$(\$49,056 / \$1,000,000) * (360 / 184) * 100 = 9.60\%$$

Thus, the dealer needs to charge the client 9.6% to break even on this transaction, taking into account liquidity and interest-rate risk.

*Step Five:* Add a spread to the break-even rate to cover overhead, transaction charges, and credit risk. In this example, if the dealer determined that it needed to add on 20 basis points (bp) to cover its costs and make its desired profit, the dealer would quote its client a rate of 9.8%.

As another example, assuming that today is September 15, 1990, determine what rate a dealer would have to quote a client on a

30/360 basis to break even on a nine-month loan, one year from now, given the following market interest rates:

**Table 20.1** *Hypothetical Market Rates*

| Time Frame | Investment Return (actual/360) | Loan Rate (actual/actual) |
|---|---|---|
| 12 Months | 11.05% | 11.30% |
| 15 Months | 10.95% | 11.20% |
| 18 Months | 9.75% | 10.90% |
| 21 Months | 9.20% | 10.70% |
| 24 Months | 8.90% | 10.45% |

Because this problem asks for a rate, any notational amount can be used in the calculation because the resulting forward rate will be the same. In the following problem, a $1,000,000 notational amount is used to keep the calculations simple.

As with the first example, the first step is to determine how much the dealer needs to borrow presently in order to have $1 million in one year. According to the preceding table of current rates, the dealer can earn 11.05% (on an actual/360 basis) on a 1-year investment. The amount that the dealer needs to borrow is therefore,

$$P + I = \$1,000,000$$
$$P + (P \times R \times T) = \$1,000,000$$
$$P + (P \times 0.1105 \times 365/360) = \$1,000,000$$
$$1.1120P = \$1,000,000$$
$$P = \$899,252$$
$$I = \$100,748$$

Once the loan amount is determined, the loan interest can be determined by,

$$I = P \times R \times T$$
$$I = \$899,252 \times 0.1070 \times 639/365$$
$$I = \$168,451$$

Once the interest expense and the interest income are determined, the amount that must be obtained from the client can be determined by subtracting the interest earned from the interest paid:

$$\$168,451 - \$100,748 = \$67,703$$

This amount can then be calculated into a forward rate:

$$(\$67,703 / \$1,000,000) \times (360 / 270) = 9.03\%$$

Thus, the break-even rate is 9.03%. What should be learned from the preceding examples is that the lower the dealer's interest expense, and the higher its interest income, the lower the break-even yield the dealer has to charge its clients.

# APPLICATIONS OF FORWARD RATE AGREEMENTS

As we have seen in the preceding examples, Forward Rate Agreements (FRAs) allow borrowers to fix the interest rate they will pay on their future loans. Borrowers may want to fix the rate on their future loans presently because (1) they expect interest rates to rise and want to eliminate the risk of having to pay a higher rate, or (2) they are preparing budgets, proposals, or proformas, and want to fix their future loan rates in order to remove one source of variance in their calculations. (Note that although an FRA allows a borrower to fix an interest rate on a future loan, it does not guarantee that the rate will be attractive.) Although an FRA protects a borrower against a rise in interest rates, it also eliminates the possibility that the borrower will benefit from a *decline* in interest rates. Thus, FRAs offer borrowers a symmetric risk/reward pattern: the elimination of the possibility of paying a higher rate also eliminates the possibility of paying a lower rate.

## Creating Synthetic Cash Instruments with FRAs

A borrower who wants to borrow money for two years at a fixed rate has numerous alternatives. For example, the borrower can borrow presently

- for two years at a fixed rate.

- for one year and enter into a 1-year FRA a year later to fix the rate for the second year.
- for six months and enter into a series of three successive six-month FRAs in order to fix the rate for the next year and a half.
- for six months and enter into a 1-year FRA six months from now, and a six-month FRA 18 months from now to fix the rate for the next year and a half.

A sensible borrower who wishes to borrow for two years will, of course, choose whatever funding alternative offers the lowest cost. On the other side of the transaction, a sensible lender who wants to lend for two years will choose whatever lending alternative offers the highest yield. By the actions of numerous borrowers and lenders, any significant differences in the yields of the various alternatives should be satisfactorily arbitraged.

## FLOATING-RATE FRAS

Whereas locking in a fixed-rate on a future loan is the most common use of FRAs, there is no reason that the same concept cannot be applied to locking in the future rate on a floating-rate loan. Assume that the following table represents the current investment and loan rates available to a dealer. A client, anticipating a severe credit crunch, would like the dealer to quote a fixed spread at which it will make a 1-year Libor-based loan, one year from now.

**Table 20.2  *Dealer's Rate Quotes (Semiannual Payments)***

|  | Invest | Borrow |
|---|---|---|
| 6 - Months | L - Flat | L + 20 bp |
| 12 - Months | L + 10 bp | L + 30 bp |
| 18 - Months | L + 20 bp | L + 45 bp |
| 24 - Months | L + 35 bp | L + 60 bp |
| 30 - Months | L + 50 bp | L + 75 bp |

The dealer can oblige its client because it can take offsetting transactions that eliminate its risk. The dealer can borrow money for two years, invest it for a year until the client needs it, and then lend it to the client. Because this FRA is tied to a floating rate, the structure of the transaction is slightly different from the structure of a fixed-rate FRA transaction. In a floating-rate FRA, the dealer borrows and then invests the full amount the client wants to borrow, and calculates the net income differential to build it into the customer's spread.

In this example, the dealer would borrow $1,000,000 for two years at L plus 60 bp, and invest $1,000,000 for one year at L plus 10 bp. The dealer would therefore sustain a minus-50 bp spread ($5,000 loss) over the first year.

Although the dealer sustains a $5,000 loss (-50 bp) in the first year, the dealer *cannot* make it up by simply adding a 50 bp spread to its loan rate in the second year (i.e, by charging L + 110). The reason is that the future value of a 50 bp loss is higher than 50 bp. In addition, the dealer would again have to add a spread to cover overhead, transaction costs, and profit.

# ADVANTAGES/DISADVANTAGES OF FRAS

The principal advantage of an FRA agreement is that it can be customized to meet a borrower's specific needs. Unlike other derivatives, an FRA can be constructed for practically any size transaction and for any term.

Although FRAs are very flexible, this flexibility is not free. They do have several disadvantages that other derivative instruments do not have. First, FRAs can be a credit risk. Because an FRA is a private agreement between two participants, both are exposed to the risk that the other will default on its obligations under the contract. Second, FRAs are not liquid. Once two participants enter into an FRA contract, the only way either can get out of it is to renegotiate with the other, assuming the other is willing. Third, with FRAs, one participant often has a trading or negotiating advantage over the other. Because of this, less knowledgeable participants run the risk of being exploited.

# 21

# INTEREST RATE FUTURES CONTRACTS

## INTRODUCTION

Interest rate futures contracts (IRFs) and FRAs can be used to hedge the same types of interest rate exposures. However, although IRFs and FRAs are *functionally* very similar, they are *structurally* very different. Perhaps the easiest way to introduce IRFs is to compare and contrast them with FRAs. The following is an examination of the characteristics of FRAs and IRFs as listed in Table 21.1.

- Whereas FRAs are private contracts involving only two participants who negotiate and trade directly with each other, IRFs are traded on public securities exchanges between participants who negotiate and trade indirectly.

- Whereas FRAs are regulated only by general contract law, IRFs are regulated by the Commodities Futures Trading Commission (CFTC) and/or the Securities and Exchange Commission (SEC).

- Whereas two participants can enter into an FRA for any underlying instrument or index rate, IRFs are only available for the most common underlying bonds and index rates.

- Whereas the two participants in an FRA are free to negotiate any mutually acceptable contract terms and conditions (size, maturity, security deposits, and so on), in an IRF, all of the terms and conditions are established by the exchange.

- Participants entering into an FRA usually need to shop around in order to determine which counterpart offers the best terms. In addition, securing an FRA sometimes requires lengthy negotiations over the contract's terms and conditions. In the IRF market, however, at any one time there is only one price--and no need to negotiate over terms--so transactions can be consummated much faster.

- In both FRAs and IRFs, one participant may have access to better information than the other, putting the latter at a disadvantage.

- Whereas both participants in an FRA are exposed to credit risk, in an IRF transaction the exchange guarantees all trades and thus virtually eliminates credit risk.

- Once an FRA is created, its terms cannot usually be changed, except by mutual consent of the participants. However, for IRFs, the exchange always reserves the right to change the contract terms if it is deemed necessary in order to maintain an orderly market.

- Whereas FRAs are not liquid instruments, IRFs trade freely and are normally very liquid.

- Both FRAs and IRFs have symmetric risk/reward patterns, meaning that if they are used to hedge against sustaining a loss from an unfavorable price move, they also eliminate the possibility of incurring a gain from a favorable price move.

- FRAs, by their very nature, eliminate the possibility of anonymity. IRFs, however, allow all but the largest of market participants to remain anonymous.

- Because the FRA market is an "over the counter" market with numerous dealers that all have their own borrowing rates, investment rates, and required spreads, it is often impossible to say what the true yield or price is for a given FRA at any time. However, in the IRF market, there is only one price--or one yield--which is, by definition, the true "future yield."

- There are no regulations that limit either the number or amount of FRA agreements into which a borrower or lender can enter. IRF exchanges, on the other hand, place strict limits on the size of IRFs that market participants are allowed to build. The exchanges impose these limits so that no participant can "corner" the market.

- Although FRAs and IRFs both fix a future yield, neither guarantees that the yield will be good. In fact, by definition, in FRAs and IRFs, the only way one participant can profit is for the other to take a loss. Thus, both markets are "net sum/zero loss" games.

- Both FRAs and IRFs are often used to hedge each other. This means that the FRA yields will impact IRF yields and visa versa. The two market's are also arbitraged against each other.

Table 21.1 *Comparison of Forwards and Futures*

| Characteristics of Instruments | FRAs | IRFs |
|---|---|---|
| Traded on an exchange | NO | YES |
| Regulated by the CFTC & SEC | NO | YES |
| Can have any underlying instrument | YES | NO |
| Contract terms are negotiable | YES | NO |
| Can be entered into instantly | NO | YES |
| Parties may have information gap | YES | YES |
| Contract has credit risk | YES | NO |
| Contract has "term" risk | NO | YES |
| Contract is liquid | NO | YES |
| Symmetric risk reward pattern | YES | YES |
| Provides anonymity | NO | YES |
| Allows for true price discovery | NO | YES |
| Has position limits | NO | YES |
| Guarantees a "good" price | NO | NO |

# MAJOR ADVANTAGES OF INTEREST RATE FUTURES CONTRACTS

Of all the differences between FRAs and IRFs, the most important are that IRFs are *liquid*, and also *have no credit risk*. They offer both of these advantages because of the unique role that the exchange plays in the overall process. Consider the following example, which illustrates how an exchange can create liquidity and eliminate credit risk. (For this example we will use a gold futures contract since gold is the simplest future to understand and price--after all, gold has no intermediate cashflows like bonds, doesn't spoil like crops, and doesn't have to be refined like oil.)

On January 15, 1991, one market participant makes the decision to sell 1,000 ounces of gold in July of the same year. Another market participant wants to buy 1,000 ounces of gold in July. If the fair 6-month forward price of gold were $400, the two market participants could simply enter into an FRA. While an FRA would allow both parties to eliminate their price risk, it would also expose both participants to liquidity risk and credit risk. In order to avoid these risks, the two participants would have to use an IRF instead of an FRA. Because each gold IRF is for 100 ounces of gold, the two parties could accomplish their objectives by instructing their respective brokers to execute the following IRF market transactions on their behalf:

**Figure 21.1** *Entering Trades on an Exchange*

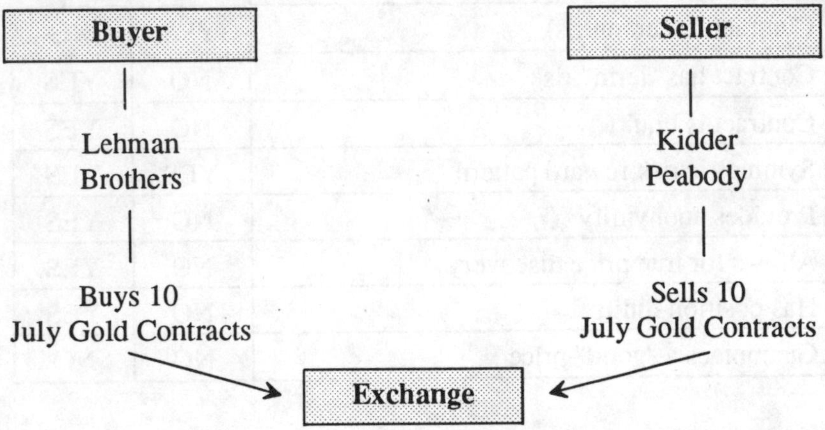

The two brokers enter into the transaction in which Kidder Peabody, Inc.® sells 10 IRFs and Lehman Brothers, Inc.® buys 10 IRFs at the current price of $400 per ounce. Immediately upon the execution of these transactions, the buyer is obligated to buy 1,000 ounces of gold in 6 months at $400 per ounce, and the seller is obligated to sell 1,000 ounces of gold in 6 months. Because IRF transactions are executed via brokers, neither the participants (nor their brokers) know the identities of the counterparts. Despite the anonymity IRFs provide, neither participant is exposed to credit risk *because the exchange guarantees all trades*. Thus, the brokers on the floor who effect this transaction are not only creating a contract that obligates their respective clients, but are also acting as agents of the exchange itself.

Futures exchanges can afford to extend a credit guarantee to all of the participants who use the exchange to trade because of the way the exchanges are structured, and because of the eight steps the exchanges take in order to reduce their credit losses.

(1) The exchanges hold the brokers responsible for their clients' obligations. Thus, in the preceding example, Lehman Brothers, Inc.® is responsible for the buyer's obligations and Kidder Peabody, Inc.® is responsible for the seller's. If a client fails to meet its obligations for any reason, its broker then becomes fully liable. Thus, each customer's obligation is guaranteed by the broker who executed the transaction on the client's behalf.

(2) If a broker who is a member of the exchange fails, all of the other members of the exchange become liable for the broker's debts and its customers' debts. Thus, each customer's obligation is secured, indirectly, by *every* broker who is a member of the exchange.

(3) The exchanges require all brokers who transact business on the exchanges to post security deposits and meet certain minimum capital requirements. The exchanges also monitors the financial condition of the brokers who transact business on the floor on a continual basis.

(4) The exchanges maintain their own reserve accounts and carry insurance policies.

(5) The exchanges require all customers to post a security deposit, commonly referred to as a "margin," when they establish their future positions. The amount of margin each customer is required to post is determined by three factors:

- Whether the customer is a bona fide hedger or a speculator. Whereas the exchange might require a hedger to post a margin requirement of 5% of the contract's face value, a speculator's margin requirement might be 10%. For the 10 gold contracts in this example, a hedger would have a $20,000 margin requirement (5% of the $400,000 total value--10 contracts * 100 ounces per contract * $400 per ounce) whereas a speculator would have to post a $40,000 margin requirement (10% of the $400,000 total value--10 contracts * 100 ounces per contract * $400 per ounce).

- The client's credit rating. Although the minimum margin requirements are set by the exchange, most brokers require all but their most creditworthy customers to post a higher margin requirement than the minimum level required by the exchange.

However, clients can post their margin in T-Bills so that their security deposit continues to earn them interest. (In this respect, margin for future's positions is very different from equity margin.)

- The recent volatility of the underlying instrument. During periods when the underlying instrument is particularly volatile, the exchanges and the brokers often raise their margin requirements in order to protect themselves against credit risk. For example, after Iraq invaded Kuwait (in 1990) and the price of crude oil became extremely volatile, the margin requirement for oil futures more than tripled.

(6) Every customer's position is "marked to the market" on a daily basis, and all losses must be settled daily. To illustrate how this works, assume that the buyer in the preceding example is a hedger and the seller is a speculator. The buyer must post a $20,000 margin deposit and the seller must post a $40,000 margin deposit.

If the next day the price of the July gold contract rose to $403, then after the close of trading the seller would owe the buyer $3 per ounce. Because the seller is short the equivalent of 1,000 ounces, the seller would owe the buyer $3,000. Thus, $3,000 would be taken out of the seller's margin account by Kidder, which would remit it to the exchange, which would in turn pass it on to Lehman, which would in turn credit it to the buyer's margin account.

If, on the second day, the price of the July gold contract fell back to $401, then after the close of trading the buyer would owe the seller $2 per ounce. Because the buyer is long $1,000 ounces, the buyer would owe the seller $2,000. Thus, $2,000 would be taken out of the buyers margin account by Lehman, which would remit it to the exchange, which would in turn pass it on to Kidder, which would in turn credit it to the seller's margin account.

**Table 21.2** *Adjusting Margin Account Balances for a 10-Contract (1,000 Ounce) Position*

|  | Price of Gold | Long's Margin Balance | Short's Margin Balance |
|---|---|---|---|
| Day 0 | $400.00 | $20,000 | $40,000 |
| Day 1 | $402.00 | $22,000 | $38,000 |
| Day 2 | $395.00 | $15,000 | $45,000 |

| Day 3 | $401.50 | $21,500 | $38,500 |
|---|---|---|---|
| Day 4 | $403.75 | $23,750 | $36,250 |
| Day 5 | $405.25 | $25,250 | $34,750 |
| Day 6 | $403.00 | $23,000 | $37,000 |
| Day 7 | $407.00 | $27,000 | $33,000 |
| Day 8 | $409.75 | $29,750 | $30,250 |
| Day 9 | $407.00 | $27,000 | $33,000 |
| Day 10 | $408.50 | $28,500 | $31,500 |
| Day 11 | $410.00 | $30,000 | $30,000 |
| Day 12 | $412.10 | $32,100 | $27,900 |

(7) When the market moves against customers and the value of their margin accounts decreases by a significant percentage, the customers' brokers will require that the customers either replace their lost margin or close out their future's positions. Customers can close out their positions by taking an "offsetting position." For example, the hedger who bought 10 contracts can close out its position by selling 10 contracts.

Usually, brokers will allow their customers to lose 30%-40% of their margin before issuing an infamous "margin call." When a margin call is issued, customers usually have just 24 hours to meet it. Because all future's losses have to be met daily, investors can be forced out of the market by temporarily adverse price moves. In the preceding example, if the price of July gold suddenly rose to $420, the speculator's margin account would be debited by $20,000. Because the speculator's account was depleted by 50%, Kidder would issue a margin call. If the speculator was either unable or unwilling to meet the margin call, Kidder would insist that the speculator close out its position by buying 10 contracts at the then-current price. Because the speculator originally sold the equivalent of 1,000 ounces of gold for $400 each, and then bought the equivalent of 1,000 ounces of gold for $420 each, the speculator's overall loss is $20,000, and that amount would have already been subtracted from the speculator's margin account. Thus, neither Kidder nor the exchange have any real credit risk exposure.

Because the speculator is now out of the market, even if the price of July gold was to subsequently decline to $300 per ounce, the speculator cannot profit from this favorable price change. (Because of the requirement to cover all losses daily and to always maintain a acceptable margin balance, future's market participants sometimes compare being closed out of future's positions by margin calls to having to fold in a poker game while holding a straight flush, because of an inability to call a small raise.)

(8) If either participant in the preceding transaction does not close out its position prior to the delivery date, and elects instead to use the exchange's delivery procedures, the delivery will occur at the *current* spot price. The reason is that the future price and the spot price must be the same when the contract expires, or else the opportunity for arbitrage would exist. For example, if the price of the July gold contract is $390 on the last day of the contract, then the spot price of gold is also $390, and delivery will occur at $390.

Because the future price is $390, a total of $10,000 has been transferred from the buyer's margin account to the seller's margin account. If both participants in the above example elected to use the exchange's delivery procedures, then the hedger would accept delivery of 1,000 ounces of gold from the exchange, and would pay $390 per ounce. The speculator would deliver 1,000 ounces of gold to the exchange, which would pay the speculator $390 per ounce. When this price is added to the change in the margin balances, both participants end up netting the price at which they originally entered into the contract.

For the buyer, the total cost of acquiring an ounce of gold is $390, paid to the exchange, plus a $10 loss in the margin account, for a total cost of $400. For the seller, the total sales revenue per ounce are the $390 received from the exchange plus the $10 credit in the margin account, for a total of $400. The advantage of having delivery occur at the then-current spot price is that neither participant can obtain a better price than the price offered by the exchange and, thus, there is no incentive for either to not honor its commitment.

# INTEREST RATE FUTURES CONTRACTS SPECIFICATIONS AND APPLICATIONS

## Treasury Bill Contracts

The underlying instrument of T-Bill contracts is $1,000,000 face value of 90-day T-Bills. The price quote of the T-Bill contract is expressed as 100 points minus the T-Bill's yield. Thus, a price quote of 92.13 points equates to a yield of:

$$100 - 92.13 \text{ points} = 7.87\%$$

The minimum price change, often referred to as a "tick," is an .01. Thus, the minimum price change of a contract that is currently quoted at 92.13 points is either to 92.14 points or 92.12 points. Because an .01 is equal to a "percent of a percent" of the contract, its dollar value is equal to:

$$1\% \text{ of } \$1,000,000 = \$10,000$$
$$1\% \text{ of } \$10,000 = \$100$$

Because the T-Bill only lasts for a quarter of a year, the value of an .01 equals $100 / 4 = $25. Thus, every time the value of the T-Bill IRF changes by an .01, $25 changes hands.

There are four T-Bill contracts per year: March, June, September, and December. *The expiration months refer to when the IRF contracts expire, not when the underlying T-Bills mature.* When a contract expires, the short (i.e., the seller) must deliver to the exchange T-Bills that mature in 90 or 91 days from the delivery date. The delivery schedule is timed to coincide with the days when the one year T-Bills have three months left until they mature.

Consider a specific example: Suppose on September 13, 1990, the December T-Bill contract is quoted at 91.14 points. This price quote means that an investor who goes long (i.e., buys) one T-Bill contract is agreeing to buy $1,000,000 face value of 90- or 91-day T-Bills upon the contract's expiration in December at whatever price equals a yield of 8.86% (100 minus 91.14 points). Thus, by going long one December contract, the long is agreeing to pay a price of:

$$\text{Discount} = \text{Face} * \text{Yield} * \text{Time}$$
$$\text{Discount} = \$1,000,000 * .0886 * 90/360$$

(assuming a 90-day T-Bill is delivered)
Discount = $22,150
Purchase Price = $977,850

It should be noted that although the price that both the buyer and the seller agree to is $977,850, both will obtain this price *indirectly*. The actual exchange of the T-Bills upon the expiration of the contract will occur at the then-current price of a three-month T-Bill. The difference between the December spot price and the $977,850 will be credited to the winner's margin account and debited from the loser's margin account as part of the daily mark-to-the-market process.

Suppose upon expiration of the above contract the three-month T-Bill rate is 7.95%. This means that the price quote for the IRF has changed from 91.14 points to 92.05 points--up 89 ticks. Because each tick is worth $25, a total of $2,275 (91 * $25) is transferred from the short's margin account to the long's margin account (whenever the price of an IRF contract rises, it is the long who profits).

At delivery, the short will deliver T-Bills to the exchange for a price of:

Discount = Principal * Rate * Time
Discount = $1,000,000 * .0795 * 90/360
Discount = $19,875
Delivery Price = $980,125

However, because the short's margin account will be down $2,275, the net proceeds are:

$980,125 - $2,275 = $977,850

The long, of course, will pay $980,125 for the T-Bills, but will have a profit of $2,275 in its margin account, and so will pay a net $977,850.

### Determining the Fair Yield of a Treasury Bill Interest Rate Future

The fair price of a T-Bill IRF is determined exactly the same way in which the fair price of an FRA is determined. In the previous chapter, FRAs were priced by replicating the FRA with cash market positions and determining the net yield of those positions. Every IRF price can be determined the same way.

For example, suppose on October 24, 1990, an investor was concerned that interest rates were going to decline and wanted to lock in a rate of return for an investment 45 days into the future. The investor could secure the rate by buying the December T-Bill IRF. In order to determine what price is fair for the IRF future, the investor needs to replicate the contract transaction exclusively with cash market transactions--just as FRAs are priced by their offsetting cash market transactions. To offset being long a 90-day T-Bill in 45 days, the required cash market positions is buying a 135-day T-Bill and shorting a 45-day T-Bill. If the current T-Bill rates are:

**Table 21.3** *Creating Synthetic Long Position*

| Short 45-day | Synthetic 90-day Long Position |
|---|---|
| T-Bill at 8.70% | 45 Days Forward |

| Long 135-day |
|---|
| T-Bill at 9.60% |

Given these two yields, the fair yield of the synthetic 90-day long's position 45 days into the future can then be calculated by a three-step process:

*Step One*: Determining the interest income of the long's position:

$$P + I = \$1,000,000$$
$$P + (P * R * T) = \$1,000,000$$
$$P + (P * .0960 * 135/360) = \$1,000,000$$
$$1.0360P = \$1,000,000$$
$$P = \$965,250.97$$
$$\text{Thus, } I = \$34,749.03$$

*Step Two*: Determining the interest expense of the short's position:

$$P + I = \$1,000,000$$
$$P + (P * R * T) = \$1,000,000$$
$$P + (P * .0870 * 45/360) = \$1,000,000$$
$$1.0109P = \$1,000,000$$

$$P = \$989{,}241.99$$
$$\text{Thus, } I = \$10{,}758.01$$

In order to be at equilibrium, the synthetic 90-day instrument has to offer a return of:

$$\$34{,}749.03 - \$10{,}758.01 = \$23{,}991.02$$

Which equates to a fair annualized return of:

$$(\$23{,}991.02 / \$976{,}008.98) * (360 / 90) = 9.83\%$$

and a fair price quote of: $(100 - 9.83\%) = 90.17$

If the actual price of the December T-Bill IRF was significantly lower than 90.17 points (and the yield was significantly higher than 9.83%), no knowledgeable investor would want to sell T-Bills in the IRF market. Instead, the sellers would create the equivalent of the IRF contract by using the cash market equivalents. If the actual price of the December T-Bill IRF was significantly higher than 90.17 points (and the yield was significantly lower than 9.83%), no knowledgeable investor would want to buy T-Bills in the IRF market. Instead, the buyers would also create the equivalent of the IRF contract by using the cash market equivalents. Thus, if the price of the IRF deviates from its cash market equivalent, either the buyers or the sellers will boycott the contract. In addition, any time there is a discrepancy between the price of the IRF and its cash equivalents, arbitrageurs will buy the cheaper alternative and sell the more expensive alternative and, in the process, push the market back toward equilibrium.

## Using Treasury Bill Interest Rate Futures as Hedges

Treasury Bill IRFs can be used to hedge both short and long positions. For example, suppose in June, 1990, the treasurer of a subsidiary of a multinational construction firm was informed that at the end of September she would be receiving $5,000,000--which she would have to invest for three months. At the end of this time (in December), she will disperse the funds to various subcontractors.

The treasurer usually invests in T-Bills. The treasurer's risk is, therefore, that between July and September, T-Bill rates will decline. If they do, the interest income the treasurer earns between September and December will also decline. To hedge this risk, the treasurer needs to establish a T-Bill IRF position that will generate a profit equal to the amount of interest income she will lose if T-Bill rates decline between July and September. Thus, if between July and the end of September interest rates were to fall by 0.18%, the treasurer would want her hedge to generate a profit of:

$$\$5,000,000 * 0.0018 * 90/360 = \$2,250$$

Because the value of each .01 for the T-Bill IRF is equal to $25 per contract, the treasurer would have to buy five Sept. T-Bill contracts.

$$5 \text{ IRF contracts} * 18 \text{ ticks} * \$25 \text{ per tick} = \$2,250$$

As another example, T-Bill IRFs can be used to effectively convert a floating-rate corporate note (FRN) into the equivalent of a fixed-rate note:

Suppose it is April 3, 1990, and an investor owns $10,000,000 (face value) of FRNs that have the following characteristics: (1) The note's coupon equals the three-month T-Bill rate plus 50 bp, and (2) the coupon is reset in March, June, September, and December. Although the investor generally expects interest rates to rise over the long term, the investor is concerned that interest rates might decline over the next six months or so. If interest rates do decline, the yield that the investor will earn from the FRN's will also decline.

To hedge against this risk, the investor needs to establish a position in which every time interest rates decline, the loss of income is offset by a profit on the hedge. Because the reset dates of the FRNs over the next six months are in June and September, the investor needs to go long 10 June T-Bill IRFs and 10 September T-Bill IRFs. If market interest rates decline, the loss of interest income will be offset by an increase in the investor's margin account. If market interest rates rise, the increase in interest income will be offset by a decrease in the investor's margin account.

It should be noted that this type of hedge is not perfect, because the gain or loss on the IRF position is paid at the start of the hedge period. In the preceding example, the June IRF was used to hedge the investor's risk from June to September. If interest rates rise and the value of the IRF falls, the loss will be paid in June--whereas the higher interest earned on the note will not be paid until September. This "cashflow mismatch" can be very significant for large IRF positions, and may need to be hedged separately.

Also, if the FRN's coupon was reset semiannually (i.e., in June and December), the coupon would still be hedged with a combination of the June and September IRF contracts. This combination can hedge a six-month exposure because of the arbitrage theory of interest rates (i.e., the sum of two successive three-month interest rates must equal the six-month rate), otherwise the opportunity for arbitrage will exist.

**Table 21.4** *Arbitrage of Forward Rates*

| 3-Month IRF | 3-Month IRF |
|---|---|
| at Rate 1 | at Rate 2 |

Can Offset:

| 6-Month Risk |
|---|
| at the Equivalent of Rate 1 and Rate 2 |

## The Eurodollar Contract

The Eurodollar contract is, structurally, very similar to the T-Bill contract. The contract's face value is $1,000,000, the price quote is 100 points minus the contract's yield, and the value of a tick is $25. The four main differences between this contract and the T-Bill contract are

- that the three-month Eurodollar deposit rate is the underlying interest rate. (The Eurodollar rate is defined as the average rate that several London banks are willing to pay for 90-day US$ dollar deposits.)

- that there is no actual "delivery." The last day of the contract is just like any other because any change in the index rate is marked to the market. Any losses or gains are debited or credited to the customer's margin accounts. (Because, by definition, a Eurodollar can not exist in the U.S., they cannot be delivered in the U.S.)

- that the Eurodollar contract is significantly more liquid than the T-Bill contract. The reason is that the Eurodollar contract offers a better correlation with general market interest rates that the T-bill Contract. The government's cost of financing often declines as general interest rates rise--because of a flight to quality.

- The T-bill contract generally only goes out about two years into the future (i.e. eight three month contracts). However, the Eurodollar contract goes out about four years into the future. As we shall see, this allows us the opportunity to use this contract to hedge swaps.

## Treasury Bond Contract

The underlying instrument in the Treasury Bond (T-Bond) contract is 100,000 face amount of a hypothetical, 8%, 20-year Treasury Bonds that *never* age. In other words, the maturity date of this hypothetical bond gets one day longer as each day passes so that we are always trading a 20-year 8% Treasury Bond. The price quote of this contract is expressed in points and 32nds of a point just like Treasury Bonds in the cash market. Because each contract is for 100 bonds, the value of each point is $1,000 (100 * $10). Thus, a T-Bond future with a price quote of:

- 94.12 = ( 94 * $1,000) + (12/32 * $1,000) = $ 94,375
- 104.30 = (104 * $1,000) + (30/32 * $1,000) = $104,937.50

### Delivery Procedure

On the delivery date, if the price of the September IRF were 104.30 points, this would imply that the short would have to deliver to the long 100 8% 20-year bonds--and receive $104,937.50 in return as payment.

Because there are no 8% 20-year bonds, the short cannot actually deliver these bonds, and the T-Bond contract has to have an alternative delivery procedure. Under the terms of the contract, the short can elect to deliver 100 of any T-Bond that has at *least* 15 years of life remaining from the first day of the delivery month to the earlier of the maturity date or call date. Thus, an investor who is short one December-91 T-Bond contract can deliver 100 of any T-Bond, as long as the bond does not mature (or have a call date) prior to December 1, 2006. For each T-Bond contract there are usually between 20 and 25 different T-Bonds that meet this delivery criteria. Therefore, the shorts can choose from between approximately 25 different bonds when they are deciding which bond to deliver. Of course, each of the different deliverable bonds will have different maturities, coupons, volatilities, and market values.

If the shorts were to fulfill their obligation by simply delivering 100 of any T-Bond to the long--and in exchange for the bonds receive the closing price of the IRF contract--this IRF contract would fail. For example, if the closing price of the IRF was 104.30 points and the market value of one of the deliverable bonds was 92.16 points, the short could buy 100 bonds in the open market for $92,500, deliver them, and receive $104,937.50.

In order to make the T-Bond contract more equitable to the longs, the contract has to have some way of compensating them for the difference in the relative values of the different deliverable bonds. The way that the delivery price is adjusted to reflect the relative attractiveness of the bond that's being delivered is to multiply the closing price of the IRF by the "conversion factor" for the deliverable bond. This conversion factor is approximately equal to:

*The price, in dollars, that the bond would be selling for if it were priced to offer an 8% YTM --or YTC, (Yield to Call) if that price is lower on the first day of the delivery period, divided by 1,000.*

As an illustration, the approximate conversion factors of the following three bonds, if they are going to be delivered against the June, 1991, T-Bond contract, would be calculated as follows:

7 1/4% of May, 2016
8 1/2% of February, 2020
12 1/2% of August, 2009 / 2014

For the 7 1/4% of May, 2016, the calculation is:

The time from June 1, 1991, to May 15, 2016, *in quarters* is:
June 1, 1991, to March 1, 2016 = 99 quarters
March 1, 2016, to May 15, 2016 = 0.82 quarters

Thus, *rounded to the nearest quarter*, there are 99 quarters from June 1, 1991. The price this bond would be selling for, if it matured 99 quarters from the delivery date and offered an 8% YTM, would be approximately:

**Table 21.5 *Conversion Factor Calculation***

| Keystrokes For 7 1/4% of May, 2016 |
|---|
| 8.00 [i] |
| 7.25 [PMT] |

| |
|---|
| 6.011991 [Enter] |
| 3.012016 [F] [Price] |
| Price = $919.53 |
| Conversion Factor = $919.53 / $1,000 = 0.9195 |

Repeating this procedure for the other two bonds, we can calculate their conversion factors to be:

**Table 21.6** *Conversion Factor Calculation*

| Keystrokes For 8 1/2% of February, 2020 |
|---|
| 8.00 [i] |
| 8.5 [PMT] |
| 6.011991 [Enter] |
| 12.012019 [F] [Price] |
| Price = $1,055.82 |
| Conversion Factor = $1,052.82 / $1,000 = 1.0528 |

**Table 21.7** *Conversion Factor Calculation*

| Keystrokes For 12 1/2% of August, 2009 / 2014 |
|---|
| 8.00 [i] |
| 7.25 [PMT] |
| 6.011991 [Enter] |
| 6.012009 [F] [Price] * Note use of Call Date |
| Price = $929.09 |
| Conversion Factor = $929.09 / $1,000 = 0.9291 |

Once the conversion factor for each deliverable bond is determined, the price that the short will receive from the exchange if a specific T-Bond issue is delivered is determined by multiplying the closing value of the IRF by the bond's conversion factor. If the closing value of the IRF is $104,937.50, then the short will receive:

**Table 21.8** *Calculation of Delivery Prices*

| Bond Number | IRF Price | Conversion Factor | Delivery Price |
|---|---|---|---|
| 1 | $104,937.50 | CF = 0.9591 | $100,645.56 |
| 2 | $104,937.50 | CF = 1.0528 | $110,478.20 |
| 3 | $104,937.50 | CF = 0.9291 | $97,497.43 |

(Note that the short is also entitled to receive accrued interest on the delivered bonds.)

### Advantages That the Shorts Have Under This contract

In the T-Bond contract, the shorts have several advantages over the longs. The first of these advantages is that it is the short who initiates the delivery process and thus it is the short that decides whether to close out its position by delivering or by taking an offsetting long position. The long can not force a short to deliver. Instead, the long must wait for a short to elect to deliver or close out its position by taking an offsetting short position.

Because the short has this alternative, the short will do whatever is in its best interest. If the market value of any deliverable bond happens to be lower than the bond's delivery price, the shorts will elect to deliver--and make a *delivery profit*. For example, the delivery price of the 7 1/4% of may 2016 $100,645.56, plus accrued interest. If the market value of 100 of these bonds was $99,837.50, the short could make a delivery profit of $808.06 by buying 100 of these bonds in the open market for $99,837.50 (plus accrued interest) and then delivering it against a short T-Bond IRF position, in exchange for $100,645.56 plus accrued interest.

The deliverable bond whose market value is the furthest beneath its delivery price is commonly referred to as the *least expensive to deliver*. (If no deliverable bond's market value is below its delivery price, then the bond that is the *least expensive to deliver* is the bond whose market value is the least above its delivery price.) If the market price of every deliverable bond is above its delivery price, the shorts will close out their positions by taking an offsetting futures position instead of electing to deliver.

On the other hand, the longs cannot force the shorts to deliver. Thus, if the longs want to close out their positions, they can either take an offsetting position, or wait for the shorts to deliver. Because they cannot force a delivery, the longs cannot hope to obtain a delivery profit.

The second advantage that the short has is that since there are usually over 20 deliverable issues, the short only needs one of the deliverable bond's market value to dip below its delivery price in order to make a profit on the delivery.

The third advantage that the short has is often referred to as the daily timing advantage. The T-Bond Future stops trading at 3.00 PM EST. Thus at 3.00 PM the closing price of the future is fixed and since the conversion value for each bond is also fixed, the delivery price is fixed. Although the delivery price is fixed at 3:00 PM, the cash market for T-Bonds remains open to between 5:00 PM and 6:00 PM. Thus, each day there are approximately 2 1/2 hours during which the market value of one or more deliverable bonds might decline to a price below the delivery price. In addition, the shorts can notify the exchange of their intentions to deliver bonds as late as 8:00 p.m. EST. Thus, they can exploit any weakness in the bond market that occurs after 3:00 PM. by waiting until 5:30 PM to buy bonds cheap and then make a profit by delivering them.

The fourth advantage that short has in the T-Bond contract is the length of the delivery period. The T-Bond contract delivery period extends from the first business day of the delivery month to the last business day of the delivery month. Thus, the shorts usually have more than 20 different business days to try to make a delivery profit.

The fifth advantage that the shorts have is often referred to as the end-of-the-month advantage. Although delivery can occur on any day during the delivery month, the IRF contract stops trading eight business days before the end of the delivery month. Thus, on the last day of trading, the delivery price is fixed for the remainder of the delivery month. This gives the shorts eight days during which the market value of one or more deliverable bonds might decline to a price below the delivery price. During this time, longs cannot take an offsetting position because trading has ceased. Thus, they are somewhat at the mercy of the shorts.

## *Quantifying the Short's Advantages*

Under the terms of the T-Bond contract, the shorts have the right to decide whether to deliver bonds, which bonds to deliver, and when to deliver them. In effect, the shorts are granted some very valuable options under the terms of this contract. Although the longs must grant these options to the shorts because of the way the T-Bond contract is written, the longs are not willing to grant the shorts these options for free. The more sophisticated longs will value these options and subtract their value from the fair future price of the contract.

## *Determining the Value of a T-Bond Future*

Like other IRF contracts, the fair value of the T-Bond IRF contract can be determined by the net yield of its offsetting cash market transactions, or by the current value of the underlying instrument plus the "cost of carry." In addition, the fair value of this IRF has to be adjusted in order to reflect the value of the embedded delivery options as discussed above. However, there is more to calculating the fair market value of the T-Bond contract than a simple addition problem.

First, since there are more than 20 different underlying bonds that can be delivered against each T-Bond Future contract, the value of the futures contract depends on which underlying instrument is used to perform the spot + cost of carry calculation. Although there are more than 20 different deliverable bonds, the T-Bond Future contract is usually priced from whatever T-Bond is presently the cheapest to deliver, because that is the bond most likely to be delivered. (Of course, the bond that is the cheapest to deliver changes from time to time, and when it does, so does the value of the T-Bond Future.)

Once the correct underlying instrument to use is determined, the next step is to calculate the cost of carry. In order to do this, it is necessary to determine the:

- daily income (DI) the bond generates,
- daily expense (DE) of financing the position,
- number of days between the present and the IRF's delivery date (ΔDYS),

and then complete the following formula:

$$\text{Cost of Carry} = [\Delta DYS * (DI - DE)]$$

Although this calculation may appear simple, it can actually be somewhat tricky. Consider the following example:

Suppose that on September 10, 1990, an investor wanted to determine the fair market value of the December T-Bond contract. Assume that (1) the T-Bond which is the least expensive to deliver is the 8.75% of August, 2020, (2) the market value of this bond is 100.19 points, and (3) the bond can be financed via a "repo" at 6.15%

How would the investor calculate the fair market value of the contract? The first variable, the bond's daily income (DI), is equal to the underlying bond's daily interest income. However, the bond's daily interest income is dependent on the number of days in the interest period (181, 182, 183, or 184). For the preceding bond, the daily interest income would be:

$$DI = P * R * T = (\$1,000 * 0.04375 * 1/184) = \$0.2378$$

However, as the bond moves from one interest period to another, the amount of daily interest income changes because the denominator in the time factor changes. Thus, the cost of carry will change from one payment period to another. The second variable, the daily expense (DE) of financing the bond position, is also:

$$DE = P * R * T$$

However, in this case the time factor is quoted on a 360-day basis, because repos are generally quoted on an actual/360 basis. Additionally, the amount that has to be financed is the total purchase price of the bond, *including accrued interest*. After all, the accrued interest has to be paid when the bond is purchased, and the money has to be obtained somehow.

Thus, the total amount being financed would be:

$$\text{Market Price} + \text{Accrued Interest}$$

$$[\$1,005.94 + (P * R * T)]$$

$$[\$1,005.94 + (1,000 * 0.04375 * 36/184)] = \$1,014.50$$

The DE interest expense would therefore be:

$$DE = P * R * T$$

$$DE = \$1,014.50 * 0.0615 * 1/360) = \$0.1733$$

Thus, the *daily* cost of carry is:

$$(\$0.2378 - \$0.1733) = \$0.0645.$$

(Note that at the next interest payment date, the bond will generate an interest payment, reducing the amount that has to be financed by the amount of the interest payment. Thus, the principal component in the preceding equation changes as time passes. As it changes, so does the cost of carry.)

The final component in the cost of carry equation is the number of days from the present to the delivery date. Because delivery can occur on any business day during the delivery month, the number of days cannot be determined with absolute certainty. However, we can make a reasonable guess when delivery will occur based on the interest income an investor earns compared to the interest expense the investor incurs in financing the position.

If the cost of carry is positive (i.e., the DI is greater than the DE), shorts will wait as long as possible to deliver their bonds, so that they can earn the spread for as long as possible. If the cost of carry is negative (i.e., the DI is less than the DE), shorts will deliver as soon as possible, so that they can limit their cashflow losses.

Thus, if the DI is greater than the DE, the number of days in the cost of carry calculation will equal the number of days from the present to the last possible delivery date; and if the DI is less than the DE, the number of days in the cost of carry calculation will equal the number of days from the present to the first possible delivery date. (The DI is greater than the DE when the yield curve has a positive slope, and vice versa.)

Thus, in the preceding example, the cost of carry is equal to:

$$(\$0.0645 * 102 \text{ days}) = \$6.58$$

Once the cost of carry is determined, the fair market value of the T-Bond Future can be determined by using the following formula:

(Current Value of the Cheapest to Deliver / Cheapest to Deliver's Conversion Factor) + the Cost of Carry - the Value of the Delivery Options = Value of the T-Bond Future.

In this case:

- the value of the cheapest to deliver is $1005.94
- the conversion factor of the cheapest to deliver is 1.0577
- the cost of carry is a *negative* $6.48 (a gain is a negative cost)
- the value of the delivery options is $12.60

Thus the fair market value of the T-Bond Future is:

$$\{[(\$1005.94 \, / \, 1.0577) - \$6.48] - \$12.60\} = \$931.98$$

## Hedging Portfolios with Treasury Bond Contracts

Consider the following example:

Suppose it is October 13, 1990, and an investor owns a portfolio of Treasury Bonds that has a face value of $65,000,000, and a current market value of $59,876,765. The investor is concerned that long-term interest rates will rise between now and the end of the year, and wants to eliminate the possibility of taking a loss. The investor has several options, including:

- simply selling the bonds.
- taking an offsetting short position in the cash market.
- taking a "synthetic" short position in the T-Bond Future.

The first two alternatives are very costly. The third may be the most practical, but in order to be effective, the investor must calculate how many T-Bond Futures contracts are needed to establish a valid hedge.

For any valid IRF hedge:

$$\text{Size}_B * \text{Volatility}_B = \text{Size}_F * \text{Volatility}_F$$

For the bond portfolio, the size is equal to its *market value,* and the volatility is best measured by the portfolio's modified duration (MD). If the portfolio's MD is 7.32 years, then:

$$\$59,876,765 * 7.32 = \text{Size}_F * \text{Volatility}_F$$

For the futures side of the equation, the volatility of the contract needs to be calculated to determine how many contracts are needed.

Because the T-Bond Future is priced off of the T-Bond that is the cheapest to deliver, when the price of the cheapest to deliver changes by $5.00, the value of the T-Bond Future also changes by $5.00. Thus, the volatility of the T-Bond Contract is equal to the volatility of the cheapest to deliver T-Bond. Further, as the volatility of this bond changes, so does the volatility of the T-Bond Future. If the volatility of the cheapest to deliver, again measured by the bond's MD were 6.15 years, the number of T-Bond Future Contracts necessary to hedge the portfolio would be:

$$\$59,876,765 * 7.32 = \text{Size}_F * 6.15$$

$$\text{Size} = \$71,267,954 \text{ worth of T-Bond Futures}$$

Thus, 713 T-Bond contracts would be needed since each contract has a face value of $100,000 per contract. Thus to hedge this portfolio, an the investor would have to sell 713 T-Bond contracts.

Another methodology that can be used to calculate the number of future's contracts needed is to:

- determine the portfolio's target volatility (i.e., the desired value of an .01).
- determine the portfolio's current volatility (i.e., the current value of an .01).
- use the following formula to calculate the number of contracts necessary to adjust the volatility of the portfolio:

(Value of an .01 for Your Target Portfolio - Value of an .01 of Your Current Portfolio) / (Value of an .01 for 100 of the Cheapest to Deliver / Cheapest to Deliver's Conversion Factor)

For example, suppose an investor who owned a portfolio with a market value of $108,658,900 and an MD of 5.41 years expected market interest rates to decline and wanted to *increase* the portfolio's volatility by 30%. How many T-Bond contracts would be necessary to accomplish this goal if the value of an .01 for the cheapest to deliver T-Bond was $0.6655, and its conversion factor was 0.9982?

The value of an .01 for the bond is:

$$\$108,658,900 * 5.41 * 0.0001 = \$58,784$$

The target volatility is:

$$\$58,784 * 1.3 = \$76,420$$

The number of contracts necessary is:

$$(\$76,420 - \$58,784) / (66.55 / 0.9982) = 265$$

Thus, the investor would have to buy 265 contracts to increase the portfolio's volatility by 30%.

### Related Contracts

Although the preceding section focuses on the T-Bond contracts, the 10-year T-Note contract and the 5-year T-Note contract are structurally very similar. For both these contracts, the underlying instrument is a hypothetical 8% note. Each contract has numerous deliverable issues, all of which have their own conversion factor.

# 22

# INTEREST RATE SWAPS

## INTRODUCTION

An interest rate swap is a private contract between two parties in which one party agrees to pay to the second party a stream of fixed-rate interest payments on a fixed notional amount of principal for a fixed time period in exchange for receiving from the second party a stream of floating rate interest payments on the same notional amount of prinipal for the same time period.

**Figure 22.1** *Basic Swap Structure*

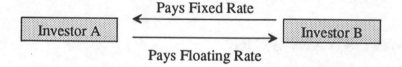

## FUNDING / INVESTMENT ALTERNATIVES

Because of the derivatives market and the swap market, market participants who want to obtain fixed-rate financing (or make fixed-rate investments) can accomplish their goal by borrowing (investing)

- a fixed rate.
- at a floating rate and entering into a series of FRAs to effectively convert the floating rate into a fixed rate.
- at a floating rate and entering into a series of IRF contracts to convert the floating rate into a fixed rate.
- at a floating rate and swapping the floating interest payments for fixed-rate payments.

Similarly, because of the derivatives market and the swap market, market participants who want to obtain floating-rate financing (or make floating-rate investments) can accomplish their goal by borrowing (investing)

- at a floating rate.
- at a fixed rate and entering into a series of FRAs to effectively convert the fixed rate into a floating rate.
- at a fixed rate and entering into a series of IRF contracts to convert the fixed rate into a floating rate.
- at a fixed rate and swapping the fixed interest payments for a series of floating-rate payments.

The alternative that particular market participants will select in order to acheive their objectives depends upon

- the market participants' degree of knowledge.
- how much "ongoing management" the market participant is willing to do.
- which alternative offers the lowest all-in interest expense or the highest all-in investment return.

## WHY SWAPS WORK

Two knowledgeable and well-informed participants will only enter into a swap when *both* parties stand to benefit. In other words, *both* parties have to be able to obtain a lower financing expense (or a higher investment return) by acting together than they could obtain by acting independently. Initially, it might seem illogical that both parties to a swap would be able to benefit - after all, in most derivative market transactions, one party benefits at the expense of the other. However, both participants can benefit from a swap because swap allow both parties to exploit their *comparable advantage*. The following examples illustrate this doctrine. Suppose the following conditions exist in the market:

**Table 22.1** *Representative Loan Rates*

|  | AAA | BBB | Delta |
|---|---|---|---|
| **3-Year Fixed Rate** | 9.00% | 11.00% | 200 bp |
| **3-Year Floating Rate** | L + 20 bp | L + 70 bp | 50 bp |

Given these rates, let's assume that a:

- AAA Rated Company wants to borrow at a floating rate.
- BBB Rated Company wants to borrow at a fixed rate.

The two companies could, of course, act independently and complete their borrowing separately. If they elected to do so, the

- AAA Rated Company would borrow at the current floating rate available to companies with its high credit rating (i.e., L + 20 bp).
- BBB Rated Company would borrow at the current fixed rate available for companies with its lower credit rating (i.e., 11.00%).

However, if the two companies did elect to act independently, they would sacrifice their comparative advantage because they would not be borrowing in the markets where they have their relative strength.

- The AAA Rated company is stronger in the fixed-rate market, where it can borrow at a rate that is 200 bp *below* the rate at which the BBB Rated company can borrow.
- The BBB Rated company, on the other hand, is stronger in the floating-rate market, where it only has to pay a 50 bp spread *above* the rate at which the AAA Rated company can borrow.

By borrowing in the markets where they are relatively weak, the two companies would collectively be sacrificing the difference between the deltas (spreads) of the two markets. Thus, since there is a 200 bp spread in the fixed rate market, and a 50 bp spread in the floating rate market, the difference between the spreads is 150 bps. By borrowing indepentently, the two companies would sacrifice this 150 bps. However, by entering into a swap, the two companies could collectively capture this 150 bps. Assuming, that the two companies elected to split this 150 bps equally, each company could expect to end up with the type of financing it wants -- and a savings of 75 bp over the rate it could get by borrowing independently.

**Table 22.2  *Interest Rates with and without a Swap***

|  | Without Swap | With Swap | Spread |
|---|---|---|---|
| AAA Company | L + 20 bp | L - 55 bp | 75 bp |
| BBB Company | 11 | 10.25 | 75 bp |

In order to accomplish these objectives, this swap would be structured as follows:

**Figure 22.2** *Summary of Swap Cash Flows*

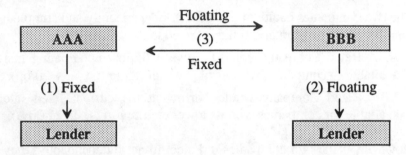

*Step One*: The AAA Rated Company borrows at a fixed rate because that is the market where it is stronger.

*Step Two*: The BBB Rated company borrows at a floating rate because that is the market where it is stronger.

*Step Three*:

- For the AAA Rated Company to end up with a floating rate, it must pay a floating rate to, and receive a fixed rate from, the BBB Rated Company. Given the above structure, the AAA Rated Company's net interest expense is equal to the floating rate it pays +/- the spread between the fixed rate it pays and the fixed rate it receives.

- For the BBB Rated Company to end up with a fixed rate, it must pay a fixed rate to, and receive a floating rate from, the AAA Rated Company. Given the above structure, the BBB Rated Company's net interest expense is equal to the fixed rate it pays +/- the spread between the floating rate it pays and the floating rate it receives.

By convention, the intercompany floating-rate payment is usually set at Libor flat, and the fixed-rate side of the swap is adjusted so that each party receives the yield it negatiates in the transaction. In this example, the 150 bp is being split equally, so therefore the fixed rate is set so that both companies benefit by 75 bp. In order for both companies to benefit by 75 bp, the fixed rate has to be:

**Figure 22.3** *Determining the Fixed Rate*

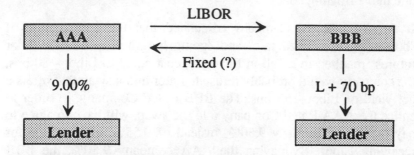

For the AAA Rated Company, the yield is =

(9.00%) - (L) + (Fixed) = (L - 55 bp)

For the BBB Rated Company, the yield is =

(L + 70) + (L) - (Fixed) = 10.25%

The only value for "Fixed" that will make both of the above equations true is 9.55%. Thus, the fixed payment is 9.55%.

## DETERMINING THE BENEFIT SPLIT

In the preceding example, we assumed that the two companies were going to split the 150 bps that are made available by this swap evenly. In actual practice, both parties do not usually benefit equally from the swap transaction. The reason for this is that, since both parties can acheive their objectives in other ways, they wiill not enter into a swap unless it provides an all-in cost that is competitive with their other alternatives.

As we examined at the beginning of this chapter, either company can also use FRAs or IRFs to convert fixed- into floating-rate funding or floating- into fixed-rate funding. Thus, both companies can borrow in the market where they are strongest--and use other derivative instruments to obtain the type of funding (fixed or floating) that they want

For example, the AAA-rated company can also obtain floating-rate financing by borrowing at a fixed rate--and then taking a long position in a 3-year series of Eurodollar IRFs to convert the fixed rate into a floating rate.

If the AAA Rated Company calculated that the combination of "borrowing at a fixed rate" and "going long a strip of Eurodollar futures" resulted in an all-in financing cost equal to Libor - 80 bps, the company would probably refuse to enter into a swap that offers a net yield of Libor - 55 bps. The BBB Rated Company, in order to entice the AAA Rated Company into the swap, will have to agree to pay the AAA company 9.80%, instead of 9.55%, in exchange for receiving Libor. By paying the AAA company 9.80%, the BBB Rated Company allows the AAA company to net the same all-in yield (Libor - 80bps) that it could obtain on its own via the Eurodollar Market. The BBB-rated company can also use IRFs or FRAs to obtain its goal of fixed-rate financing by borrowing at a floating rate and shorting a matching 3-year series of Eurodollar IRFs. Thus, it will not agree to a swap in which its net yield is less than the fixed rate it can create on its own.

Thus, the fixed interest rate that can be obtained by buying or selling an equivalent strip of Eurodollar Futures will be equal to the "fair rate" to pay or receive in an interest rate swap.

## Limiting the Credit Risk of Interest Rate Swap Transactions

Because interest rate swaps are private transactions executed between two parties, they have credit risk. Fortunately however, interest rate swaps are structured so that credit risk is kept to a minimum. For example:

- There is no initial exchange of principal at the start of the transaction, nor reexchange of principal at the transaction's conclusion. It would not make any sense for the two parties to exchange, or reexchange, the same amount of the same currency.

- With regards to the intermediate payments, only the net differential between the fixed rate and the floating rate is exchanged between the two participants. It would make no sense for the first party to pay the second party $100,000, while the second party pays the first party $87,500, when a single payment of $12,500 from the first party to the second would accomplish the same goal.

Thus, the credit risk of an interest rate swap is limited to the difference between the periodic cash flows. In the following table, the credit risk is illustrated for various Libor rates. As can be seen, the credit risk, compared to the size of the transaction, is minimal.

**Table 22.3 *Cash Payments as the Libor Rate Fluctuates (per mm)***

| Reset Date | Libor Rate | Variable Payment | Fixed Payment | Net Payment | Paid To |
|---|---|---|---|---|---|
| 1 | 8.85 | $44,250 | $47,750 | $3,500 | AAA |
| 2 | 9.9 | $49,500 | $47,750 | $1,750 | BBB |
| 3 | 10.25 | $51,250 | $47,750 | $3,500 | BBB |
| 4 | 9.4 | $47,000 | $47,750 | $750 | AAA |
| 5 | 11.05 | $55,250 | $47,750 | $7,500 | BBB |
| 6 | 10.5 | $52,500 | $47,750 | $4,750 | BBB |

## ASSET SWAPS

Although most people think of interest rate swaps as a way of decreasing interest expense, interest rate swaps can just as easily be used to increase investment returns. Consider the following example:

Assume that Investor One wants to make an AA-rated, 2-year fixed-rate investment and that Investor Two wants to make a BBB minus-rated, 2-year floating-rate investment.

**Table 22.4 *Representative Investment Rates***

| | AA Rated | BBB- Rated | Delta |
|---|---|---|---|
| 2-Year Fixed Rate Investments | 9.00% | 10.50% | 150 |
| 2-Year Floating Rate Investments | L + 25 bp | L + 75 bp | 50 |
| | | Difference = | 100 |

The two investors can, of course, invest independently of each other. However, if they do, they will be investing in the markets where they are comparatively weak. Because they would both be investing in the market where they are weak, they would be sacrificing the yield difference between the deltas (i.e., 100 bps). It would be more sensible for the investors to enter into the following swap:

**Figure 22.4** *Determining the Fixed Rate*

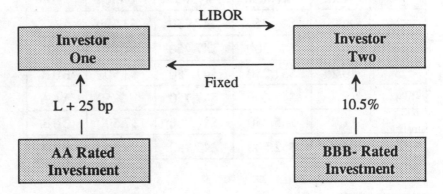

This swap allows both investors to invest in the market where they are strongest. Thus,

- Investor One invests in the floating-rate instrument because it only has to sacrifice 50 bp in return in order to obtain the credit quality it requires. (If Investor One invested directly at a fixed rate, it would have to sacrifice 150 bp in yield in order to obtain the credit quality it desires.)

- Investor Two invests at a fixed rate, where it receives a 150 bp spread in exchange for accepting the lower credit risk. (If Investor Two invested directly at a floating rate, it would receive only a 50 bp spread in exchange for accepting the lower credit quality.)

For the investors to end up with the type of investment they desire, they can enter into a swap in which Investor One pays a floating rate to Investor Two--and Investor Two pays a fixed rate to Investor One. The floating rate is again set to Libor, and the fixed rate is set so that each investor receives the portion of the 100 bp difference in the deltas that it negotiates. If the 100 bp were split equally, the fixed rate would be set as follows:

**Figure 22.5** *Final Swap Structure*

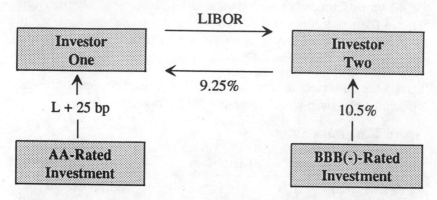

Thus, Investor One nets a 9.50% fixed rate and Investor Two nets a Libor + 125 bp. (Note that for Investor One to meet its objective of having its investment be AA-rated, Investor Two must have at least an AA credit rating.)

## USING SWAPS TO ADJUST THE "BASIS"

Another common type of swap is the swap that is used to substitute one index rate for another. Thus, it is used to substitute the T-Bills rate for the Libor rate, or the Libor rate for the Commercial Paper (CP) rate, or the CP rate for the Prime rate. By using this swap, any borrower paying a rate assigned to a specific index, or any investor receiving a rate assigned to a specific index, can substitute another index. For example, assume that the following market conditions exist for FRNs that are tied to the following rates:

**Table 22.5** *Representative Basis Rates*

|  | AAA | BBB+ | Delta |
|---|---|---|---|
| Six-month Libor | L + 10 bp | L + 50 bp | 40 |
| Six-month CP | CP + 20 bp | CP + 100 bp | 80 |
|  |  | Difference = | 40 |

The AAA Rated Company wants to issue FRNs tied to Libor, and a BBB+ Rated Company wants to issue FRNs tied to the CP rate. If the companies issue their securities independently, they will sacrifice the 40 bp difference between deltas. Both issuers can alternatively achieve their objectives and save a net 40 bp in interest expense if the AAA Rated company issues CP-based FRNs, the BBB+ Rated company issues Libor-based FRNs, and the issuers enter into a swap.

If the companies elect to split the 40 bp difference between the deltas differently, the swap would resemble the following:

**Figure 22.6** *Basis Swap*

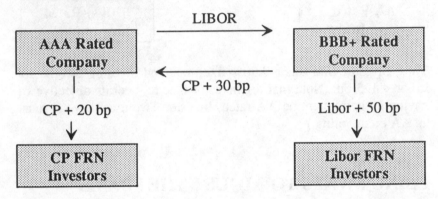

In this swap, the AAA Rated company pays CP + 20 bp to its investors, receives CP + 30 bp from the BBB+ Rated company, and pays Libor to the BBB+ Rated company for a net interest expense of Libor - 10 bp. The BBB+ Rated company, on the other hand, pays Libor + 50 to its investors, receives Libor from the AAA Rated company, and pays CP + 30 bp, for a net interest expense of CP + 80 bp.

## MANAGING THE CREDIT RISK OF INTEREST RATE SWAP TRANSACTIONS

As we examined earlier, the credit risk of interest rate swap transactions is kept to a minimum by the way swap transactions are structured. Because the only difference between the fixed rate and the floating rate is actually exchanged, the credit risk is limited to this amount. Although the credit risk may be small compared to the size of the transaction, it must still be managed.

Different market participants have different ways of dealing with credit risk. For example, most swaps include a provision for automatic suspension of payments by the non-defaulting participant, in the event one participant defaults. Other swaps include a provision that the split of the difference of the deltas changes if the credit quality of one of the participants changes. Also, some market participants require their less creditworthy counterparts to post a security deposit.

## THE ROLE OF THE DEALERS

The role of dealers in the interest rate swap market has changed over the past few years. When this market first formed, dealers acted strictly as brokers. In this capacity, they provided advice to market participants, made introductions to prospective counterparts, and provided prototype documentation.

Presently, the role of dealers has evolved into that of "principal." In order to accommodate clients, dealers are ready to act as counterparts, regardless of the side of the swap that the client wants. For example, if the client wants to receive a fixed rate and pay a floating rate, the dealer will agree to pay the fixed rate and receive the floating rate.

## QUOTING INTEREST RATE SWAPS

Because interest rates are so volatile, it is difficult to quote interest rate swaps. Whereas the floating-rate side of the swap is usually set at six-month Libor, the fixed-rate side of the swap changes with every interest fluctuation in the market. Rather than quoting the fixed-rate side of the swap as a yield, it is generally quoted as a spread over the Treasury Security that has the same maturity. Thus, the fixed-rate side of a 5-year swap will be quoted as a spread over a 5-year Treasury Note, and a 3-year swap will be quoted as a spread over a 3-year Treasury Note. The advantage of this approach is that, although market interest rates change constantly, dealers change their spreads much less frequently. Thus, a quote based on the spread is good for a longer period of time, giving clients time to get quotes from several dealers before committing to a transaction.

# HEDGING A DEALER'S SWAP BOOK

By entering into swap transactions with clients, the dealer exposes itself to interest rate risk. If the dealer receives a fixed rate and pays a floating rate, its risk is that interest rates will rise. If they do, the present value of the future fixed-rate interest payments will, of course, decline. If the dealer receives a floating rate and pays a fixed rate, the dealer's risk is that interest rates will decline, reducing the present value of the floating interest rate payments. Regardless of the dealer's interest rate exposure, it will usually be hedged unless the dealer wants to speculate. One way that a dealer can hedge the interest rate risk of a swap is to enter into another swap for the same notational amount, with the dealer taking the opposite side of the transaction.

As is normally the case, if the floating-rate portion of both swaps is equal to the six-month Libor rate, the dealer will both pay and receive the same interest rate on the floating side of the swaps. Thus, the floating-rate side is a "wash" from the dealer's point of view. Therefore, in order to cover its costs and make a profit, the dealer must receive a higher spread over Treasuries on the fixed-rate side than it pays.

Usually, a dealer will quote the rates at which it will enter into swaps by quoting the spreads. Thus, a dealer might quote a 5-year swap as "68 by 60," meaning that (1) it will pay a fixed rate equal to the 5-year Treasury rate on the day the swap is started, plus 60 bp, in exchange for receiving six-month Libor, and (2) it will accept a fixed rate equal to the 5-year Treasury rate on the day the swap is started, plus 68 bp, in exchange for paying six-month Libor.

The 8-point spread covers the dealer's costs and, hopefully, allows the dealer to make a profit. (The spread between the two rates typically ranges between 6 and 18 bps, depending on the maturity of the transaction.) If the dealer is unable to offset the transaction with another swap, the dealer has to use a series of Eurodollar IRFs contracts to hedge its swap position. However, if Eurodollar IRFs are used to hedge the interest rate risk of a swap book, there is an additional complication that must be taken into account: as interest rates fall, the spread of swaps over the corresponding Treasuries tends to widen. This has implications for the value of the fixed-income stream, aside from the straight discount effect of using a different interest rate.

When interest rates rise, the spread of the fixed-income side of a swap over the corresponding Treasury Bonds tends to decline. This makes existing fixed-income streams more valuable at the higher spreads. Thus, if the dealer is receiving fixed-income payments, the payments become more valuable if interest rates rise, partially offsetting the decrease in their value because of interest-rate increase. However, if interest rates fall, the spread widens, reducing the value of the existing payment stream and partially negating the increase in the value of the payment stream that resulted from the decline in interest rates. Naturally, the impact is reversed if the dealer is paying a fixed rate and receiving a floating rate.

# 23

# INTEREST RATE OPTIONS

## INTRODUCTION

Interest rate options are the most flexible and, in many ways, the most powerful tools that market participants have at their disposal. There are numerous option strategies that market participants can employ that are designed to accomplish a wide variety of objectives. However, although options are certainly useful, they can also provide unwary or uninformed market participants with some very unpleasant surprises. Thus its important to make sure you really understand options before you use them.

## OPTION BASICS AND TERMINOLOGY

There are two basic types of options. *Call options* are contracts in which buyers (i.e., the *longs*) have the right, though *not the obligation*, to purchase a certain quantity of a certain security, currency, notational index, commodity, or future's contract, for a certain price (referred to as the "strike price"), on or until a certain date (the expiration date).

For example, a single call option might entitle the long to buy

- 100 shares of IBM Stock at a price of $105 any time during the next three months.
- $1,000,000 (face value) of T-Bills at a price of 92.16 points any time during the next 10 days.
- one July domestic sugar IRF contract at a price of $0.23/lb. any time during the next two years.

*Put options* are contracts in which the buyers (i.e., the longs) have the right, though *not the obligation*, to sell a certain quantity of a certain security, currency, commodity, or IRF contract for a fixed price on or until a certain date.

For example, a single put option might entitle the long to sell

- one U.S. T-Bond IRF contract at a price of 94.14 points any time during the next two years.

- the notational S&P 500 Index at a value of 350 any time during the next six months.

- 62,500 West German [Whole German?] marks at a price of $0.75 cents per mark for the next three months.

## The Longs' Position

The reason these contracts are called *options* is that the longs have the choice of whether or not to exercise (i.e. use) them. Call options are usually exercised when the option's strike price is below the market value of the underlying instrument, and put options are usually exercised when the strike price is above the market value of the underlying instrument. For example, if a call option allowed an investor to buy 100 ounces of gold at $400 per ounce, and the market price of gold was $420, the investor would exercise the option because it would allow the investor to acquire gold below the current market price. Even if the investor had no desire to actually own the gold, the investor would still either exercise the option (because the gold could be resold at an immediate $20 profit) or sell the option to someone else who did want to own gold.

When an investor can acquire an immediate profit from just the exercise of an option and the disposal of the underlying instrument in the open market, the option is said to be "in the money." (Note that the definition of "in the money" makes no provision for either the cost of the option itself or the transaction costs incurred by the option's exercise.) If the investor would lose money by simultaneously exercising the option and disposing of the underlying instrument, the option is said to be "out of the money." If the option's strike price is equal to the market price of the underlying instrument, the option is said to be "at the money." Thus, the relationship between the market value (MV) of the underlying instrument and the option's strike price (SP) is:

**Table 23.1** *Relationship between the Market Value and the Strike Price*

|  | Calls | Puts |
|---|---|---|
| **"In the Money"** | MV > SP | MV < SP |
| **"At the Money"** | MV = SP | MV = SP |
| **"Out of the Money"** | MV < SP | MV > SP |

(Note that "at the money" is often used to describe the option whose strike price is closest to the market value of the underlying instrument, even if it is not exactly the same.)

The option's price is composed of two components: intrinsic value and time value. The intrinsic value is the value that can be immediately acquired by exercising the option. The time value is equal to the total option price minus its intrinsic value. For example, if the T-Bond future's contract were trading at 93.16 points and the market value of the 95 point put option were $4,000, the option's intrinsic value would be $1,500 [(95 points - 93.16 points) times $1,000], and its time value would be $2,500 ($4,000 - $1,500).

## The Shorts' Position

Whereas the longs have the choice of using their options, the sellers (i.e., the *shorts)* do not have a choice. Instead, they have a *contingent* obligation. If the longs exercise their options, the shorts must, in the case of call options, *sell* the underlying instrument to them at the option's strike price, and, in the case of put options, *buy* the underlying instrument from them at the option's strike price.

Because the longs may or may not exercise their options, the short's obligation is contingent upon their actions. Thus, the first difference between options and other derivatives we have examined (forwards, futures, and swaps) is that, whereas entering into a forward, future, or swap creates an *absolute obligation* for both the long and the short, entering into an option *does not create an absolute obligation* for either party. It is the contingent nature of options that gives them their flexibility and allows us to design and implement so many different option strategies.

## Determining the Value of an Option

In previous chapters we determined the value of various interest rate derivatives by first generating Spot Rate Yield Curves for the various markets. The accuracy of our valuation was limited only by the accuracy of our spot curve. We can also determine the value of an interest rate option, although not with the same degree of accuracy as for the other derivative instruments. The mathematics of option pricing is extremely well documented and is presented in great detail in option textbooks. However, although most option textbooks do an excellent job of discussing the mathematics of option pricing, they often don't adequately examine, from a conceptual point of view, the variables that influence the value of an option and how those variables interact with each other. Therefore, this section examines these variables, including:

- the option's exercise provisions.
- the volatility of the underlying instrument.
- the option's strike price relative to the initial value of the underlying instrument.
- changes in the value of the underlying instrument.
- the time remaining until the option expires.
- the leverage the option provides.
- the level of market interest rates.
- the transaction costs involved.

## Exercise Provisions

An option contract will either be defined as an American Option or a European Option, depending on when the investor who is buying elects to exercise. Options that are exercised any business day from the day they are purchased to the day they expire are commonly referred to as American Options. European Options, on the other hand, may only be exercised on the day they expire.

Initially, it might seem that of two options that differ only regarding their exercise provisions, the American Option would be more valuable than the European Option. After all, because the value of an option can change radically over time, there is always some probability that an option that was very valuable at sometime during its life would become worthless by the time it reached its expiration date. Because an option can be valuable during its life and worthless on its expiration date, it might seem that the ability to exercise an option early is always useful and, thus, that an American Option would be more valuable. However, the right to exercise the option prior to expiration is not always useful.

For a call option on an interest rate instrument, it is *almost never* advantageous to exercise the option early. Whereas the market value of a call option may certainly rise and then decline, so can the value of the underlying instrument. Thus, exercising the call option early will only substitute one risk for another--namely, the risk that the value of the underlying instrument will decline for the risk that the value of the call option will decline.

Whereas the underlying instrument can be sold, so can the option itself, and thus, exercising the option often only increases the investor's transaction charges. In addition, in order to exercise a call option, the option-holder will have to buy the underlying instrument at a price equal to the strike price. Thus, by exercising the call option, the option-holder loses whatever interest could have been earned by *not* exercising the option, but instead investing the strike price in an investment offering the risk free rate of return.

Thus, by exercising a call option early instead of simply selling it, an investor sustains a loss of interest income and an increase in transaction costs. Therefore, exercising call options early is seldom valuable (assuming the option is selling for its fair market value).

For put options on interest rate instruments, the reverse is true. With these options, an American Option is almost always more valuable than a European Option. The reason early exercise can make sense with a put option is that the option-holder sells the underlying instrument at the strike price, receives cash, and can then earn interest by reinvesting the cash at the risk free rate until the expiration date. Thus, delaying the exercise of a put option can "cost" the option-holder interest. Because exercising a call option requires an outlay of cash and exercising a put option generates an inflow of cash, an "at the money" put option is worth less than an "at the money" call option.

## Volatility of the Underlying Instrument

The volatility of the underlying instrument also plays a role in determining the value of an option. Naturally, the higher the volatility, the greater the value of an option (either a call or a put) on that underlying instrument. The reason for the direct relationship between volatility and the option's price is that the higher the volatility of the underlying instrument, the higher the probability that the option will experience large, potentially profitable price changes. Naturally, the higher the probability of large price change, the more valuable an option becomes to a buyer--and the riskier it becomes for the seller. Most parameters that influence the value of an option can be determined with a high degree of certainty. *However, although the value of the option depends on the future volatility of the underlying instrument, the future volatility of the instrument can only be estimated.*

Complicating this further is the fact that there is no best way to estimate the volatility of an underlying instrument. Some market participants estimate the future volatility of the underlying instrument by analyzing statistically the historical volatility of the instrument. For example, by analyzing the historical price changes of the instrument, it might be determined that the average price change of the instrument per specific time frame was $5/month, or $0.087/day, or $20/year. (Naturally, the average price change can also be expressed on a percentage basis.)

Given the current price of the underlying instrument and the average price change per time period, it is possible to create a price/probability lattice for the underlying instrument over the term of the option's life. As a first example, assume that the current market value of the underlying instrument is $100, and its historical volatility is $2/month. Assume also that, historically, it is just as likely that the value of the instrument will rise as it is that the value of the instrument will decline. If the term of the option were six months, the price lattice would resemble the one in figure 23.1.

Naturally, for any given month, the value of the underlying instrument will probably change by some other price than $2 ($2 is just the *average* price change). Because the actual price changes will probably be greater than or less than $2, the price of the instrument at the end of six months will probably not equal one of the values in the preceding figure. As we shall see, this will not matter.

**Figure 23.1** *Possible Prices of an Underlying that Has an Average Price Change of $2/Month Over a Six-Month Time Frame*

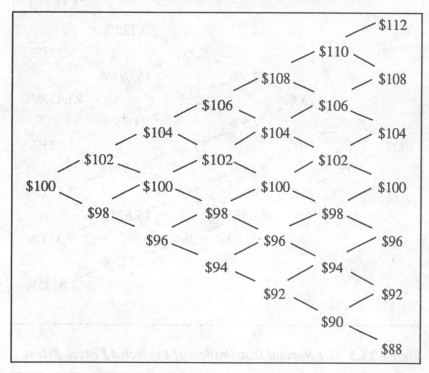

After the price lattice is constructed, the next step is to calculate the probability that the underlying instrument will be at each of the preceding prices. Because there is a 50% probability that the value of the instrument will rise, we can use that percentage to determine the probability of each of the prices. Thus, in the first month there is a 50% chance that the instrument will rise to $102, and a 50% chance that it will drop to $98. In the second month, there is again a 50% chance of an increase or decrease from each of the one-month values etc.

Once these two lattices have been created and both the instrument's future prices and the respective probabilities of those prices have been determined, the data can then be used to calculate the standard deviation and the normal distribution (i.e., the Figure 23.3) of the instrument's potential future prices.

**Figure 23.2** *Probability of the Various Future Prices Over a Six Month Period*

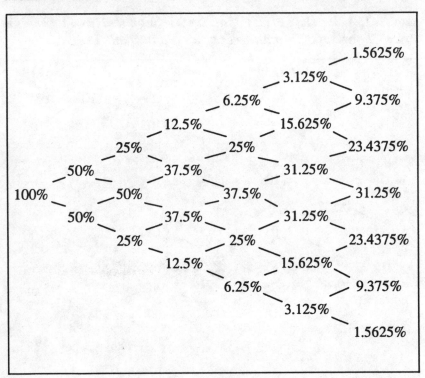

**Figure 23.3** *The Normal Distribution of Projected Future Prices*

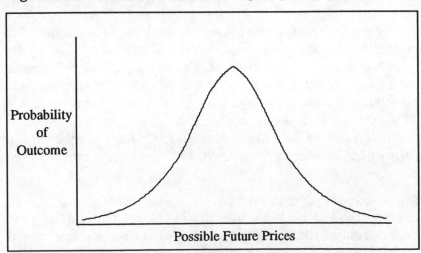

From this bell-shaped curve, the probability of each future price can be determined, as can the probability that the price of the underlying instrument will equal or exceed an option's strike price. As an illustration, consider the following example:

Suppose there is a series of European call options on the preceding underlying instrument with strike prices ranging from 88 to 112 in 2-point increments. On its expiration date, any call option will only be valuable if the market value of the instrument is greater than the option's strike price. By examining the bell-shaped curve, we can determine what the probability is that the instrument's market value will exceed each strike price. For example, if we consider the option with the 110 strike price, we know that the option will only be valuable on its expiration date if the market value of the instrument is greater than 110 when the option expires. The probability of the instrument's market value being greater than 110 on the option's expiration date is equal to the area under the curve in "Area A," divided by the total area under the curve. The size of Area A, as well as the total area under the curve, can be determined by statistical techniques.

For the option with the 102 strike price, the probability that the option would be worth something at expiration would be equal to Area B, divided by the total area under the curve.

**Figure 23.4** *Probability Distribution*

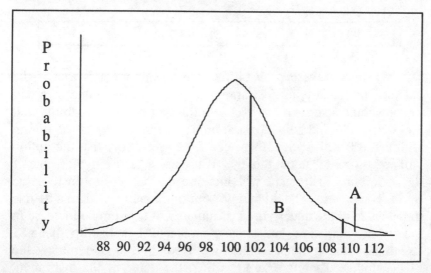

By looking at the area to the right of each strike price relative to the area under the entire curve, the probability that each option will end up "in the money" can be determined. In this example, the approximate probability that each option will be "in the money" when it expires is illustrated in the following table:

**Table 23.2** *Probability of Various Strikes Being "In the Money"*

| Strike Price | Approximate Probability of the Option Being "In the Money" |
|:---:|:---:|
| 112 | 1.20% |
| 110 | 2.05% |
| 108 | 5.13% |
| 106 | 11.10% |
| 104 | 20.09% |
| 102 | 48.40% |
| 100 | 50.00% |
| 98 | 51.60% |
| 96 | 79.91% |
| 94 | 88.90% |
| 92 | 94.87% |
| 90 | 97.95% |
| 88 | 98.80% |

The reason that these probabilities are so important is that if the value of the underlying instrument rises by $1, the value of a call option should also increase by $1, multiplied by the probability that the option will end being "in the money." In the case of the option with the 100 strike price, there is a 50% probability that the option will end up being "in the money." If it does, a $1 rise in the value of the underlying instrument will increase the option's intrinsic value by $1. If the option should end up "out of the money," then a $1 rise in the value of the underlying instrument will result in no increase in the option's intrinsic value. Thus, there is a 50% probability that a $1 rise in the value of the instrument will result in a $1 gain in the value of the option. Therefore, a $1 rise in the value of the instrument should result in a $0.50 increase in the value of the option ($1.00 * 0.5 = $0.50). Likewise, a $1 drop in the value of the instrument would result in a $0.50 decline in the value of this option.

As another example, the probability that the 104 call option will end up "in the money" is 20.09%. Thus, there is a 20.09% chance that the option will be worth $1 more upon expiration and a 79.01% chance that the option will be "out of the money," and thus, worth nothing, when the option expires. If there is a 20.09% chance that the option will be worth a dollar more upon expiration, this option's price should increase (or decrease) by 0.2009 multiplied by $1, or $0.21, in response to a $1 increase (or decrease) in the value of the underlying instrument.

As a final example, if the price of the underlying instrument falls by a dollar, there is a 94.87% chance that the option with the 92 strike price will be worth $1 less upon expiration. Thus, we would expect the value of the 92 call option to decrease by $0.95 if the value of the instrument fell by $1.

The probability that the option will end up being "in the money" is referred to as the option's *delta*. An option's *delta* can also be defined as the change in the value of the option, divided by the change in the value of the underlying instrument. For call options, *delta* is a positive number, meaning that the value of the option increases as the value of the underlying instrument rises. For put options, *delta* is a negative number, meaning that the value of the option falls as the value of the instrument rises. Although the calculation of an option's *delta* appears to be reasonably simple, there are two complications that can lead to errors:

First, is the fact that the instrument's future volatility cannot be known with certainty. If the instrument's volatility is incorrect, the distribution curve will also be incorrect. (Naturally, using the wrong distribution curve will result in the wrong *deltas*.) The preceding example used historical data to predict the instrument's future volatility--a very common practice in option-pricing models. However, there is no guarantee that the instrument's future volatility will be equal to its past volatility. Instead of using historical data, many proprietary models use their own economic models to predict volatility, and therefore the accuracy of their *delta* calculations is dependent on the accuracy of their models.

The second complication is the way the original price and probability lattices are constructed. The lattice, and therefore the distribution curve, will be slightly different depending on whether hourly, daily, weekly, or monthly data is used to construct it. Because there is no best way to construct the curve, different market participants, using the same market data, could reasonably come up with slightly different distribution curves.

It is worth noting also that although quantifying or estimating the volatility of the instrument is an essential step in determining the value of an option, this calculation can also be done in reverse. Given the current market price of an option and the current market price of the instrument, the volatility that relates the two figures can be calculated. This volatility is, by definition, the average volatility of all the market participants, and is commonly referred to as the *implied volatility*. Naturally, the volatility of the underlying instrument is constantly changing, and so this calculation needs to be performed frequently.

### Impact That a Change in the Value of the Underlying Instrument Has on the Option's Delta

In the preceding example, the relationship between the price of the option, its strike price, and the value of the instrument was explored. Our conclusion was that, for a given change in the value of the underlying instrument, the value of the option would change by a factor equal to the change in the value of the instrument multiplied by the probability that the option will end up being "in the money." Although this is true for very small changes in the value of the instrument, it is not true for larger changes. The reason is that every time the value of the instrument changes, so does the price lattice, and every time the price lattice changes, so does the distribution curve. Every time this curve changes, so does the probability that a given option, with a given strike price, will end up being "in the money."

Consider the preceding example if the price of the underlying rises suddenly by $3, and as a result, the distribution curve shifts three points to the right.

The shift of the distribution curve to the right naturally influences the probability that the various options will end up being "in the money." The new approximate probabilities are illustrated in Table 23.3.

**Figure 23.5** *New Probability Distributions of Strike Prices*

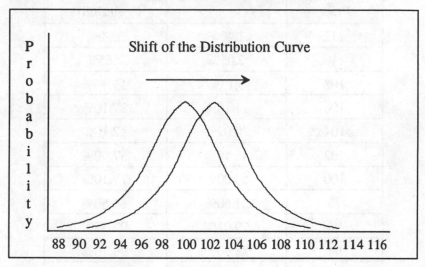

The curve would naturally shift to the right, because the new price lattice for the instrument would start at $103, instead of $100.

**Figure 23.6** *Revised Price Lattice of the Underlying*

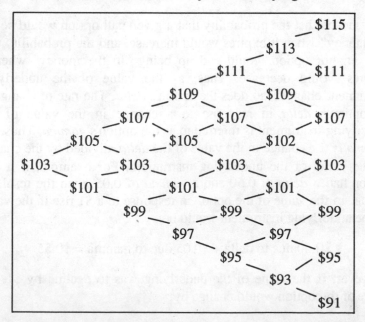

**Table 23.3** *The Probabilities That the Various Strike Prices Will Be in the Money after the Price of the Underlying Rises*

| Strike Price | Old Probability | New Probability |
|:---:|:---:|:---:|
| 112 | 1.20% | 3.30% |
| 110 | 2.05% | 7.65% |
| 108 | 5.13% | 15.40% |
| 106 | 11.10% | 27.10% |
| 104 | 20.09% | 42.10% |
| 102 | 48.40% | 57.90% |
| 100 | 50.00% | 77.10% |
| 98 | 51.60% | 84.60% |
| 96 | 79.91% | 92.35% |
| 94 | 88.90% | 96.70% |
| 92 | 94.87% | 98.75% |
| 90 | 97.95% | 99.6% |
| 88 | 98.80% | 99.9% |

This means that the probability that a given call option would be "in the money" when it expires would increase, and the probability that a given put option would end up being "in the money" when it expires would decrease. Thus, as the value of the underlying instrument changes, so does the option's *delta*. The rate of change in an option's *delta* in response to a change in the value of the underlying instrument is referred to as the option's *gamma*. Thus, the *gamma is* the change in the value of the *delta*, divided by the change in the value of the underlying instrument. For example, if a call option had a *delta* of 0.50 and a *gamma* of 0.05, then the resulting change in the value of the option in response to a $1 rise in the value of the underlying instrument would be:

$$\$0.50 \text{ due to delta} + \$0.05 \text{ due to gamma} = \$0.55$$

However, if the value of the underlying was to decline by $1, the value of the option would change by:

$0.50 due to delta - $0.05 due to gamma = $0.45

The relationship between *gamma* and *delta* is conceptually very similar to the relationship between convexity and duration. Whereas *gamma* measures the change in an option's *delta* in response to a change in the value of the underlying instrument, convexity measures the change in a bond's duration in response to a change in market interest rates.

## Time Remaining until the Option Expires

If all other factors are equal, the longer the term of the option, the greater its value. This is true for both calls and puts. Intuitively, this is sensible, because the longer the term of the option, the more time it has for its value to change. Thus, buyers should be willing to pay more for options with longer terms, and sellers should demand higher premiums for them. To quantify the difference, consider how the underlying instrument's price lattice is influenced by increasing the number of steps in the lattice. As the number of steps increases, both the maximum price changes and the range of possible future values increases. Likewise, as time passes, both the maximum price changes and the range of possible future values decreases.

Thus, as time passes, both the height and the breadth of the distribution curve declines, and so does the probability that some of the call options will end up being "in the money." For example, consider the call option with the 106 strike price. When there are six months until the option expires, there is a reasonable probability that the option will end up "in the money." However, if time passes and the price of the underlying instrument remains constant, the probability that the option will end up "in the money" declines. As it does, so will the value of the option, its *delta*, and its *gamma*.

Because we are dealing with a normal distribution curve, the relationship between the passage of time and the erosion of an option's time premium is *not linear*. In other words, the *rate of decline* in Area A, relative to the total area under the curve, *increases* as time passes. The fewer the number of time periods remaining, the greater the decline in Area A, relative to the area under the curve. Thus, the rate of decay of an option's time premium increases (when expressed in dollars) in an ever-increasing manner as time passes. The rate of decay of an option's time premium per day is referred to as the option's *theta*.

**Figure 23.7** *Changing Probability Distribution as Time Passes*

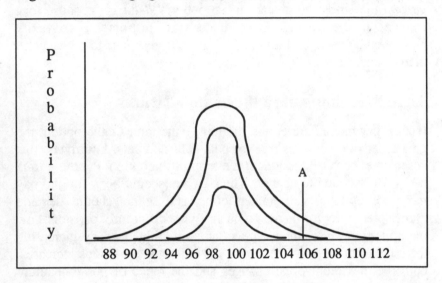

For the buyers of options, *theta* is almost always a negative number and, thus, the lower its value the better. (The only exception being European put options, in those rare cases when they are trading below the option's intrinsic value.) For this reason, options are often referred to as *wasting assets*. For the sellers of options, however, the higher the *theta*, the better. The value of *theta* is very low when the option has a long remaining life. Thus, the passage of a single day will not have a very great impact on the value of the option. However, because the value of *theta* increases steadily as the option gets closer to expiration, the value of *theta* increases. For example, an option with a year until expiration and a premium of $400 might have a *theta* of $1, meaning that the value of the option would decline by $1/day if the price of the underlying instrument remained unchanged. However, as the option moved closer to expiration, the *theta* might increase to $5/day, meaning that every day the price of the option would decline by $5--assuming again that the value of the underlying instrument remains unchanged.

Expressed graphically, the price path of an option as time passes would resemble the path illustrated in Figure 23.8.

**Figure 23.8** *Impact of Theta on Option's Value*

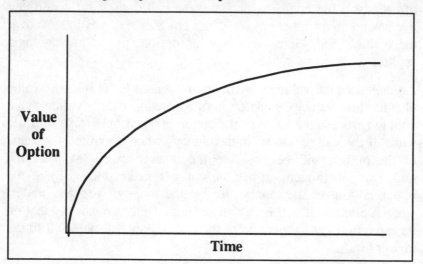

In addition to the remaining life of the option, the other principal factor that influences the *theta* of an option is whether the option is in, at, or "out of the money." Generally, for options on the same underlying instrument with the same expiration date, the further the option is "out of the money," the higher its *theta* will be (expressed as a percentage of the option's value). Again, this is the result of "shrinking" a bell-shaped curve. Thus, in the preceding example, the 110 call option would have a higher *theta* than the 104 option (expressed as a percentage of its value), because it is further "out of the money."

## Leverage and the Level of Market Interest Rates

Changing market interest rates will also influence the value of an option. The relationship between interest rates and the value of options is very complex, because changing interest rates will have a different impact on different options depending on:

- whether the option in question is a put or a call.

- whether the underlying instrument will make any dividend or interest payments prior to the day the option expires.

- how sensitive the value of the underlying instrument is to changes in interest rates.

- whether the option is an American Option or a European Option.

The simplest relationship between market interest rates and the value of options is the one between European call options on underlying instruments that neither pay dividends nor accrue or pay interest over the option's life. Given this type of option, the following logic applies:

An option's total value is, by definition, equal to its intrinsic value plus its time value. On the option's expiration date, its time value goes to zero and the value of the option is equal only to its intrinsic value. If the call option is "in the money" when it expires, the value of the option will be equal to the market value (MV) of the underlying instrument, minus the option's strike price (SP). If the option is "out of the money" (or "at the money," for that matter) when it expires, it will be worth nothing. Thus, we can say that on its expiration date, the value of the call option will be equal to the greater of:

$$(MV - SP) \text{ or } 0$$

Prior to the option's expiration date, the option may also have time value. The option's time value, in turn, is composed of two components: the leverage factor and the choice factor.

Time Value = Leverage Factor + Choice Factor

The first component, the leverage factor, arises from the fact that by owning the call option, you can delay the purchase of the underlying instrument at the strike price until the option's expiration date. The money that you would have had to pay to buy the instrument can, therefore, be invested from the purchase date of the option to the option's expiration date, and interest can be earned. The amount of interest that can be earned, expressed on a present-value basis, is equal to the option's strike price, minus the present value of the strike price.

The choice factor is the "value" of *not having to buy the underlying instrument* at the strike price if the instrument can be purchased for less than the strike price in the open market. From a net financial point of view, the value of not having to buy the instrument is equal to the value of buying it at a price below the strike price, and then selling it at the strike price. The ability to sell the instrument at the strike price is, of course, the definition of a put option. Thus, the value of not having to buy the instrument at the strike price is equal to the value of a put option for the same underlying instrument at the same strike price. The conclusion, therefore, is:

Option's Value (OV) = Intrinsic Value + Time Value

or

OV = Intrinsic Value + Leverage Value + Choice Value

Replacing these terms with their equivalent values gives us the following formula:

**Table 23.4** *Alternative Values for a Call*

| Intrinsic Value | Leverage Value | Choice Value |
|:---:|:---:|:---:|
| (MV - SP) | [SP - PV(SP)] | P |

thus:

$$OV = (MV - SP) + [SP-PV(SP)] + P$$

which can be simplified to:

$$OV = MV - PV(SP) + P$$

Thus, this is the formula for the value of a European call option, where the underlying instrument generates no cash flows. By applying the same logic to a European put option, we can determine that the value of a put option is equal to:

Intrinsic Value + Leverage Value + Choice Value

Replacing these terms with their equivalent values gives us the following formula:

**Table 23.5** *Alternative Values for a Put*

| Intrinsic Value | Leverage Value | Choice Value |
|:---:|:---:|:---:|
| (SP - MV) | [PV(SP) - SP] | C |

which can be simplified to: PV(SP) - MV + C

From these equations, we can conclude that as interest rates rise, the PV of the strike price (i.e., the PV(SP)) will decline, and therefore the value of a call option will rise and the value of a put option will fall, as long as the underlying instrument makes no payments during its life. Naturally, if the instrument generates some cash flows (dividends or interest), these cash flows will influence the attractiveness of buying or selling an option, compared to simply taking a position in the underlying instrument.

## Transaction Charges

The last major factor to consider when evaluating an option is the influence of the obligatory transaction charges. When the value of a forward or future contract is determined, the influence of transaction charges can often be ignored because they are often negligible in relation to the size of the underlying instrument contract. However, transaction costs cannot be ignored in options transactions because these costs are not negligible relative to the size of the transaction. The principal reason that transaction costs are higher for options transactions is that option contracts are generally less liquid than other derivative instruments. Consider the September T-Bond IRF contract versus the options on this same contract. Whereas all the buyers and sellers of the IRF are trading just one contract, there are often 15 call options and 15 put options on just the September IRF contract alone. The greater the number of option contracts the lower the liquidity of each contract.

The four principal transaction costs associated with option transactions are:

- The bid/ask spread, which for options, is often relatively high, because of the lower liquidity.

- The financing cost (gain). The cost of buying the option must be financed, and the proceeds from selling the option can be reinvested.

- The commission and/or overhead. Customers pay commissions when they buy and when they sell, and also have some overhead costs. Dealers have very substantial overhead costs.

- The slippage. Because most option contracts are not very liquid, trying to buy or sell a large quantity of contracts at any one time can disturb the market. Thus, if you enter a market order to buy 100 call options when the option is trading at 1 and 3/4 by 2, because of its lack of liquidity, the order might actually get filled with 20 contracts at 2, another 20 at 2 1/8, 50 at 2 1/4, and the last

10 at 2 3/8. Depending on how much the contract is not liquid, slippage can be the largest component of the overall transaction costs.

# MODELING CONSIDERATIONS AND LIMITATIONS

In order to be accurate, an option pricing model must incorporate all of the variables discussed above. In addition, all of the preceding factors are interrelated to some degree. Because changing one variable will usually influence several others, we cannot simply change one variable and recalculate the option's value.

Also, adding complexity to any pricing model is the fact that different variables have different influences on the options of different types of underlying instruments. Thus, separate models often need to be developed for each type of underlying instrument.

# USING OPTIONS AS HEDGING VEHICLES

In previous chapters, the risk/reward pattern of forwards and futures was examined, and it was demonstrated that their risk/reward patterns were both *symmetric* and *absolute*.

*Symmetric* means that when these instruments are used for hedging purposes, they can eliminate the possibility of risk from an unfavorable price change--but only by *also eliminating* the possibility of reward from a favorable price change. *Absolute* means that these instruments create an absolute obligation for both buyers and sellers. Because forward and future obligations are absolute, they can only be used to hedge risks that are also absolute, regarding their size and timing.

Options, on the other hand, are *neither* symmetric *nor* absolute. Because their risk/reward patterns are different from the patterns of futures and forwards, they can be used in different ways and applied to different situations. Consider the following examples:

Suppose an investor is buying 50 million floating rate notes (FRNs) that are tied to the six-month Libor rate. The risk, as an investor, is that the Libor rate will decline, reducing the interest income. The investor would like to hedge against that risk, but does not want to sacrifice the upside potential if the Libor rate should rise instead. In effect, the investor wants a hedge that has an asymmetric risk/reward pattern, one that pays the investor if interest rates fall, but does not eliminate the upside if interest rates rise. The only way to establish a hedge with an asymmetric risk/reward pattern is to use options.

As another example, consider why options can be used to hedge a portfolio of fixed-rate residential mortgages. A portfolio of 30-year mortgages might have an average life of 10 years, because some of the homeowners will undoubtedly move, trade up, default, or pay off their mortgages. When homeowners want to prepay their mortgages for whatever reason, they can do so without penalty, because almost all mortgages in the U.S. have an embedded option that entitles them to this choice. (An embedded option is not a separate contract, but instead is simply a part of the underlying instrument itself.)

This option grants the homeowners the right to prepay their mortgages at any time without penalty. Because this option is embedded into the contract, mortgage-holders have effectively "sold" this option to the homeowner. Thus, the mortgage-holders are selling these options and the homeowners are buying them. Because this option grants the homeowner the right to buy back their mortgages, the option is a call option. Because the homeowners are buying these options, the homeowners decide when to use it. Obviously, the homeowner will exercise this option and buy back their mortgages when it is advantageous to do so (i.e., when interest rates drop and the homeowners can refinance at a lower rate). Thus, by utilizing or not utilizing this option, the homeowner can adjust the duration of the mortgage (see Chapter 11 for a more complete definition).

For the mortgage holder, this option creates a very definite and substantial risk. If interest rates fall, the mortgage's duration will be shortened, because the homeowner will refinance--just when the investor would like the investment's duration to be longer. If they rise, the mortgage's duration will be lengthened, because the homeowner will not refinance--just when the investor would like the investment's duration to be shorter.

Because mortgage holders do not know which way interest rates will move in the future, they do not know whether to hedge the portfolio against the risk that the portfolio's duration will get shorter or longer. Also, they do not know how much of a hedge they will need. The only way to hedge a risk where neither the type of exposure nor the magnitude of exposure is known with certainty is with options. In order to hedge both risks that interest rates will either rise or fall, investors would have to own *both* call options and put options. If an investor owned both in sufficient quantity, the investor could choose which options to exercise, what quantity of option to exercise, and when to exercise the options in order to offset the influence of the homeowner's options. Thus, the options would be used to hedge other options, and in fact, the only way to hedge an option is with another option.

# 24

# OTHER INTEREST RATE DERIVATIVES

---

## INTRODUCTION

In addition to forwards, futures, swaps, and options on forwards, there are many other interest rate derivatives available currently in the market. Some of the popular derivatives include forward swaps, swap facilities or spread locks, "swaptions," interest rate caps, floors, and collars, and participating rate agreements.

This chapter defines each of the these derivatives, describes the situations in which they are commonly employed, discusses how each is priced, and provides some examples of how they can be used to accomplish specific investment goals and objectives.

## FORWARD SWAPS

A forward swap is simply an interest rate swap that is scheduled to begin at some future time. Market participants use forward swaps

- to fix the refinancing rate of a fixed-rate liability that matures or can be called at some future time. For example, a company that was refinancing some 3-year notes in a year might enter into a forward swap to lock in a 3-year rate, one year into the future.

- fix the rate of a future liability such as project financing or construction loan draw-downs. For example, a builder planning on drawing against a $100 million Libor-based LOC over a 2-year period, starting in six months, might want to fix the rate now.

As with all derivatives, the price of a forward swap is equal to the sum of the cost of hedging the transaction, the transaction costs and expenses, and the dealer's profit.

For example, suppose "XYZ," Inc. can borrow at Libor + 25 bp and that the company expected to borrow $100 million for three years, two years from now. If the company wanted to lock in the rate presently, it could ask its dealer for a 3-year swap, two years forward, in which it would receive a fixed rate and pay a floating rate. The dealer can quote the client a rate because it can hedge the transaction by entering into the following swaps against Libor flat:

**Figure 24.1** *Forward Swap Arbitrage*

| 2-year swap in which | 3-year forward swap in which |
|---|---|
| dealer pays a fixed rate | dealer pays a fixed rate |

| 5-year swap in which the dealer |
|---|
| receives a fixed rate |

By entering into a 5-year swap in which the dealer receives a fixed rate and pays Libor, the dealer locks in a fixed rate for the entire 5-year period. The dealer then enters into a 2-year swap to "store the swap" for two years until it is needed to meet the client's 3-year need. The price is determined the same way in which the forward rate agreement is priced. The sum of the 2-year component and the 3-year component must equal the sum of the 5-year component, or else the opportunity for arbitrage would exist.

Given that the 2-year swap rate is 8.5%, and the 5-year swap rate is 9.5%, the yield of a 3-year swap, two years forward, can be calculated as follows (using a $1,000,000 notational amount). The total cash in and cash out from the dealer's point of view would be:

**Table 24.1** *The Cash Flows of a Forward Swap from the Dealer's Point of View*

| Period | Fixed Rate Received | Fixed Rate Paid Out 2-Year | Fixed Rate Paid Out 3-Year |
|---|---|---|---|
| 1 | $47,500 | $42,250 | $0 |
| 2 | $47,500 | $42,250 | $0 |
| 3 | $47,500 | $42,250 | $0 |

| | | | |
|---|---|---|---|
| 4 | $47,500 | $42,250 | $0 |
| 5 | $47,500 | $0.00 | ? |
| 6 | $47,500 | $0.00 | ? |
| 7 | $47,500 | $0.00 | ? |
| 8 | $47,500 | $0.00 | ? |
| 9 | $47,500 | $0.00 | ? |
| 10 | $47,500 | $0.00 | ? |

Note that for the first four periods, the dealer would receive $5,250 more dollars than would be paid out. These dollars could be invested at a conservative rate (e.g., 6%) and the dollars, plus the interest earned, can be used to supplement the payments made by the dealer on the forward swap.

For example, four payments of $5,250 each, reinvested at 6% per year (3% per period), would grow to be:

- setting n = 4
- setting i = 3%
- setting PMT = $5,250
- setting PV = 0
- solving for FV = $21,964

This sum, if invested at 3% per period, can generate six payments of:

- setting n = 6
- setting i = 3%
- setting FV = 0
- solving for PV = $21,964
- solving for the PMT = $4,054

Adding this $4,054 to the $47,500 the dealer receives from the 5-year swap means that the dealer can afford to make six payments of $51,554 on the 3-year swap, two years forward (ignoring for now the transaction costs and profit). Thus, the rate on the 3-year swap, two years forward, would be:

$$[(\$51,554 * 2) / \$1,000,000] * 100 = 10.31\%$$

From this 10.31%, the dealer would subtract a spread to account for transaction costs and profit, and might quote the client a yield of 10.10% on the swap in exchange for paying Libor. Because the client can borrow at Libor + 25 bp, the total cost of 3-year fixed-rate interest, two years forward, would be:

$$10.31\% + 0.25\% = 10.56\%$$

A forward swap, like other swaps, is an absolute transaction, meaning that once the participants agree to enter the transaction, they must complete it on schedule (i.e., a forward swap is not an option).

# THE SWAP FACILITY OR SPREAD LOCK

A spread lock facility is an agreement between a client and a dealer in which

- the client agrees to execute a swap transaction with a dealer within a certain period of time, usually 30 to 120 days.
- the dealer agrees to hold the swap spread (over the corresponding Treasury) constant until the swap transaction is executed.

For example, a client might agree to enter into a $50 million 4-year swap within the next 90 days, at a spread of 55 bp over the 4-year Treasury. Once the transaction is agreed to, the client must exercise the swap within the 90 days. Thus, a swap facility or spread lock is not an option.

The reason spread locks are useful is that the "spreads" of swaps over their corresponding Treasuries change as market interest rates change. When market interest rates decline, more clients want to lock in a fixed rate. By the law of supply and demand, as more and more clients want to lock in a fixed rate, the swap spreads tend to widen. Market participants who expect interest rates to decline can protect themselves from the increase in the swap spread by entering into a spread lock facility. A participant and a dealer can therefore speculate about the direction of interest rates.

Depending on how the contract is written, when the swap facility is exercised, the start date for the swap can either be the date the spread lock was entered into or the date the facility is exercised.

## "SWAPTIONS"

A "swaption" is an option to enter a swap. The option can either give the holder the right to pay a fixed rate and receive a floating rate, and vice versa.

The *fixed side* of the swap is quoted, thus, investors who are purchasing buyer's options have the right, though not the obligation, to enter into a swap in which they will pay a fixed rate. They benefit if interest rates rise above the strike yield, because by exercising their options, they can enter into a swap at a lower market rate (i.e., paying 9% in exchange for receiving Libor payments, instead of paying 10% for the same Libor payments).

Investors who are selling buyer's options have a contingent obligation to receive a fixed rate and pay a floating rate. They benefit when interest rates drop below the strike yield, because the options will not be exercised and, thus, they will be able to keep the premiums they received when they sold the options.

Investors who are buying receiver's options have the right to pay a floating rate in exchange for receiving a fixed rate. They benefit as interest rates fall below the strike yield, because they can use their options to obtain an above-market fixed-rate stream of payments in exchange for their floating-rate payments.

Investors who are selling receiver's options have a contingent obligation to deliver fixed-rate payments in exchange for floating-rate payments. They benefit when interest rates rise above the strike yield, because the options will not be exercised then, and therefore, they will be able to keep the premiums they received when they sold the options.

"Swaptions" are categorized as either *standard* or *reversible* depending on the exercise provisions. When standard options are exercised, a new swap is started. When reversible options are exercised, the participants take a position in an existing swap. To avoid the complications of early exercise, most "swaptions" have European exercise provisions.

# CAPS, FLOORS, AND COLLARS

## Floating-Rate Cap

A floating-rate cap is a contract between two participants in which the maximum rate that the borrower will have to pay on a floating-rate debt is fixed. For example, suppose a company borrows $100 million for five years at an interest rate of Libor + 50 bp. If the company wants to protect itself against rising interest rates, it can purchase a 10% Libor cap from a dealer. If the Libor rate rises above 10% (and thus, the company's interest expense rises above 10.5%), the dealer pays the incremental difference. Thus, if the Libor rate were to rise to 11%, the dealer would pay the company 1%.

A cap is the functional equivalent of a series of interest rate call options (just as an interest rate swap is the functional equivalent of a series of forward rate agreements). The buyer of the cap is long the call options, whereas the seller is short them. The price of a cap must equal the value of the equivalent series of call options, otherwise the opportunity for arbitrage would exist.

## Floating-Rate Floor

A floating-rate floor is a contract between two participants in which the minimum rate that the borrower will receive on a floating-rate investment is fixed. For example, suppose a company buys $50 million of 2-year FRNs that pay Libor + 50 bp. If the company wants to protect itself against falling interest rates, it can purchase an 8% floor from a dealer. If the Libor declines below 8% (and thus the company's interest income falls below 8.5%), the dealer pays the incremental difference. Thus, if the Libor rate fell to 7%, the dealer would pay the company 1%.

A floor is the functional equivalent of a series of interest rate put options (just as an interest rate swap is the functional equivalent of a series of forward rate agreements). The buyer of the floor is long the put options, whereas the seller is short them. The price of a floor must equal the value of the equivalent series of put options, otherwise the opportunity for arbitrage would exist.

## Floating-Rate Collars

A floating-rate collar is a combination of a cap and a floor. For example, a borrower can *buy a cap* in order to limit how high its interest payments can rise, and can also *sell a floor,* which limits how low its interest expense can drop. The money received from selling the floor can offset the cost of buying the cap. Similarly, an investor can sell a cap and buy a floor, and in doing so limit its maximum interest income, but guarantee itself a minimum interest rate. An interest rate swap is in some ways a collar.

Consider a plain interest rate swap in which the fixed payment is 9.5% of the notational amount. One way to think of the fixed side of a swap is as the equivalent of a 9.5% cap and a 9.5% floor. Other collars can be priced as the series of the equivalent underlying instrument options.

# PARTICIPATING RATE AGREEMENTS

Related closely to caps, floors, and collars are Participating Rate Agreements (PRAs), which are contracts usually between borrowers and dealers. According to a PRA

- the borrower fixes the maximum rate it will have to pay (i.e., the cap rate).
- the borrower fixes a floor rate that may or may not be the same as the cap rate.
- if the index rate drops below the floor rate, the dealer and the borrower split the difference in a predetermined manner.

For example, suppose that "XYZ", Inc. had a $50 million outstanding loan at Libor flat, and the company elected to buy a 2-year PRA that had the following provisions: a 12% Libor cap rate, a 10% Libor floor rate, and a 50/50 participating split. If the Libor rate rose to

- 14%, the borrower would have to pay 12% because of the cap.
- 11%, the borrower would have to pay 11%.
- 8%, the borrower would have to pay 9% because of the floor. Although the PRA has a 10% floor, it also has a 50/50 participation split, and thus, the 2% loss is sustained 50% by the

borrower and 50% by the dealer. Because the rate is 8% and the borrower must pay half of the 2% differential between the floor rate and the index rate, the borrower's cost is 9%.

In order to hedge a PRA, a dealer

- enters into a swap in which it pays a fixed rate equal to the PRA's floor rate. The swap should be on the same notational amount as the PRA ($50 million in this example).

- buys a floor at a rate equal to the PRA's floor rate on a notational amount equal to the size of the PRA, multiplied by the participant's percentage ($50 million * 0.5 = $25 million).

Thus, the net transactions necessary to enter and hedge a PRA include, in this case, XYZ, Inc. borrowing at a floating rate (Libor + spread) from a lender, and then entering into a PRA in which it

- receives $\Delta$ between Libor and 12% if Libor is greater than 12%.

- pays 1/2 $\Delta$ Libor and 10% if Libor is less than 10%.

The dealer enters into a $50 million PRA with XYZ, Inc. and

- receives a fee.

- pays the $\Delta$ between Libor and 12% if Libor is > than 12%.

- receives 1/2 the $\Delta$ between Libor and 10% if Libor is < than 10%.

The dealer then enters into a $50 million swap with a counterpart and

- pays a 10% fixed rate.

- receives Libor.

The dealer also purchases a $25 million 10% floor and

- pays a fee.

- receives $\Delta$ Libor and 10% if Libor is less than 10%.

The first counterpart (C-1) enters into a $50 million swap with the dealer and

- pays Libor.

- receives a 10% fixed rate.

The second counterpart (C-2) sells a $25 million 10% floor to the dealer and

- receives a fee.
- pays Δ Libor and 10% if Libor is less than 10%.

The following chart describes the impact of various Libor rates:

**Table 24.2** *Impact of Various Libor Rates*

| L | XYZ's Cash Flow | Dealer's Cash Flow |
|---|---|---|
| 6 | Pays fee to dealer<br>Pays 6% to lender<br>Pays 2% to dealer<br>Net 8% + fee | Receives fee from XYZ<br>Receives 2% from XYZ<br>Pays 10% to (C-1)<br>Receives 6% from (C-1)<br>Receives 4% on $25 million or<br>2% on $50 million from (C-2)<br>Pays fee to (C-2)<br>Net = 0% + Δ fees |
| 10 | Pays fee to dealer<br>Pays 10% to lender<br>Net 10% + Fee | Receives fee from XYZ<br>Pays 10% to (C-1)<br>Receives 10% from (C-1)<br>Pays fee to (C-2)<br>Net = 0% + Δ fees |
| 11 | Pays fee to dealer<br>Pays 11% to lender<br>Net 11% + fee | Receives fee From XYZ<br>Pays 10% to (C-1)<br>Receives 11% from (C-1)<br>Pays fee to (C-2)<br>Net = 1% + Δ fees |
| 12 | Pays fee to dealer<br>Pays 12% to lender<br>Net 12% + fee | Receives fee from XYZ<br>Pays 10% to (C-1)<br>Receives 12% from (C-1)<br>Pays fee to (C-2)<br>Net = 2% + Δ fees |

| 16 | Pays fee to dealer<br>Pays 16% to lender<br>Receives 4% from dealer<br>Net 12% + fee | Receives fee from XYZ<br>Pays 4% to XYZ<br>Pays 10% to (C-1)<br>Receives 16% from (C-1)<br>Pays fee to (C-2)<br>Net = 0% + $\Delta$ fees |

# 25

## CURRENCY FORWARDS

### INTRODUCTION

In this age of "globalization," an ever-increasing number of companies are seizing opportunities on a global basis and are therefore exposed to foreign exchange (FX) risk. Companies typically manage their foreign exchange risk in one or more of the following ways:

- Refusing to do business in any currency other than their "reference" currency.

- Investing only in instruments that are denominated in currencies that are expected to strengthen relative to their reference currency.

- Limiting the currencies in which they will invoice to those they expect to strengthen relative to their reference currency.

- Limiting the currencies in which they will agree to be invoiced to those currencies they expect to weaken relative to their reference currency.

- Borrowing money only in currencies that they expect to weaken relative to their reference currency.

- Taking long or short spot positions in the currency market in order to offset their currency exposures.

- Taking long or short forward and/or future positions to offset their currency exposures.

- Taking long or short positions in currency swaps.

- Utilizing a variety of option strategies.

The choice of alternative(s) that an company will utilize in any situation depends on the specifics of the situation, including:

- The expertise level of the company's managers.

- The magnitude of the potential loss.

- The investor's projections regarding future FX rates and interest rates.
- The ability to quantify, accurately, the size and timing of its currency exposures.

Normally, a specific FX exposure can be hedged in a variety of different ways. Those parties exposed to the risk need to find the best overall hedging strategy to each foreign exchange exposure. In order to decide which strategy is the best one to use, the cost associated with implementing each strategy must be weighed against how well the strategy meets the investor's needs and objectives. However, it is sometimes very difficult to determine the total cost of hedging strategies. In addition to all of the *direct* expenses associated with implementing the hedging strategy, there are often *indirect* expenses also, such as administrative expenses, management time, and related overhead that have to be considered.

## CURRENCY NOTATION

In the remainder of this section, we use the following notation:

Currency bought / Currency sold.

For example, if British pounds were purchased with U.S. dollars, the notation would be £/US$ = 0.8877, meaning that one U.S. dollar would buy .8877 British pounds. However, if U.S. dollars were purchased with pounds, the notation would be US$/£ = 1.1265.

In addition, we use the following abbreviations in this section and in the examples that follow:

| | |
|---|---|
| U.S. dollars | US$ |
| Canadian dollars | C$ |
| Australian dollars | A$ |
| German marks | DM |
| Swiss francs | SF |
| French francs | FF |
| British pounds | £ |
| Japanese yen | ¥ |
| New Zealand dollar | NZ$ |
| Hong Kong dollar | HK$ |

# NON-DERIVATIVE-RELATED HEDGING METHODS

The most common method of hedging currency risk is to elect to deal only in one currency. For example, business owners/managers whose suppliers are all in the United States, and whose customers are all in the U.S., and who only do business in U.S., might conclude that it is not exposed to currency risk. However, this conclusion is often wrong! One reason is that the company might have foreign competitors. For example, if a U.S. company had Japanese competitors and the value of the US$ were to rise against the ¥, the Japanese company would be able to lower its prices in US$, and yet still earn as many ¥.

Another way that investors and businesses sometimes hedge currency risk is by taking only long positions (investments and receivables) in currencies that are expected to increase in value compared to the reference currency, and short positions (loans and payables) in currencies that are expected to weaken. Of course, this is not really hedging, but instead is simple speculation. Like any speculation, it will be profitable or unprofitable based on the accuracy of the underlying assumptions.

Finally, some business owners hedge the FX exposures created by their business ventures by taking offsetting spot positions. For example, if a company undertook a business venture that was expected to generate an incoming cashflow of 1.5 MM DMs in one year, the company might also short, or sell, 1.5 MM DMs for one year (or more accurately, the present value of the 1.5 MM DMs). The hedger takes these spot positions in the hope that the exposures will cancel each other out - i.e. any loss incurred by the conversion of the DMs coming from the business venture into dollars will be offset by an equal gain on closing out the short position by converting dollars into DMs. As we shall see, all derivative instruments are priced off of this simple spot hedge.

# PRICING CURRENCY FORWARDS

Like interest rate forwards, the price of currency forwards is determined almost exclusively by the cost of carrying the forward position. The market's expectations about the future strength or weakness of one currency compared to another determines the *spot exchange rate*. However, the forward rate is determined almost exclusively by the respective Spot Rate Yield Curves of the two currencies. Like other forward prices or rates, any significant imbalances are quickly corrected by arbitrageurs. To illustrate how the cost of carry and forward equilibrium exchange rates are calculated, consider the following example:

Assume that the current £/US$ exchange rate is 0.8877. In other words, one US dollar buys 0.8877 British pounds. (Note the rate at which pounds can buy US$ would be the inverse of this exchange rate, or 1/.8877 = 1.1265 - excluding dealer spreads and commissions.) Assume also that the 1-year, risk-free rate of return is 8% (expressed on a discounted basis) in the U.S. and 10% (also on a discounted basis) in the U.K. Given this information, the 1-year forward exchange rate can be calculated. As with any forward rate, the correct forward rate is the exchange rate that will eliminate any possibility of arbitrage. Thus, *the return offered by investing in the US$ instrument must be the same as the return offered by*

- converting the dollars into pounds in the spot market.
- simultaneously entering into a forward rate agreement (FRA) to fix the rate at which the pounds can be reconverted into dollars in one year.
- investing the pounds for one year at the risk-free rate of return.
- reconverting the pounds (P + I) into dollars in one year.

**Figure 25.1 *Dollar and Pound Investment Alternatives for One Year***

```
           US$ ——————— 8% A/360 ——————— US$
            |                             |
   US$/£ = 0.8877                  £/US$ = (?)
            |                             |
            £ ——————— 10% A/360 ——————— £
```

In the preceding figure, an investor holding US$ would have two ways to earn a guaranteed rate of return over the next year:

- The investor could invest in the risk-free US$ vehicle and earn an 8% rate of return.

- The investor could convert dollars into pounds at a 0.8877 exchange rate, simultaneously enter into a 1-year FRA to convert the pounds back into dollars at a predetermined exchange rate, and invest the pounds for one year at 10%.

If the predetermined exchange rate is the correct forward rate (i.e., the market is in equilibrium), which alternative the investor uses to lock in a one year return should be irrelevant. They should both offer the same yield - assuming the same initial investment. Assuming that a $1,000,000 investment is made, an investor buying the US$ investment would earn:

$$Interest = (P * R * T)$$

$$Interest = (US\$1,000,000 * 0.08 * 365/360) = \$81,111$$

$$Total\ return = P + I = US\$1,081,111$$

If the forward exchange rate correct and the market is in equilibrium, then converting the 1 MM $US into pounds, investing the pounds for one year, and then reconverting the pounds into dollars in one year (at the forward rate), should net the investor the same US$ 1,081,111.

Converting $1 million into pounds at the current spot rate would net £887,700 ($1,000,000 * 0.8877). If this £887,700 were invested at 10%, it would generate £90,003 [£887,700 * (0.10) * (365/360)] for a total of £977,703 (£90,003 + £887,700). Thus, in one year, US$1,081,111 must equal £977,703.

Thus, the 1-year US$/£ exchange rate must be:

US$ 1,081,111 / £ 977,703 = 1.1058 (one Pound buys 1.1058 US$)

£ 977,703/US$ 1,081,111 = .9044 (one US$ buys .9044 Pounds)

Therefore, in order for this market to be in equilibrium, the one year forward rate must be US$/£ = 1.1058. If the 1-year FX rate in the market were significantly different than this figure, the opportunity for arbitrage would exist, and the market would quickly be brought into balance.

Suppose, the 1-year US$/£ forward rate rose to 1.1316, while the spot rate and risk-free rates remained the same. Because the forward rate is too high, the opportunity exists to earn a risk-free rate by simultaneously borrowing dollars, converting them into pounds, entering into a 1-year FRA to fix the forward exchange rate, and investing the pounds for one year:

**Figure 25.2 *Arbitrage Possibility of Mispriced Forward Rates***

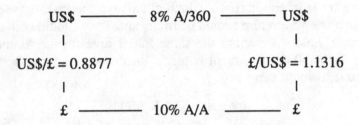

Borrowing $1,000,000 at 8% for one year would mean incurring an $81,111 interest expense. Converting the dollars into pounds, investing the pounds, and then converting the pounds back into dollars, would net:

$$\$1,000,000 * 0.8877 = £887,700$$

$$£887,700 * 0.10 * 365/360 = £90,003$$

$$£90,003 * 1.1316 = \$101,847$$

Thus, even after incurring $81,111 interest expense, this series of transactions would still generate a profit of $20,736 ($101,847 - $81,111).

If this no-cost, risk-free opportunity for profit presented itself, every knowledgeable market participant would take advantage by borrowing dollars, using those dollars to buy pounds in the spot market, and investing the pounds at the current spot rate, while simultaneously selling pounds in the forward market. Their concerted actions would cause the value of the pound to rise in the spot market and decline in the forward market (compared to the dollar), and might even cause U.S. interest rates to rise and British interest rates to fall. This process would continue until the respective market offered no opportunity for a risk-free profit.

## Calculating the True Forward Rate

In the preceding example, we calculated the hypothetical 1-year $US/£ forward rate to be 1.1058, and stated that at this rate, there is no opportunity to generate arbitrage profits. It is important to note, however, that this calculation gives us only a theoretical approximation. It would be detrimental to trade currencies or quote forward rates to customers based on the rates calculated by the method used in the preceding example. The reason this method cannot be used is that it excludes several important factors that can have an impact on the profitability of a transaction.

First, the preceding calculation excludes transaction costs. If the total transaction costs were $150/million for the US$ investment alternative, and £800/million for the pound conversion/pound investment/dollar reconversion, then the true forward rate would be slightly different. For example, the US$ investment would really net the investor $1,080,961 * $1,081,111 - $150). Thus, in order for the market to be in equilibrium, the 1-year US$/£ forward rate would have to *net* the investor $1,080,961 after transaction costs:

**Figure 25.3** *Calculating the Forward Rate when Transaction Costs Are Included*

```
   $1,000,000  ——— 8% - $150 ———  $1,080,961

        |                              |

   US$/£ = 0.8877                 £/US$ = (?)

        |                              |

    £887,700   ——— 10% - £800 ———   £976,903
```

By including transaction charges, the 1-year £/US$ FX changes to 1.1065 ($1,080,961 / £976,903), from 1.1058. This is not a big difference unless large currency transactions are being used.

The second factor overlooked in the initial calculation is the impact that taxes may have in determining the correct forward rate. The reason taxes may influence forward FX rates is that they may have different impacts on the different currencies--even if tax rates are the same on both currencies. For example, if both alternatives were subject to a 30% tax rate, then the after-tax, after-transaction-cost forward rate would be:

**Figure 25.4** *Calculating the Forward Rate when Both Taxes and Transaction Costs Are Included*

$$\$1,000,000 \longrightarrow (8\% * 0.7) - \$150 \longrightarrow \$1,056,628$$

$$US\$/£ = 0.8877 \qquad\qquad £/US\$ = (?)$$

$$£887,700 \longrightarrow (10\% * 0.7) - £800 \longrightarrow £949,039$$

$$\$1,000,000 + (\$1,000,000 * 0.056 * 365/360) - \$150 = \$1,056,628$$

$$£887,700 + £887,700 * 0.07 * 365/360) - £800 = £949,039$$

Thus, the US\$ / £ = \$1,056,628 / £949,039 = 1.1134

The difference in the pre-tax and after-tax forward rate is more pronounced if the two investment options are subject to *different* tax rates, as is sometimes the case. (Note that the FX transactions of dealers and their customers are often subject to very different tax treatments.)

## Quoting Forward Rates to Clients

When a dealer quotes a forward FX rate to a client, it first calculates its break-even rate and then adjusts that rate to reflect the overhead and other costs it incurs, and the profit margin it wants to make. For example, suppose a U.S. multinational corporation has a German subsidiary and wants to reconvert 5,000,000 DM in six months, but wants to fix its future exchange rate now. The corporation may be concerned that the DM will weaken against the US\$ over the next six months. If it does, the company will end up with fewer dollars, unless it hedges itself against this risk by entering into an FRA. For a dealer to quote its client a forward FX rate, the dealer first has to decide what spot transactions it needs to enter in order to hedge its two exposures, which are:

- the liquidity risk. The dealer must be sure that it will have the necessary dollars available for the client when required.

- the exchange rate exposure. The dealer must be sure that the forward FX rate it quotes will insure that the dealer does not incur a currency loss.

The dealer can, of course, offset both exposures by entering into the following series of spot market transactions:

- The dealer can make a US$ investment presently that will provide enough dollars in six months to pay for the client's DMs.
- The dealer can obtain the dollars to make the preceding investment by borrowing DMs now, and then converting them into US$ in the spot market.
- When the six months are over, the dealer can use the DMs it receives from the client to repay its DM loan, and use the maturing dollar investment to pay the client.

Because the dealer knows the interest rate it will have to pay to borrow DMs for six months, the current DM/US$ spot rate, and the interest rate it will earn on its US$ investment, it can calculate the forward rate it needs to break-even, or cover the cost of establishing this position. For example, if the bank can invest its US$ at 6.35% and must pay 7.13% on its DM loan, and the current exchange rate is DM/US$ 1.1612, then the dealer's cashflows would be as follows (assuming that there are no taxes or transaction costs):

**Figure 25.5  *Forward Rate Calculation***

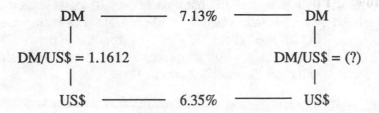

Given this situation, the dealer will receive DM 5,000,000 in six months from its client, and therefore will want its short position (the amount it borrows plus the interest it accrues) to be equal to DM 5,000,000 in six months.

$$P + I = DM\ 5,000,000$$
$$\text{since } I = (P * R * T), \text{ then}$$
$$P + (P * R * T) = DM\ 5,000,000$$
$$P + (P * 0.0713 * 183/360) = DM\ 5,000,000$$
$$P + (0.0362P) = DM\ 5,000,000$$
$$1.0362P = DM\ 5,000,000$$
$$P = DM\ 4,825,118$$

Thus, if the dealer borrowed DM 4,825,118 now, and paid the prevailing interest rate of 6-Month DM loans, it would be DM 5,000,000 in debt in six months. This debt could be retired by the payment that the client wants to make to the dealer.

Next, the dealer has to determine how many dollars to pay the client in 6-months for its DM 5,000,000. Well, the DM 4,825,118 the dealer borrows today can be converted into:

$$DM\ 4.825,118 * 1.1612 = US\$\ 5,602,927$$

These dollars could then be invested for six months at 6.35%. If the dollars were invested, they would grow to:

$$I = P * R * T$$
$$I = \$5,602,927 * 0.0635 * 183/360 = \$180,858$$
$$P + I = \$5,783,784\ \text{six months}$$

If the client is going to pay the dealer DM5,000,000 in six- months, the dealer can pay the client $5,783,784. Thus, the break-even US$/DM 6-month forward rate is 0.8645 (or DM/US$ = 1.1568). Although the dealer's break even rate is $5,783,784, this does not mean that the dealer will offer to pay its client this sum in exchange for the client's DM 5,000,000 in six months. The bank will offer the client fewer dollars so that the bank can cover its costs, expenses, and related overhead, and, hopefully, make a profit. For example, the bank might offer the client $5,700,000 for the client's DM 5,000,000, but most clients will get quotes from two or three dealers to see which will offer the most dollars for DMs.

In addition to keeping its operations efficient, there are two other ways that a dealer can gain a competitive advantage. As has been stated, there are three variables that determine a dealer's break-even forward rate: the spot rate, the interest rate a dealer earns on its investment, and the interest rate it pays on its debt. Whereas most major dealers can buy and sell currencies at the same spot rates, different dealers can sometimes borrow and/or invest at different rates, giving them a higher or lower break-even rate than their competitors--and a competitive advantage (or disadvantage). (Note that whereas in the preceding example the dealer elected to hedge both its liquidity risk and FX risk, the dealer could have elected to remain unhedged and, in effect, speculate on the future direction of interest and/or currency rates.)

As another example, suppose a U.S. business had to pay its Japanese supplier ¥460,125,000 in 120 days, and the client was worried that the value of the dollar compared to the yen would decline between now and then. The client might ask its dealer for a forward quote so that it could lock in its US$/¥ forward FX rate. In this case, the dealer could hedge its exposures by borrowing dollars, converting them into yen, and investing the yen until they would be needed by the client. Given the following spot rates, we can calculate the dealer's break-even forward rate, excluding transaction charges and taxes:

- The 120-day yen interest rate is 4.67%.
- The 120-day US$ interest rate is 8.95%.
- The current spot rate is ¥/US$ = 140.

To hedge its risk, the dealer first needs to calculate how many yen it needs to invest now at 4.67% in order to have the ¥460,125,000 that its client requires in 120 days.

$$\text{Because the interest is equal to } (P * R * T),$$
$$P + (P * R * T) = ¥460,125,000$$
$$P + (P * 0.0467 * 120/360) = ¥460,125,000$$
$$P + (0.0156P) = ¥460,125,000$$
$$1.0156\,P = ¥460,125,000$$
$$P = ¥453,072,176 \text{ and}$$
$$I = ¥7,052,828 \ (¥460,125,000 - ¥453,072,172)$$

Once the dealer determines it needs ¥453,072,172, the next step is to calculate how many dollars the dealer needs to borrow in order to be able to obtain ¥453,072,172 in the spot market. At the current spot rate of 140 ¥/US$, the dealer will have to borrow ¥453,072,172, or $3,236,230. Over the 120 days that the dealer borrows the $3,326.230, it will, of course, have to pay interest. The break-even rate will allow the bank to be reimbursed for its interest expense.

$$I = (P * R * T)$$

Therefore,

$$I = (\$3,236,230 * 0.0895 * 120/360) = \$96,548$$

Thus, in exchange for receiving ¥460,125,000 from its dealer in 120 days, the client will have to pay the dealer $3,332,778 ($3,236,230 +

$96,548) plus a spread so that the dealer can cover its expenses and make a profit. Thus, the US$/¥ break-even forward rate is $3,332,778 / ¥460,125,000, or 0.007243.

The actual forward rate will depend on the spread the dealer adds to its break-even rate.

## Sample Currency Problems

1. On September 1, 1990, you are given the following data:

- The spot rate US$/DM is 0.8675.
- The nine-month US$ risk-free rate is 7.89% (discounted yield expressed on an actual/360 basis).
- The nine-month DM risk-free rate is 6.91% (discounted yield expressed on an actual/360 basis).

What would the forward rate be on June 1, 1991, in order to eliminate the possibility of arbitrage?

What would the forward rate be if the investor was subject to 20% taxation on its US$ investments, and 30% on its DM investments?

2. A client has to pay a supplier £16,789,000 in 200 days and wants to hedge its FX risk by locking in its forward price in dollars. The client asks a dealer for a forward quote. Given the below data, calculate the dealer's quote.

- The spot rate US$/£ is 1.1414.
- The 200-day US$ risk-free rate is 8.91% (actual/360)
- The 200-day £ risk-free rate is 7.82% (actual/actual).
- The dealer's transaction charges are $460, its overhead is $500 per transaction, and it wants to make a $2,750 profit on the transaction.

### Answer to Problem One

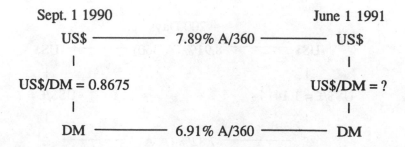

US$ Investment

$$P * R * T$$
$$1,000,000 * 0.0789 * 273/360 = \$59,832.50$$

DM Investment

$$1,000,000 / 0.8675 = \text{DM } 1,152,737.75$$
$$P * R * T$$
$$\text{DM } 1,152,737.75 * 0.0691 * 273/360 = \text{DM60,404.42}$$

Thus on June 1, 1991

$$\$1,000,000 + \$59,832.50 =$$
$$\text{DM } 1,152,737.75 + \text{DM } 60,404.42$$
or
$$\$1,059,832.50 / \text{DM } 1,213,142.17 =$$
$$\text{US\$/DM} = 0.8736 \text{ Forward Rate}$$

After-Tax Forward Rate:

$$\text{US\$ Interest } \$59,832.50 * 0.8 = \$47,866.00$$

$$\text{DM Interest } \$60,404.42 * 0.7 = \text{DM } 42,283.10$$

Thus, on June 1, 1991

$$\$1,000,000 + \$47,866.00 =$$
$$\text{DM } 1,152.737.75 + \text{DM } 42,283.10$$
$$\text{US\$/DM} = 0.8769 \text{ Forward Rate}$$

## Answer to Problem Two

```
                    200 Days
  US$ ————— 8.91% (A/360) ————— US$
   |                              |
US$/£ = 1.1414              US$/£ = ?
   |                              |
   £  ————— 7.82% (A/A) ————— £
```

**US$ Investment:**

$$\$1,000,000 * 0.0891 * 200/360 = \$49,500.00$$
$$\text{Total Dollars} = \$1,049,500$$

**£ Investment:**

$$£876,117.05 * 0.0782 * 200/365 = £37,541.02$$
$$\text{Total Pounds} = £913,658.07$$

**Forward Rate:**

$$\text{US\$/£} = \$1,049,500 / £913,658.07 = 1.1487$$
$$£16,789,000 * 1.1487 = \$19,285,174.80$$
$$\text{Plus Fees and Profit of } \$3710.00$$
$$\text{Final Quote} = \$19,288,884.80$$

# 26

## CURRENCY FUTURES

## INTRODUCTION

Currency futures evolved from currency forwards in much the same way that interest rate futures evolved from interest rate forwards. As a result, many of the relationships between currency forwards and currency futures are identical to those between interest rate forwards and interest rate futures.

## ADVANTAGES OF CURRENCY FUTURES

Currency futures offer three advantages over currency forwards:

- Currency futures have no credit risk because the exchange guarantees all trades. Currency exchanges can afford to extend this "blanket" credit guarantee because they use the same credit management techniques that are used with other futures contracts.

- Currency futures are liquid. Because the exchange fixes all of the contract's terms and conditions, and because the exchange maintains a clearing house, currency futures are free to trade.

- Currency futures provide an efficient pricing mechanism.

(Note that these are the same advantages that interest rate futures offer over interest rate forwards.)

## DISADVANTAGES OF CURRENCY FUTURES

The principal disadvantage of currency futures compared to currency forwards is that currency futures contracts are completely inflexible regarding size, expiration date, and being "marked to the market" (same as interest rate futures).

# PRICING CURRENCY FUTURES

Currency futures are priced the same way that currency forwards are priced: by starting with the spot rate and using the interest rate differential to determine the future exchange rate. Depending on the details of the calculation, taxes and transaction charges may also be included in the calculation.

## Contract Terms

The major currency contracts in the U.S. are included in the following table:

**Table 26.1** *Common FX Future Contracts*

|  | Contract Size | Value of an .01 |
|---|---|---|
| **Japanese yen** | 12,500,000 yen | $12.50 |
| **German deutschemark** | 125,000 marks | $12.50 |
| **Canadian dollar** | 100,000 dollars | $10.00 |
| **British pound** | 62,500 pounds | $6.25* |
| **Swiss francs** | 100,000 dollars | $12.50 |
| **Australian dollars** | 100,000 dollars | $10.00 |

(*Note that for the British pound contract, the minimum price change is .02 and thus, even though the value of an .01 is $6.25, the minimum price change is actually $12.50.)

For these currency futures contracts, the

- *long* (the buyer) buys the foreign currency and sells the U.S. dollar at the agreed upon futures price.
- *short* (the seller) sells the foreign currency and buys the U.S. dollar at the agreed upon futures price.

For example, suppose on March 8, 1991, an investor wanted to buy 312,500 British pounds for delivery in June, 1991, while another investor wanted to sell 312,5000 British pounds, also for delivery in

June. Both investors could accomplish their objectives by entering into the following series of transactions:

**Figure 26.1** *Example FX Future Trade*

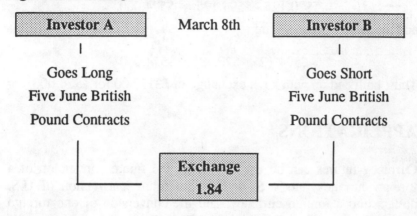

Because the contract is originally entered into at an exchange rate of 1.8368, the buyer and seller are both agreeing that the value of 312,500 British pounds in June is:

$$1.8368 * 312,500 = \$574,000$$

As with all futures contracts, this figure will be obtained through the purchase/sale of pounds for dollars at the spot rate in June, plus or minus the credit or debit to each investor's margin account. For example, suppose that on the contract's expiration date in June the spot rate is 1.9012. This means that the buyer will have to pay the clearing house

$$1.9012 * £312,500 = \$594,125$$

in order to receive £312,500. Likewise, the seller will receive $594,125 from the clearing house in exchange for £312,500.

The margin transfer between them will be

$$1.9012 - 1.8368 = 644 \text{ ticks}$$

$$644 \text{ ticks} * 5 \text{ contracts} * \$6.25 \text{ per tick} = \$20,125$$

This amount would be credited to the long's account and subtracted from the short's account because the price quote rose. Thus, the buyer's cost is

$$\$20,125 - \$594,125 = -\$574,000,$$

and the seller's proceeds are

$$\$594,125 - \$20,125 = \$574,000$$

Thus, both end up with a net exchange of £312,500 for $574,000.

## APPLICATIONS

Currency futures can be used to hedge the future conversion of a foreign currency into U.S. dollars, the future conversion of U.S. dollars into a foreign currency, and the conversion of one foreign currency into another. Consider the following examples:

### *Example One:*

Suppose that in June, 1992, a U.S. printing firm purchases a new printing press from a German company. The size of the contract is 10 million DM with terms net payable in 90 days. The current DM spot rate is 0.6405 (DM/US$ = 0.6405). The U.S. company's risk is that the value of the DM will rise against the dollar. If it does, it will take more dollars to buy the 10 million DM necessary to settle the account.

There are two ways the U.S. company can hedge this risk:

- It can convert the US$ into DM now, at the spot rate, and then invest the DM for 90 days until the bill becomes due. (The number of dollars necessary can be determined by discounting the 10 million DM by the 90-day DM interest rate, and then multiplying the number of DM by 0.6405.)
- The U.S. company can arrange to buy the 10 million DM it needs in three months by going long 80 three-month DM contracts:

$$80 \text{ contracts} * 125,000 \text{ DM/contract} = 10 \text{ million DM}$$

If the price of the DM is 0.6370 three months into the future, the buyer can lock in a cost of:

$$10,000,000 \text{ DM} * 0.6370 = \$637,000$$

Thus, the U.S. company knows that in three months the DM it needs will cost \$637,000. By using futures contracts, the U.S. company is free to invest its dollars for three months.

There are two points worth noting: First, if the markets are in equilibrium, both methods of hedging the FX risk will result in the same cost to the U.S. company (any significant difference should be arbitraged away). Second, regardless of which alternative the U.S. company uses to lock in the cost of the DM it needs, there is no guarantee that the cost locked in will be a good one. The value of a DM could always decline compared to the dollar over the next 90 days. (Thus, the risk/reward pattern of currency futures is symmetric, as with interest rate futures.)

## Example Two:

Suppose that in February, 1992, a U.S. firm agrees to provide some consulting services to a Canadian firm. The U.S. company estimates that the project will take 90 days and cost \$400,000. In addition, the contract states that the firm will be billed in Canadian dollars upon completion of the work, and that it will have 30 days to settle the account. How can the U.S. firm determine how many Canadian dollars to bill its client while hedging itself against FX risk?

Because the U.S. company will be paid in 120 days (90 days for the project plus 30 days for billing), it can use the June contract to hedge the currency risk. If the current price of the June contract were 0.8557 (Canadian/US\$ = 0.8557), then the U.S. company should price its contract at:

$$\$400,000 / 0.8557 = 467,454 \text{ Canadian dollars}$$

Because the U.S. company's risk is that the Canadian dollar will decline against the U.S. dollar, the U.S. company should hedge this risk by shorting five Canadian dollar contracts. (Note that the company will be slightly over-hedged.) The combination of receiving 467,454 Canadian dollars and locking in a conversion rate of 0.8557 should net the U.S. company the \$400,000 it requires.

## Example Three:

Suppose that on March 15, 1992, a U.S. manufacturer buys some components from a Japanese firm and sells its finished goods in Great Britain (U.K.). Assuming that the U.S. company generally pays its bills in three months, has payables of 1,096,000,000 yen, gets paid in six months, and has receivables of 4,324,324 pounds, how can it hedge its FX risk?

**Figure 26.2** *Multicurrency Transaction*

The U.S. company's risk regarding its receivables is that the value of the pound will decline relative to the dollar (or that the dollar will rise relative to the pound). If the pound declines, when the company receives the pounds from its customer in six months, the pounds will buy fewer dollars.

The U.S. company's risk regarding its payables is that the value of the yen will rise relative to the dollar (or that the dollar will decline relative to the yen). If the yen rises relative to the dollar, when the company pays its supplier in three months, its dollars will buy fewer yen.

Thus, the U.S. company has a six-month risk that the dollar will rise relative to the pound and a three-month risk that the dollar will fall relative to the yen. If the U.S. company has a six-month risk that the dollar will rise and a three-month risk that the dollar will decline, can these risks offset each other, leaving, perhaps, a three-month risk--three months forward--that the dollar will rise? The answer is no. There is no guarantee that the dollar will change the same way against the pound as it does against the yen. Thus, these two risks cannot offset each other. Instead, they have to be hedged separately.

Because the first risk is that the dollar will rise relative to the pound, this risk must be hedged by taking a position that profits if the opposite happens. The position that would profit if the pound rises relative to the dollar is being "long" pounds and "short" dollars. Going long the pound contract is the equivalent of going long pounds and short dollars:

$$4,324,324 / 62,500 = 69 \text{ September contracts}$$

Because the second risk is that the dollar will decline relative to the yen, this must be hedged by taking a position that profits if the yen declines relative to the dollar. The position that would profit if the yen declines relative to the dollar is being short yen and long dollars. Going short the yen contract is the equivalent of going short yen and long dollars.

$$1,096,000,000 / 12,500,000 = 88 \text{ June contracts}$$

The net effect of these futures positions is that for the first three months, the U.S. company is, relative to pounds, long pounds and short dollars, and, relative to yen, long dollars and short yen.

The long dollar positions and the short dollar positions largely cancel each other out, leaving a three-month position of long pounds and short yen, which is the opposite of the company's cash position of short pounds and long yen. For the second three-month period, the company's futures position is equal to long pounds and short dollars, which offsets the company's remaining long pounds/short dollars cash position.

## NEW CONTRACTS

Several futures exchanges have recently announced plans to create some additional currency futures contracts, including

- deutschemarks vs. pounds.
- deutschemarks vs. swiss franc
- yen vs. deutschemarks.

Several others are planned, as well. Assuming that these contracts are successful, a U.S. company will be able to hedge the type of cross-currency risk in the preceding example by using one futures contract instead of two.

# 27

# CURRENCY SWAPS

## INTRODUCTION

A currency swap is a transaction in which a stream of cashflows in one currency is exchanged for a stream of cashflows in another currency. For example, an individual or an institution might want to swap a series of fixed US$ payments for a stream of fixed payments in Japanese Yen (¥) or a stream of floating-rate payments in German Deutschemarks (DM).

There are several reasons why a company might want to convert a stream of cashflows in one currency into a stream of cashflows in another currency. Companies that make foreign investments will receive their dividends, interest payments, principal payments, and/or sales proceeds in a foreign currency. Since they are receiving payments in a foreign currency, they are exposed to the risk that the value of that foreign currency will decline relative to their reference currency--decreasing their return when measured in their reference currency.

Likewise, a company that borrows in a foreign currency must make a stream of interest and principal payments in that foreign currency. Companies that borrow in foreign currencies and are exposed to the risk that the value of the foreign currency will rise relative to their reference currency--increasing their interest expense when measured in their reference currency.

Because currency swaps can largely eliminate the currency risk inherent in paying or receiving a stream of payments in a foreign currency, they allow both borrowers and investors to pursue attractive investment/funding opportunities on a global basis. In addition, by combining a currency swap and an interest-rate swap a company can convert a fixed-income stream in one currency into a floating-rate income stream in another currency, and vice versa.

# THE STRUCTURE OF CURRENCY SWAPS

Perhaps the easiest way to explore the structure of a currency swap is to compare it to an interest-rate swap. While both currency swaps and interest-rate swaps involve the exchange of one stream of cashflows for another, they have some very important differences in the way in which the swaps are structured. To illustrate these differences let's compare a 100 MM US$ interest rate swap and a 100 MM US$/£ currency swap.

## Start of the Swap

In our discussion of interest rate swaps, we noted that at the start of the swap there was no exchange of cashflows between the parties because it would make no sense for two parties to pay each other identical sums of the same currency. (It would make no sense for both parties to both pay and receive 100 MM US$). However, in the case of currency swaps, the two parties actually do have to swap initial cashflows. The parties would have to swap 100 MM US$ for an equal value of British Pounds where the equal value is determined by the current spot rate.

## During the Swap

In our discussion of interest rate swaps, we noted that the only intermediate cashflows are the net difference between the fixed and floating rate interest payments. (It would make no sense for one party to cut a check for 5 MM US$ to the counterparty and receive a check for 4 MM US$ from the counterparty when the paying of 1 MM US$ to the counterparty would accomplish the same net exchange.) However, in the case of currency swaps, the two parties do have to swap the entire cashflows since different currencies can not be netted-out against each other.

## Conclusion of the Swap

In our discussion of interest rate swaps, we noted that there is no re-exchange of principal since there was no initial exchange of principal. However, in the case of currency swaps, the two parties do have to re-exchange the principal.

The net effect of these differences between interest-rate and currency swaps is that, given the same notational amount, the cashflows in an interest-rate swap are much smaller than the cashflows in a currency swap. Since the cashflows in a currency swap are much larger than the cashflows in an interest-rate swap, the credit risk of a currency swap is much greater than that of an comparably sized interest rate swap.

For example, assume that a U.S. company wants to purchase DM50,000,000 face amount of 8%, three-year German Bonds which are selling at par and pay interest semiannually. Currently, the US$/DM rate is 1.5000 (i.e., it takes 1.5 US$ to buy one German DM). Because the bonds will pay both interest and principal in DMs, the U.S. company is exposed to the risk that the value of the DM will decline relative to the value of the dollar. If the value of the DM declines against the dollar, the company will net fewer dollars when it converts the DMs it receives. The investor's cashflows from these bonds would be as follows:

**Table 27.1  *The Cash Market Transaction***

| Start of the investment | The U.S. company purchases the German bonds for a price of 50 MM DM. |
|---|---|
| 6, 12, 18, 24, and 30 months | The U.S. company receives 2 million DM interest payments from the bonds. |
| 36 months | The U.S. company receives a 2 million DM interest payment and a 50 million DM principal payment as the bond's mature. |

To hedge this income stream against currency risk, the company could, when it buys the bonds, *simultaneously enter into an agreement with another party in which it will agree to swap the DMs for a fixed number of U.S. Dollars*. The swap transaction would be structured as follows:

**Table 27.2  *The Swap Transaction***

| Start of the transaction | The U.S. company pays the contraparty 75 MM US$ in exchange for 50 MM DMs. |
|---|---|

| 6, 12, 18, 24, and 30 months | The U.S. company remits the 2 million DM interest payments it receives from the bonds to the contraparty in exchange for a fixed number of US$. Each exchange occurs at the forward FX rate determined at the start of the swap or its IRR equivalent (discussed below). |
| --- | --- |
| 36 months | The U.S. company remits the 52 million DMs payment (the principal and the last interest payment) it receives from the bonds to the contraparty in exchange for a fixed number of US$. The exchange occurs at the forward FX rate determined at the start of the swap or its IRR equivalent (discussed below). |

**Figure 27.1** *Basic Fixed - Fixed Currency Swap*

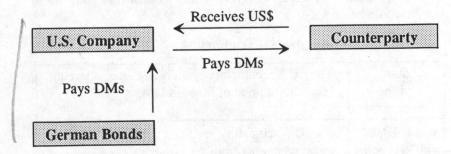

By combining the cash market transactions and the swap transactions, the U.S. investor ends up with the following net cashflows:

**Table 27.3** *Combined Transactions*

| Start of the transaction | The U.S. company's initial investment is $75 million |
| --- | --- |
| 6, 12, 18, 24, and 30 months | The U.S. company receives a predetermined number of US$. |
| 36 months | The U.S. company receives a predetermined number of US$. |

Thus, by entering into this swap transaction, the U.S. company effectively eliminates its DM exposure and has created, synthetically, a US$ investment.

# PRICING CURRENCY SWAPS

In the preceding example, the U.S. company protected itself from the currency risk of its German bond investment by entering into a swap that fixed the number of US$ the U.S. company will receive in exchange for the projected DM payments it will receive from its investment in the German Bonds. Because both sides of this transaction are *fixed*, it is easy to determine exactly how many US$ the U.S. company will receive in exchange for its DMs.

Currency swaps are priced like interest-rate swaps. An interest-rate swap is functionally the same as a series of forward rate agreements (FRAs) and is priced as such. A currency swap is functionally the same as a series of forward FX agreements and is priced as such. Thus, the number of US$ the U.S. company will receive in this swap is roughly equivalent to the number of dollars that the company would receive if it entered into a series of currency forwards.

For example, if the forward rate calculation detailed in the previous chapter gave us the following future FX rates, then the future cashflows from a series of currency forwards would be:

**Table 27.4  *U.S. Dollar Cashflows from Swap***

| Time of Payment | Future DM Cashflow | Forward 6-Month US$/DM Rates | Future US$ Total |
|---|---|---|---|
| 6 months | 2 million DM | 1.49 | $2,970,000 |
| 12 months | 2 million DM | 1.47 | $2,935,000 |
| 18 months | 2 million DM | 1.44 | $2,877,000 |
| 24 months | 2 million DM | 1.42 | $2,830,000 |
| 30 months | 2 million DM | 1.39 | $2,770,000 |
| 36 months | 52 million DM | 1.35 | $70,330,000 |

Once the U.S. company's future cashflows from the FX forwards are determined, the IRR of the US dollar cashflows can be calculated. However, if each cashflow is different, it makes this transaction cumbersome, difficult to quote, and difficult for accounting purposes. It would make more sense to restructure the cashflows so that the IRR stays the same, the initial investment and principal payments are equal, and each interest payment is equal. The IRR calculation is as follows:

**Table 27.5 *IRR Calculation***

| Keystrokes |
|---|
| -$75,000,000 [g] [CFo] |
| $2,970,000 [g] [CFj] |
| $2,935,000 [g] [CFj] |
| $2,877,000 [g] [CFj] |
| $2,830,000 [g] [CFj] |
| $2,770,000 [g] [CFj] |
| $70,330,000 [g] [CFj] |
| [F] [IRR] |
| 2.2527% Per Period |

Once the IRR is determined, the interest payment can be calculated:

**Table 27.6 *Payment Calculation***

| Keystrokes |
|---|
| 75,000,000 [CHS] [PV] |
| 6 [n] |
| 2.2527 [i] |
| 75,000,000 [FV] |
| [PMT] = $1,689,553.37 |

Thus, the net swap can be:

**Table 27.7** *Net Swap Cashflows*

|  | DM Cashflows | US$ Cashflows |
|---|---|---|
| Initial Cashflow | 50,000,000 DM | $75,000,000.00 |
| Intermediate Cashflows | 2,000,000 DM | $1,689,553.37 |
| Final Cashflow | 52,000,000 DM | $76,689,553.37 |

Because both participants in a swap have the alternative of using forwards instead of swaps to hedge their risk, the price of swaps is tied directly to the forward market. Further, because the forward rates are determined from the cash market rates, the swap rate is tied directly to the cash market, as well.

As another example, assume that a British company is willing to lend its U.S. subsidiary the equivalent of $50,000,000 for two years at a rate of six-month US$ Libor + 50 bp. Although the parent company is willing to accept the credit risk associated with making this loan to its subsidiary, it does not want to assume the currency risk because it thinks the US$ will decline relative to the pound. The British company would also prefer to have the interest rate on this loan be a fixed-rate instead of a floating-rate because it expects interest rates in both the U.S. and U.K. to decline, and does not want to have its income stream reduced over time. Thus, ideally, the British firm would like to enter a swap with a counterparty in which it would pay the counterparty a floating interest rate equal to the US$ 6-Month Libor rate and receive in return a fixed-rate denominated in pounds.

The question is, how do you price a swap in which a floating-rate US$ payment stream is swapped for a fixed-rate payment stream of British Pounds? Like any derivative instrument, the price of the instrument is equal to the cost of hedging the transaction. Because all of the various derivative instruments are priced of off the cash market, either directly or indirectly, the cost of hedging the transaction should be the same, regardless of whether the dealer uses cash market transactions or other derivative instruments to hedge the transaction.

To calculate the cost of hedging this swap, we need the following information:

■ the current US$/£ spot rate (in our example 2.000)

- the notational amount (in our example $50 MM)
- the rates at which the company can borrow and invest in both the US market and the UK market (given in the table below)

**Figure 27.2** *Cashflows in a Fixed/Floating Currency Swap*

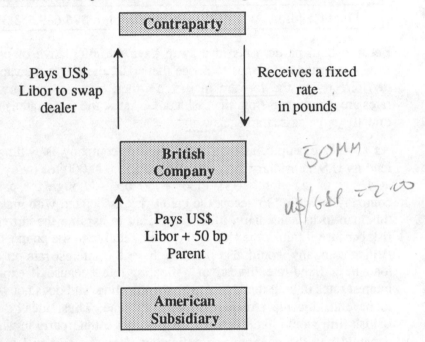

**Table 27.8** *Current Interest Rates at Which the Company Can Borrow and Invest*

| | US$ Fixed Rates (Actual/360) (Borrow - Invest) | UK£ Fixed Rates (Actual/Actual) (Borrow - Invest) |
|---|---|---|
| 6 Months (183 days) | 8.50% - 8.45% | 10.50% - 10.45% |
| 12 Months (366 days) | 8.80% - 8.75% | 10.20% - 10.15% |
| 18 Months (549 days) | 9.90% - 9.85% | 10.05% - 10.00% |
| 24 Months (731 days) | 10.30% - 10.25% | 10.00% - 9.95% |

Hedging this transaction requires three steps:

- Converting the floating rate portion (i.e., Libor) of the subsidiary's payment into a fixed payment in US$.

- Determining the total amount of the company's fixed income US$ cashflows.

- Converting the fixed US$ cashflows into fixed Sterling cashflows. The first step, converting the Libor portion of the US$ payments that the subsidiary pays to its parent into a fixed-rate stream of dollar payments rate, can be accomplished by taking the offsetting series of cash market transactions:

**Table 27.9  *Corresponding Cash Market Positions***

| Period | Rate |
|---|---|
| 0-6 Months | Current 6-Month Rate |
| 7-12 Months | 6-Month Rate,   6 Months Forward |
| 13-18 Months | 6-Month Rate, 12 Months Forward |
| 19-24 Months | 6-Month Rate, 18 Months Forward |

By taking offsetting cash market positions at the appropriate spot rates, the various forward rates can be determined. (The following calculation is described in greater detail in Chapter 20). It is at these forward rates that Libor can be swapped for fixed.

### *Six-month rate, six months forward:*

Determining how much to borrow and interest income.

$$P + I = \$50,000,000$$
$$P + (P * R * T) = \$50,000,000$$
$$P + (P * 0.0845 * 183/360) = \$50,000,000$$
$$1.0430P = \$50,000,000$$
$$P = \$47,940,745.22$$
$$I = \$2,059,254.78$$

Determining the interest expense.

$$I = P * R * T$$
$$I = \$47,940,745.22 * 0.0880 * 366/360 \text{ (leap year)}$$
$$I = \$4,289,098.67$$

Determining the forward rate.

$$\text{Forward Interest} = \$4,289,098.67 - \$2,059,254.78$$

$$\text{Forward Interest} = \$2,229,843.89$$
$$\text{Rate} = (\$2,229,843.89 \,/\, \$50,000,000) * 360/183$$
$$\text{Rate} = 8.77\%$$

### Six-month rate, twelve months forward:

Determining how much to borrow.

$$P + I = \$50,000,000$$
$$P + (P * R * T) \, \$50,000,000$$
$$P + (P * 0.0875 * 366/360) = \$50,000,000$$
$$1.0890P = \$50,000.000$$
$$P = \$45,915,439.08$$
$$I = \$4,084,560.92$$

Determining the interest expense.

$$I = P * R * T$$
$$I = \$45,915,439.08 * 0.099 * 549/360$$
$$I = \$6,932,083.41$$

Determining the forward rate.

$$\text{Forward Interest} = \$6,932,083.41 - \$4,084,560.92$$
$$\text{Forward Interest} = \$2,847,522.49$$
$$\text{Rate} = \$2,847,522.49 \,/\, \$50,000,000 * 360/183$$
$$\text{Rate} = 11.20\%$$

### Six-month rate, eighteen months forward:

Determining how much to borrow.

$$P + I = \$50,000,000$$
$$P + (P * R * T) = \$50,000,000$$
$$P + (P * 0.0985 * 549/360) = \$50,000,000$$
$$1.1502P = \$50,000,000$$
$$P = \$43,470,228.33$$
$$I = \$6,529,771.67$$

Determining the interest expense.

$$I = P * R * T$$
$$I = \$43,470,228 * 0.1030 * 731/360$$
$$I = \$9,091,677.44$$

Determining the forward rate.

$$Forward\ Interest = \$9,091,677.44 - \$6,529,771.67$$
$$Forward\ Interest = \$2,561,905.77$$
$$Rate = (\$2,561,905.77/\ \$50,000,000) * 360/182$$
$$Rate = 10.14\%$$

**Table 27.10** *Forward Rates and Corresponding Interest Payments*

| Period | Forward Rate | Fixed Payment |
|--------|--------------|---------------|
| 0-6 months | 8.45% A/360 | $2,147,708.33 |
| 7-12 months | 8.77% A/360 | $2,229,041.67 |
| 13-18 months | 11.20% A/360 | $2,846,666.67 |
| 19-24 months | 10.14% A/360 | $2,563,166.67 |

Once the payments that should be swapped for the Libor payments have been determined, the spread should be added to each payment and the principal should be added to the last payment in order to determine the total fixed dollar payment that the subsidiary would pay to the parent company.

**Table 27.11** *Interest Payments Plus the Spread*

| Fixed Payment | Spread | Principal | Total Interest |
|---------------|--------|-----------|----------------|
| $2,147,708.33 | $250,000 | $0.00 | $2,397,708.33 |
| $2,229,041.67 | $250,000 | $0.00 | $2,479,041.67 |
| $2,846,666.67 | $250,000 | $0.00 | $3,096,666,67 |
| $2,563,166.67 | $250,000 | $50,000,000 | $52,813,166.67 |

Once the total US$ cashflows are calculated, the company can then determine how many pounds it would need to receive in exchange for the cashflow. To make this calculation:

- each future US$ cashflow should be discounted by the rate at which the company could earn from the start date until the cashflow was received.

- the PV of these future cashflows should be converted into pounds at the spot rate.

- The pounds should then be invested over the same time frame in order to determine.

**Table 27.12** *Dollars Converted into Pounds*

| Time Frame | Discount Rate | Future Cashflow | Present Value |
|---|---|---|---|
| 6 months | 8.45% | $2,397,708.33 | $2,147,708.33 |
| 12 months | 8.75% | $2,479,041.67 | $2,276,525.74 |
| 18 months | 9.85% | $3,096,666,67 | $2,692,256.14 |
| 24 months | 10.25% | $52,813,166.67 | $43,714,734.05 |

**Table 27.13** *Converting Dollars into Pounds at the Spot Rate*

| Present Value of Future US$ Cashflow | Can be Converted Into Pounds at the Current Spot Rate |
|---|---|
| $2,147,708.33 | £1,073,854.17 |
| $2,276,525.74 | £1,138,262.87 |
| $2,692,256.14 | £1,346,128.07 |
| $43,714,734.05 | £21,857,367.03 |

**Table 27.14** *Calculating the Future Value of the Pounds*

| PV of Pounds | Yield | # Days | Interest in Pounds | Total Future Cashflow |
|---|---|---|---|---|
| £1,073,854.17 | 10.45% | 183/366 | £56,108.88 | £1,129,963.05 |
| £1,138,262.87 | 10.15% | 366/366 | £115,533.68 | £1,253,796.55 |
| £1,346,128.07 | 10.00% | 549/365 | £202,472.41 | £1,548,600.48 |
| £21,857,367.03 | 9.95% | 731/365 | £4,355,574.42 | £26,212,941.45 |

Thus the British company could receive US$ 6 month Libor from its subsidiary and pass it straight through to a counterparty in exchange for the four above cashflows. Of course, since each of the cashflows is different, it would make more sense for accounting purposes to restructure the cashflows so that the interest payments would be equal.

The IRR of the above cashflows would be calculated as follows:

**Table 27.15** *IRR Calculation*

| Keystrokes |
| --- |
| -$25,000,000.00 [g] [CFo] |
| 1,129,963.05 [g] [CFj] |
| 1,253,796.55 [g] [CFj] |
| 1,548,600.48 [g] [CFj] |
| 26,212,941.45 [g] [CFj] |
| [F] [IRR] |
| 5.1311% per period |

Once the IRR is determined, we can establish what the interest payments would have to be in order to have the same IRR with the first payment and last payment being the same.

**Table 27.16** *Payment Calculation*

| Keystrokes |
| --- |
| -25,000,000 [PV] |
| 4 [n] |
| 5.1311 [i] |
| 25,000,000 [FV] |
| [PMT] |
| $1,282,784.41 |

Thus, given the above data, a two year stream of floating rate interest payments pegged at US$ 6-Month Libor + 50 bps could be fairly swapped for a fixed stream of semiannual interest payments denominated in British Pounds at a 10.16% annual (51.3% per period) interest rate.

# PART V
# Fixed-Income Portfolio Management

# 28

# INTRODUCTION TO FIXED-INCOME PORTFOLIO MANAGEMENT

## INTRODUCTION

There are almost as many portfolio management strategies as there are investors. The reason for this diversity is that different investors have different objectives, preferences, restrictions, degrees of expertise, information resources, access to analytic tools, and so on. For example, some of the many fixed-income portfolio management strategies that investors have employed successfully include

- either having 100% of their money invested in T-Bills or 100% in long-term Government Zeros, depending on which way they expect interest rates to move.

- simply buying and holding a representative bond index.

- adopting a formula that is designed to force them to buy low and sell high.

- using sophisticated computer programs to identify and exploit arbitrage opportunities.

- moving money between different types of securities based on their yield spreads.

- moving money between short- and long-term bonds based upon the shape of the yield curve.

Portfolio management has undergone tremendous advances over the past decade. Quantitative theories and analyses have evolved so that a portfolio's risk level and projected return within a given period of time can be estimated with a reasonable degree of accuracy. The advent of new investment vehicles and a global investment perspective have made the science of portfolio management even more exciting and challenging.

However, one consequence of the advances in portfolio management is that the gap between the "knows" and the "know nots" is widening. The investors who have substantial knowledge of modern quantitative portfolio management strategies, and who have access to state-of-the-art resources and analytics, have a tremendous advantage over less knowledgeable investors.

Whereas portfolio management is too broad to be examined thoroughly in this text, we can examine the basic quantitative theories that are the foundation for much of the advanced work performed during the past decade. (Many aspects of these theories were developed by individuals who were awarded the Nobel Prize in Economics for their work.)

## THEORY OF PORTFOLIO MANAGEMENT

According to classic portfolio management theory, one of the primary objectives of portfolio management is to determine which portfolio, out of all the possible portfolios, offers investors the highest risk-adjusted return over a specific investment horizon. Note that because many investors have to adhere to certain investment restrictions, they are forced to accept a lower risk-adjusted return than the maximum possible. For example, whereas most investors are willing to invest in Treasury Bonds, few investors have both the desire and freedom to invest in "seaweed." Thus, even if seaweed were to offer a higher risk-adjusted return than Treasury Bonds, few investors would be willing to invest in seaweed. Strict interpretation of academic theory suggests that this preference for the investment vehicle with the lower risk-adjusted return is illogical. Investors who are more comfortable investing in T-Bonds than in seaweed would probably disagree.

Similarly, academic theory suggests that investors should have no preference for the source(s) of the risk that they assume, or the currencies in which their investments are denominated and instead should focus strictly on the risk-adjusted return. However, since investors do have preferences regarding these criteria, few investors actually have optimized portfolios.

Thus, from a practical viewpoint, the primary objectives of most investors differs somewhat from the objectives suggested by classic portfolio management theory. The investment objective of most investors is to *maximize their risk-adjusted return over a given investment period and within a given set of investment preferences and restrictions.* Thus, before a portfolio can be designed, the investor's preferences and restrictions must be carefully defined.

## Investor's Risk Tolerance

The most important preferences and/or restrictions that need to be defined relate to the investor's willingness to accept risk. Some of the questions that need to be answered regarding risk are:

- What sources of risk does the investor prefer to accept?
- How does the investor define risk?
- What total level of risk can the investor accept?

Concerning the sources of risk that the investor can accept, theoretically it should make no difference what the source of risk is, as long as that risk can be accurately quantified. Obviously, if an investor loses $100,000 from credit losses or from currency conversion losses, the net result is the same $100,000 loss. However, for both logical and emotional reasons, investors have strong preferences regarding the sources of risk to which they are willing to be exposed. Some investors feel that they have specific knowledge that allows them to manage certain sources of risk better than others. Other investors simply refuse to accept certain types of risk for emotional or philosophical reasons. Some of the common sources of risk that portfolio's can be exposed to include:

**Table 28.1** *Some Potential Investment Risks*

| | |
|---|---|
| credit risk | fraud risk |
| currency risk | sovereign risk |
| liquidity risk | reinvestment risk |
| market risk | spread risk |
| management fee/expense risk | liquidity risk |
| hedging expense risk | valuation risk |
| management time risk | information risk |

As might be assumed, when investors select the sources of risk that they are willing to accept, they are also defining the investment vehicles that can be included in their portfolios. Investors cannot include vehicles in their portfolios that would expose them to sources of risk that they are unwilling to accept. Consequently, if an investor refuses to accept currency risk, credit risk, or market risk, there will be a limit to the types of investment vehicles that can be included in the investor's portfolio. Of course, once the investment vehicles that can be included in the portfolio are determined, so is the portfolio's return. Thus, when investors define the sources of risk that they are willing to accept, they are also defining, to a large extent, their portfolio's composition and maximum possible return.

The next step is to determine the investor's definition of risk. Academic studies and experienced investors frequently define risk in terms of the variance of the portfolio's possible returns compared to its expected return. For example, a portfolio's risk might be defined as a standard deviation of 6.13% for a portfolio with a 12% expected return over a 5-year investment period. (Note that the distribution of the possible returns of a portfolio do not always take the shape of a normal distribution curve, and thus, more advanced analysis is sometimes required.)

**Figure 28.1** *Distribution of Possible Returns*

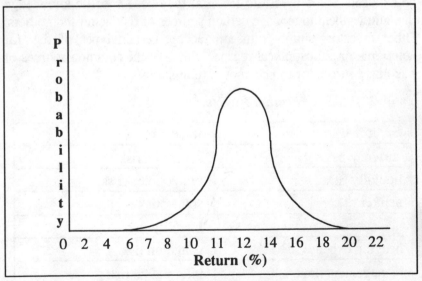

Instead of defining risk and reward in terms of the portfolio's mean and standard deviation, many investors prefer to have the risk of their portfolios expressed in terms of the possible absolute returns and their respective probabilities.

**Table 28.2** *Probability of Returns for Portfolio "A" Over a 5-Year Investment Period*

| Return | Probability | Return | Probability |
|--------|-------------|--------|-------------|
| < 4% | < .01% | 12%-14% | 17.50% |
| 4%-6% | 4.50% | 14%-16% | 14.00% |
| 6%-8% | 9.00% | 16%-18% | 9.00% |
| 8%-10% | 14.00% | 18%-20% | 4.50% |
| 10%-12% | 17.50% | 20%> | < .01% |

(Note that the portfolio's SD and probability tables are two ways of expressing the same information.) Now that we have been introduced to risk, let us examine risk in greater detail.

# THE RISKS INHERENT IN INVESTING IN A SINGLE INVESTMENT VEHICLE

A single investment vehicle exposes investors to two types of risk:

- Systematic risk, which is the risk inherent in the investment vehicle that arises from the investment vehicle's asset class. In other words, some of the risk of owning stock in IBM arises from the fact that the investment is equity. Some of the risk of buying IBM's bonds arises from the fact that they are corporate bonds. And some of the risk inherent in a New York City bond arises from the fact that it is a municipal bond.

- Non-systematic risk, which is the risk inherent in the investment vehicle that is completely different from systematic risk. In other words, some of the risk of owning an IBM bond arises from the fact that the investment is specifically IBM's debt, as opposed to corporate debt generally.

To calculate the systematic and non-systematic risk of an individual security, it is necessary to monitor both the performance of the security and the whole market. From the performance data, a *regression analysis* is performed to determine the extent of the relationship between general market movements and the price movements of the individual security.

Normally, the formula for a security's regression line is: $Y = a + b(x)$, where

- $b$ = slope of the regression line
- $a$ = the $y$ intercept
- $x$ = the value of the independent variable. In our example, the independent variable is the percentage change in the value of the whole market.
- $Y$ = the value of the dependent variable. In our example, the dependent variable is the percentage change in the value of the individual security.

**Figure 28.2** *Regression (Characteristic) Line*

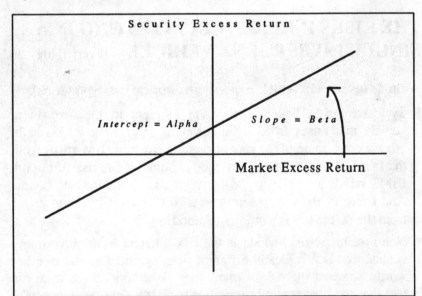

The slope of the regression line (b) is equal to the security's systematic risk. A slope of 45° equates to a systematic risk of "1,"

meaning that a 1% rise or decline in the market will cause a 1% rise or decline in the value of the security. A slope of 22.5° would translate into a *beta* of "0.5," meaning that the security's value would change by 1/2% for every 1% change in the market.

The security's non-systematic risk is the point where the security's regression line crosses the *y* intercept. (Note that by examining statistically the dispersion of the actual data points around the regression line, it is also possible to determine the reliability of the regression calculation.) Because an investment vehicle's standard deviation is a measure of the vehicle's risk, we can conclude that:

For a single investment vehicle, the total level of risk is *equal to the vehicle's standard deviation which, in turn, is equal to the vehicle's systematic plus non-systematic risk.*

# THE RISKS INHERENT IN INVESTING IN TWO INVESTMENT VEHICLES

Although the risk of a single investment vehicle is equal to its standard deviation, the same *cannot* be said of a portfolio that is composed of two investment vehicles. The reason for this is that the non-systematic risk component is reduced by diversifying the portfolio. Because the standard deviation is the sum of both the systematic and non-systematic risk, and because a portion of the non-systematic risk can be diversified away, the typical standard deviation calculation *over-estimates* the risk level of a portfolio with two investment vehicles. For a portfolio with two or more investment vehicles, the total level of risk is *equal to the systematic risk, plus the portion of the non-systematic risk that is not diversified away.*

The question provoked by the preceding statement is, how much of the non-systematic risk is eliminated by adding the second investment vehicle? The answer depends on the degree of correlation between the two investment vehicles. Correlation is the degree to which the returns (or prices) of different assets simultaneously move in the same direction. The correlation between two assets can range from being perfectly positive to perfectly negative.

If two assets have perfectly positive correlation (represented by "+1"), the yields (or the prices) of the two assets *always* change in the same direction. Expressed graphically, the price changes over time of two assets with perfectly positive correlation are illustrated in Figure 28.3.

**Figure 28.3 *Perfectly Positive Correlation***

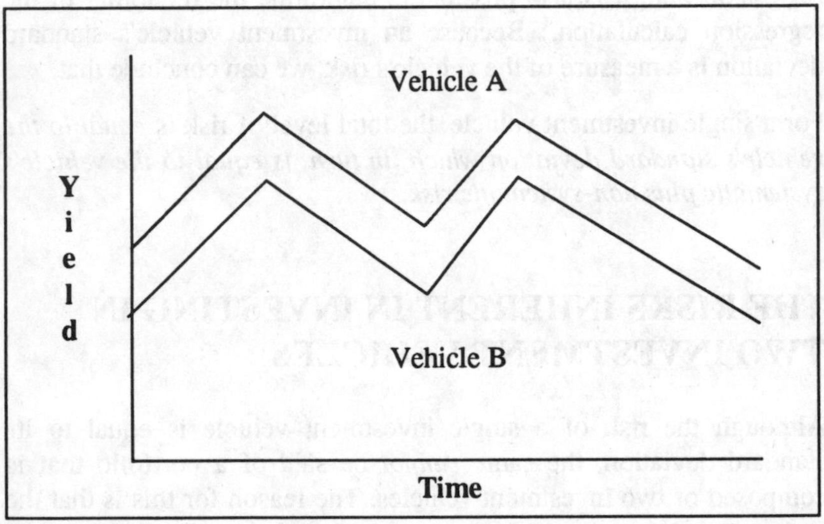

On the other hand, if two assets have perfectly negative correlation (represented by "-1"), the prices of the two assets always change in the opposite direction. Expressed graphically, the price changes over time of two assets with perfectly negative correlation are illustrated in Figure 28.4.

Of course, it is also possible for the price changes of two assets or commodities to be completely unrelated. If there is no relationship between the price changes of two assets or commodities, the assets will have "zero" correlation (represented by "0"). For example, changes in the price of celery may have no relationship whatever to changes in the price of computer chips. Thus, if two assets have zero correlation, when the price of one asset rises, it provides no indication as to whether the price of the second asset is likely to rise or fall (expressed graphically in Figure 28.5).

**Figure 28.4** *Perfectly Negative Correlation*

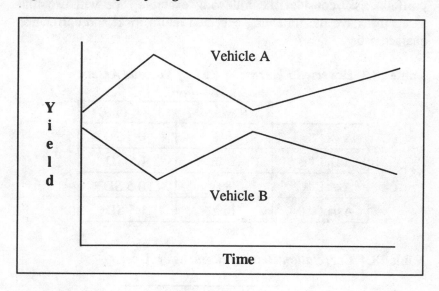

**Figure 28.5** *Zero Correlation*

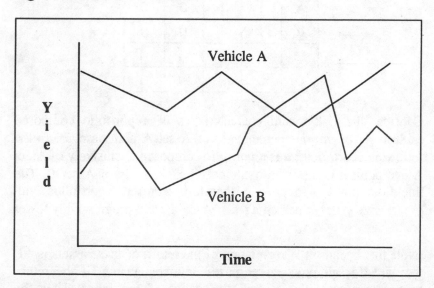

Financial assets rarely exhibit either perfectly positive, perfectly negative, or zero correlations with each other. For example, very similar assets might exhibit correlations of +0.95 or +0.96, but will probably not have a correlation of +1.

In order to illustrate how negative correlation can be used to reduce portfolio risk, consider the following example. We will use four assets that have the following expected return, risk, and correlation characteristics:

**Table 28.3 *Expected Return and Risk of Various Assets***

|  | Reward | Risk in SD |
|---|---|---|
| Asset "A" | 8% | 0.5 SD |
| Asset "B" | 16% | 1.5 SD |
| Asset "C" | 8% | 0.5 SD |
| Asset "D" | 16% | 1.5 SD |

**Table 28.4 *Correlation Between Returns of Assets***

|  | A | B | C | D |
|---|---|---|---|---|
| A | 1 | 1 | 0 | 0 |
| B | 1 | 1 | 0 | 0 |
| C | 0 | 0 | -1 | -1 |
| D | 0 | 0 | -1 | -1 |

Consider the risk/reward characteristics of a portfolio composed exclusively of various percentages of Asset A and Asset B. In the following chart, point *a* is a portfolio composed exclusively of Asset A and point *b* is a portfolio composed exclusively of Asset B. The line from point *a* to point *b* therefore represents portfolios with progressively larger percentages of Asset B, and progressively lower percentages of Asset A.

(Note that because the correlation of the return of these assets is +1, they are, for all practical purposes, interchangeable. If the return from one asset falls, so will the return of the other. Thus, by combining Asset A with Asset B, there is no net reduction in risk.)

**Figure 28.6** *Combination of Asset A and Asset B*

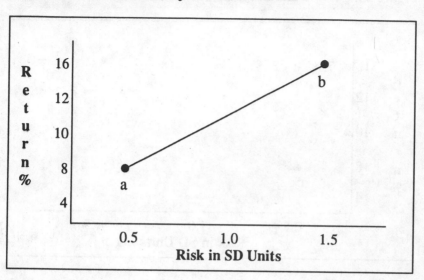

As another example, consider the risk/reward characteristics of a portfolio composed exclusively of various percentages of Asset C and Asset D. In the following chart, point *c* is a portfolio composed exclusively of Asset C and point *d* is a portfolio composed exclusively of Asset D. The line from point *c* to point *d* therefore represents portfolios with progressively larger percentages of Asset D. If we start with a portfolio composed exclusively of Asset C and then add progressively larger percentages of Asset D, the return increases initially (because Asset D offers a higher return) while the risk decreases (because the risk of asset C is offset by the risk of Asset D).

Since Asset D is three times as volatile as Asset C, and since the assets have perfect negative correlation, if the yield of Asset C changes by X, the yield of Asset D will change by a *negative* 3X. Thus a portfolio that is composed of three parts Asset C and one part of Asset D, will have *no* risk because the risks of Asset C and Asset D would exactly offset each other.

However, although the weighted average risk is reduced to zero, the reward of the portfolio would be:

$$(0.75 * 8\%) + (0.25 * 16\%) = 10\%$$

**Figure 28.7** *Combination of Asset C and Asset D*

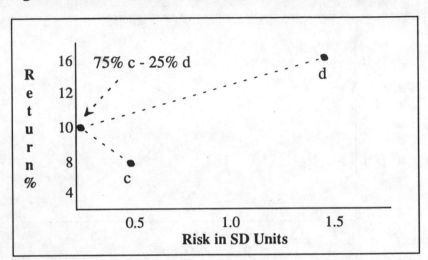

If the percentage of Asset D in the portfolio is increased beyond 1:3, both the portfolio's overall level of risk and its overall level of return increase. Despite the fact that Asset A and Asset B have the same returns and volatilities as Asset C and Asset D, the combination of Asset C and Asset D *always* yields more than an equal combination of Asset A and Asset B. (The only place where the yields are equal is where the portfolio is composed exclusively of one asset or the other.) Likewise, for any level of risk, a portfolio composed of Asset C and Asset D will offer a higher return than a portfolio composed of Asset A and Asset B.

In this example, we were able to create a truly risk-free portfolio using Asset C and Asset D, because the correlation of the assets was -1. Because perfectly negative correlations do not exist, neither does the risk-free portfolio. However, the stronger the negative correlation between the two assets, the closer the combination can come to being risk-free. (See Figure 28.7)

As the negative correlation of the two assets increases, the risk/reward ratio of the portfolio combinations gets closer to the c - d path than the a - b path. Finally, it should be noted that although these calculations are very useful, they are not always accurate. Most correlation studies are based on historical data. However, there are no firm rules regarding how much historical data should be used in the correlation calculations. If the calculations are performed with five years of data instead of one year, the correlations are different. In addition, there is no guarantee that the past relationship between two investment vehicles will continue in the future.

**Figure 28.8** *Portfolios Composed of Two Assets with Imperfect Correlation Are Between the Extremes*

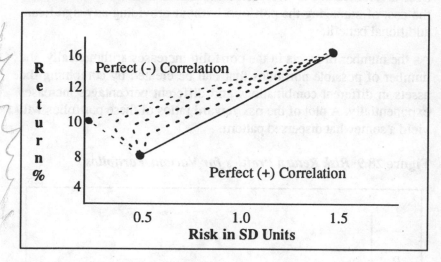

# THE RISKS INHERENT IN INVESTING IN NUMEROUS INVESTMENT VEHICLES

In the preceding example, the entire portfolio consisted of two investment vehicles. Whereas this example may be based on a simple portfolio, the same logic and reasoning can be applied to portfolios composed of hundreds--or even thousands--of different investment vehicles from different asset classes. The only significant difference between calculating the risk/reward possibilities of a portfolio of two investment vehicles and a portfolio of numerous investment vehicles is that the mathematics are more complex.

As additional investment vehicles are added to the portfolio, the amount of non-systematic risk generally declines and may be eliminated, leaving the total risk of the portfolio to be reduced to only the systematic risk. Surprisingly, not too much diversification is required in order to largely eliminate non-systematic risk. (Depending on how correlated the individual securities are, non-systematic risk can be virtually eliminated by as few as 10 securities.)

It is important to know how many securities are needed in order to largely eliminate non-systematic risk so that unnecessary over-diversification is avoided. Over-diversification only increases the cost of managing the portfolio without providing any significant additional benefit.

As the number of assets in the portfolio increases arithmetically, the number of possible portfolios that can be created by combining the assets in different combinations and different percentages increases exponentially. A plot of the risk/reward ratios of these portfolios will yield a somewhat dispersed pattern.

**Figure 28.9** *Risk Return Profiles for Various Portfolios*

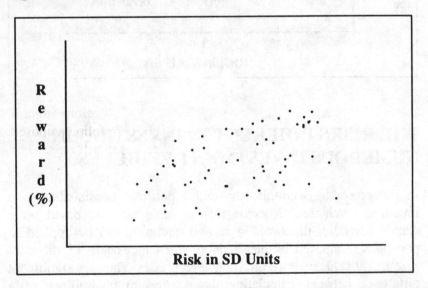

By systematically creating different portfolios from the available assets and plotting the risk/reward characteristics of each portfolio, it is possible to determine which portfolio offers the highest reward for each level of risk. A line connecting these portfolios would form a curve that is commonly referred to as the "efficient frontier":

**Figure 28.10** *The Efficient Frontier*

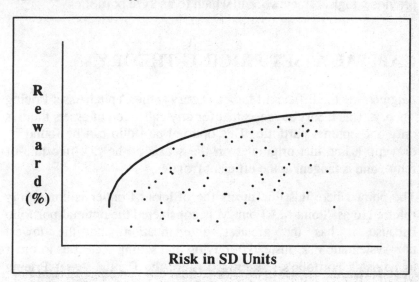

In the portfolio that had only two vehicles, the extremes were defined by a portfolio composed of only one asset. That is also true for the efficient frontier. The high end of the frontier is a portfolio composed exclusively of the highest risk (and therefore highest reward asset), and the low end of the frontier is a portfolio composed exclusively of the asset with the lowest risk/reward ratio. The portfolios near the extremes of the frontier generally have few securities, whereas the portfolios near the middle of the efficient frontier are composed of all the assets available.

Proponents of the Efficient Market Theory believe that it is illogical to own a portfolio that is not on the efficient frontier because they offer the highest risk for every level of return. They also believe that the best way to adjust the risk/reward ratio of a portfolio is to *alter the asset mix,* so that the portfolio always stays on the efficient frontier. Thus, proponents of this theory would try to slide up and down the efficient frontier if they wanted to change their risk/reward ratio.

Detractors of the Efficient Market Theory firmly believe that this entire theory is built on assumptions that are not necessarily valid in practice. For example, this theory assumes that investors can buy or sell any amount of any security without influencing the market and without incurring significant transaction costs.    Although the

Efficient Market Theory may not be entirely accurate, it does provide a logical framework in which to analyze portfolios.

# CAPITAL ASSET PRICING THEORY

Augmenting the Efficient Market Theory is the Capital Asset Pricing Theory. This theory suggests that for any collection of assets there is only one optimal portfolio. This optimal portfolio can be found by drawing a line that originates on the *y* axis at the risk-free rate of return and is tangent to the efficient frontier.

The point where this line meets the efficient frontier is commonly referred to as "Point M." Point M is considered the optimal portfolio because it has the greatest diversification and the lowest non-systematic risk. Instead of buying and selling securities in order to adjust a portfolio's risk/reward ratio, the Capital Asset Pricing Theory suggests that portfolio managers buy only the optimum portfolio and then use "leverage" to adjust the portfolio's risk/reward ratio. By either borrowing or lending money at the risk-free rate, the portfolio manager can take any risk/reward position along the line *RMZ*. Note that the line *RMZ* offers investors a more attractive risk/reward ratio than the efficient frontier at every point except Point M. Thus, by using leverage, investors can improve their risk/reward ratios over what the efficient frontier would allow.

**Figure 28.11** *Capital Market Line*

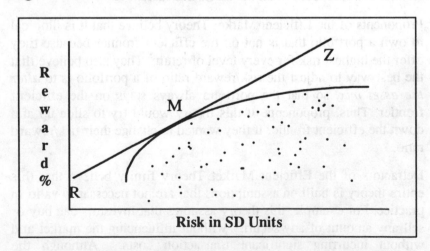

# WHY EVERY PORTFOLIO ISN'T OPTIMIZED

Although the Efficient Market Theory and the Capital Asset Pricing Theory illustrate how to optimize a portfolio, most investors elect to own portfolios that are not optimized.

There are several reasons that investors and portfolio managers elect to have non-optimized portfolios:

- First, the correct academic method of portfolio management makes no provision for emotional response, despite that making investment decisions is an extremely emotional process. The pain of taking losses, the ecstasy of large gains, and the temptation to play a hunch can all influence the decisions an investor makes. Regardless of whether investors are making decisions about their own money or someone else's, it is very difficult for them to remain emotionally detached.

- Second, this method of portfolio management assumes that investors are both logical and knowledgeable, although few are either.

- Third, performing the analysis required to properly implement this strategy is so time-consuming that most investors do not have the patience.

- Fourth, this strategy can be very expensive and is often only worthwhile when applied to very large portfolios.

- Fifth, the portfolio management process outlined includes no provision for the influence that personal relationships and "old-fashioned salesmanship" have on the investment decisions that investors make.

Because of these factors, very few portfolios are actually managed in an academically correct manner. Instead, most investors allow their personalities and preferences to influence their portfolio management strategies, despite that academic theory suggests that any deviation from the classic approach can only worsen the investor's risk/reward ratio. In addition, even those investors who want to manage their portfolios in an academically correct way often have to take shortcuts in order to make the process practical.

# 29

# OVERVIEW OF FIXED-INCOME PORTFOLIO STRATEGIES

## INTRODUCTION

Because of the nature of fixed-income securities, fixed-income portfolio management lends itself to a variety of quantitative portfolio management techniques. Both the potential risk and the potential reward of fixed-income instruments can be estimated by a variety of quantitative and statistical techniques.

The first decision an investor has to make regarding a fixed-income portfolio is whether to manage it on a passive or an active basis. Investors who select a passive strategy will attempt to earn a *market* rate of return instead of trying to "beat" the market. Investors who select an active strategy will try to *beat* the market. (By trying to beat the market, the investor will take calculated risks that, if successful, will offer the investor a higher return than the projected return of the passive strategies.)

The decision of whether an investor should pursue an active or a passive strategy depends on a variety of factors, including

- how much uncertainty (on both a relative and absolute basis) the investor can tolerate regarding the portfolio's return. The more uncertainty the investor can tolerate, the more freedom the investor has to pursue an active strategy.
- whether the portfolio is being used to fund a specific liability schedule. If the portfolio's cash flows have to fund a specific liability schedule, the investor will usually favor a passive strategy.
- how much work the investor wants to do. Active portfolio management strategies require more work on the part of the investor than most passive strategies.

- the types of information and analytical tools that the investor can access. Active portfolio management strategies require access to more information and analytical tools than most passive strategies.

- whether the investor is more interested in getting good performance or avoiding poor performance. Many investors, especially professional portfolio managers, are more interested in avoiding poor performance than they are in achieving excellent performance. Passive approaches seldom result in bad performance (measured on a relative basis), therefore are favored by the investors whose goal is to avoid bad performance.

- whether the investor feels that they can gain an advantage over the market. For example, some portfolio managers believe that their organizations do a superior job of credit analysis, economic analysis, trade executions, and so on. Unless investors feel that they can gain an advantage of some kind, it makes little sense to pursue an active strategy.

- whether the investor believes in the Efficient Market Theory, which suggests that it is impossible to beat the market because the prices of securities already reflect all the information that is or can be known about the security. Not all investors subscribe to this theory (at least not completely).

## EVOLUTION OF THE EFFICIENT MARKET THEORY

The Efficient Market Theory has really evolved into four separate theories, each of which has its own proponents and detractors:

- The *Strong* Efficient Market Theory suggests that all information is useless, because the prices of securities already reflect all the information that is or can be known.

- The *Moderate* Efficient Market Theory suggests that all publicly available information is useless, but that private information (i.e., inside information) is useful.

- The *Weak* Efficient Market Theory suggests that whereas current information may be useful, all historical price information is useless and, therefore, technical analysis is worthless.

- The *Inefficient* Market Theory suggests that all information is at least somewhat valuable.

Investors who are proponents of either the Strong or Moderate Efficient Market Theories tend to favor passive strategies because they do not believe that it is possible to beat the market.

## PASSIVE PORTFOLIO MANAGEMENT

The five classic passive portfolio management strategies include structuring

- the portfolio so that it is on the Efficient Frontier.
- the portfolio so that it is on the "Capital Market Line."
- a "Ladder Portfolio."
- an "Immunized Portfolio."
- a "Dedicated Portfolio."

Each of these strategies have their advantages and disadvantages. Whereas all of the strategies are passive, they differ regarding whether they

- require sophisticated analytical tools.
- require the use of "leverage."
- lock in a specific return.
- require significant ongoing maintenance.

## CREATING OPTIMAL PASSIVE PORTFOLIOS

Passive strategies are designed to allow investors to earn a market rate of return in exchange for accepting a market level of risk (the scope of what constitutes *market* is defined by the investor). Using techniques that are closely related to the techniques examined in the previous chapter, it is possible to approximate what level of risk, and potential return, the *market* offers. To determine this, it is essential to know

- the investor's time period.
- the type(s) of fixed-income vehicles that the investor is willing to include in the portfolio.

- the restriction(s) that the investor elects to adopt regarding the minimum and maximum percentage (if any) of each type of security in the portfolio.
- the historical price data for each type of security and the software necessary to analyze it.
- the investor's attitude toward using leverage.

Given the preceding information, it is possible to calculate both the efficient frontier and the capital market line (as the investor defines it). Once these are determined, the investor can select where, along these lines, they want the portfolio to be. By implementing this logical quantitative approach to portfolio design, the investor can determine which portfolio offers the highest return for a given level of risk. For example, if the investor were willing to accept 1.5 SD units of risk and the efficient frontier and capital markets line were as illustrated, the investor's return would be:

**Figure 29.1 *Risk and Reward Portfolio***

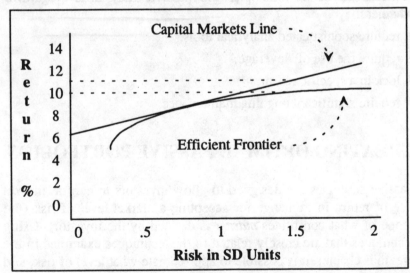

- 11% if the investor wanted to use leverage.
- 10% if the investor did not want to use leverage.

Because these portfolios represent the highest possible return for a given level of risk, they are optimized. Whereas this quantitative approach allows investors to optimize their returns, it has two significant disadvantages:

- In order to implement this strategy, the investor has to have access to a tremendous amount of data and some very sophisticated analytical tools.
- Although this strategy will optimize the investor's return, the return that it projects is just an approximation.

Therefore, these optimized strategies are inappropriate for investors who either lack access to sophisticated analytical tools or who desire to have a high degree of certainty regarding their portfolio's future return.

## Ladder Portfolios

Investors who lack access to sophisticated analytical tools, and yet want to earn a market rate of return, have an alternative strategy that they can implement. The strategy that they can use is to build a ladder portfolio, which is a portfolio composed of bonds with an orderly series of maturities. As one bond matures, the proceeds are used to buy the next one in the series. For example, suppose an investor builds a $1,000,000 10-year ladder portfolio with 1-year intervals. As time passes, the bonds will age and, in one year, the first $100,000 of bonds will mature. The proceeds from the maturing bonds are then used to purchase the new 10-year Treasury Bond. Thus, the ladder approach operates something like a treadmill, with the proceeds of each maturing issue being used to purchase the new long issue.

Over a long enough time frame (10 or more years), this approach will generate a market rate of return. However, over shorter time frames, the return will not be optimized. Thus, the drawback of this approach is a less-than-optimized return in exchange for simplicity. (Note that this approach provides no estimate of what the investor's actual return will be.)

## Immunized Portfolios

As examined in Chapters 11 and 12, an immunized portfolio is a portfolio in which the weighted average duration of the assets is equal to the weighted average duration of the liabilities. Because of this, both the assets and liabilities will have the same volatility. However, because the duration of the assets and the liabilities will change at different rates, and because they will have different convexities, immunized portfolios need to be periodically rebalanced. Building a portfolio like this is easy. An investor could, for example, simply combine T-Bills and long-term Zeros in the right percentages to create a portfolio with any duration from 90 days to more than 28 years. Or an investor could combine the Treasury Long Bond with a short position in the T-Bond futures market at the right percentages.

However, although there is a vast number of ways to build a portfolio whose weighted average duration matches the weighted average duration of a liability schedule, only one portfolio will offer the highest return (be optimized). Determining which qualified portfolio offers the highest yield requires very sophisticated analytical tools. Also, the construction of an immunized portfolio is complicated by the fact that, in addition to obtaining a high yield, investors should also seek portfolios with favorable convexity whose rebalancing costs are expected to be low, and whose cash flows closely match those of the liabilities. In other words, it might be worth giving up five bp in yield in order to obtain a portfolio with lower maintenance costs and higher convexity. Performing this type of analysis adds an additional element of convexity to the optimization calculation.

Because any capital gain or loss that the investor experiences from an immunized portfolio is offset by an equal yet opposite increase or decrease in the reinvestment income, immunized portfolios allow investors to predict what their return will be over a specific investment period. Because an investor can determine what a portfolio's yield will be, investors can effectively use immunized portfolios to meet a specific set of liabilities.

## Dedicated Portfolios

Another passive strategy that is effectively used to fund a specific set of liabilities is to establish a dedicated portfolio, which is a portfolio in which the cash flows generated by the portfolio are designed to match, as closely as possible, the liability schedule. For example, suppose an investor wants to fund the following liability schedule: $1 million/year for the next 20 years.

In a cash-matched or "dedicated" portfolio, every liability is met with a corresponding cash flow. For example, if the investor could buy $20 million (face value) of U.S. Government Zero Coupon Bonds whose maturities coincidentally corresponded exactly with the liabilities, the portfolio's cash flows would match the liabilities exactly. Although this portfolio would be matched exactly, it would probably also be very expensive. Consider the cost of funding the liabilities, using the following Treasury Bond Yield Curve. If the liabilities were funded with Zero Coupon Bonds at the yields in the Treasury Bond Curve, the total cost of funding the liabilities would be $9,964,640.

**Figure 29.2  *Treasury Yield Curve***

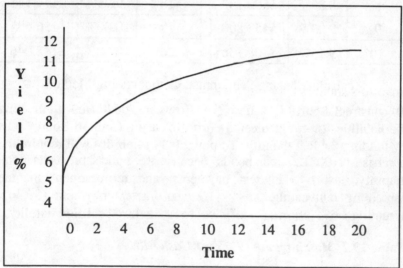

From this yield curve we can calculate the cost of buying the bonds necessary to fund the liabilities.

Of course, whereas Zero Coupon Bonds may be the simplest way of funding the liabilities, there are other ways that may be less costly. Suppose that instead of using Zero Coupon Bonds, the investor used Coupon Bonds.

(For illustrative purposes only, we will assume that the yield curve for Coupon Bonds and Zero Coupon Bonds are identical.)

**Table 29.1** *Pricing the Individual Cash Flows*

| Maturity | Yield | Price * | Maturity | Yield | Price * |
|----------|-------|---------|----------|--------|---------|
| 1 | 5.00% | $951,814 | 11 | 9.30% | $367,906 |
| 2 | 6.00% | $888,487 | 12 | 9.40% | $332,108 |
| 3 | 6.80% | $818,232 | 13 | 9.50% | $299,223 |
| 4 | 7.40% | $747,773 | 14 | 9.60% | $269,082 |
| 5 | 8.00% | $675,564 | 15 | 9.70% | $241,517 |
| 6 | 8.40% | $610,362 | 16 | 9.80% | $229,989 |
| 7 | 8.65% | $552,793 | 17 | 9.90% | $193,463 |
| 8 | 8.85% | $500,182 | 18 | 9.95% | $174,144 |
| 9 | 9.00% | $452,800 | 19 | 10.00% | $156,605 |
| 10 | 9.15% | $408,736 | 20 | 10.00% | $142,046 |

*calculated using Semiannual Compounding Method

To construct a portfolio whose cash flows are "dedicated" to meeting the liabilities (i.e., a dedicated portfolio) using Coupon Bonds, start by funding the last liability. To pay this last liability will require the purchase of 908 20-year bonds, because the bond's proceeds upon maturity, last two interest payments, and reinvestment income earned by reinvesting the 19 1/2-year interest payment ($1,362, assuming a 6% return), is sufficient to retire the $1 million liability.

**Table 29.2** *Matching the 19½ Year Cash Flow*

| | |
|---|---|
| Maturity proceeds | $908,000 |
| 20th year interest payments | $90,800 |
| Interest earned by reinvesting 19 1/2-year payment for six months at 6% | $1,362 |
| Total | $1,000,162 |

However, in addition to retiring this last liability, these bonds also generate $90,800 of interest and $1,362 of "interest on interest" in each of the earlier years. This interest and "interest on interest" can be used to partially meet the earlier liabilities. Thus, by buying 908 long-term bonds, the last liability is completely eliminated, and each of the earlier liabilities is reduced by approximately $92,162, to $907,838.

The next step in creating this dedicated portfolio is to buy enough 19-year bonds to fund the remaining $907,838 19-year liability. Because 19-year bonds are also yielding 10%, it will take 825 of them to fund the liability. The contributions are:

**Table 29.3** *Matching the 19-Year Cash Flow*

| Maturity proceeds | $825,000 |
|---|---|
| 20th year interest payments | $82,500 |
| Interest earned by reinvesting 18 1/2-year payments for six months at 6% | $1,238 |
| Total | $908,738 |

In addition to paying the 19-year liability, the interest and the "interest on interest" generated in the earlier years reduces the 18 earlier liabilities to $825,000. By continuing this process, all of the liabilities can be funded. The cost of funding this set of liabilities with Coupon Bonds is significantly lower than the cost of funding it with Zeros, despite our assumption of an equal yield curve. The reason for this difference is that when Coupon Bonds are used to fund the liabilities, long-term, higher yielding assets fund the short-term liabilities (i.e., the interest payments of the long-term bonds are used to pay the short-term liabilities).

In practice, of course, creating a dedicated portfolio is complicated by the fact that

- the bonds will not mature on the day that the liabilities become due.
- the bonds will not be purchased at value.
- the investor may elect to borrow for short periods of time in order to meet funding dates.

Thus, once the investor defines the types of bonds that can be included in the portfolio and how much leverage can be used, it again falls to complicated software tools to determine the one portfolio that will fund the liabilities at the lowest cost.

The similarities and differences of the different strategies are summarized in the following table:

**Table 29.4** *Passive Fixed-Income Strategies*

| Strategy | Requires Leverage | Requires Analytics | Return is Known | Requires Maintenance |
|---|---|---|---|---|
| Efficient Frontier | No | Yes | No | No |
| Capital Market Line | Yes | Yes | No | No |
| Ladder | No | No | No | No |
| Immunized | No | Yes | Yes | Yes |
| Dedicated | No | Yes | Yes | No |

# ACTIVE PORTFOLIO MANAGEMENT

Investors who use active portfolio management strategies try to beat the market as it is defined by them. Thus, investors who prefer active management attempt to earn a return that is higher than the return offered by the optimized passive portfolio composed of the same types of securities. Modern portfolio theory acknowledges that it is possible to earn an *absolute return* that is higher than the efficient frontier or the capital market line, respectively. However, modern portfolio theory also suggests that any time you deviate from the optimized passive portfolio, your *risk-adjusted return* declines. This means that whereas an investor may be able to beat the market, the odds are stacked against the investor. The longer an investor tries to beat the market, the higher the odds become.

In order to overcome this disadvantage, investors taking an active approach to managing their portfolios need to have a significant advantage over other investors. Many investors believe that they have an actual advantage in one or more of the following areas:

- predicting interest rate movements.
- effectively utilizing derivative instruments.
- predicting exchange-rate movements.
- performing credit analysis.

For example, investors who believe that they have an above-average ability in predicting interest rate movements will actively increase or decrease the weighted average duration of their portfolios in an attempt to maximize their capital gains while minimizing their capital losses. Investors who believe that they have an above-average ability in predicting exchange rates will move money between investments denominated in different currencies with the same objective. If the investor has an actual advantage, and if the market is either weakly efficient of inefficient, the investor may indeed be able to outperform the passive portfolios.